Advance Praise for

BRAVE NEW
CLASSROOMS

"Brave New Classrooms represents a landmark book in its examination of the complex relationship among the diverse demands of democracy, higher education, and electronic learning. Cutting beneath the surface of hype and superficiality, it offers a complex, erudite, and invigorating analysis of both the dangers and possibilities of e-learning within an ever-increasing corporatized world. This book is crucial reading for those individuals and groups concerned about the future of higher education and the importance of democratic public spheres."

Henry Giroux, Author of Take Back Higher Education
and Stormy Weather: Katrina and the Politics of Disposability

"This thought-provoking collection provides a welcome antidote to the utopian and dystopian positions that tend to dominate discussions of educational technology. The volume's critical perspective on e-learning deserves the attention of educators and policy-makers alike."

Mark Warschauer, Department of Education, University of California, Irvine

"Brave New Classrooms represents a bold and important contribution to scholarship on e-learning. The book provides a critical, clear-sighted examination of precisely what is at stake in the competing rhetorics, practices, pedagogies, and politics surrounding online education. Of particular significance is the way the collection brings together many neglected yet urgently needed concerns: how to resist, adapt and engage e-learning technologies in ways that support democratic educational potentials; how to situate contemporary e-learning in terms of the particular economic, institutional, and sociopolitical contexts in which it is embedded; an exploration of teacher-driven practices and pedagogies that represent an alternative critical politics of online education."

*Chris Werry, Associate Professor of Rhetoric and Writing Studies,
San Diego State University*

BRAVE NEW CLASSROOMS

Steve Jones
General Editor

Vol. 37

PETER LANG
New York • Washington, D.C./Baltimore • Bern
Frankfurt am Main • Berlin • Brussels • Vienna • Oxford

BRAVE NEW CLASSROOMS

Democratic Education & the Internet

Edited by
Joe Lockard & Mark Pegrum

PETER LANG
New York • Washington, D.C./Baltimore • Bern
Frankfurt am Main • Berlin • Brussels • Vienna • Oxford

Library of Congress Cataloging-in-Publication Data

Brave new classrooms: democratic education and the Internet /
edited by Joe Lockard and Mark Pegrum.
p. cm. — (Digital formations; v. 37)
Includes bibliographical references and index.
1. Critical pedagogy—United States. 2. Internet in education.
3. Education—Effect of technological innovations on.
I. Pegrum, Mark. II. Title.
LC196.5.U6P44   371.35'8—dc22   2006023641
ISBN-13: 978-0-8204-8123-4
ISBN-10: 0-8204-8123-8
ISSN 1526-3169

Bibliographic information published by **Die Deutsche Bibliothek**.
Die Deutsche Bibliothek lists this publication in the "Deutsche
Nationalbibliografie"; detailed bibliographic data is available
on the Internet at http://dnb.ddb.de/.

Cover illustration: El Lissitzky, *Victory Over the Sun: The New Man,* 1923.
Photo credit: Tate Gallery, London / Art Resource, NY
© 2006 Artists Rights Society (ARS), New York / VG Bild-Kunst, Bonn
Lockard author photo by Montye Fuse; Pegrum author photo by Stephen Morris

The paper in this book meets the guidelines for permanence and durability
of the Committee on Production Guidelines for Book Longevity
of the Council of Library Resources.

© 2007 Peter Lang Publishing, Inc., New York
29 Broadway, 18th floor, New York, NY 10006
www.peterlang.com

Printed in the United States of America

For Ewa

— JL

For Stephen

— MP

Contents

Section III: Pedagogies of Resistance

Acknowledgments

The co-editors wish to acknowledge the supportive comment and assistance of Steven Jones, Series Editor, and Damon Zucca and Sophie Appel at Peter Lang. We are especially grateful to the wonderful, cheerful, and invaluable work of April Brannon, without whose marathon-trained skills it is difficult to conceive this project would ever have come to a successful completion. A grant from Arizona State University's Institute for Humanities Research provided partial assistance for manuscript preparation, and Joe wishes to acknowledge discussions with his colleagues on the IT Committee at the College of Liberal Arts and Sciences, Arizona State University. Sincere thanks are due to Anne-Marie Chase for her help in the camera-ready formatting of the finalized manuscript.

Mark would also like to thank Bridget Cook and Marion Spöring for their companionship and support on shared, early forays into online program delivery; for many long, inspirational discussions of e-learning; and for their invaluable collaboration on conference papers which helped shape his thinking about this field.

Most importantly, we both express our appreciation toward the contributors to this volume who have entrusted us with their work. Pedagogical and political critiques of electronic education are in too-short supply, and our authors have contributed significantly toward meeting this urgent need.

Joe Lockard and Mark Pegrum

From Counterdiscourses to Counterpedagogies: An Introduction

Joe Lockard and Mark Pegrum

The early, halcyon days of electronic education are gone. There is no longer a unifying belief, common during the Internet boom of the early 1990s, that this new medium provides a means for universal educational development. Many who embraced personal computers and the Internet, and who devoted their work to creating new forms of electronic education, have grown dissatisfied with trends toward commodification and corporatization, a paucity of critical thought in e-learning, poor quality and inappropriate uses of distance learning, hierarchical organization, and the growing exploitation of teaching labor. In short, the apparent democratic potential that inhered to electronic education increasingly seems a chimera. How can its original promise be recovered, or was it a case of hopeless naïveté?

Discussions of democratic practice within e-learning, unfortunately, are not common. When the topic does appear, it is too often phrased within bland, highly circumscribed, or lip-service definitions of democracy. For many, access equates with democracy, but there is much more to the concept of democracy than this. Like other forms of education, e-learning has an anti-democratic, even authoritarian potential residing alongside democratic content and practices. With the advance of globalist neoliberalism, the potential use of electronic education as a tool to bolster an anti-democratic agenda is an issue of rising concern.

Continual discussions of democracy in education are crucial to defining what we mean in using this concept; in the instance of electronic education this social conversation has become an insistent need. Dissatisfaction with and cynicism toward e-learning is more manifest than ever today, largely because of prolonged and evident degradation of its social contribution, as online education is turned into yet another cash-flow opportunity. A cadre of experienced teachers, among whom are numerous early adopters of electronic classwork and the Internet, are voicing their critiques of e-learning.

This volume assembles a collective, democratic critique of e-learning. Its contributors may agree or disagree on specific arguments; however, all agree on the central value of active, participatory democracy in the discussion. The political goal of this book lies in encouraging its readers to join that discussion.

Many of the chapters are multi-faceted tracts examining a range of positive and negative discourses around e-learning, while offering their own warnings and suggestions about the way we teach and learn online. The chapters have been loosely grouped according to their dominant ethos: a focus on discourses of resistance; a highlighting of points which require resistance; or a move toward pedagogies which combine a resistance to the more troubling aspects of e-learning with a determination to exploit its democratizing potential.

Section I: Discourses of Resistance

The first, short section of this volume considers the emergence of discourses of resistance to current developments in e-learning.

Mark Pegrum opens the collection with a discussion of online learning as the site of an intense clash between competing philosophies, with the positivist, techno-rationalist agendas of governments and corporations servicing the knowledge economy pitted against the oppositional discourses of educators of all kinds. The latter group, ranging from liberals through constructivists to postmodernists, typically seeks to foreground pedagogical concerns and the sociopolitical implications of teaching and learning. Both sides view e-learning as a field in which their own aims may be realized.

A close examination of Socrates and Plato, two of the figures most frequently invoked in pedagogical discussions of e-learning, reveals these philosophers to have been far more ambiguous figures than is commonly realized by oppositional educators, who draw very selectively on their philosophies in an attempt to bolster contemporary arguments. Nevertheless, the aspects of their work which are highlighted reveal a great deal about the current educational predicament, and it is concluded that this selective concentration on the two ancient teachers serves to create a point of focus for the resistance strategies of quite disparate groups of online educators.

In a similar vein, *Mary Low O'Sullivan* and *Tom Palaskas* contrast the neoliberal discourse focused on the economic value of higher education with the discourse of educators. Following Martin Hall, they consider three discourses which present alternatives to the neoliberal vision: (1) a utopian discourse foregrounding the democratizing potential of e-learning; (2) a dystopian discourse focusing on the digital divide, the downgrading of the role of academics and experienced teachers, and limited learning designs; and (3) a utilitarian position centered on the role played by information and communication technologies (ICTs) in the shift to a post-Fordist model of education, and their effects on student and staff participation.

Indicating the limitations of both the utopian and dystopian positions, and while recognizing the danger of the prioritization of financial issues in the utilitarian model, the authors conclude that only the last of these offers the hope of finding a balance between economic and pedagogical considerations—a way of accommodating some of the demands of educators while acknowledging contemporary financial constraints. The extent to which educational discourses will prevail over neoliberal discourses is currently undecidable, say O'Sullivan and Palaskas, but chapters such as their own and the others in this volume are at the very least evidence of the existence of counterdiscourses to today's dominant neoliberal philosophies.

Section II: Points of Resistance

In one sense, the second section takes a step back, focusing on some of the areas which have caused the emergence and continue to fuel the development of the vociferous discourses of resistance explored in the first section. In essence, it examines the dangers of e-learning, many of them associated with the rise of neoliberal paradigms and the intrusion of market models into education, leading to the increasing corporatization of higher learning.

Robin Goodfellow's chapter, while internationally focused, takes the UK's Open University (OU), the model for many other open and distance learning providers, as a key example of the changes occurring around the world as universities attempt to adapt their social missions to neoliberal paradigms and increasing economic competition.

Today's promotion by governments of lifelong learning agendas, together with the idea that investing in widened participation in higher education is likely to enhance national productivity in the information and service industries, has created an implicit link between the right to higher education and a responsibility to become and remain employable in the so-called knowledge society. This obligation is reinforced by the penetration of information technology-related practices and values into subject and study skills curricula across the range of post-compulsory education.

Consequently, an organization such as the OU finds itself struggling to reconcile ideologies—of social justice, of national economic interest and corporate survival—which do not sit easily together. As the OU attempts to preserve its original commitment to equity as a social and political ideal, it is becoming clear that technologies of e-learning and discourses of participation cannot always be regarded as its allies.

Martha Henn McCormick takes an equally broad view of e-learning, which she examines through the lens of postcolonial theory, asking, as she does so, whether the Internet is by its very nature an instrument of neocolonialism. Notwithstanding the widely held view that sharing technology internationally is a positive phenomenon, it may be impossible to do so without imposing the cultural values inherent in that technology. In other words, it may be impossible not to impose Western ideology through e-learning.

Many Internet users, McCormick observes, are content to follow regulations whose origins are unclear and whose presuppositions are not questioned, and, more importantly, to punish rogue users who contravene these rules. Much has been said about the multiplicity of cultures, voices and modes of discourse which mingle in cyberspace, and yet online interaction is subject to strongly norming patterns and practices which limit the extent of the supposed diversity. If the potential of e-learning to foster democracy and diversity is to be realized, we must interrogate the silent assumptions which underpin it. Failing to do so, she concludes, means acquiescing to a new form of cultural hegemony.

Unease over the intrusion of economics into academia is evidenced by *Marjorie D. Kibby*, who warns starkly of the danger of e-learning being driven by an economic agenda. She acknowledges that the Internet has the potential to provide a democratic space where students are exposed to a range of discourses and ideas, and where they can discuss and debate varying viewpoints as they come to appreciate the ways in which "truth" is socially determined. Hybrid courses, she says, seem to provide the maximum flexibility, allowing for the greatest range of learning styles and most varied forms of interaction, and thereby fostering the construction of just such a democratic learning space.

However, as universities become increasingly subject to market values and job training replaces more traditional education, and in the wake of the failure of many purely online ventures, there is a danger that the development of hybrid courses is being hijacked by those who are primarily interested in creating economically viable educational products and increasing market share and income. The more that e-learning is driven by an economic agenda, she argues, the more we are likely to see the implementation of standardized information-delivery models of learning and the loss of the exceptional potential for open dialog and democratic learning represented by hybrid courses.

Robert Samuels' chapter highlights the dangers of e-learning for academic staff and functions as a warning about the co-option of disparate discourses, including apparently progressive educational ones, by those with corporatizing, globalizing agendas. He begins by foregrounding the conflicting demands placed on today's universities, which are expected to embrace e-learning yet simultaneously retain a critical distance to it; to be egalitarian institutions providing wider access while competing with each other for students-turned-consumers; and to stand above society and yet become core to the new social order.

In this contradictory situation, he argues, the growing corporatization of higher education is often camouflaged by the use of progressive educational discourses, including the rhetoric of social constructionism, student-centeredness, flexibility and information sharing, all of which may entail a devaluing and downsizing of staff, a process in which staff themselves collaborate in fostering such pedagogies. Drawing on and simultaneously critiquing the work of Chris Werry, Samuels argues that it is problematic to be democratic in non-democratic, hierarchical institutions where academic staff often have little say in high-level decisions. The democratization of classrooms, says Samuels, must be matched by an engagement with university power structures. Current critical pedagogies with their simple, polarized oppositional stances may ultimately function to justify administrators' decisions to pare back academic staff levels.

Turning to the impact of online learning on students, *Kerri-Lee Krause* problematizes the notion of a homogenous e-generation and the appropriateness of a one-size-fits-all approach to their education. Drawing on research which demonstrates that many students perceive e-learning as a matter of convenience rather than a means of enhancing learning, much less building a learning community, she goes on to show that the construction of a learning community online is further hampered by differential attitudes to and uses of ICTs across demographic subgroups.

Reporting on a large-scale survey of first year undergraduates at nine Australian universities, she details the considerable influence of age, gender, socioeconomic status, and rural–urban differences on patterns of ICT usage. Krause concludes that educational policy must become more responsive to the needs of varying student groups. Moreover, she argues, e-learning must not be driven by technological innovations but, while inevitably influenced by these, must prioritize pedagogy.

Kate Kiefer, focusing on composition courses, observes that hybrid and online classes mean that students unable to attend campus-based classes will have access to instruction, theoretically broadening the student base, encouraging more voices to be heard, and thereby promoting democratization.

She suggests, however, that the reality is quite different from this idealized scenario.

Kiefer focuses on three major "deficits" of online writing classes. The first is the nature of the classroom support software, which does not provide effectively for interaction; the second is time constraints on students who are juggling jobs, families, and study. The third is the prevalence of market models of education: when learning is a means to an end and the degree is regarded as a commodity, the interaction and shared knowledge building necessary for educational democratization are so far from being a priority for students that they are actively resisted.

Students' preconceptions of their roles in online and hybrid courses and the limitations of technology combine, then, to work against community building in e-learning. The online environment reduces opportunities for the democratic exchange of ideas so significantly, concludes Kiefer, that writing teachers should be skeptical of claims for the efficacy of these classes.

Tara Brabazon focuses on students' use of the search engine Google. Recent years, she contends, have seen an influx of techno-positivists and neophiliacs into schools and universities, all of them far more focused on technology than on teaching and learning. In the process, the ability to think critically and assess the appropriateness of the technology has been lost.

This chapter addresses the consequences of such developments in terms of the assimilation of information by students. The problem is that information, through Google, is seen to be both abundant and cheap, and information searching has become standardized and fast. However, the skills required to judge and evaluate the information retrieved from the web are not so easily acquired, and students who lack such skills are likely to base their work on material that is ideologically loaded and lacking in depth.

Some of the time, reading must be slow and methodical, and involve media other than the Internet. Important learning experiences cannot always be convenient and flexible, argues Brabazon, while discipline and motivation are required for scholarship. In today's ideologically charged mediascape, with its sound-bite solutions to complex issues, such scholarly qualities are all the more important, and are not likely to be fostered by Google.

Bettina Fabos agrees that there are major problems with students' web-based research, which draws increasingly on commercial websites. This trend is all the more worrying because students conduct most of their research online and fail to question the validity of the information they encounter. Like Brabazon, Fabos considers that commercial search engines seriously undermine the web's educational potential.

It is imperative for educators to move away from supposedly objective research assignments based on factual information and toward projects which highlight the partial, biased nature of all information. Using the example of an assignment about perspectives on obesity, she demonstrates how students can be trained to discern the ideological coloring of "facts" found in a variety of texts, on- and offline. At the same time, students can be encouraged to come up with their own ideas, and their own concrete ideologies. This process, concludes Fabos, may well entail orienting students away from the Internet, which is a commercial medium first and an information tool only second, and pointing them back toward libraries and books.

Section III: Pedagogies of Resistance

The final section considers how educators might engage with e-learning in ways that minimize the dangers examined in the previous section and maximize the opportunities for promoting educational democracy. While, on the surface, the authors take rather disparate approaches—ranging from the promotion of hybrid learning to the critical engagement of academics, from the retention of a sense of embodiment to a renewed focus on the humanities—they do in fact share an important common theme. All consider that we are still very much in the early days of e-learning and that, whatever the pressures of neoliberalism and globalizing ideologies, of commodification and corporatization of higher learning, we, as academics and teachers, retain a significant ability to influence the future direction(s) taken by e-learning. It is, at least in part, up to us to channel online learning in directions which we consider to be pedagogically sound, socially beneficial, and maximally democratic.

In a world-spanning philosophical chapter, *Charles Ess* argues that the goals of a global liberal arts education, conjoining Western and Eastern sources from Socrates to Confucius, must focus on "virtue first," that is, on the pursuit of human excellence. Ess asks whether such excellence can be taught online, and whether the epistemological humility required for human beings to co-exist harmoniously in a multicultural world can be fostered through e-learning.

He notes that, in addition to the real costs of online education, important gender and cultural issues have moderated early enthusiasm for e-learning. Echoing McCormick's postcolonial argument, he explains that because computer-mediated communication (CMC) embeds specific cultural and social values, it has tended to downplay the values of others, both within and beyond Western societies, its culturally imperialistic nature leading to conflicts with local values in South Asia and elsewhere.

Taking up and expanding on Hubert Dreyfus' pedagogical taxonomy, which emphasizes the role of embodiment in the teaching/learning process, Ess claims that achieving the goal of human excellence means training people to be capable of sound *judgment*, which is crucial not only to professional success, but also ethical and political life. This, he says, necessitates human teachers who incarnate the skills and judgment students need to acquire. Ess' analysis, finally, supports the recent turn toward blended classrooms that seek to exploit the distinctive advantages of both embodied and disembodied teaching.

T. Mills Kelly considers the influence of digital technology on the teaching and learning of history. He takes as an article of faith neither the proposition that the more technology is used in a course, the better students learn, nor the proposition that the use of digital technology in teaching history is somehow ruining students' ability to learn about the past in an authentic way. Instead of positioning himself in one or the other of these frequently polemical camps, Kelly demonstrates that the use of technology in teaching can have both positive and negative results—often at the same time.

Without attacking those on either side of the debate about technology and student learning, Kelly proposes that online technology, properly used, can help educators solve certain thorny pedagogical problems and can help students arrive at new or different conclusions about the past that may well be unavailable to them from print sources. Like Ess, then, he does not advocate the general adoption of technology, but sees real value in its implementation in specific learning situations, where the technology is harnessed to particular educational aims rather than the other way around.

Edward Hamilton and *Andrew Feenberg*, tapping into a core theme of this volume, see e-learning as the object of an intensely polarized debate over the future of higher education. For them, one side portrays educational technologies as neoliberal instruments of administrative and commercial control, while the other views them as neutral factors whose alignment with particular politico-economic interests is accidental. In both cases, technology is seen deterministically as a *fait accompli* with respect to the consequences of its development and implementation.

Hamilton and Feenberg propose an alternative critical politics of online education. After examining the *representational* capacities of the computer as a medium of information delivery, they examine its *relational* capacities based on its communicative potential. Computer-assisted instruction (CAI), where the computer stands in for the teacher, and CMC, where it stands in for the classroom, represent two different pathways for e-learning. It is not yet clear which pathway will be taken in the future. Despite the growing influence of administrators, the state and corporate interests in universities, academic staff are still able to intervene in institutional change and attempt to redirect online education as a transformative movement. The critical politics proposed by Hamilton and Feenberg is, crucially, based not on academics' critical opposition to e-learning, but on their critical engagement with it.

Tina S. Kazan emphasizes the importance of fostering a critical stance among students. Reflecting on cultural representations of the tension between embodied and online identity in movies such as *You've Got Mail* and *The Net*, Kazan goes on to show that similar issues surface in educational contexts, where online presence can facilitate both disclosure and concealment.

As we incorporate technology into our classrooms, students can exploit gaps between their culturally read bodies and their identities as they explore various constructions of "selves." The real challenge is to help them find ways to embody their texts online, and learn a range of strategies to create persuasive online and offline selves. Like Ess, Kazan insists that teaching remains a situated, embodied practice, and that the online arena must not become a place to eliminate bodies. Indeed, students must learn to listen to the silences of cyberspace, in which the body may often reside. Bearing this in mind, the peculiarities of the medium mean that e-learning may offer much more ready opportunities than face-to-face classrooms for the development of critical awareness regarding the self, others, and embodiment.

Drawing on a republican theory of citizenship that promotes participation in public judgment about the collective good, *Darin Barney* identifies three ways in which technology challenges citizenship: as a potential means of citizenship practice, as a potential object of political judgment, and as the necessary context of citizenship activity. He then proceeds to examine possible educational responses to each of these challenges. These include developing sufficient facility with technology to use it comfortably for purposes of information sharing and dialog; developing the critical technological literacy necessary to engage in public discussion of and judgments about technology; and an immersion in the humanities, the only major discipline in which the question of ends—the question of the "good life"—is regarded as still open to discussion and debate.

It is argued that while the practical and epistemological contradictions between these responses are significant, the demands of citizenship in technological societies are such that an accommodation between them must be sought. The current struggle between neoliberal and democratizing educational discourses, the outcome of which remains uncertain, renders such educational intervention all the more urgent.

Closing the volume with a "Manifesto for Democratic Education and the Internet," *Joe Lockard* details aspects of e-learning which are to be avoided or treated with caution, while proposing ways of drawing out its pedagogical, social, and democratic benefits.

We should reject the electronic classroom, he suggests, insofar as it displaces physical communities, but embrace its ability to link people, real-place educational spaces, and learning cultures in new and imaginative ways. Against the tendency to substitute e-learning for face-to-face learning, he insists that we should seek means of using the former to complement the latter. We must continue to see teachers and students as whole individuals, resist inappropriate e-pedagogies, and learn electronic self-reliance. If social issues such as class are present in online as in face-to-face teaching, both modes can be used to overcome such privilege. If e-learning is easily co-opted in the corporatization of higher education, it can equally be used to resist commercialization and social control, and to promote self-realization, collaborative labor, and anti-capitalist work. Finally, if academic staff are to continue to have influence over online education and pedagogy, the organization of their labor should be supported.

High-quality public education can be obstructed or advanced by e-learning. As so many of the authors in this volume have indicated, it is up to us to engage critically with the technology and work to exploit its most promising potentialities.

I: Discourses of Resistance

Chapter 1

Socrates and Plato Meet Neoliberalism in the Virtual Agora: Online Dialog and the Development of Oppositional Pedagogies

Mark Pegrum

An early contributor to debates on the emerging paradigm of e-learning, Andrew Feenberg, observed that technology is "not a destiny but a scene of struggle" (1991: 14; cf. Hamilton & Feenberg, this volume). There are many educators who are currently engaged in a struggle against the neoliberal tendency to portray the roll-out of e-learning technology as agentless, inevitable and inevitably beneficial for humanity at large. At stake is the way online education is envisaged, designed and deployed. Specifically, it is a struggle to counter the positivist, techno-rationalist agendas of governments bowing to corporate demands for a standardized workforce to service the so-called knowledge economy; it is a struggle to resist the corporatization, marketization and bureaucratization of learning. Its proponents insist, rather, on foregrounding pedagogical concerns and the social, cultural and political implications of teaching and learning. The struggle pervades all levels and aspects of education, but it obtains a particular salience within e-learning, currently anchored predominantly within higher education, because of the intrinsic features and potentialities of this mode of learning. And while the predicament in the main derives from and is inherent to the late capitalist economies of the West, it is spread internationally through Western discoursal hegemony—and nothing propels it faster than the proliferation of online distance learning courses marketed and sold by Western institutions to the waiting world.

A key point of contention is the nature of the interaction between teachers and students. Under increasing pressure in many contexts to function as purveyors of prepackaged knowledge, guardians of standardization and guarantors of systemic accountability, teachers are called upon by oppositional thinkers to embrace constructivist or postmodernist approaches, encourage dialog and multiply perspectives, resisting the simplistic closure inherent in rationalist agendas. Significantly, there is a wide consensus that just as the possibilities of standardized knowledge delivery and technocratic skills training are enhanced by e-learning, so too are the opportunities for a radical democratization of education and the structures of authority in which it is embedded, including, clearly, the relations of teachers and students. Conscious of its historical positioning, the literature addressing these issues freely draws on a long heritage of educational philosophy to define and bolster its position. Among all the pre-twentieth-century referents, perhaps the most frequent recourse is two of the earliest Western teachers who remain household names today, Socrates and Plato.

Although the general literature on pedagogy is not lacking in deferential nods to Socrates and Plato, there is a striking concentration of references to these figures in works on e-learning. Some authors take a cautionary stance: Azevedo calls a 1998 article "Computers Don't Teach—People Teach: The Socrates Online Method." Allen (2002) warns that many slick e-learning systems draw on "shop-worn, passive learning paradigms that Socrates spurned in the fifth century BC," the alternative being a constructivist/discovery learning paradigm containing "elements of th[e] Socratic model." In their study of effective teaching with technology, Bates and Poole (2003) lament what they see as the gulf between the Socratic ideal and the reality of "one size fits all" tendencies in contemporary higher education (12–13). Strikingly, Brabazon gives her 2002 book, on the threat to the quality of education posed by some e-learning paradigms, the title *Digital Hemlock*.

Socrates is widely viewed as an appropriate model for online teachers. Having detailed a depth education model for e-learning, Weigel (2001) introduces a quote from Socrates, implicitly highlighting the applicability of a Socratic attitude (139–140), while Kettner-Polley (1999) suggests that a Socratic method is the only viable or credible mode of instruction in a virtual learning environment (VLE). Burniske and Monke (2001) also advocate Socratic principles in online education, as do Hardin (2004) and Walker (2005). In 2003, Trufant displays supreme confidence in entitling an article "Move Over

Socrates: Online Discussion Is Here." Many agree that an online transformation is already underway whereby the teacher is naturally becoming a "Socratic tutor" (Hardaway 2005) or even a "Digital Socrates" (Coppola et al. 2002).

While most references in recent years have been to Socrates, Plato also figures in e-learning discussions. As early as 1991, Bolter registered the tentative quality of the text preserved in Plato's dialogs, and facilitated in an online environment (55–56); he is echoed by Morrell (2000) who asks: "can the new technology actually help realize the person-to-person encounters that Plato believed were a better means of conveying knowledge than the written word?" (64).

This is to say nothing of the academic and commercial e-learning organizations, projects and software which bear the name of one or other of these thinkers because of a perceived or desired connection with their ideas. Examples include the Italian e-Socrates virtual school; the online Socrates Café for school students run by the Department of Education in Tasmania, Australia; the US-based e-Socrates consultancy; the Socrates Distance Learning Technologies Group, also US-based; the Socrates 2.0 e-learning application from Digital Samba; and Project Plato (*Providing Learning And Teaching Online*) at the University of Adelaide, Australia. Older companies such as Plato Learning, already involved in educational software design prior to the advent of the Internet, may benefit from and reinforce this trend, while many other organizations whose names are not directly linked to the philosophers are still keen to promote such an association; thus the UK-based BrightWave e-learning consultancy, for example, states that its "designs and scripts are written in the spirit of Socrates" (BrightIdeas 2005).

On the other hand, the heritage of Socrates and Plato may be problematic for those with different agendas or priorities. For example, Spicer (2003) finds a hindrance in the fact that, as he puts it, the Socratic ideal "is not a scalable model" (148). Indeed it is not. Nor, as the foregoing quotations suggest, is scalability the only respect in which Socrates and Plato serve to highlight the clashes between very different approaches to education. However, before going on to examine in more detail the perceived heritage of these thinkers, what they mean today and to whom, it is firstly necessary to have a clearer conception of the parameters of the contemporary struggle around online education.

Virtual Learning: The Battle Lines

It has long been recognized that both repressive and liberating possibilities inhere in Western educational institutions. Serving, on the one hand, purposes of ideological control, they have also been semi-autonomous loci for the promotion of societal democratization and equalization. But if there have been moments of general liberalization such as that widely experienced in the sixties, then recent years have seen the erosion of past gains. With the gradual retreat of the state from the public sphere and the transformation of the state-as-provider into the state-as-contractor (Scott 1995: 171), Western education has become increasingly subject to the economics of the market and the creed of neoliberalism, where the state's overwhelming objective is to supply the standardized workforce—that is, human capital with transferable skills—necessary to compete in the ever more globalized knowledge-based economy (Aronowitz 2000; Geiger 2004; Giroux 2002, 2003; Lauzon 1999; Noble 2002a; Taylor et al. 2002; Yorke & Knight 2002). The confluence of neoliberalism and the neoconservative tide sweeping the West has ensured governmental mandates to establish more centralized control of education, including the imposition of bureaucratic accountability and standardized testing (Aronowitz & Giroux 1991; Mathison & Ross 2002; Pegrum 2004). While this is particularly true at compulsory levels, similar tendencies are manifesting themselves in the post-compulsory sphere. Higher education, in the worst-case scenario, is being reduced to "the handmaiden of corporate culture" (Giroux 2002), or the "university.com" (Katz 2000: 37), with faculty having little time or autonomy to maintain distance to political and economic structures, or cultivate the social critique and alternative perspectives traditionally regarded as integral to their roles (Aronowitz 2000: 13; Filmer 1997; Miyoshi 1998).

In 1997, Stuart Parker outlined a "two stories" thesis, in which he observed that there are two competing stories of education (implicitly, in the West): "In one there is a vocabulary of means, efficiency, universals, law-like generalization and bureaucracy; in the other, one of autonomy, emancipation, uniqueness, democracy, ends and values" (3). And to be sure, arrayed against the arguably growing power of positivist or techno-rationalist agendas, there are numerous countervailing movements, philosophies and practices which are not entirely compatible with each other, but which do have in common their oppositional stance. In the ebb and flow of the struggle over education, they have experienced varying degrees of success in varying contexts. Key examples drawn from the confused continuum ranging from liberal progressivism to postmodernism would include: Paulo Freire's emancipatory pedagogy (1996);

work on higher-order cognitive skills, with roots in the 1956 taxonomy of Benjamin Bloom et al., or deep learning, often inspired by constructivism; the broad constructivist movement, derived from the cognitive constructivism of Jean Piaget and the social constructivism of Lev Vygotsky; Howard Gardner's work on multiple intelligences (1983, 1999); the critical pedagogy of Henry Giroux, Peter McLaren and others who, inspired by Freire, move well beyond him to draw heavily on postmodern insights, though they arguably continue to operate within the project of modernity (Pennycook 2001; Usher & Edwards 1994); the multiliteracies of The New London Group (2000); the postmethod language pedagogy of Kumaravadivelu (2001, 2003); and numerous overtly postmodern approaches such as that of Parker (1997) or the critical applied linguistics of Pennycook (2001).

In a curious echo of Giroux's comment on higher education cited above, Lauzon suggests that educational technology is the handmaiden of the social order (1999: 266). More than that, as Noble (2002a) has argued, today's technological revolution effectively camouflages "the commercialization of higher education" (26) with its penchant for "the technologically prepackaged course" (32). Much has been written about the dangers of offering "education in a box" (Werry 2002a), of treating knowledge as a product to be downloaded (Greenwald & Rosner 2003), or of the potential lack of coherence of modular programs (Fay 2002), especially those making use of the transferable "learning objects" advocated by many (Rosenberg 2001: 170–172; Wiley et al. 2000).

Against the simplistic application of Parker's "first story," however, the e-learning medium, with its potential for interactivity, also lends itself to the realization of the aims of constructivists, critical pedagogues and postmodernists: in short, those who are writing the "second story," even if the latter is far from being a single narrative thread. (Although Parker regards postmodernists as transcending both stories, for the purposes of this chapter they are grouped with the second story, of which they compose a highly radicalized version which promotes a relativistic textuality unbound from overarching modernist aims such as democratization.) In their own ways, all oppose "a pedagogy and politics of certainty" (Giroux 2003: 14) and espouse an acceptance of "relativism as a positive position" (Laurillard 2002: 12). Teachers, in this view, are not disseminators of pre-established facts or the coaches of clearly defined skills; nor can students be viewed as empty vessels, passively waiting for knowledge. Rather, education is an exploratory partnership.

The frequent invocations of Socrates and Plato in the literature of oppositional pedagogy function either to bolster resistance to the "first story" or as building blocks for the "second story" in its many versions. Yet this begs a number of questions: What do Socrates and Plato, standing at the beginning of the tradition of rational(-ist) philosophy, have to say to educators and thinkers struggling against the creeping rationalization of twenty-first-century education? Can they really inform our discussions of education in cyberspace, or are they being misread or misused? In sum: How legitimate, and how useful, are the weapons Socrates and Plato have to offer today's educational philosophers and oppositional intellectuals on the front lines in the world of e-learning?

Socrates and Plato

Socrates was born at the peak of Athenian power, lived through the Golden Age of Pericles, and died as the star of his polis was waning in the wake of the Peloponnesian War. It was Athens on the wane which, in 399 BCE, executed Socrates for his beliefs, or arguably for his challenging of Athenian beliefs, by requiring him to drink the poison hemlock; and it was at this time, or shortly thereafter, that his teaching was set down in the form of dialogs by his pupil, Plato. It was also in Athens, in a grove named after the mythical Academus, that Plato later founded his Academy, launching the traditions of academia which, in altered form, still inform our universities today.

Much ink and many keystrokes have contributed to debating the so-called Socratic Problem which, given that Socrates seemingly wrote nothing himself, turns on the issue of where the influence of the historical Socrates ends and that of Plato—or other commentators such as Xenophon, Aeschines, Aristophanes and Plato's pupil Aristotle—begins. Unlikely ever to be conclusively settled, there is nevertheless some consensus that over the course of Plato's dialogs the non-doctrinaire Socrates gradually becomes a mouthpiece for the universalizing Platonic philosophical system (e.g., see Vlastos 1991, 1996a on Socrates$_E$ and Socrates$_M$; Graham 1996 on Early Dialogue Theory; Hackforth 1996), with the shift being perhaps most obviously visible in the *Meno* (at 81a;[1] see Guthrie 1956: 25; cf. Vlastos 1991: 54, 1996a: 144). There is inevitable overlap, however, as Plato struggles to preserve the Socratic method rather than the details of Socrates' arguments, before developing his own, very personal philosophy from his master's beginnings.

This overlap should be borne in mind in the following examination of four key aspects of their work, two nominally associated with Socrates and two with Plato, as should the fact that not only is Socrates to some extent a construct of Plato's but both are constructs of ours, especially at such historical distance. The second and third aspects, which concern the specific features of Socratic–Platonic philosophy most often mentioned by oppositional educators, are in many ways framed by the first and fourth aspects, which provide essential contextualization of the more specific ideas.

Socrates as Gadfly

"But Socrates, I have no way of telling you what I have in mind, for whatever proposition we put forward goes around and refuses to stay put where we establish it." Thus, in one of Plato's earliest works, Euthyphro demonstrates the effect on established opinion of the Socratic method (*Euthyphro* 11b). Also known as the *elenchus*, in the early dialogs it consists of Socrates' examination of a definition solicited from an interlocutor and his undermining of it through a rational demonstration of its inconsistency with the interlocutor's other beliefs. Many of the dialogs are *aporetic* since they end in a puzzle with no obvious positive solution, and to that extent may be seen as negative.

Socrates himself professes not to know anything, as expressed most famously in the *Apology*, the account of his trial, where the status of the wisest man in Athens attributed to him by the Delphic Oracle is seen to rest on the fact that unlike other men he is at least aware that he knows nothing (20d–23b). Notwithstanding the fact that Socrates' claims of ignorance may be deceptively complex, resting on a question of definitions or categories of knowledge (Lesher 1996; Vlastos 1996b; Woodruff 1996), it has been widely argued that he is less a teacher and more "a fellow searcher" (Hackforth 1996: 6). Certainly, Socrates maintains at his trial that he has "never been anyone's teacher" (*Apology* 33a) and that his purpose has only ever been to ask difficult questions for, he says, "the unexamined life is not worth living" (38a). In fact, he claims to have been attached to Athens "as upon a great and noble horse which was somewhat sluggish because of its size and needed to be stirred up by a kind of gadfly" (30e). In other words, Socrates, the gadfly, has been attempting to rouse Athens from its comfortable sleep. The moral overtones of the quest are apparent when Socrates, in full recognition of his unpopularity and outsider status, describes his typical manner of address to a fellow Athenian:

> Good Sir, you are an Athenian, a citizen of the greatest city with the greatest reputation for both wisdom and power; are you not ashamed of your eagerness to possess as much wealth, reputation and honors as possible, while you do not care for nor give thought to wisdom or truth, or the best possible state of your soul? (29d–e)

He is often seen in counterpoint to the traveling Sophists who made a living from selling lessons, particularly in rhetorical skills, and who, despite the fact that some were important thinkers and that even Socrates accorded a degree of respect to the great Sophist, Protagoras, have generally come to be associated with the deceptive manipulation of words. Thus Socrates, who seemingly never charged for conversational services, warns: "And watch, or the sophist might deceive us in advertising what he sells, the way merchants who market food for the body do" (*Protagoras* 313d).

It is but a small step to link Socrates, if loosely and somewhat naïvely, with the deconstructive practices of our own time or with the intellectual guerrilla theme which runs, now implicitly, now explicitly, through postmodernism, for example in Deleuze's (1973) advocacy of nomadic struggles against centralized societal structures, or Foucault's (1976) valorization of a multiplicity of transitory, mobile resistances (126–127). It is tempting, also, to insert Socrates' name among those of the "edifying philosophers" described by Rorty (1980). Focusing on the likes of Wittgenstein and Heidegger, but with minor reference to Nietzsche and Derrida, Rorty brackets together those thinkers who, rather than offering constructive arguments, "are *intentionally* peripheral" and "destroy for the sake of their own generation" (369). Such a move is supported by one of the charges brought against Socrates by the Athenian Court, namely that he "is guilty of corrupting the young and of not believing in the gods in whom the city believes, but in other new spiritual things" (*Apology* 24b–c). The myth of the cave in Plato's *Republic* also underlines this conception, suggesting that a man would be killed by the cave dwellers for trying to puncture their illusions and point them toward the light (517a). Of course, Socrates' antagonism vis-à-vis the state is also paralleled by his opposition to the Sophists' selling of knowledge that might be of little real value, a situation with clear analogies to the current commercialization and packaging of education.

In a time of crisis, there is a propensity to return to the old certainties and suppress those who question them. Parallels might be noted between the Athens of Socrates' day, recovering from the shock of its humiliation at the hands of the Spartans, and the New York of our own time. Perhaps Socrates seemed a threat to the fragile and recently resuscitated fledgling democracy of Athens (Gallop 1999: xviii); certainly terrorists are viewed as a threat to contemporary Western democracy. The tendency may well be for democracy concerned for its defense to become less democratic—or to be reduced to a set of sacred principles, as immune to challenge as the old Greek gods. Needless to say, if September 11 is leading to a tightening of educational screws (Decoo 2001; Giroux 2002; Noble 2002a: 93–95), this is likely to mean a further clampdown on alternatives to neoliberalism and neoconservatism. Significantly, commenting on the potential for the development of critical thinking in e-learning, Burniske and Monke note that there are always dangers: "It's the kind of education that got Socrates hemlocked" (2001: 260).

Although Socrates might have denied being a teacher, he would doubtless not have been impressed by what Apple (1986) calls the deskilling of today's teachers—their reduction to the role of bureaucratic technicians—or their market-driven reinvention as customer-oriented "digital butlers" (Brabazon 2002: 187; cf. Brabazon, this volume). Parker's "first story" requires a bureaucracy which "runs to a belief that in education there is a single right answer, and that managers know it, and precipitates a lack of trust of the underlings which necessitates a strong police force of inspectors" (1997: 4). This can only mean that it is time for new gadflies to emerge from among the underlings. Indeed, this process has already begun with the appearance of vociferous oppositional thinkers, perhaps most notably those with a postmodern bent.

It is not difficult to see, given aspects of congruence between Socrates' responses to his own situation and contemporary oppositional stances on education, why today's educators might turn to him for inspiration. Brabazon reflects the admiration of many teachers and reveals something of why Socrates is still meaningful in the cyber-era when she notes that "Socrates remains a beacon for educators, and not because he provided the answers to complex theorems or conducted the perfect proof. Instead, he had the courage to ask difficult questions" (2002: vii).

And yet all of the above rests on a somewhat selective reading of Socrates, focused primarily on the early dialogs. Even these are arguably underpinned by a belief in universal goodness, and in the hands of Plato, the literary Socrates moves ever more explicitly toward absolutes, transcendent truth—and a rejection of Protagoras' dictum that "man is the measure of all things" in the late dialog *Theaetetus*. Such a refusal of relativism, while likely to be problematic for most progressives among today's oppositional educators, leaves no room at all for the contextualization and particularity central to approaches which draw on postmodern insights. The move toward the Platonic philosophical system, however, begins much earlier; and it has been suggested, for example, that in Plato's middle-period *Republic*, the enlightened Guardians who are to take care of the ignorant cave dwellers seem like "intellectual imperialists in a dark place" (Williams 1998: 38).[2] Is this equally true of Socrates? Certainly, insofar as he becomes a mouthpiece for Platonic philosophy, he is more like Rorty's "systematic philosophers" or foundational thinkers who seek "universal commensuration in a final vocabulary" and "build for eternity" (1980: 368–369).

Nor can it have escaped notice that many postmodernist philosophers regard Socrates, who from the outset works with an implicit belief in the supremacy of reason as the basis of his method, as standing at the beginning of the universalizing rational tradition which they oppose. Lyotard (1976), hammering out his own take on the nomadic guerrilla theme, advocates small-scale attacks and retortions which specifically "belong to a logic which is that of the sophists and rhetoricians of the first generation, not of the logician" (153; my translation). Whatever degree of system building may or may not be attributed to Socrates, there is little doubt that he heads the tradition of logicians, of rationalists, with which postmodernism takes issue.

It is equally important to consider who else, in recent decades, has made use of Socrates to push other agendas. In particular, his name is often found adorning neoconservative proposals for a return to canonicity. One notable example which might alarm liberals and postmodernists alike is *The Closing of the American Mind*, whose author, Allan Bloom, describing what he sees as the crisis of universities, notes that "contemplation of Socrates is our most urgent task" (1988: 312). Similarly, in *Cultural Literacy*, E.D. Hirsch, a self-confessed enemy of pluralism in education, opposes to "the curriculum of cultural fragmentation and illiteracy" (1987: 144), his own, co-authored list of core knowledge, which does not omit to feature "Socrates," "Plato" and "Platonism."

Socratic philosophy is sufficiently complex—some might argue, sufficiently divided against itself—to allow for alternative readings and manipulations. Those who draw on it to support a contemporary oppositional stance should be aware that they are adopting some ideas to the exclusion of others, and that the aspects adopted reveal as much about them as about Socrates. Nowhere is this more evident than in the appropriation of the model of Socratic dialog, undoubtedly the single feature which has found the most resonance with today's online educators, and to which we now turn.

Socrates as Dialogist

Expert opinion lends credence to the contemporary appeal of Socratic dialog. Thus, Plato translator W.K.C. Guthrie indicates that early and middle-period Platonic dialog:

> cannot be analysed and presented as a collection of neatly tied and labelled parcels of philosophical doctrine. At least, to do so would be to travesty Plato, who made it clear that he did not believe philosophy could be retailed in that way. It could only be a product of living contact between mind and mind, in which one strikes sparks from the other as steel from flint. (1956: 9–10)

For his part, Myles Burnyeat, scholar of ancient philosophy, sees the real benefit of Socratic dialog in that:

> You end up not with a firm answer, but with a much better grasp of the problem than you had before. Whether you are a twentieth-century reader or an ancient reader, you have been drawn into the problem; you are left still wanting to get the answer, and feeling that perhaps you can contribute. (Magee 1987: 16)

Clearer support for the shift from a transmission to a dialogic model of education, one centered on co-operative exploration, multiple perspectives and resistance to closure, would be difficult to find, unless perhaps in the words of Socrates himself. In the *Meno*, he makes it apparent that the teacher can act as a guide but cannot give the student knowledge, which the latter will arrive at "without having been taught but only questioned," a process leading the student to "find the knowledge within himself" (85d).[3] A corollary of such a stance is a democratization of student and teacher roles. During his debate with Protagoras, Socrates announces: "I am primarily interested in testing the argument, although it may happen both that the questioner, myself, and my respondent wind up being tested" (*Protagoras* 333c). Later in the same dialog, Socrates invites Protagoras to engage in a joint investigation of the topic under discussion (347c; cf. 361d). Protagoras is of course a figure of high intellectual caliber, but Socrates likewise expresses to the young Meno his wish "to examine and seek together with" him a possible answer to the question of what virtue is (*Meno* 80d). This is because, says Socrates: "I myself do not have the answer when I perplex others, but I am more perplexed than anyone when I cause perplexity in others" (80c). Far from being a fount of wisdom, the teacher is, as Hackett was seen to say earlier, a fellow searcher or, in updated pedagogical terminology, a fellow member (if a relatively experienced one) of a community of inquiry.

From Freire's statement that "there is no oppressive reality which is not at the same time necessarily antidialogical" (1996: 121) to Giroux's insistence on the importance of "revitalizing public dialogue" (2002), dialog has been regarded by oppositional educators as crucial both in wider society and in education itself; this is as true of constructivism (R. Vanden in Lauzon 1999: 263; Whittle et al. 2000) as of postmodernism (Parker 1997; Usher & Edwards 1994). A penchant for dialog of a Socratic nature might even be regarded as a key difference between the two competing stories of education. Burniske states:

> In essence, I'm describing a division between the Land of Answers and the Sea of Questions. Administrators step off *terra firma* when they enter a classroom in which

> Socratic methods lead to an infinite exploration; teachers, meanwhile, bemoan the tedium of simplistic answers they must endure upon the shore of supposed "faculty meetings" run by administrators. (Burniske & Monke 2001: 89)

It has often been remarked that new technologies tend to amplify certain values and downplay others (Burniske & Monke 2001: 20–26; Garrison & Anderson 2003: 5–7). It is axiomatic for oppositional educators that a VLE can and should function as a modern-day, virtual agora which "takes dialogue as the fundamental way of inquiry" (E. Christiansen & L. Dirckinck-Holmfeld in Palloff & Pratt 2001: 32–33); that "cyber learning has electronic dialogue at its heart" (Maeroff 2003: 61); that online interaction facilitates the "dialogue across difference" which is much more difficult in a face-to-face class (Lauzon 1999: 273, with reference to Burbules & Rice 1991); in sum, that the nature of the online environment and its supporting technology can massively assist the shift away from transmission models of education to interactive, collaborative and dialogic ones (Brown 2001; Coomey & Stephenson 2001; Harasim 1989; Lapadat 2002). Notwithstanding warnings of the dangers inhering to various aspects of the Enlightenment-derived model of autonomous speaking subjects engaged in rational, consensual dialog (Ellsworth 1989; Giroux 1997: 222; Parker 1997: 153–154; Pennycook 2001: 119), especially across languages and cultures (Cameron 2002; Goodfellow 2003a, b; cf. Ess, this volume; McCormick, this volume), the shift to a dialogic approach—most commonly an asynchronous one, with the flexibility and reflection time this offers—is broadly promoted as a means of achieving the co-operation, multivocality and openness which are typically opposed to techno-rationalist models of knowledge delivery.

Not surprisingly, for many embattled educators this shift occurs under the aegis of Socrates. Bates and Poole believe that "Plato's Socratic Method," by which they mean "small group discussions led by an experienced academic," is facilitated by online technology (2003: 100). As noted earlier, Azevedo (1998) advocates "The Socrates Online Method," while Kettner-Polley (1999) sees no real alternative to "a Socratic method of instruction" online. For Trufant (2003), threaded online discussion "is simply the Socratic method brought forward to a new environment" (2). When Burniske and Monke speak of "embracing the spirit of ancient discourse rather than modern sound bites" in an email exchange (2001: 229), it is not difficult to guess what—and whom—they have in mind. It has even been claimed that there is empirical evidence of a shift underway through which the teaching persona is becoming "a kind of a 'Digital Socrates,' which [sic] shifts from conveying information to raising questions and engaging in dialogue" (Coppola et al. 2002: 186).

As seen above, by its very nature educational dialog can promote a radical democratization of student–teacher relations. This again is a theme found throughout oppositional pedagogy with its emphasis on respectful interaction where teachers relinquish some control, but it is especially pronounced in e-learning. Goodfellow (2001) notes the widespread agreement in the literature that "the passing of responsibility for learning from the teacher to the student is one of the characteristics of progressive pedagogy in general and online educational innovation in particular." This paradigm is facilitated in VLEs by an embedded pedagogy which makes learner control a dominant feature (Doherty 1998), while the teacher becomes "a member of a learning team" (Ryan et al. 2000: 112) who contributes along with students to a jointly constructed knowledge space (Doherty 1998). Possibilities for negotiated syllabi and curricula are also opened up.

This does not mean that the teacher's role is any less crucial or demanding than in traditional pedagogy. To the contrary, Pegrum and Spöring (2004), following Pegrum and Cook (2003), have argued that a teacher who takes seriously the need for both exploratory dialog and learner empowerment finds him-/herself faced with a rather complex and at least tripartite role in online discussion, where he/she must fulfill the following functions:

1. *Teacher*: structuring learning experiences and initiating discussion, which he/she must then guide and facilitate, offering direct input where factual issues arise but for the most part supporting students in developing and synthesizing their own ideas.

2. *Monitor*: knowing when to step back and observe from a distance, allowing students to interact with each other in "the creation of new patterns of understanding built on the foundation of shared individual perspectives" (Belanger & Jordan 2000: 23).

3. *Learner*: knowing when to step back in as a peer among peers, i.e., where he/she is also a learner, thereby approximating the Freirean (1996) ideal of everyone being simultaneously a teacher and a student.

It is nevertheless important to guard against a pervasive disingenuousness in accounts of student and teacher roles: teachers are not really equal to students, which becomes particularly clear in the common practice of assessing online discussions as a means of ensuring full participation (Goodfellow 2001, 2003a). Nor ought they to be seen as equal, since it is precisely their superior specialist knowledge and depth of experience, often hard-won, which qualifies them to organize learning events, guide students and moderate discussions (cf. Brabazon 2002; Garrison & Anderson 2003), though this is a position into which, over time, learners should be able and encouraged to grow. That said, the dialog which is enabled by the opening up of authoritarian, hierarchical teacher–student structures to allow broad participation and, where appropriate, questioning of or disagreement with the teacher, in short, where there is an increasingly "distributed teaching presence" (Garrison & Anderson 2003: 72), produces spectacular, creative results. This involves an interweaving of ideas to generate an organic and rich intertextuality, a "plurivocal record of inquiry" (R.L. Bangert-Drowns in Lapadat 2002) unconstrained by requirements for linear development, and with latitude for the parallel expression of minority perspectives (Graddol 1989).

To all appearances, especially if we allow that teacher and student roles are to be complementary rather than structurally equal, the Socratic dialogs are a step on the path to this kind of distributed teaching presence and plurivocality; or more accurately, today's educators are taking a step back in that direction, to a moment just prior to the rise of the linear texts which have shaped Western civilization and mediated educational authority for more than two millennia. And yet, when the part played by Socrates is compared with the roles outlined by Pegrum and Spöring above, or the resulting dialogs are measured against the notion of unrestricted intertextuality, major differences become manifest.

By his own account, Socrates goes some way toward fulfilling the first role of facilitating the development of the students' own ideas, as suggested by his self-description as a midwife in the *Theaetetus* (149a–151b). Nevertheless, despite meta-dialogic comments such as this, or those cited earlier, in practice the support and guidance required of a teacher as the senior member of a learning team are little in evidence, as we witness Socrates often harrying his interlocutors into an acceptance of his own stance, not infrequently making them appear ridiculous in the process. Poor Meno does not stand a chance and reproaches Socrates:

> you seem, in appearance and in every other way, to be like the broad torpedo fish [sting ray], for it too makes anyone who comes close and touches it feel numb, and you now seem to have had that kind of effect on me, for both my mind and my tongue are numb, and I have no answer to give you. (*Meno* 80a–b)

The issue of whether Socrates feels the same way aside (80c), we might ask whether this is a useful state to which to bring an interlocutor, whose contribution to the dialog in any case largely consists of frequently intoned replies such as: "Yes," "Certainly," "So it seems," and "That is so," interspersed with longer versions: "That seems to me to be an excellent answer, Socrates" (76d), "I think it must necessarily be as you say" (79a), "That seems indisputable, Socrates" (85e), "Somehow, Socrates, I think that what you say is right" (86b), "In this too I think you are right, Socrates" (86c), "What you say, Socrates, seems to me quite right" (89a), "I cannot tell, Socrates ..." (95c), "By all means tell me" (97d), "Yes, by Zeus, Socrates, it seems to be something like that" (98a), "I think you are right in this too" (98b), "It is likely to be as you say, Socrates" (99b), all of which lead up to Meno's final humble avowal: "I think that is an excellent way to put it, Socrates" (100b). This does not sound much like teamwork.

In fact, the adversarial nature of some dialogs makes the other speakers seem less like interlocutors than opponents, while many speakers are little more than caricatures, a backdrop against which an idealized Socrates can shine.[4] Nor are Socrates' arguments always justifiable or fair (Guthrie 1956: 19–20), and the same might be said of his often rather one-sided questioning, not to mention its sometimes destructive effects. Small wonder that Thrasymachus admonishes Socrates in the *Republic*: "You know very well that it is easier to ask questions than answer them" (336c). Bernard Williams comments that a substantial number of characters in the dialogs as well as Plato's subsequent readers see:

> the question and answer form as itself a rhetorical contrivance, one that helps Socrates to force his opponents down a favoured train of thought, often a chain of misleading analogies, instead of giving them a chance to stand back and ask what other kinds of consideration might bear on the issue. (1998: 12)

Indeed, Socrates' conversations do not generally seem open-ended but rather pre-planned and hence do not correspond to the wishes of today's educators for unpredictable, opportunistic dialog (Garrison & Anderson 2003: 117; Morgan 2000; Muirhead 2001: 108). Aronowitz (2000: 190) views the Socratic method as a closed instructional strategy with single right answers, while Laurillard also rejects the espousal of Socratic dialog as an educational ideal. In her analysis of Socrates' conversation with the slave which occurs within the aforementioned *Meno*, she comments:

> In essence it is a strategy designed to reduce his interlocutor to helplessness, when they are ready to capitulate to anything he says: "let it be as you say", "certainly, Socrates". It is extremely authoritarian. The Socratic method is not, as it is often described, a tutorial method that allows the student to come to an understanding of what they know. It is a rhetorical method that gives all the responsibility to, and therefore achieves all the benefit for, the teacher. (2002: 76)

As we have seen, Meno, the slave's master, does not fare much better at Socrates' hands. Ultimately, as Szlezák observes, "[t]here is no conversation among equals in Plato" (1999: 106). This is the case even with much more sophisticated interlocutors than Meno; for if in the early aporetic dialogs, the intention is for the superior interlocutor to bring the conversational partner to a recognition of his own ignorance of the subject at hand, then in later pieces it seems to be to lead the partner in the direction of some higher Platonic truth.

Whatever his meta-dialogic claims, then, it is apparent that Socrates fails to fulfill the first of Pegrum and Spöring's roles in that he does little to foster the development of the students' own ideas, and is in no sense merely a guide or facilitator. Moreover, and again despite protestations of ignorance, he rarely if ever steps into the third role of a learner among learners. Finally, he actively blocks the kind of student–student exchanges at the heart of the second role, where the teacher is to monitor from a distance. Rather, discussion is controlled by and channeled through Socrates so that other participants do not discuss issues directly with one another (Szlezák 1999: 23, 104–105). Not for Socrates the role of weaver (Feenberg 1989) or e-moderator (Salmon 2000) of others' contributions! In the final analysis, this refusal of the possibilities of distributed teaching severely limits the potential for plurivocality, or for the intertextual richness which is the main outcome of well-guided online discussion.

To be fair, the three-role model presented above is no more than an idealization. Furthermore, it is only one among an abundance of such models, but it is certain that Socrates' strategies would be found similarly wanting by comparison with almost any progressive, democratic or critical model which might serve to guide today's online education. It is probably inevitable, on the other hand, that educators fall short of models, and it is surely unrealistic to expect a historical figure to live up to externally imposed ideals which relate to an age far removed from his own. In brief, it is possible to continue to draw inspiration from some aspects of his work, notably his meta-dialogic comments, but in the knowledge that the Socratic ideal, as commonly conceived of nowadays by oppositional educators, is rarely exemplified by Socrates' dialogs themselves.

Plato as Tentative

You know, Phaedrus, writing shares a strange feature with painting. The offsprings [sic] of painting stand there as if they are alive, but if anyone asks them anything, they remain most solemnly silent. The same is true of written words. You'd think they were speaking as if they had some understanding, but if you question anything that has been said because you want to learn more, it continues to signify just that very same thing forever. (*Phaedrus* 275d–e)

Thus Socrates gives his opinion on writing, a view shared by his pupil and literary animator, Plato, who attempted to preserve the aura of speech as far as possible within the constraints of the writing technologies of his day: that is, through the dialogic presentation of Socrates' and his own philosophy. While there are various implications and interpretations of Plato's assertion of the primacy of speech over writing, speech—or at least the use of the dialogic form in writing—seems to impart a certain tentativeness to the discussion (this idea is supported by Plato's willingness to question his own conclusions, as forcefully demonstrated in the *Parmenides* where the tables are turned on the literary Socrates). At the same time, as suggested earlier, it implicitly valorizes the interaction of minds, rather than the transmission of a set of ideas from one person to another.

Bolter (1991) views the electronic medium as fostering the tentativeness which Plato sought to preserve in his dialogs (55–56). This dovetails with later characterizations of online discussion as inquiring, experimental and hypothetical (Morgan 2000), and with the move away from teaching as a dealership in pre-established knowledge. Plato, argues Morrell (2000), recognized the danger of extracting ideas from discourse and encoding them in text. Morrell suggests that although online technology risks being turned to the ends of knowledge transmission, it might equally be used to encourage the person-to-person encounters on which Plato placed such value (63–64). The cautious and provisional nature of such encounters is necessarily opposed to the certainties of techno-rationalism.

In a sense, by combining the interactive nature of dialog with the reflective aspects of writing online (Garrison & Anderson 2003: 6, 26; Warschauer 1999: 6), we may have stumbled across a resolution of the interaction/reflection dilemma which has haunted the West ever since Plato began to set down Socrates' speech in writing. Plato's was undoubtedly an uneasy compromise position. To the extent that online discussion represents a viable resolution of his dilemma, it reinforces the case for the use of written dialog in cyberspace, especially in light of emerging evidence that text is more conducive to effective educational discussion than the budding audio or video channels (Lapadat 2002; Richards 2000: 66). On the one hand, it overcomes many of the limitations of spoken classroom-based discourse, where interactivity comes at the price of reflection and there is no record which can be revisited and reworked; and on the other hand, it transcends unidirectional modes, notably the use of prepackaged distance learning materials where student response is limited to little more than mid-course and end-of-course essays.

And yet, as always, it is necessary to beware the possibility of transposing present concerns into the past. It has been suggested, for example, that Plato's use of dialog is less about reproducing oral tentativeness and more about the demonstration of steps toward a correct *homology*, or agreement, and that the apparent openness of the dialogs indicates that they are merely an introduction to a more sophisticated oral philosophy, initiation into which is reserved for those deemed to be ready (Szlezák 1999). Difficult as it may be to adjudicate among competing views on Platonic tentativeness, at the very least we are compelled to remember that what we seek and seem to find in Plato may or may not correspond to his original intentions and philosophy, although it certainly corresponds to present needs.

Plato as Educator

If Socrates' role as a foundational or systematic philosopher can be seen in balance with his role as a peripheral thinker, a guerrilla, a gadfly, the same is not true of Plato, whose systematic philosophy overshadows all other aspects of his life and work. Nevertheless, just as Socrates' gadfly role lends him a measure of credibility and authenticity in the eyes of today's oppositional educators— whatever the details of his philosophy—Plato's theoretical privileging and practical promotion of education has helped him to be viewed, too, as a possible comrade-in-arms. For higher education there can be no symbolically greater figure, especially given that the closure in 529 CE of his Academy, generally recognized as the forerunner of today's universities, effectively capped institutional secular education until toward the end of the Dark Ages when it began to reemerge in the fledgling universities of Western Europe.

Today there is a move in the direction of treating schooling and education in general as a private good (Geiger 2004: 66; Giroux 2003: 7). After all, marketization, with its corollary of privatization, entails viewing society as "a collection of possessive individuals" and downgrading a sense of the common good (Apple 1995: xvii). In education this means a tendency to treat students as "customers" and "consumers" (Giroux 2002), the latter being, as Bourdieu has noted, "the commercial substitute for the citizen" (1998: 25). In such a context it is salutary to recall Plato's unswerving commitment to education as a state responsibility, as seen in the *Republic* and the *Laws*. This corresponds to his broader belief that there is nothing worse than the splintering of the common good into selfish, competitive individualism undergirded by the inequitable distribution of wealth: "Is there any greater evil we can mention for a city than that which tears it apart and makes it many instead of one? Or any greater good than that which binds it together and makes it one?" (*Republic* 462a–b).

With a little adjustment, significant tracts of the *Republic* could be read as a critique of (neo-)liberalism and a defense of the collective or common interest—in which Plato sees education playing a pivotal role. Education is viewed as a long-term process aimed at developing character as much as specific knowledge or skills, in which respect it might be contrasted with the "short-termism" of utilitarian agendas (Fay 2002) and their targeted, just-in-time nature. In an uncanny anticipation of contemporary concerns, which in fact belies their contemporary nature, Plato has Socrates announce:

> Education isn't what some people declare it to be, namely, putting knowledge into souls that lack it, like putting sight into blind eyes. [...] Education takes for granted that sight is there but that it isn't turned the right way or looking where it ought to look, and it tries to redirect it appropriately. (*Republic* 518b–d)

It is unsurprising, then, that today's educators turn so often to the Socratic–Platonic duo. And yet Plato is "not a good nineteenth-century liberal" (Lee 2003: xlix), much less a constructivist or a postmodernist. His attack on individualism and the breakdown of society extends to a savage critique of democracy (e.g., *Republic* 488a–489a) and its champions such as Pericles (e.g. *Gorgias* 515d–516d). Instead he proposes a totalitarian, rigidly stratified and heavily censored society, critiqued, notably, by Karl Popper in 1945 in the wake of Europe's mid-twentieth-century experiences with fascism (Popper 1966). As outlined in the *Republic*, education would be the preserve of the upper stratum, the Guardians, the most gifted of whom, destined to be Rulers, would progress eventually toward an understanding of the Good. This aim relates in turn to Plato's essentialist, anti-historicist Theory of Forms, which posits absolute, eternal realities set apart from the transient and imperfect sensory world. If Plato's elite education system mitigates against the kind of "anytime, anyplace, anyone" education or its more emphatic "everyone, every place, all the time" form championed by proponents of online learning such as Duderstadt (2000: 330), his essentialism and dualism are utterly incompatible with constructivism, critical pedagogy or postmodern positions.

While wholly opposed to Plato's solution, Popper (1966) grants that the philosopher's diagnosis of the social problems of his time was largely correct, and argues that he was advocating a return to tribalism in the face of strains attributable to the rise of democracy and individualism (171) in the shift to an "open society" (173). This is particularly significant in our own postmodern age, as tribalism and fundamentalism increasingly rear their heads in both local and international contexts. Indeed, as Popper observes, "[i]n spite of Socrates' warning against misanthropy and misology, [Plato] was led to distrust man and to fear argument" (200). Popper suggests in effect that we should read Socrates *against* Plato, recognizing the fundamental opposition of their stances. This in itself indicates the dangers inherent in any easy appropriation of the work of either, and particularly in the all-too-easy and all-too-common conflation of the two figures.

Thus, it is apparent that key facets of Plato's work—primarily his maintenance of the dialogic form and the assumed espousal of tentativeness and interaction as core values—can be readily and helpfully contextualized within some parts of his broader philosophy, particularly his views on state education as a countermeasure to the atomization of society. However, there are other aspects of his thinking which are seriously at variance with contemporary oppositional pedagogical stances, arguably even more so than in the case of Socrates, his master, with whom he may in fact have less in common than is often supposed.

Socrates and Plato: Ideal Teachers for the Virtual Agora?

At present, institutions of higher education continue to provide some space for teachers and students to challenge the epochal creed of neoliberalism and its associated discourses. If today's language of managerialism "walks blithely over a whole tradition of Western philosophy, crushing all subtleties and distinctions" (Watson 2003: 27), then it may be that a resuscitation of the philosophical tradition is in order. If it is a case of "winning back democracy from technocracy" (Bourdieu 1998: 26), perhaps it is time to revisit our proto-democratic roots in Athens. If "[t]here is a tissue of continuity and commitment that connects teachers, from Socrates to the present" (Brabazon 2002: 127), then it may be apposite for those under threat from standardization and deskilling to appeal to the respected teachers of the past. And if online educators see in e-learning new possibilities for exploratory dialog as a medium for the democratization and pluralization which are increasingly marginalized in state-governed or commercial education, why should they not find non-virtual precedents in Ancient Greece?

On the other hand, the frequent invocation of Socrates and Plato by today's oppositional educators working within e-learning would seem to indicate that many are looking, ironically, for an authoritative approach to anti-authoritarianism. One of the dangers of such a stance is illustrated by the increasingly unreflective association of online learning with Socratic and Platonic ideals made not only by educators but also by commercial enterprises, as seen at the outset of this chapter. Merely invoking the name of one or other of these thinkers seems to function as a guarantee of educational progressiveness, forestalling closer and more probing questioning.

If the canons of the conservatives are to be interrogated, so too must the use of all foundational figures, including Socrates and Plato. Such an interrogation, as in this chapter, highlights our tendency to (re-)read the past selectively. If Socrates overturned clichés, undermined certainty, promoted self-examination and drew his fellow citizens into dialog, he also bullied his interlocutors, valorized the reason whose reincarnation as techno-rationalism haunts us more than two millennia later, and rejected relativity, while moving, in the hands of his pupil and scribe, ever closer to the eternal and innate truths of the Platonic system. Socrates the gadfly became, and perhaps always was, Socrates the builder of a new establishment. Plato, despite apparently accentuating open dialog, tentativeness and interactivity, was never anything other than the builder of a new establishment, one whose prioritization of education appeals to contemporary critical thinkers, but whose elitism and essentialism are more likely to resonate with neoconservative agendas.

It is apparent that Socrates and Plato simply cannot answer the contemporary call to "reject [ ] finality and certainty for the voice of difference and dialogue" (Aronowitz & Giroux 1991: 188), whether on- or offline. In other words, there can be no simple remedies in an appeal to these figures—and why should there be? Their responses were crafted for their own world, in which the Enlightenment was still 2000 years away. The adherents of the "second story," it was suggested above, are a disparate group and are in part defined by the fact that they do not look for simple answers or easy solutions. Bearing this in mind, today's oppositional educators should be prepared to draw from Socrates and Plato as and when appropriate, but should be wary of seeking definitive guidance from the figures of the past, or of using their names as simple shorthand for the strategies being developed to deal with the exigencies of the present time.

It would be difficult to contend that, on balance, Socrates and Plato are forces for openness, egalitarianism or multiplicity. Nevertheless, there are aspects of their philosophy, such as the Socratic meta-dialogic commentary and Platonic tentativeness, which can be disentangled from their wider work and pressed into service in current critiques of pedagogical practice. What is more, the inspiration to be found in their work can help to link various strands and sites of resistance. Socrates the gadfly and Plato the educator speak a language understood by many of today's beleaguered teachers, and can thereby contribute a certain amount to what might best be described as an unholy alliance—coalesced under increasing pressure from neoliberalism, with its positivist and techno-rationalist discourses—in search of the most effective oppositional pedagogies.

Notes

1. Quotations from Plato's works are normally referenced by means of the Stephanus numbers printed in the margins of the texts. These correspond to the pages and sections of the 1578 Greek edition of Plato's texts by Henri Estienne, and allow easy comparison across translations and editions. All quotations in this chapter are from Plato (1997).

2. Williams goes on to argue that Plato cannot really have conceived of the Guardians in this way. Nonetheless, this does not alter the fact that readers of the *Republic* are likely to come away with such an impression, or that this might be the net effect of Plato's scheme.

3. The *Meno* is the dialog that signals the shift to the Platonic system whereby learning is merely recollection of what the immortal soul already knows, which is Socrates' explanation as to why the student is able to find this knowledge within himself. However, this does not invalidate the principle of the learner arriving at knowledge through guided questioning by the teacher, but without prepackaged answers being handed over.

4. An exception is the late dialog *Parmenides*, where Plato is querying the underpinnings of his own *Republic*.

Chapter 2

The Political Economy of the "New" Discourse of Higher Education

Mary Low O'Sullivan and Tom Palaskas

The revolution in communications and information technologies and the much touted emergence of the information society means that this is a time of rapid change in all sectors of society; in the way people will spend and organize their lives, blurring the boundaries between work and leisure, for example. These new realities bring with them new learning needs (Carnoy 1999; Davies 1998; Galbreath 1999; Reigeluth 1992; Reigeluth & Garfinkle 1992; Trilling & Hood 1999). The development of online learning, e-learning or networked learning resulting from the emergence of the Internet and the World Wide Web has been embraced by educators and educational institutions as a means of meeting these new learning needs (Davies 1998; Harasim et al. 1995; O'Tuathail & McCormack 1998; Palloff & Pratt 1999). Educators who have been at the forefront of online learning, such as Harasim et al. (1995) and Palloff and Pratt (1999), have focused on the potential of the Internet and World Wide Web to transform teaching and learning practices. Harasim et al. (1995) are optimistic in stating that online learning will result in "expanded educational access" (273) and that people will be able to access "the educational services that best suit their needs" (269–270). However, we argue that there are different purposes of online learning as there are many different players within the current higher education context. The purpose of online learning as conceptualized by those who espouse an educational social constructivist agenda differs from the purpose of those who view online learning as an instrument of a neoliberal economic agenda (Greener & Perriton 2005; O'Tuathail & McCormack 1998; cf. Pegrum, this volume).

Similarly, the economic and technological transformations which are currently occurring in our world are interpreted differently by various social agents depending on their positionality in society. Thus the "new learning needs" are given different meanings by different players in the higher education enterprise. For example, the set of "new learning needs" as conceptualized by educators and educationists who have a social constructivist agenda would differ from the conceptions of those actors who pursue a neoliberal agenda. Educators who view their role as that of critical or transformative intellectuals (Aronowitz & Giroux 1985: 36–43) assume that a university education involves participants engaging in vibrant and critical debates "about the kind of society we want to live in" (Smyth & Hattam 2000: 157; cf. McLaren 2003). However, agents working for the Organization for Economic Cooperation and Development (OECD) and the World Bank have emphasized the economic importance of higher education and training (Gibbons 1998). The neoliberal discourse on higher education focuses on the development of "human resources" in terms of "upskilling and increasing of competencies for workers," seen as essential for nation-states to successfully compete in today's international marketplace (Giroux & Myrsiades 2001; Peters & Roberts 2000: 125).

In the dominant discourse of neoliberalism, the source of national comparative advantage now consists of knowledge and skills. Research and scientific knowledge are given value according to economics and productivity terms (Levin 2002; Peters & Roberts 2000; Torres & Schugurensky 2002). As a consequence of changing economic and political conditions arising from the emergence of the new regime of flexible accumulation, the competitive state form has replaced the traditional Keynesian state (Bonal 2003: 160). At the level of the nation-state, Australia, like many developed countries, is currently engendering change in its higher education sector in order to provide the kinds of higher education services that Australia and its citizens will require so as to compete successfully in the "new knowledge-based world economy" (Considine et al. 2001). Colin Gordon's insight into the neoliberal view of education is illuminating here. Gordon (1991) analyzed the neoliberal conception of work as the worker's "use of resources of skill, aptitude and competence which comprise the worker's human capital, to obtain earnings which constitute the revenue on that capital" (44). According to Gordon, from such a worker's viewpoint, education is an investment in order to acquire the aptitudes required to be an effective entrepreneur of him/herself. This view of education is consonant with the "notion of the individual as enterprise" and part of the process of "capitalization of the meaning of life" (ibid.). Within this paradigm of education and work, the single most important question is whether *all* Australian citizens will have *access* to these higher educational services when they require them. While this chapter emphasizes the Australian experience as empirical evidence, our approach is global as well in that we also refer to trends in the United States, the United Kingdom, Canada and other countries which engage with the global economy—and where the success of higher education institutions, such as universities, is measured by how much they contribute to the economy (Aronowitz 2000).

The development of online learning in higher education is occurring at a time when there is an international convergence of higher education reforms in many societies across the world (Currie 2005; Ginsburg et al. 2003; Torres & Schugurensky 2002; Twombly 1997). Higher education institutions from Latin America to Australia are under great pressure to change their organizational culture and structure as a result of the nation-state's new control strategies to make universities give up much of their institutional autonomy to respond to market forces (Currie 2005; Marginson & Considine 2000; Torres & Schugurensky 2002). Therefore, online learning, while seen by educators and educationists as holding out promise in the provision of new opportunities for facilitating critical learning, must also be located in the context of a political economy and field of power in which the Internet and the World Wide Web are constituent parts.

Matrices of Power and Knowledge

Foucault has demonstrated the connection between knowledge and power. According to Foucault, the existence of any particular discourse of knowledge and truth makes possible a particular set of power relations. Conversely, the existence of a particular set of power relations makes possible some discourses of truth while silencing others. The goal of any critical work is to attempt to elucidate the connections between the dominant regimes of thought and disciplinary practice and people's lived experience. Fields of knowledge are historically situated discursive formations. As Rouse (1994) puts it, for Foucault:

> Knowledge is established not only in relation to a field of statements but also of objects, instruments, practices, research programs, skills, social networks, and institutions. Some elements of such an epistemic field reinforce and strengthen one another, and are taken up, extended and reproduced in other contexts; others remain isolated from, or conflict with, these emergent "strategies" and eventually become forgotten curiosities. The configuration of knowledge requires that these heterogeneous elements be adequately adapted to one another, and that their mutual alignment be sustained over time. (110)

Power relations are constituted from these "strategies." Foucault's work demonstrates how knowledge and power are intricately intertwined and how they come together in specific historical epochs. The relationship between knowledge and power is a dynamic one and differs significantly in different domains (Rouse 1994). Foucault's analysis of discourse is "about events" which render certain statements possible and how these events correlate "with other previous or simultaneous events, discursive or otherwise" (Foucault 1991: 59). He focuses on the facts and conditions which allow certain discourses to be manifest in society and on the transformations which such discourses effect.

This chapter's theoretical framework is underpinned by Foucault's insight that power is established, naturalized and modified through discourses generated by the various agents or social groups involved in human interrelationships and networks. We attempt to analyze intertwined discourses of the economic, political and educational systems of modern societies, using Foucault's archeology of knowledge to discern how a dominant discourse promotes and naturalizes the commodification and marketing of higher education courses. In doing so, we wish to draw attention to questions of power, access and equity at the same time that we, as educators, focus our discourse and energy on devising ways of improving pedagogy and access to higher education through the use of technology. Thus the "new" discourse of higher education can be juxtaposed with the discourse of educators and educationists to examine questions of power, hegemony and the place of education within society.

The "New" Discourse of Higher Education in the Knowledge-Based Economy

The new discourse of higher education is constituted by persons involved in the "coordination" of the relations between the nation-state, the market and higher education, that is postsecondary education (Huisman et al. 2001). The balance between the agents of influence that shape national higher education policy—the academic oligarchy, the state and the market—will have important consequences for academics and students in terms of access to key resources. The neoliberal agenda which promotes the market poses a grave challenge to "the notion that higher education is primarily a citizen's right and a social investment" (Torres & Schugurensky 2002: 427).

The key question is how the neoliberal higher education agenda is implemented and legitimated by new government strategies within the economic and political context of twenty-first century capitalism. This agenda promotes a paradigm shift from "busy workers" to "busy learners," where "busy learners outperform busy workers. When our workforce is aligned with learning and action, things get done" (Lenderman & Sandelands 2002: 383). At the level of the nation-state, the shift from Keynesian welfare to competition has meant "the prioritising of accumulation over legitimation" (Bonal 2003: 165). According to Peters and Roberts (2000), the neoliberal paradigm of economic restructuring entails:

> the abolition of subsidies and tariffs; the floating of exchange rates; the privitisation of state assets; encouragement of foreign direct investment; tax reforms; and the "downsizing" and commercialisation of the public sector [as well as] the rise of finance capitalism, supported by the emergence of new information and communications technologies, and a series of agreements concerning the liberalisation of world trade. (125)

The policy agendas of most Western countries have more or less followed the path mapped out by this neoliberal paradigm (Helleiner 2003). Many developing countries have also been pushed by powerful multilateral agencies and states into following such a path (Ginsburg et al. 2003).

Peter McLaren (2003) presents a more critical perspective on the growth of hegemonic neoliberalism, writing that:

> Neoliberalism [...] refers to a corporate domination of society that supports state enforcement of the unregulated market, engages in the oppression of nonmarket forces and antimarket policies, guts free public services, eliminates social subsidies, offers limitless concessions to transnational corporations, enthrones a neomercantilist public policy agenda, establishes the market as the patron of educational reform, and permits private interests to control most of social life in the pursuit of profits for the few (i.e. through lowering taxes on the wealthy, scrapping environmental regulations and dismantling public education and social welfare programs). (70)

Since the collapse of the Soviet Union in 1991 and with it the supposed demise of any alternative system to capitalism, there seems to be a general acceptance of "the seeming inevitability of capital" (65).

Bourdieu's volume, *Acts of Resistance*, highlights the workings of power through the current dominant political and economic discourse:

> Everywhere we hear it said, all day long—and this is what gives the dominant discourse its strength—that there is nothing to put forward in opposition to the neo-liberal view, that it has succeeded in presenting itself as self-evident, that there is no alternative. If it is taken for granted in this way, this is as a result of a whole labour of symbolic inculcation in which journalists and ordinary citizens participate passively and, above all, a certain number of intellectuals participate actively.

Our understanding of the workings of power is aided by Gramsci's concept of hegemony, which elucidates the fact that effective dominant discourses and ideologies become naturalized as part of the human subjects' consciousness (Wasson 2004: 180). In short, "[t]he most effective use of power occurs when those with power are able to get those with less power to interpret the world from the former's point of view" (Mumby & Clair 1997, cited in ibid.). An all-encompassing dominant ideology is most effective when it naturalizes power relations in a society and depoliticizes the social. However, this hegemony "must be fought for constantly in order to be maintained" (Aronowitz & Giroux 1985: 89).

There have been major changes in economic and social policy since the mid-1970s in Western countries (Jessop 2002). These changes have been referred to as post-Fordism (Hardt & Negri 2004: 112). As Jessop (2002) points out, there is a move toward "new techno-economic paradigms" which are now subsumed under a single paradigm of the "knowledge-based economy" or KBE (97). Furthermore, according to Jessop:

> This paradigm [KBE] has become hegemonic as a rationale and strategic guide for economic, political and social restructuring, resonates across many different systems and the lifeworld, and reflects the general importance attributed [...] to knowledge as a "factor of production" in the post-Fordist labour process [...]. (ibid.)

In addition to the technological changes in the economic and labor processes, institutional innovations are required to reorganize society for a new regime of accumulation. The KBE "enables the re-thinking of social, material, and spatio-temporal relations among economic and extra-economic activities, institutions, and systems and their encompassing civil society" (Jessop 2004: 166).

Within hegemonic neoliberalism, the KBE has become the master economic narrative driving changes in Western societies and gaining resonance in, for example, the reorganization of higher educational institutions. The typical Western nation-state has begun to relinquish its role as the guardian of the public interest in line with the decline of the Keynesian welfare state. Thus the state's role in social functions, such as education, health and welfare, has been gradually wound back (Bourdieu 1998).

In order to be competitive in the international market of the global economy, the nation-state has adopted market mechanisms in the creation of its regulatory framework for public administration and the distribution of goods and services within society. The state has a pivotal role to play in order for capital to thrive (Miyoshi 1996). In the regime of flexible accumulation and postmodern production, the state's role is to facilitate the development of "immaterial labor," which involves workers in the creation of "knowledge, information [and] communication" (Hardt & Negri 2004: 108). Thus, the state's regulation of citizen's lives under neoliberalism involves enforcing conformity with the interests of collective capital under contemporary economic and political conditions.

Neoliberalism and the "New" Discourse of Higher Education

The discourse of neoliberalism, which promotes the imperative and logic of the market, has spawned the "new" discourse of higher education. The language of economic rationality permeates the symbolic domain of governments as politicians and technocrats alike extol the virtues of the market. In the neoliberal view that economic forces cannot be resisted in any area of social life, the state's withdrawal or preparation to withdraw from sectors of social life for which it has held responsibility—such as education, health, social welfare and public service broadcasting—is presented as natural and not open to challenge (Bourdieu 1998). Institutions of higher education, such as universities, have responded in different ways to this neoliberal view of the changed role of the state, depending on the positionality of various agents performing different forms of coordination.

Changes are currently underway in the areas of certification and state-controlled sectors of higher education. The instruments of funding, regulation, planning and evaluation have provided governments (in Australia, the European Union, the United States, Canada) with ways to determine the forms of coordination, thus affecting the autonomy of academics to carry out research and teaching according to the values of their profession (Huisman et al. 2001). Within the past three decades, academia, which traditionally operated under its own norms and values, has become subjected to the demands of government accountability mechanisms, subsumed under the rubric of quality assurance. This has occurred in the context of the introduction of market coordination or market mechanisms into the higher education sector.

Political Economy of the "New" Discourse of Higher Education

Under the impact of shifting material and cultural conditions of existence, pedagogical work and the boundaries of education are being redefined (Rizvi & Lingard 1997). Although new spaces are being opened up for potentially empowering models of pedagogy, there is a need to pay attention to wider questions of power relations and the place of education in its sociopolitical context.

If international competitiveness is determined by the production of knowledge for economic gain, the main role universities can play in this scheme is to produce the knowledge workers needed to increase economic productivity and to engage "in scientific and technological areas that feed high-tech productivity" (Torres & Schugurensky 2002: 432). Currie (2005) maintains that this move, whereby the university changes from being a community of scholars into the university as corporation, is predominantly an Anglo-American one. Giroux, in his argument for defending "higher education as a resource vital to the democratic and civic life of the nation" (2001: 5), has traced the commercialization and vocationalization of American higher education, where the distinction between higher education and business has become increasingly blurred as the central purpose of the university has become aligned with meeting the workforce needs of multinational corporations (Aronowitz 2000; Giroux 2001; Peters & Roberts 2000). According to Giroux (2001) and Aronowitz (2000), many American universities have redefined themselves in the image of the all-powerful and pervasive corporations in the pursuit of efficiency and cost effectiveness. Australian universities, like their counterparts in North America, South America, the United Kingdom and Asia, have been forced to follow the trend of increasing reliance on private funding for survival. Within this context, government subsidies have been drastically reduced and higher education institutions have had to compete with other national research agencies for funding and with other universities for students. In some cases, there has been wholesale adoption of a business culture which emphasizes performance, specifically productivity among staff (Levin 2002). Other preferred organizational behavior of the business culture has been adopted, with the emphasis on the goals of survival, efficiency, control and growth (ibid.).

Thus, in most advanced capitalist states including Australia, higher education as a non-market public service funded through taxation has been gradually replaced by markets and the extension of principles of capitalist production. In his work on competition and control in higher education, Marginson (1997) traces the emergence of a market system in the provision of higher education in Australia to the Dawkins reforms of 1987 to 1989. The implementation of these reforms resulted in a unified national system of higher education, which the federal government has subsequently proceeded to marketize. Thus, the transition from an elite to a mass higher education system in Australia has followed the pattern of most OECD countries, involving a move toward a decentralized, market-oriented system. The main features in this process include "greater financial autonomy of institutions, competitive allocations, contract-based planning, and growing income from commercial sources and fees" (OECD 1990, cited in Marginson 1997: 223). On the other hand, the federal government has maintained its regulatory control of the higher education system in Australia through determining "the rules of the game [and] the forms and limits of what could be achieved, so that the system-institution could be steered in less onerous fashion by remote control" (222).

The reforms to modernize and marketize higher education institutions in Australia have been implemented and effectively legitimized through the "new" discourse of higher education. This new discourse of higher education has been constituted and promulgated by the key agents or persons involved in national policy formulation and the senior managers or academic oligarchy involved in the coordination of the relations between the state and higher education institutions. The actors in higher education have been constituted essentially as economic actors and higher education institutions as "self-entrepreneurial universities" (Marginson 1997). The Dawkins reforms provided the catalyst for the redefinition of identities, missions and the *modus operandi* of Australian universities, thus linking and rewarding innovation and entrepreneurialism. These reforms have created a new institutional type called the *enterprise university* (Marginson & Considine 2000). It is a type of institutional capitalism (Torres & Schugurensky 2002), but it is not identical to the business form whose bottom line is profit-making.

The use of marketplace metaphors has emerged in the language of senior university actors as the success of university leaders is measured and rewarded according to a university's financial health. University activities and relationships are now couched in such metaphors as: *the corporate university, collegial entrepreneurialism, customers, clients, stakeholders, branding, key performance indicators* and *service level agreements*, for example. The neoliberal "universalist message of liberation" (Bourdieu 1998: 31) permeates the field of higher education in the form of "enterprise ideology" (Wasson 2004: 175).

The student participating in higher education has come to be viewed not as a recipient "of a citizen entitlement but as [a] choice-making investor in the self" (Marginson 1997: 223). In Australia, this process began with the introduction of the *Higher Education Contribution Scheme* for domestic students in 1989, while full fees for international students were approved in 1985. This universal user charge has been rationalized on the basis that students will be able to improve their social and economic standing as a result of having the opportunity to access higher education. The Labor government which introduced this reform prioritized access, and the income-contingent feature of the scheme meant that it still had some redistributional role. However, the notions of "user pays" and the "student-as-investor in the self" have contributed toward constituting higher education squarely as an economic activity involving "a private investment in human capital" (236).

The Liberal-National Party government which has been in power in Australia since 1996 has emphasized the private benefits that accrue to participants in higher education to justify subsequent increases in user payments. As a result of a major review of higher education initiated by the Minister for Education, Science and Training in 2002 (in *Higher Education at the Crossroads* 2002) and a series of issue papers which followed—allowing for at least some consultation with and input from the major "stakeholders"—a raft of reforms moving higher education institutions toward greater financial autonomy, along with the introduction of the notion of student loans, were passed in the *Higher Education Support Act 2003*. In the name of diversity and the provision of choice, specific reforms, such as fee deregulation, are now being implemented.

Thus, the current dominant discourse of higher education has reconceptualized students as consumers who have a "desire for an educational product, rather than being co-travelers on an educational journey" (Greener & Perriton 2005: 67). In this context, new technologies of online learning play an ambivalent role since, as Greener and Perriton note, "networked learning, far from being a pedagogy that opposes the commodification of learning, can easily be coopted as a method in the commercialization of education" (68). In the remaining sections of this chapter, we present a discourse on the use of information and communication technologies (ICTs) by educationists and educators to highlight the complex interplay between the progressive democratic potential often claimed for online learning and the economics of higher education provision.

What Is the Internet's Role in the Democratic Provision of Higher Education?

The adoption and application of ICTs in higher education is associated with multiple perspectives about their efficacy and impact on the democratization of the educational process. In the subsequent section, sociopolitical, economic and pedagogical agendas driving the implementation of ICTs are discussed, and inferences drawn regarding their potential to constrain or foster democratization.

Unsurprisingly, there is hesitancy about ICTs as a force for democratization in education. On the one hand, access to information and the ability to communicate across time and space has positive outcomes for the provision of education to learners with widely varying profiles and needs. On the other hand, the promise of the technology can be constrained by incompatibilities with the organizational structures of the institutions that host it, the political and social agendas driving its application, the poor quality of student access to the networks that support it, and the low degree of efficacy of the pedagogical frameworks that surround its use.

According to Hall (1999), there are three prevailing philosophical positions regarding the role of ICTs and their impact on the democratization of education. Firstly, a "utopian" position views the use of ICTs in higher education as democratizing because technology has the potential to increase access to education for all. Anticipated benefits include the use of ICTs to support discipline-specific and work-based virtual communities, sometimes referred to as "communities of practice" (Wenger 1998). It is argued that the old dichotomy of "individual" and "community" is made redundant because the communication needs of both can be met concurrently online (Hall 1999). The possible global and multicultural constitution of virtual communities is also seen to enhance opportunities for critical reflection as both staff and students are engaged directly in "comparisons and contrasts of approaches and cultures" (Davis 1999). These communication networks are considered to offer enhanced opportunities for staff development and teacher training (ibid.), with a leveling of hierarchical differences between learners and a fostering of collaborative and constructivist approaches to learning (Hodgson 2002, cited in Greener & Perriton 2005: 73). In particular, there is seen to be a shift in the role of the teacher to a facilitative position, relinquishing a large measure of authority to the individual learner who is required to demonstrate self-management and a high degree of metacognitive skill in taking ownership of learning (Greener & Perriton 2005).

The "dystopian" position, however, considers that the use of ICTs in higher education can undermine the democratic process. It is suggested that ICTs tend to increase gaps in power and wealth, allowing those in certain groups to strengthen their control over others. In this way, it is possible to marginalize communities as opposed to empowering them as the utopians suggest. Hall (1999) argues that ICTs allow "virtual communities to form that are exclusive to specific power blocks, bolstered by data and an information-rich environment, to the exclusion and marginalization of non-community members."

The role of the teacher also poses problems in the dystopian perspective. A facilitator's role does not always carry with it content expertise, and the increasing employment by universities of sessional and casual teaching staff compounds the problem. Moreover, it is argued that the quality of interaction between teacher and student suffers because "facilitation," by definition, is less engaging than "teaching," resulting in poorer communication and learning. Paradoxically, better communication is a central benefit espoused by supporters of ICTs in learning and teaching.

Opponents also point out that the potential for increased and flexible access to education for all is limited by the very nature of the medium delivering that access. To realize the full potential of the Internet, broadband access is required. The media-rich content that adds value to the learning experience is either not produced because of resourcing constraints at universities, or when incorporated, requires substantial bandwidth to be viewed. Although it is now considered the norm for students to have Internet access in Western educational settings, there is no presumption that the Internet connections available to off-campus students have broadband capability. Therefore, the combination of limited learning designs and limited broadband connections results in the majority of learning resources delivered by universities being text-based.

Coates et al. (2005) suggest that "the textual nature of the Internet may reinforce conceptions of teaching as the transmission of decontextualized and discrete pieces of information." The hypermedia character of the Internet and the flexibility of access are such that students often experience fragmentation in place, time and content. This is compounded by the possibility of following a wide variety of different routes through the material. Building conceptual schemata that tie discrete areas of content together in a timely manner, and making the cognitive links between that content and the learning objectives of a unit of study, is more difficult in a virtual environment due to the very nature of hypermedia and hypertext.

An additional point that concerns those with a dystopian view of ICTs in education is that information often seems to be equated to knowledge. Opponents of the utopian perspective argue that it is the quality of a learner's cognitive processing and the degree of knowledge construction that takes place after exposure to online information that results in effective learning (Bransford et al. 2000; Gagné et al. 1988; Jonassen 1994). There is a case to be made that in a world awash with information easily accessed and shared through ICTs, there is a shortfall of knowledge.

A third perspective on ICTs in higher education and their potential for democratization can be labeled "utilitarian" (Hall 1999). The use of ICTs in institutional settings can facilitate alternative approaches to governance and participatory democracy. From an administrative perspective, the ability to conduct planning activities in which all stakeholders are actively involved in an open and timely sharing of information has transformed aspects of institutional governance. However, the fostering of participatory democracy in this way is in contrast to the long cherished independence and autonomy of the academic. The somewhat unstructured and chaotic environment resulting from this independence makes it difficult for management to implement and meet quality assurance targets which are increasingly linked to the receipt of funding. From a learning and teaching standpoint, Coates et al. (2005: 25) state that the systematic delivery of tuition through Learning Management Systems (LMS) "[o]ffers universities a hitherto undreamt-of capacity to control and regulate teaching." The order and consistency resulting from the use of ICTs in this way does undermine academic independence, but it also creates a structured environment with respect to quality assurance, that can maintain the institution's financial viability. By association, therefore, a stronger institution can result in increased job security for its staff, albeit at the cost of academic independence.

Historically, the university represented the amalgamation of the finest intellect, committed students, wisdom and knowledge encapsulated in books, and dedicated study spaces, often cohabited by both scholars and students (Hall 1995: 2). Educational opportunity was available to few. The post–World War II advent of mass education placed increasing pressure on this historical model to cope with a larger number of students seeking higher education. This pressure was caused by several factors. Firstly, the post-war economic boom and the associated requirement for a highly educated workforce in Western countries swelled the number of applicants. Secondly, increased prosperity and the broader distribution of wealth across social divides helped to break down the notion that a university education was only to be associated with wealth and social position. Thirdly, the decline of colonialism was manifested in the creation of new nations whose development depended on raising the educational levels of their citizens. In most cases, the preferred source of higher education among those citizens was Western universities. Finally, the demand for a skilled workforce in Western democracies required a rapid increase in the number of workers, which in most cases could only be achieved through large immigration programs. The consequent swelling of populations in nations like Canada, Australia and New Zealand puts great pressure on higher education systems as the children of the migrants reached enrollment age. This led to an increase in class sizes and the size of universities, as well as the creation of additional campuses, and a fundamental change to the organizational model of the university itself (Bates 2000: 36–40; Hall 1999: 2).

The effect of the trend toward mass education was that the historical model of a university with scarce resources only available to the elite was transformed under scientific rationalism to cope with the ever-increasing number of students seeking a curriculum that offered relevance and employability as prime outcomes. The notion of a university became that of a production center in which the main goal was to process as many students as possible in the most efficient and cost-effective manner. This "Fordist" organizational model was characterized by large class sizes due to economies of scale, hierarchical management, division of labor and a predominance of managerial decision-making over "collegial" decision-making (Bates 2000).

The Fordist model tended to treat students as raw materials in a production process whose success was measured not by individual learning but by number of graduates and norm-referenced grades, frequently adjusted to suit an impersonal mean score. Other manifestations of the Fordist model included transmissive tuition methods aimed at achieving efficiency in educational delivery over and above student-centeredness. Despite the somewhat rigid curriculum and the unilateral nature of the educational process, the Fordist university model did partially democratize access to higher education. However, requirements for an adaptable vision, operational flexibility including a flexible allocation of resources, a proactive approach to meeting student needs, and academic programs that are scalable as well as easily and rapidly modified to meet different student and market profiles have resulted in a different organizational structure. These organizational elements characterize the post-Fordist university model (Bates 2000: 39–42).

The transition from a Fordist to a post-Fordist model in educational institutions was in large part a reaction to pressures on the Fordist structures that had reached the limit of physical growth and could not accommodate continuing demands for higher education places. It is fortuitous that this limit was reached at a time when the Internet provided the means to distribute education to off-campus students.

Distance education expanded rapidly as the networking and communication capabilities of the new Internet technologies took education right into the homes of students. Contemporary "distance education" and "open learning" are logical successors to the traditional correspondence school, with email and online communication playing a large role in many courses, allowing geographically dispersed students to communicate more easily with their teachers.

The quickening pace of change in the workplace now requires many employees to continue to engage in formal learning through their productive lives. This need is a factor in the transformation process and a new role for universities that sits well with the post-Fordist model, which has emerged to address the specialized development needs of lifelong learners (Brown & Duguid 1996). In both a corporate training context and in a higher or vocational education sense, the pursuit of learning is frequently facilitated by the use of ICTs.

The perspectives represented by utopian, dystopian and utilitarian philosophical positions on ICTs provide a useful framework for addressing concerns about the role of technology in the democratic provision of higher education. The utopian ideal that electronically connected learning communities, strengthened by a virtual and collective consciousness, would dissolve traditional barriers to education seems to be only partially fulfilled. Inroads are being made, however, as the price of technology falls and attempts are made to broaden access to educational opportunities across the digital divide. For example, the $100 laptop project, a non-profit educational initiative, aims to distribute millions of laptops to children for whom access to the educational opportunities afforded by ICTs and the Internet is far from achievable at present. This project should significantly enhance educational opportunities if its goals are met (MIT Media Lab, n.d.). Access to the ICTs in this way will add value and enhance the impact of free educational content available through open courseware projects in the United States, Japan and China, demonstrating that at least some utopian ideals are achievable.

For these reasons, dystopian fears that the digital divide is widening cannot be fully justified in every case. The job opportunities and related economic benefits associated with information technology and the affordances it provides for further and higher education in India, for example, have resulted in the rapid expansion of an educated middle class with some positive flow-on benefits for the nation's poorest people. Other dystopian predictions concerning the formation of virtual communities of an exclusive, information-rich elite class have also not been fully borne out. The recent exponential growth in the use of blogs and wikis fosters independent web publishing and provides the means to edit any page in a wiki-enabled website. Such ICTs encourage the democratic use of the web, and in educational contexts can promote the democratic expression of student views in networked learning environments.

The utilitarian vision of ICTs, while raising concerns about the prioritization of financial viability to the detriment of learning and teaching, can achieve a balance in purpose and means. Given the funding concerns of many higher education institutions, the possibility of maintaining fiscal viability through efficiencies brought about by the deployment of ICTs is an option for serious consideration, given that a balance can be struck between increasing efficiency and maintaining quality in learning and teaching.

These three perspectives on ICTs provide a counterbalance to the valorization of the market in providing choice and the type of educational product that students as customers will want to purchase. The appropriation of ICTs in education so that universities can compete in a global market is quite problematic given that "all things are not equal" within the social contexts of the prospective consumers.

Conclusion

In this chapter, we have attempted to analyze the proposition of educators such as Harasim et al. that networked or online learning "offers the possibility of bringing equal learning opportunities to learners whenever they need them and wherever they may be" (1995: 278). We have indicated that a new discourse of higher education has emerged to legitimize and naturalize the rise of market mechanisms in the public sector of education in general, and more specifically post-compulsory or higher education. We may still press for the universality of higher learning and defend it as a public good. However, a powerful discourse is pushing for universities to be run on market principles. Within this context, the nation-state continues to assume its role in the reproduction of labor power. The agents or persons who hold the pivotal roles in national educational policy formulation now find new ways to impart direction and purpose in the higher education sector. As Hardt and Negri argue, the role of the collective mass of citizenry, if not individuals, has been heightened under neoliberalism. The language of economic rationalism that pervades higher education is a conforming response, one that emphasizes that individuals can find their proper role in new markets through higher education. Thus state-sponsored higher education has become one means through which neoliberal values obtain communication. It serves as a social node through which individual citizens can establish their connection with the market and enrich their social utility.

The second section of this chapter examined three (educational) perspectives on ICTs as a way of balancing out the first section's macroargument about neoliberal discourse in higher education. What readers really want to know at this point is to what degree will educational discourses prevail over, or make inroads into, the dominant neoliberal discourse? This question needs to be broached here. It is probably impossible to answer at the current historical juncture, but it should at least be raised.

Online learning, made possible by the advances in ICTs, has implications for corporate universities as it opens up new avenues in the economics of education, while for educators it raises the possibility of radical change in pedagogy in terms of democratizing the learning and teaching processes. As social demands for access to higher education increase as a result of the perception that having degrees provides the means to improve one's life chances in the global economy, "universal access" has been redefined in terms of the purchasing power of the student, now conceptualized as a consumer, client or customer. However, analyses of the current context as provided by chapters in this volume comprise a counterdiscourse which highlights the fact that the development of market mechanisms in higher education is not inherently linear and the consequences of the trend are currently not graspable. This counterdiscourse is a form of resistance, which puts human agency back into the picture.

II: Points of Resistance

Chapter 3

From "Equal Access" to "Widening Participation": The Discourse of Equity in the Age of E-learning

Robin Goodfellow

The Open Learning System has the political mandate to espouse the educational cause of the marginalised sections of Society.
—Roy (2002)

Higher Education as a Basic Human Right

Education is enshrined as a basic human right in the United Nations' Universal Declaration of Human Rights of 1948 (Article 26). This declaration specifies three levels of basic right to education, with a corresponding onus on nations to provide (i) free compulsory elementary education for all, (ii) general availability of technical and professional education, and (iii) equality of access to higher education "on the basis of merit." The commitment to free compulsory elementary education gives governments clear targets to aim at, but the right to technical, professional, and higher education leaves considerable room for political reinterpretation. Moreover, the construction of the right to higher education as being available on the basis of merit is ideologically equivocal. The idea of merit suggests intellectual fitness and a capacity to benefit, and while the underlying intent is that this should be the main factor determining access, rather than social status or ability to pay, many social egalitarians (including Michael Young, one of the founders of the British Open University [OU]) reject the notion that social advantage should accrue from attributes, intellectual or otherwise, which are inherent in some people but not in others.

In the half-century that has passed since these principles were declared, the world has made progress in terms of the number of children and young people attending schools and colleges (Perraton 2000: 2–3). However, whereas the developed and industrialized countries (Western Europe, North America, Japan, Australasia, etc.) and some of the more advanced countries of the developing world (India, Thailand) have also seen a considerable increase in the proportions of their school populations which go on to benefit from higher education in some form, in the developing world in general and in Africa in particular, this proportion is still less than 10% (Gourley 2004; Perraton 2000: 3).

What are the means by which these richer countries have created educational equity for significant proportions of their own populations? Has it been achieved in an egalitarian manner, or through the creation of meritocracies? And can these means be universally applied, in this more globalized age, to the extension of the same rights to all the world's people? To address these questions we need to look at the field of open and distance education (ODE), which bears much of the responsibility for the expansion of mass post-compulsory education over the post-war period, and we need to look at current developments in e-learning, in which much of the promise for the future resides. In particular, we need to look at some of the ideological, political, economic, technical, and entrepreneurial factors which have shaped distance teaching practices and the systems in which they are embedded.

In this chapter I will focus specifically on the British OU, not only because it has been my own employer since 1996 and is the context with which I am most familiar, but also because it was the first of the open universities and has been hugely influential in legitimizing, and serving as a model for, a number of similar initiatives in other countries (Perraton 2000: 84). Distance education was not, of course, invented by the OU; it grew out of the marriage in the 1920s of correspondence teaching, which had been around in Europe and the United States since the late 1800s, and the new technologies of radio broadcasting (McIsaac & Gunawardena 1996). However, the system of ODE which the OU has been practicing since 1969 is generally regarded as the most successful model to date for distance education on a large scale (Keegan 1986). It has been influential in the development of mass distance education systems in several other countries, including in Asia and other developing areas (Perraton 2000: 84–85). So a discussion of how the OU currently conceives its mission with regard to the fundamental questions of equity of opportunity at the higher education level could be considered relevant to most other open universities that have adopted this model.

The Age of E-learning

When we talk about open universities and mass distance education, we usually refer to systems that are publicly owned and government-funded, and thus politically accountable. Such systems have tended to actively embrace educational technologies, not only as a means to widen access, but also as a way of reducing the costs of teaching on a large scale. ODE in the current context also encompasses what is now called e-learning. This, at its most generic, is simply the use of digital technologies to connect learners with sources of teaching, but in the wider contexts of globalization and the economic development of countries, the practices of e-learning have acquired a much profounder significance. Indeed, they are demonstrating an apparent potential to fragment those same systems of mass distance education, and to cause us to have to redefine the concept of access and the very distinctions between technical, professional, and higher education on which the traditional commitment to the right to post-compulsory education is based. Many ODE providers employ e-learning technologies, but the arena has come to be dominated by organizations which are, to varying degrees, privately owned and engaged in the electronic delivery of distance education primarily and explicitly for profit. Such organizations have mushroomed in recent times, and are not confined to the advanced industrialized countries (King 2003 cites Malaysia and South Africa as sites of expansion of "for-profit" e-learning). However, the most commercially successful are currently US publicly listed companies, for example, the Apollo Group, which includes the University of Phoenix Online, and the Sylvan Group (ibid. 5). The success of the Apollo Group, which was ranked higher for market capitalization in Arizona in 2005 than all but one of the state's most successful companies (Wiles 2005), demonstrates that the for-profit e-learning industry is capable of outstripping traditional industries in some areas. These organizations have been highly influential in determining the nature of the market for private e-learning provision internationally, and have recently begun to influence the thinking of public and non-profit institutions, including the traditional ODE leaders such as the OU, with regard to their strategies for increasing and retaining student numbers in an international market.

How do these public and for-profit ODE and e-learning organizations conceive their missions in terms of equity? Are they able to serve, simultaneously, a commitment to education as a basic human right, the requirements of individual and national economic development, and the desire for corporate profit? What impact has the rise of for-profit e-learning organizations, such as the University of Phoenix Online, had on the way that non-profit providers, such as the British OU, represent their purposes, to themselves, and to the world? To address these questions we need to look at the way that terms, such as "access" and "participation," are used in institutional and pedagogical discourses as proxies for the right to equity in the opportunity for higher education.

Discourses of Equity in Distance Education

Institutions belonging to both non-profit and for-profit sectors publicly espouse social goals such as the expansion of opportunity, widening of participation, enriching of lives, etc. In this they are honoring traditions of discourse about education as a social good that today are universal. However, there are different ways of conceptualizing these goals and different motives underlying the commitment to them.

Roy (2002), in the quote which prefaces this chapter, argues that ODE has a political mandate to serve the cause of marginalized sections of society. There have been, broadly, two different viewpoints underlying the political commitment to access to higher education on the part of national governments of Organization for Economic Cooperation and Development (OECD) countries in the 1960s–1970s and the 1980s–1990s (Jakupec 2000: 68–70). The early period is associated with Keynesian "welfare state" ideologies, and the later with neoliberal "economic rationalist" ideologies. These viewpoints construct access to tertiary education respectively as: a political catalyst for social equality and mobility; and necessarily aligned with national economic priorities (68). Roy, along with other voices within the Asian Association of Open Universities, argues that economic rationalism and globalization currently threaten the historic commitment of ODE to social justice and transformative education (274).

Lockwood (2002, citing Hawkridge's 1995 address to the International Council for Distance Education World Conference) implicates technology in this threat to social justice, identifying a number of ways in which global e-learning developments may impact negatively on populations in the developing world. The chief way is by accelerating the penetration of largely Western technologically advanced and commercially oriented provision (which may involve both private companies and collaborations of universities with each other or with private companies) into the learner constituencies of other nation states. The growth of an international market for teaching and training materials, at decreasing cost and on an increasing scale of production, it is argued, leads to the imposition of the cultural values of rich and powerful communities onto the lives of the less advantaged, and the deskilling of these developing societies in respect of their ability to reproduce their own values through the development of their own educational resources.

For-profit education does not have an explicit political mandate, but a financial one imposed by customers and shareholders. This does not mean that it is free from any requirement to respond to pressures for social transformation, any more than publicly funded systems are able to ignore economic and market pressures, because it is still working largely within a regulatory system which is owned and managed by the public sector (King 2003). Like the public ODE institutions, for-profits are deploying increasingly sophisticated technologies to reach their target audiences and to enhance their reputations, and in doing so, they are implicated in the creation of conditions in which the less acceptable kinds of social consequences outlined by Lockwood and Hawkridge (above) may emerge.

Other principles, as well as equity, are thus active in the ways that access to higher education is being extended through the technologies of distance education, and however they may be represented in the discourse of involved organizations, these are not necessarily based in the social and political priorities of the communities which distance learners themselves inhabit. It would be tempting to see the obstacles to the extension of human rights through e-learning in the developing world as rooted in a fundamental contradiction between the philanthropic principle of equity and the economic principle of profit. However, closer examination of the roots of technology-based ODE as practiced by the open universities suggests that there has always been a more complex relation between ideological and technical/entrepreneurial aspects of the missions of these public distance education providers. For example, the missions of the Asian open universities have always been closely associated with national economic needs. While the public agendas of the founders of national open universities in India, Pakistan, China, Malaysia, Indonesia and the other members of the Asian Group aspired to extend access to groups who are marginalized by existing systems of formal education,[1] they also reflect an overt and pragmatic commitment to national economic and social development. The mission statement of the Indira Gandhi National Open University (IGNOU), for example, cites the objective of providing for disadvantaged segments of society and strengthening the "natural and human resources of the country through the medium of education" (IGNOU 1985).[2]

The open universities of Asia and elsewhere contributed considerably to the number of their citizens entering higher education during the last two decades of the twentieth century. India, for example, saw an annual increase of 13.1% in students enrolling in distance education courses, compared to 5.3% for those entering higher education in general (Perraton 2000: 89). But there are at least two caveats to the conclusion that the ODE movement has been the means to expand access to higher education in a universally equitable manner. The first is that, although the commitment of the open universities continues to be nominally to higher education, the majority of the courses they have provided are more properly to be described as technical and professional education, specifically in subjects such as teaching, nursing, and commerce (Perraton 2000: 92–93).[3] The second, and more important, caveat is that, while numbers of participants in post-compulsory education globally have increased overall, the proportions from low-income and marginalized groups have not (Power 2002: 54–55; Sawyer 2004). It seems that the goals of national economic development and an increasingly egalitarian social order are not necessarily both served by the access-expanding policies of governments which have created mass ODE systems to date.

Discourses of Participation and the "Marginalized"

Over the last few years, the concept of "participation" has begun to replace that of "access," as a key descriptor of the effort to extend the opportunity of higher education to a wider population. In the United Kingdom, successive Labour governments since 1997 have set targets for the percentage of the population aged between 18 and 30 to be engaged in higher education in some form. By 2004 the figure of 44% had been achieved, and the target of 50% set for 2010. However, the UK government has recently acknowledged in its white paper, "The Future of Higher Education," that the proportion of these from low-income families has not increased (DfES 2003) and there is evidence now that the 50% figure is unlikely to be achieved (Bekhradnia 2005). Expanded opportunity is now being constructed in terms of fairer access, which focuses on the identities, rather than the numbers, of those who engage in higher education (Scott 2003).

A concern with the disadvantaged has long underpinned the concept of social justice that the OU has espoused (see the next section). But, as is the case with the field of ODE in general, it is arguable whether it has contributed much to the extension of higher education to the economically marginalized. The social mandate is now being expressed through a change in the discourse of equality of opportunity, from emphasizing access for classes of people, to the participation of individuals. The OU, for example, which used to have a strategic priority to support the participation of people who had been previously disadvantaged in their pursuit of education, now represents its mission as "providing high-quality university education to all who wish to realize their ambitions and fulfill their potential" (OU, n.d.). It is arguable whether this shift of emphasis is still in line with the traditional commitment to social justice based on political egalitarianism, or whether it represents another facet of contemporary economic rationalism.

Other elements of the discourse of participation which have been inherited from UK government policy address ideas of lifelong learning enabled by ubiquitous technologies, particularly the technologies of e-learning. The discourses of e-learning and lifelong learning promoted by the UK and other Western governments still refer to equality of opportunity, just as did the original mission of the British OU, but these technologies are also implicated in the wider discourses of globalization and entrepreneurship (Edwards & Usher 2000: 52), and e-learning has come to be associated with business in a way that earlier generations of distance learning have not been. Not that the field of ODE was free of commercial associations—even in the earliest days of the OU's founding there was an opportunist strand of argument running parallel to the social agenda, as Harris (1987) has pointed out. Private commercial publishing interests, such as Pitmans, Pearson, and private colleges and universities, such as the Open Learning Centre International in the United Kingdom and DeVry University in the United States, have always sought to profit from demand for distance teaching. However, the association in the case of e-learning is both more extensive, in that there has been an explosion of initiatives aimed at establishing for-profit electronic teaching operations during the last 10 years, and more fundamental, as business studies, along with related areas such as administration and accounting, has itself become one of the subjects most taught in e-learning contexts. The University of Phoenix Online's own subject curriculum is evidence of this, with 11 of its 15 undergraduate programs related to business and/or management areas (Phoenix Program List 2004). According to Garrett (2004), Phoenix Online is a model for a form of distance education which directly addresses a demand which is not being catered for by public education providers in the United States. This is for mass-market taught programs with workplace relevance, targeting "non-traditional" learners who are defined as aged 25 and over and seeking short-term career advancement through study.

The issue for the OU today is therefore whether a mission to promote participation in what Bonk (2004) calls the coming "e-storms" in higher education being generated principally in the United States (by which he means the increased demand for convenient and career-focused post-compulsory education, and the expansion of technological "solutions" to pedagogical problems) can still be represented as a strategy to create a more just society through the extension of opportunity for higher education. Or does it signal instead a reconceptualization of the idea of social justice, in which human rights are contingent on the ability to find a place in a new kind of social and economic order, predicated on technical and occupational competencies?

Access, Social Class, and the British OU

One of the founders of the OU, Michael Young, coined the term "meritocracy" to describe a society which "sieved" people according to values laid down by an intellectual elite (Young 1958). In his view such a society would be as divisive as one based on social class. Young, and the British Labour Party of the post-war period to which he belonged, were the inheritors of a movement toward educational reform begun in 1945 and given momentum by the creation of the national welfare state in 1948. They were motivated by the inequalities of a system which selected 80% of British schoolchildren for secondary education (vocational or non-university focused) at age 11. Both the comprehensive school system which they were responsible for launching in 1964, and the OU which was founded in 1969 were, at the ideological level, expressions of their belief in the human right not to be "streamed" or treated as inferior on the grounds of either social class or intellectual merit.

The principle of "openness" in its original formulation by the founders of the OU therefore meant that the opportunity to study at tertiary level should be available to everyone who wanted it, not just those who could claim to merit it. At the time of the OU's founding, less than 16% of British school-leavers went to university, and of these only a very small proportion came from working class backgrounds. (Social class in the United Kingdom used to be determined according to categories of employment: managerial and professional, manual and casual, etc. More recently, it has come to be seen as a function of the places where people live, with neighborhoods categorized on the basis of average income, value of property, consumption patterns, etc. See Chapman 2001–2004.) Furthermore, there were very few routes to a university degree open to mature students of any class. Openness was therefore construed in constructive terms, not only through the lowering of symbolic barriers, such as entrance qualifications or age restrictions, but also through practical intervention to make it possible for the educationally marginalized to engage in study activities which had been denied to them for pragmatic reasons. This particularly applied to working class students, the disabled, the imprisoned or those in care, and to members of the police and armed forces. Openness was seen as the route to an increasing and increasingly diverse student population, which would bring both social and economic benefits to British society as a whole.

The overtly ideological character of the discourses of social equality that accompanied the establishment of the OU inevitably generated political resistance, as much from Labour's own supporters as from the conservative opposition. The decision by the Education Minister, Jennie Lee, to constitute the fledgling institution as a fully chartered university, rather than as a consortium of public education providers outside the "elite" university system (National Extension College, Workers' Educational Association, Local Authority Adult Education, Trade Unions, etc.), attracted opposition from those on the left who felt that this sold out the cause of adult education to the middle class values of the academy. It was seen by many as a betrayal of Labour's egalitarian principles. As Walter Perry, the OU's first Vice Chancellor, puts it:

> In her effort to navigate the political minefield, Jennie Lee had sought advice from the University world, ignoring the world of adult education, including extramural departments, the Workers' Educational Association and local education authorities that Harold Wilson had included in his original consortium concept. It took the Open University a very long time to overcome this resentment. (Perry 1976, quoted in Schugurensky 2001–2005)

And of course, there was strenuous opposition from the right too, objecting both to the principle of qualification-less entry to the British university system, and to the cost of setting it up, which was to be borne entirely by the public purse. Nevertheless, there was much in the idea of access to higher education for people who did not conform to the traditional profile of the university student, in order to help them make good their potential, that appealed to progressive conservatives. It enshrined the notion of university education, and the degree-level qualification, as the benchmark of educational success, and it promised a whole generation of middle class people whose education had been interrupted by the war a "second chance." Jennie Lee did her best to remove any lingering connotation of class bias: "It is not a working class university. It was never intended to be a working class university. It was planned as a university. It is the Open University" (Lee quoted in Harris 1987).

The OU was successful from the start, with 19,500 people registering for its first courses in 1971 (Schugurensky 2001–2005), and 600 of them graduating at the first degree ceremony two years later (The OU then and now 2003). Ten years later, the numbers had more than doubled and the university had proved that it was able to retain students in the notoriously precarious domain of distance learning.[4] It also established itself as a cultural influence on the British public's attitudes to higher education in a way that few other universities outside Oxbridge have. A combination of the political controversy surrounding its foundation, the enduring resonance of the images created by the film *Educating Rita*,[5] the consistent public exposure to its teaching via broadcast TV, and its success in drawing attention to its celebrity alumni guaranteed it a recognition factor that other institutions could only envy. This public image was, and is, of great business value to the university (a recent survey carried out by the Institute of Education Technology, for example, found that only 28% of new OU students in 2003 had even considered studying with another college or university). The flexibility of part-time learning at a distance for older students with families, and for professional people who cannot take time off from work, is clearly a factor in the decision of many of these students to take an OU course, but whereas in the 1970s the OU was effectively the only provider of good quality higher education of this kind, this is no longer the case.

Diversity and the OU

In 2005, the OU has grown to around 180,000 students, including 25,000 studying overseas, 10,000 registered disabled people, and 1,000 in prison, and its claim to have helped to expand the UK university population over its 35-year history is undeniable. But John Daniels, Vice Chancellor of the OU from 1996 to 2001, has also claimed that the OU has increased the social diversity of university students: "On almost any measure of the profile of the student body: gender, disability, ethnic origin, or socio-economic background, the Open University has greatly expanded the diversity of students entering higher education" (Daniels 1998).

The OU's impact on diversity has been disputed from the beginning. Harris (1987), for example, argued that it was because of the inequalities of the British education system that there was a pool of able, motivated, but insufficiently qualified students ready to seize the opportunity offered by new means of access. These students included a large number of women, which represented an increase in diversity over conventional university populations, but considerable proportions of these were from semi-professional occupations, especially teaching, which is a traditional occupation of the British middle class. These people were the disenfranchised, rather than the marginalized, in the sense that their exclusion was a function of the elitism of the British university system itself, not of fundamental inequalities in economic or social status. In the

United States, for example, where college education had never been a preserve of the elite, there was arguably no equivalent constituency for part-time higher education at a distance, at that time.

Furthermore, the last 10 years have seen a general widening of access to higher education in the United Kingdom, through reorganization of the full-time university sector (e.g., the granting of university status to polytechnics in 1993). The OU's role in this expansion has been significant, but its retention rate for students from lower-income and "non-traditional" backgrounds has been considerably worse than that of non-distance universities attempting to expand participation by the same groups. Aston and Bekhradnia (2005) compare first year withdrawal rates of 13% and 18% at two London universities with high populations of lower-income students, with the UK average for all students of 8%. By contrast, OU internal figures for students receiving financial assistance in 2002 show that over 65% did not complete the first year. But as Aston and Bekhradnia have pointed out, higher non-completion rates are the price that universities have to pay for operating open access policies.

A major part of the UK government's discourse on diversity in higher education is nowadays about increasing participation in the national economy of people from diverse backgrounds. The "salary premium" that graduates are able to command when they are employed has been an important part of this rhetoric. But the idea that adult part-timers entering higher education are more likely to be motivated by instrumental- and occupation-related considerations, rather than by cultural ones, is not borne out in the case of OU students. Motivation for studying with the OU varies considerably between individuals, and studying purely for interest or as a hobby has equal priority with looking to enhance employability either in a current or a prospective career. As OU internal surveys have repeatedly shown, new students on undergraduate courses are more likely to cite "personal development" or "interest in the subject" as their reason for doing the course, rather than "to help me progress in my employment." This is certainly the case with some of the more high-profile students taking OU courses, such as well-known actors and other personalities who clearly have little need to improve their academic profiles or their job prospects.

There are notable differences, however, for those following postgraduate programs, who are more oriented toward employment and professional goals. The majority of these students seek to use a course as a means of progressing in their employment. Furthermore, once people get beyond their first course, whatever level they are at, they are more likely to cite qualifications or credit points, rather than intrinsic interest, as a reason for studying. The OU is, of course, very keen for students to go on and seek accreditation, not only for their development, but for its own business reasons too, as competition for part-time students has increased. The emphasis which was once put on student recruitment is now moving to retention, and this may be one of the reasons why the number of postgraduate places has steadily increased (in 1996 the OU was offering 135 postgraduate courses; by 2000 this had risen to 220). This is an indication of the way that the concept of access, with its original justification in the idea of removing barriers to entry, is increasingly acquiring a more instrumental meaning as education is converted into social capital for the student, and into economic capital for the university.

The OU and E-learning

Most major organizations involved today in mass distance education via e-learning emphasize their commitment to innovation, and to being leaders in the field, as is demonstrated by these extracts from the statements of mission and/or objectives of three of the main "players:" "to be a world leader in the design, content and delivery of supported open and distance learning" (British OU, see OU 2004c); "to be a recognized player in (commercial) distance and e-learning training programmes and consultancy" (Open University of the Netherlands, see Open Universiteit Nederland 2004); and "to foster a spirit of innovation that focuses on providing academic quality, service excellence, and convenience to the working adult" (University of Phoenix, n.d.).

The original Charter of the OU established the objectives of the institution as disseminating learning and knowledge by a diversity of means including broadcasting and "technological devices appropriate to Higher Education" (OU 2004a). As Schugurensky (2001–2005) points out, the then Labour Prime Minister Harold Wilson had a fascination with technologies, particularly the broadcast methods which were being used to train engineers in the Soviet Union, and the use of teaching films by Encyclopedia Britannica in the United States. His election manifesto for 1964 argued that there was an "imperative need for a revolution in our education system which will ensure the education of all our citizens in the responsibilities of this scientific age" (*Labour Party Manifesto* 1964). TV broadcasting figured largely in the constructing of the public image of the university, but the real motive for using technology at that time was making teaching cheaper, and the real technologizing of teaching was in the development of systems for production and distribution of printed materials on a very large scale, as well as the administration of the registration, teaching and assessment of hundreds of thousands of distant students annually. As Schugurensky (2001–2005) observes:

> Staff at the Open University have titles unheard-of in other British academic institutions, for example: photographic manager, copyrights manager, director of marketing, manager of correspondence services, chief systems analyst, and project control officer.

But with the development of new information and communication technologies (ICTs) from the mid-1980s onwards, the economic argument for technology-based teaching began to be supplemented by claims for additional pedagogical benefits to be gained. The OU's approach to distance teaching had always claimed enhanced learner-centeredness and pedagogical effectiveness from the use of technologies, including print. Some very distinct print-based pedagogies were developed to support a very diverse range of student types, including the socially and educationally marginalized. Rowntree (1999), for example, describes the attention paid to active understanding and to the "voices" of students as well as of teachers, in what he calls "second and third generation" distance learning texts and practices (broadly the pre- and post-computer phases of distance teaching).

The major investment in new technologies going on across the higher education sectors, both public and private, was therefore seen as educationally, as well as economically, justified, and the OU set out to embed ICTs into all its courses and dealings with students and part-time tutors, and to propel itself to the forefront of the development of new technology-based teaching methods. John Daniels, then Vice Chancellor, wrote and spoke extensively of his vision of a future in which "mega-universities" would provide mass education globally, delivered electronically, across social and geographical boundaries (Daniels 1996).

Participation as a Metaphor for Learning

But e-learning also has another discoursal relation to the notion of participation, in the pedagogical domain. Participation as a metaphor for learning, in contrast to the more conventional acquisition model (Sfard 1998), has long been a central feature in the discourse of computer-mediated communication in education (see Bullen 1998). The online learner is usually idealized as independent and autonomous, participating fully in, and benefiting from, online discussion with peers in an unthreatening collaborative environment, where the tutor acts more as a friendly facilitator rather than as the traditional authoritative didactic figure. Learning in these contexts is seen as a function of participation in the social construction of knowledge (e.g., see Garrison & Anderson 2003).

As a corollary of this pedagogical emphasis on active participation, assessment in online courses has a strongly regulative function. In Garrison and Anderson's words: "it is clear that students must perceive participation in eLearning discussions as a major component of the programme of studies. Thus, assessment activities must be integrated within the eLearning activities" (Garrison & Anderson 2003: 95). The simplest way to do this is to specify minimum levels of contribution (e.g., the University of Phoenix Online specifies a minimum number of logins per week). In addition, guidelines can be provided as to what constitutes a "good" message, and how to interact and build on others' contributions. Due to the practical difficulties of monitoring every student's contribution in an ongoing discussion, the onus for demonstrating the value of his/her contributions is often put back onto the student, sometimes through requiring him/her to "reflect" on discussion at a later point, in order to provide evidence of his/her learning, or to demonstrate outcomes from problem-based learning or group collaboration. The use of assessment as a means of rewarding, and thus promoting, participation in online discussion is now very common in the world of e-learning. Garrison and Anderson observe that many online courses now offer 40–50% of overall course grades for this kind of participation (96).

But there is evidence from elsewhere that cultural, linguistic, and other factors of student difference do not disappear in e-learning environments, and may in some cases exacerbate effects of exclusion and marginalization (Goodfellow et al. 2001; Mavor & Traynor 2003; Reeder et al. 2004). Furthermore, as Ess (2002b) has argued, the dominance of Western, English-speaking institutions in the design and development of these systems of remote communication ensures that it is a culturally specific notion of participation that is being imposed on the otherwise heterogeneous population of e-learners. Examples of this can be seen in studies of the type which investigate participation in computer-mediated tutorials by students from different national backgrounds (e.g., Kim & Bonk 2002). The findings of these studies often reinforce the idea that characteristics of student engagement such as individualism and autonomy, valued by pedagogical thinking in the West and embedded into the design of both technical and social structures of communication in many e-learning contexts, are more often present among the participants who are schooled in Anglo/US academic environments.

Participation for Employability

Developments in the technologies of e-learning are not tied to the proliferation of interaction-based models of participation. The relation between the technologies and the social goal of widened participation has also been constructed by associating the ability to use "knowledge tools" with individual or organizational survival, in a society where competitiveness and success depend on the creation of knowledge. Romiszowski (1996) provides a good illustration of this. In his view, societies in the twenty-first century will be characterized by networks of "knowledge workers" whose primary function is to continually renew the process of knowledge creation in order to keep themselves, or their employers, ahead of the competition (25). The process of knowledge creation is dependent on personal skills of information access, location, analysis, and evaluation, which involve the manipulation of sophisticated and ever-developing software applications, and also on the performance of human "conversational networks" in which knowledge workers "collaborate participatively toward the same set of global objectives" (26). The emphasis on collaboration, on new technologies, and on competition as the key driver is highly typical of the discourse of what Gee and others have called "fast capitalism" (Gee et al. 1996) and is paradigmatic of an approach to educational opportunity which is oriented simultaneously to participation in a social order and to individual competitive advantage.

There is also an influential strand of development located predominantly in the United States and Western Europe, concerned with the design, operationalization, and ultimately marketing of technical platforms and systems which support the mass delivery of materials which are independent of any communication between or among teachers and students. Wiley (2002) calls this "automated instruction," and predicts a future collision between this model and the social-constructivist version of participation in e-learning. The assumption is that the effort of providers of teaching materials will shift away from content and the delivery of teaching to the creation of repositories of learning objects. These are essentially software objects designed for learning purposes that can be picked up and reused by different learners in different learning contexts. Such a development, it is proposed, will free educational institutions from the need to create learning materials for themselves. They will then be able to concentrate on assessment and accreditation, and on developing systems which focus on validating a learner's success at self-initiated learning. This conceptualization is closely associated with ideas of a developing global market in learning "objects," and with the participation of the (lifelong) learner as a customer in that market.

Limitations of E-learning

The valorization of information technology in relation to learning in general and lifelong learning in particular, as exemplified in the British Government's "Learning Age" papers (DfES 1998), led to the founding in the United Kingdom of the "university for industry" (later renamed "Learn Direct") which was to use "leading edge technology to make learning available at work, in learning centres, in the community, and at home" (David Blunkett, UK Education Secretary 1997–2001). Gorard et al. (2002) suggest that:

> ICT-based initiatives have formed the bulk of interventions aimed at achieving lifelong learning for all in the UK with the government keen to adhere to the notion that technology is a means through which to free learning from those characteristics that have made it traditionally unattractive or inaccessible to large sections of the population.

Inaccessibility is seen as connected with the location and convenience of learning opportunities, rather than with longer-term social, economic, and educational factors. In fact, the study by Gorard et al. reports that having access to computers and the Internet is not a significant factor determining whether people have undertaken any post-compulsory education. Thus, access to IT is not a proxy for wider participation in education, which remains largely determined by other factors. For example, those in social class AB (professional and managerial) are three times as likely to participate as class DE (manual and casual). This contradicts the assumed link between participation and electronic access which continues to characterize much of the public discourse of lifelong learning in the United Kingdom.

In fact, while the use of online communication in distance education is widespread, especially in the United States, it is not yet all pervasive. In the case of the OU, for example, while much is made publicly of the 160,000 students and tutors who are registered users of the university's email and online discussion facilities, only half of its (over 360) courses make use of the Internet for the delivery of materials or for study support (OU 2004b). The university acknowledges that it has no ambition to become an "online university," unlike, for example, the Open University of the Netherlands, which is explicitly engaged in transforming itself into a "digital university" (Curran 2001). This is partly out of a commitment to flexibility in the means of studying offered to its students, but also a product of a policy on equal opportunities that requires that technical systems are embedded in the curriculum in ways that do not undermine the ability of any students to access material or benefit from teaching. One of the roles of the Institute of Educational Technology at the OU has always been to monitor and report on levels of student access to the various media considered to have an educational application.[6] Over the years this data has played an important role in the development of the university's policies on courses which required students to use, progressively, audio tapes, video tapes and off-air recordings, stand-alone computers, email and computer conferencing, CD-ROM multimedia packages, and most recently the Internet.

E-business and the Digital Divide

It might appear, as Boshier and Onn argue (2000, quoted in Roy 2002), that the rhetoric of e-learning as e-business is a construct of a neoliberal social agenda focused on the internationalization of education as an instrument of economic globalization, rather than the democratization of educational opportunity. Certainly the apparent impact of new technologies on social structures in the developed world leaves little room for optimism as to any leveling effects they might achieve elsewhere. The tendency identified by van Dijk (2000) for technological divides to deepen, so that the gap separating the haves from the have-nots gets progressively more unbridgeable, does not augur well for the prospects of increased technical access to post-compulsory education for traditionally disadvantaged sectors, even if it does widen participation by previously uninvolved groups on the "have" side of the divide. Nevertheless, even institutions such as the OU, which are still publicly committed to a social transformative role in the wider international context, are finding themselves constrained to consider the way their social missions articulate with the conditions that commercial self-interest is creating in the global education market. This is not least because of the rapidly increasing complexity of types of institutional partnership and forms of public–private financing that have emerged in the wake of several spectacular and costly failures to turn considerable levels of investment into acceptable number of students (e.g., Columbia University's Fathom company, Cornell University's eCornell venture, the UK e-University, etc.).

Reshaping the OU's Social Mission

The OU's current priorities link its core UK objective of widening participation to the revitalization of its international focus and "global reach," and to becoming a leader in design, content, and delivery. This strategy explicitly constructs the international arena as a key area of pedagogical and institutional innovation, and stresses the pedagogic resource that the OU and developed economies represent to the international market. The impact of OU audiovisual techniques on the world in the early 1970s is presented as evidence for its capacity to exploit the global implications of newer e-learning technologies. The university thus aims to use its advantage in pedagogy and technical resources to compete in major new areas of distance education expansion, for example, India and China, focusing on reproducing itself as a large-scale provider on a global basis. It also draws on the OU's traditional social agenda, emphasizing its support for the principles agreed by UNESCO in the Dakar framework of 2000 (see "Education for All"7). These two aspects of the organization's enterprise are not seen as polarized but as complementary. Business advantage can be found in meeting what is seen as a desire on the part of the stronger developing countries to deliver low-cost mass education. The OU's resources are in both expertise and "goods" (i.e., hardware, materials, and accreditation), but the unstable economic climate for e-learning suggests that it will not be advising international clients on major investments in e-learning infrastructure of their own.

Higher Education for Economic Advantage

The two discourses of "equal access" and "widening participation" are essentially two faces of the single coin of expanded educational opportunity. Nevertheless, they involve differences in emphasis on human rights, economic priorities, and individual development. They also have different implications for the way that higher education is constructed in opposition to professional and/or occupational education, and suggest different trajectories of development for the technologies of e-learning. Finally, they also lead to different positionings of the socially disadvantaged and/or marginalized.

Historically, equity in the context of access to higher education has been presented as the equalizing across all sectors of society of the availability and the quality of teaching at this level so as to remove any physical and financial barriers to its take-up. It has been viewed as the responsibility of national governments and identified with publicly funded systems of ODE, such as the British OU, which utilizes a variety of technologies to achieve flexible, large-scale, low-cost teaching of a comparable quality with the conventional elite systems it supplements. The maintenance of intellectual and cultural parity with the curriculum and learning outcomes of these elites has been of key importance in upholding equality of access through ODE, and the representation of e-learning technologies in this perspective has emphasized their ability to reproduce teaching and learning processes characteristic of quality in conventional universities.

The success of the discourse of equality of access through ODE in highlighting its contribution to an overall increase in number of people entering higher education has been mitigated by a perceived failure of national education systems as a whole to alter the proportion of those from low-income and socially marginalized groups who do so. At the same time, the increased educational levels of populations in parts of the developing world where access has expanded have created conditions of increased global competition, for both commercial and educational opportunity. There has therefore been a shift in the ideological underpinnings of social commitment to equity in higher education in the developed countries, from the individual's right to a university education, whatever his/her circumstances or social background, to his/her opportunity to participate in post-compulsory education at some level, as part of commercial and governmental agendas for social and economic transformation.

Equity in the context of participation in this social and economic transformation has been presented within two additional frames of reference, one focusing on the theme of diversity in the social backgrounds of those who do take up enhanced opportunities, and the other emphasizing a convergence of higher education with professional, technical, and lifelong learning, and the dissemination of the opportunity for personal economic advantage. These discourses have valorized the development of educational technologies which are oriented to the customization of the teaching and learning process to local contexts of work and social life, and which are also capable of reaching educationally marginalized, but economically viable, sectors of relatively developed societies on a global level. In general, widening participation through e-learning, while inheriting the democratic connotations of personalization and choice, adds a strong implication of social responsibility—to participate "in" a social process which has to a large extent been determined by larger political and corporate interests (e.g., the so-called "knowledge society" in conditions of globalization). Access is, by contrast, a more passive concept, removing restrictions without necessarily imposing duties.

The OU's social mission, like that of other public education systems in the West, is changing through its representation as part of the discourse of equity in participation, rather than of access, and through the expression of this in the development of more complex technological systems. In attempting to retain its principles of social justice and diversity, while at the same time responding to the UK government's invoking of the national economic interest, and meeting the challenge of corporate survival in the highly commercialized conditions of global teaching with technology, the institution is trying to reconcile ideologies which many would see as incompatible. If it is the case that the notion of equity is coming to mean equal opportunity to participate in a competition for economic advantage, and if it is also the case that the cost of achieving equity is shifting from society to the individual, then it could be argued that this is a departure from the basic human right to be educated at university level. Whatever the discourse, however, if the growing investment of non-profit institutions such as the OU in the technologies of e-learning is not able to extend significant benefits of higher education to globally marginalized populations, then they will have failed in their mission of over half a century.

Notes

1. For example, marginalized groups in the Indian context identified by Sharma Sen (2002) include the differently abled, women, minorities, scheduled castes and tribes, prison inmates, senior citizens, nomads and migrants, and the geographically remote.
2. Compare this with the British OU's commitment to "promote the educational well-being of the community generally" (OU 2004a).
3. More recent figures from Murphy et al. (2003), however, suggest that in the provision of online courses, Asian universities now offer more in humanities subjects than in education.
4. Dropout rates in distance education have long been thought to be considerably higher than for face-to-face equivalents (e.g., see Kember 1995).
5. This film played on the relationship between an aspiring working class OU student and her disillusioned middle class tutor.
6. In 1996, for example, a Student Access survey showed that 25% of OU students had no access at all to a computer. By 2001 this was down to 8%.
7. See www.unesco.org/education/efa/ed_for_all/dakfram_eng.shtml

Chapter 4

Webmastered: Postcolonialism and the Internet

Martha Henn McCormick

New concepts of literary forms and modes have been proposed; new notions of the nature of literature itself, and of how it communicates, are current: new views of literature's role in relation to society flourish.
—Terence Hawkes' General Editor's Preface to *The Empire Writes Back: Theory and Practice in Post-Colonial Literatures*

Beneath the great continuities of thought, beneath the solid, homogeneous manifestations of a single mind or of a collective mentality, beneath the stubborn development of a science striving to exist and to reach completion at the very outset, beneath the persistence of a particular genre, form, discipline, or theoretical activity, one is now trying to detect the incidence of interruptions, interruptions whose status and nature vary considerably. These are epistemological acts and thresholds [...] they suspend the continuous accumulation of knowledge, interrupt its slow development, and force it to enter a new time.
—Michel Foucault, *The Archaeology of Knowledge and the Discourse on Language*

As anyone who currently teaches college-level composition courses knows, technologized information is an unavoidable tool of the contemporary pedagogical rubric. Instructors now routinely confront electronic communication media, especially if we want to encourage responsible use, by our students, of these media in the context of writing. Yet, is it possible to encourage responsible use of media that may, by their very existence, be riddled with colonizing tendencies? On the one hand, yes, the Internet contains a multitude of resources for students of postcolonialism to consult and participate in. Students may participate, for example, in listservs, where they can both hear the insights of others and share their own, developing a fuller and, ideally, a more multicultural sense of the global intellectual community. Provided, that is, that a further splintering of Internet culture does not emerge. Danny Goodman (1995) conjectures that the intellectual elite may remove themselves entirely from the great, "democratic" fray of the Internet and "hustle off to other areas that are more private and form their own new elite" (11). In the last several years, we have witnessed the creation of Value-Added Networks (VANs), Virtual Private Networks (VPNs), Intranets, Extranets, and Private Internet Exchanges, all mechanisms for greater security and exclusivity than the World Wide Web generally affords.

Looking at the World Wide Web and email communication together as aspects of the Internet, I am interested in the question of where unique and disparate societies fit into this electronic equation. One is hard pressed to discuss writing, literatures, and technologies without addressing their place in the social fabric. After all,

> [o]ne cannot but see significant links between new technologies of information, the most diverse cultural forms, and the deepest social structures caused by such large transformations in the techniques of both writing and of storing and making writing available. (Bloch & Hesse 1993: 1)

I am concerned that the relationship between the Internet (as a technology of information) and diverse cultures is a colonizing one. I believe there are inconsistencies between the insights of postcolonialism and the Internet, so highly and yet often mistakenly praised as a great equalizer.

Both the title of this chapter and the title of a 1989 book on postcolonialism (*The Empire Writes Back: Theory and Practice in Post-Colonial Literatures*) run the risk of situating the postcolonial writer in the position of respondent to the hegemony of the colonial culture. Indeed, *The Columbia Dictionary of Modern Literary and Cultural Criticism* describes postcolonialism as a "historical phase undergone by many of the world's countries after the decline of European empires by the mid-twentieth century" (Childers & Hentzi 1995: 234). By that definition, only formerly colonial states are postcolonial and, hence, only their writers postcolonialists. However, others think of postcolonialism as the (or "a") historical moment—a phase, if you will, in which we are all participating, affected by it whether we are the colonized, the colonizers, or merely witnesses. Bill Ashcroft argues that the term "postcolonial" refers to "all the culture affected by the imperial process from the moment of colonization to the present day" (as quoted in Murdoch 1995: 1060). Though rhetorically my title appears to situate the postcolonial writer as respondent, I conceive of postcolonialism as a more or less global phenomenon.

Colonialism and Language: From Cultural Reiteration to Self-Definition

In the heyday of colonialism, both education generally and literature specifically were used to inculcate the values of the colonizing power. In India, for example, the institutionalized study of the English language began in 1835, put in place by the Governor General, Lord William Bentnick, and the General Committee on Public Instruction. The Committee disagreed about what the language of public instruction should be, with some arguing for Arabic and Sanskrit and the rest arguing for English. Thomas Macaulay, Legal Member of Council, had argued as early as 1833 for the betterment of the public mind in India through a European (or, more specifically, English) model of education (Gupta 1995: 73). In his 1835 "Minute on Indian Education," he addressed the Committee on Public Instruction, declaring that:

> we are free to employ our funds as we choose; [...] we ought to employ them in teaching what is best worth knowing; that English is better worth knowing than Sanscrit (*sic*) or Arabic; that the natives are desirous to be taught English, and are not desirous to be taught Sanscrit or Arabic; [...] that it is possible to make natives of this country thoroughly good English scholars, and that to this end all our efforts should be directed. (Macaulay 1972: 249)

Macaulay argued for a "class of persons, Indian in blood and colour, but English in taste, in opinions, in morals, and in intellect" (ibid.).[1] In other words, cultivating a desire for an English sensibility was the point of the education provided, in English, to Indian colonial subjects. As Ashcroft et al. phrase it, "[t]he study of English has always been a densely political and cultural phenomenon, a practice in which language and literature have both been called into the service of a profound and embracing nationalism" (1989: 2).

Consequently, "talking back" to the colonial power often followed the model of call and response, or echoed reply. The colonized were expected to reiterate the imperialist culture. However, as postcolonialism has proliferated around the globe, as we learn more about what it means to be beyond the colonial moment, "talking back" has ceased being the recitation or rehearsal of imposed cultural values and has become instead the refutation (or at least scrutiny) of externally imposed values and the description of unique cultures by those who truly belong to them. Michael Gorra quotes a character in Rushdie's *Satanic Verses*, who says of white British society, "[t]hey have the power of description, and we succumb to the picture they construct." Continues Gorra, "[f]or seeing India, or Africa, or the Caribbean is indeed a way of ruling them. One consequence of the end of the British Empire is that they have started to describe themselves" (1994: 656).

The Internet: Colonial Terra Infirma?

As postcolonialism involves speaking for oneself rather than being "spoken for," it is particularly fruitful to examine the ways in which the ideas and ideals of postcolonialism both mesh and clash with the ideas and ideals of the Internet, which is so frequently touted as a model of democracy in action. Even Derrida, in an article in *Diacritics* analyzing the impulse to save records, has something to say about the Internet's impact on political structures:

> Electronic mail today [...] even more than the fax, is on the way to transforming the entire public and private space of humanity [...] This is not only a technique, in the ordinary and limited sense of the term: at an unprecedented rhythm, in quasi-instantaneous fashion, this instrumental possibility of production, of printing, of conservation, and of destruction of the archive must inevitably be accompanied by juridical and thus political transformations. (1995: 17–18)

In June of 1996, a conference entitled "The Global Research Village" was held in Denmark. Present at this conference were the research ministers from seven European countries plus representatives from 20 other countries, including the United States and Japan. The attendees were there to discuss the potential value of the Internet to the world community of researchers. They issued a call to world governments to achieve three goals: first, to "[i]nsure that research institutions have high-quality Internet connections" and to "support the digitization of scientific documents and the development of virtual electronic research libraries open to all researchers." Second, to "[c]ooperate in developing international legal, regulatory, and commercial standards covering such issues as copyright protection, combating the criminal uses of the Internet, and guaranteeing that the scientific community will have continued, unhindered access to the Internet." Third, to "[d]evote more foreign aid to providing good Internet connections for universities and research institutions in developing countries" (Bollag 1996: A14).

However, several problems remain unsolved in the wake of this gathering of officials, and other problems have been exacerbated. "Criminal uses of the

Internet," from many governments' perspectives, involve not just flagrant violations such as credit fraud, but also infractions against the Communications Decency Act, as in the United States, or the dissemination of neo-Nazi propaganda in Germany. And in China, not only are obscene and pornographic materials banned, but also so is any "information that jeopardizes 'public order' or 'threatens state security'" (ibid.). Human Rights Watch (2001) shows that "[s]ince 1995, when Chinese authorities began permitting commercial Internet accounts, at least 60 sets of regulations have been issued aimed at controlling Internet content" and that sending "secret" or "reactionary" materials over the Internet has been considered a capital crime since early 2001.

Global Research Village conference participants bemoaned the lack of uniformity of access policies around the globe and pushed for "international policy coordination" so that "commercial interests could [not] gain a hold over the network." However, users of the net are opposed to just this—government regulation of access. So while users hope for unlimited access predicated on a technological infrastructure provided by governments, the government participants at this conference were calling for international regulatory policies and hoping that commercial entities would assume responsibility for infrastructure development (Bollag 1996: A14).

Debates continue about Internet governance and regulation, and the role of the private versus the public sectors. Documents coming out of the World Summit on the Information Society, held in Geneva in 2003, call for the establishment of the United Nations Working Group on Internet Governance (WGIG). The WGIG Declaration of Principles states that:

> [t]he international management of the Internet should be multilateral, transparent and democratic, with the full involvement of governments, the private sector, civil society and international organizations. It should ensure an equitable distribution of resources, facilitate access for all and ensure a stable and secure functioning of the Internet, taking into account multilingualism

and that Internet management should involve all relevant civil and private stakeholders (UN 2003a). Its Plan of Action uses words such as trustworthy, transparent, non-discriminatory, open and inclusive as descriptive of the values that underlie the charge to issue a report in 2005 that defines Internet governance, identifies public policy issues, and develops:

> a common understanding of the respective roles and responsibilities of governments, existing intergovernmental and international organisations and other forums as well as the private sector and civil society from both developing and developed countries. (UN 2003b)

WGIG's Final Report was completed in June 2005; it has of course sparked controversy. The Internet Society, a professional membership society with 100 organizational and 20,000 individual members in 180 countries, has criticized the WGIG Final Report for lack of full stakeholder participation, governmental heavy-handedness and likewise an under-emphasis on the contributions of Internet users and a lack of bottom-up input (Internet Society 2005).

"Anonymous" Was an Internet User

The Internet is often described as open and available to people around the world, yet its global availability is a myth; access to it is dependent on the usual staples of worldly power: education, yes, but even more so, money and technology. What is more, possession of the requisite technology means nothing if one does not have the benefit of a reliable infrastructure of telecommunication services and steady electrical supply:

> High costs are splitting us into information haves and have-nots, thereby threatening democratic principles. Countries, too, are being divided into haves and have-nots. In many developing nations, a majority of people have no telephones or computers. Even if they did, their machines would be idle unless governments were able to invest billions of dollars in telecommunications infrastructure—primarily cables, satellites, and transmitters. And this would not bridge the gap—a third of all people in developing nations cannot read. (Swerdlow 1995: 15)

For those lucky enough to possess the know-how, technology, money to pay the bills, and infrastructure to support equipment, the Internet plays host to millions of users worldwide who, despite log-on IDs and signature files, remain essentially anonymous. And while gaining reliable access to the Internet may obviate somewhat the privilege of place (i.e., first versus third world), making dialogs international and placing whomever speaks at the center, current netiquette nonetheless enforces linguistic, grammatical, and stylistic standards and expectations. These standards and expectations contribute to the anxieties of self-presentation that one may experience on the net, despite its relative anonymity. Danny Goodman (1995) mistakenly states, for example, that age, gender, and race disappear online and that one is judged only by "ideas, grammar and spelling," (11) as if these areas are unrelated to age, race, gender, and, of course, nationality. Does having an email address or Internet or World Wide Web access mean one has sworn to uphold the "values" of the Internet? This question is particularly relevant, given that the rhetorical expectations of the Internet do run fairly high and the control and punishment mechanism of flaming is well in place.

The Internet, then, is not really a bastion of open dialog and free speech. Modes of communication are fairly regulated; listservs, for example, all come with their own rules of comportment. I surveyed the initial subscriber messages from listservs, I have joined in the past and found the following examples from the Library Reference List. Under "Etiquette": "The moderators urge all subscribers to be courteous. The moderators reserve the right to reject any posting that they consider discourteous." The moderators also include the following: "Points for Effective Computer Mediated Communication": users are told to make sure we are not misunderstanding a message we receive and to make sure that the message we send will not be misunderstood, though how we are to discern the authorial intentions of others or guarantee our own is not addressed. We are told to clearly label sarcasm and humor (the smiley face emoticon, I presume, being the Internet equivalent of the laugh track), and we are urged not to "abuse new users of computer networks for their ignorance— be patient as they first learn to crawl, then to walk" (Balraj et al. 1999). I am amused by the infantilized characterization of "newbies," as if they are the new primitivists.

I am not arguing that such setting of ground rules is ill-advised or unreasonably constraining. "Netiquette" is meant to ensure that people can have their say so long as everyone agrees to abide by certain rules of order. However, it is striking how willing Internet users are to police each other and how aggressive and even vituperative the conversation can get as soon as someone is seen to step out of line. This is especially ironic considering how resentful Internet users are of government attempts to regulate this electronic forum. And yet, there is relatively little discussion about where the rules of comportment come from, who composed them, why we all are expected to acquiesce to them, why we never revisit and reconsider them, and why we are so intent on insisting to each other that they be upheld. I am reminded, unmistakably, of the workings of cultural hegemony, the "invisible hand" of class and Western modes of discourse. And as the net becomes more and more global, as people from more and more places begin to talk with each other, those rigid and prescribed rules of discourse are used to govern the electronic conversation of peoples from very disparate cultures.

For example, in September of 1995, a question about Derek Walcott was posed, in French, by a Postcolonial List member and responded to in French by a few others. Then, another list member complained that "this discussion in French on an English-speaking list [is] more rudeness by some folks who are quick to align themselves with one of the historical metropoles that had no problem with enslaving, say, Cesaire's ancestors." A controversy exploded on the list about who had declared it English speaking and what an insistence upon English-language postings could be said to signify on a postcolonial list. People debated the idea that writing in French could be considered an imperialistic act aimed at the listserv and debated the meaning of aligning oneself with French colonization versus English colonization. Strangely, no one questioned the notion that use of a language was somehow equivalent to aligning oneself with one colonizer or another. Suddenly, the list was filled with remarks in Telugu, Punjabi, Spanish, and even pig Latin. One user commented in rather turgid prose: "The hyperdeterritorialization of the net may help toward a certain apparent linguistic reification which ought, I think, to be resisted." In other words, since people participate in net discussions from around the world and since English, for better or worse, is the most commonly used language in business, technological, and educational circles, people tend to use English on the net, too, and perhaps we should question that (*Postcolonial Archive* 1995).

True Democratization?

The following question presents itself in light of such controversies as the one I have just outlined. Have we already established a falsely naturalized electronic mode of discourse? And if so, can it be unsettled or decolonized? Is it possible that the Internet is neocolonial? John Docker describes neocolonialism as "the imposition of the metropolitan power's dominant cultural values" (1995: 445). Philip Altbach argues: "[N]eocolonialism means the impact of advanced nations on developing areas, in this case with a special reference to their educational systems and intellectual life" rather than by means of overt political control (1995: 452). If we agree that the Internet may be governed, de facto, by Western cultural values, and if we see it as an educational and/or intellectual tool, then it can be said to have neocolonial aspirations. Françoise Lionnet reminds us that "ethnocentric value judgements have no place within a truly diverse, multicultural, and multiracial [...] practice" (1995: 2). So, for that matter, does Star Trek's Prime Directive, which posits as the ultimate rule of intercultural contact a prohibition against the undue influencing of another culture's development. I do not ask you to accept a television show's creed as an argument for or against viewing the net as potentially colonial. In fact, I mention it in a devil's advocate spirit: we generally hold that sharing technological developments around the globe is a good thing, a generous thing, and the right thing to do. It may be that there is no way to share technology and, at the same time, be so culturally relativist as to avoid any imposition of the values of the cultures providing the technologies. There may be no fail-safe way to provide the technological vehicles of communication without their also becoming, in a sense, ideological overseers of that communication.

Electronic media change critical response. What is it about postcolonialism that compels me to argue that perhaps electronic media should widen their definition of acceptable forms of discourse? Well, says Joel Swerdlow, "[r]eliance on the electronic screen is part of something larger, the spread of technological civilization. George Steiner, a cultural historian [...], warns that this civilization produces a creeping sameness that threatens local cultures" (1995: 7). Meanwhile, in postcolonial zones:

> all our academic preconceptions about cultural, linguistic, or stylistic norms are constantly being put to the test by creative practices that make visible and set off the processes of adaptation, appropriation, and contestation governing the construction of identity in colonial and postcolonial contexts. (Lionnet 1995: 6)

So we have a problem of technological civilization radiating outward from its "first-world" centers that must be met with playful resistances to its "dominant conceptual paradigms" (ibid.). Ashcroft et al. write the following, regarding the development of postcolonial literatures. I think their words provide an excellent parallel logic to the need for some true liberation or democratization of the net—if, that is, you agree that the net is institutionalized:

> The institution of "Literature" in the colony is under direct control of the imperial ruling class who alone license the acceptable form and permit the publication and distribution of the resulting work. So, texts of this kind come into being within the constraints of a discourse and the institutional practice of a patronage system that limits and undercuts their assertion of a different perspective. The development of independent literatures depended upon the abrogation of this constraining power and the appropriation of language and writing for new and distinctive usages. Such an appropriation is clearly the most significant feature in the emergence of modern postcolonial literatures. (1989: 6)

You may be waiting for me to provide some concrete examples of the class and Western cultural values of the Internet, and I will offer these. First, there is the supposedly sacred nature of email as a medium that is to be free of aggressive marketing strategies. If you post email messages advertising goods or services, or send them to private accounts, be prepared for unrelenting flaming. But why is it that we believe email should be a commerce-free zone (especially when we tolerate advertising in our mailboxes and through our telephone lines and celebrate it on the World Wide Web)? Email cannot remain a commerce-free zone; it is more and more a commercial commodity. However, we are culturally disdainful of commercialization in this realm. One could read this as a vestige of upper-class distaste for the merchant classes and the sullied topic of money. We struggle to preserve this seemingly private medium from the sordidness of commerce. However, only those who exist in a thriving economy, in which income is reasonably predictable and a high standard of living reasonably guaranteed, can seriously make an argument that any forum of mass communication should be inviolably free of commercialization, for the benefit and convenience of the privileged masses.

Where the World Wide Web is concerned, there is mounting debate and even litigation surrounding trademark infringement. In 1999, American online toy marketer eToys filed suit in California against a European art group, etoy.com, on the basis of the similarity of their online identities and Uniform Resource Locators (URLs). A story on National Public Radio focused on this case and, generally, the international nature of the Internet. Reporter Madeline Brand spoke with lawyer Mark Lindsey, who makes the point that "[j]ust because the US has dominated the lucrative 'dot com' so far doesn't mean it should continue to do so." Lindsey believes that eToys may have the stronger case under US trademark law; even though etoy.com has been an Internet presence at its URL for three more years than has eToys, eToys purchased a copyright while etoy.com has not. However, Lindsey is uncertain if "from a global Internet perspective [...] that's an appropriate resolution." He points out that US companies have gotten ahead early in the registering of trademarks for Internet names and are now trying to prevent people in other countries from using similar names. The debate has mostly been a United States–European one so far, but it is likely to become ever more global in scope. Says Lindsey, "[p]eople [...] are quite concerned that the US is in essence making the Internet one of its territories" ("Is an E-Toy by Another Name the Same?").

Or consider, for example, the significance of the domain name. Your domain, that is, the part of your email address following the @, is now the object of what Danny Goodman calls "domain discrimination" (1995: 11). It is not necessarily who you know but who your Internet provider is that determines how seriously your posting may be taken. Also, many formerly colonized cultures have strong oral rather than literary traditions. Now the Internet and the ability to use computer technology generally creates a new standard of literacy, which asks cultures to move from oral to written to digitized activities in order to stay in any way competitive. Furthermore, at least in academic lists, the emphasis is most definitely placed upon conventionally expressed critical commentary. However, what if you want to offer your critical commentary in an unconventional way? With postcolonial writing, "[t]heories of style and genre, assumptions about the universal features of language, epistemological and value systems are all radically questioned" (Ashcroft et al., 1989: 11). Is this really the case on the Internet?

David Murdoch (1995) points out that "many postcolonial creative works are also critical commentaries" (1068). But most of the critical commentary I encounter on the Internet is not offered in a particularly creative or narrativized fashion. Murdoch is not the only one to make this observation. Lionnet (1995) discusses how postcolonial writers, particularly women, must function across multiple cultural boundaries, "[m]ale and female, colonial and indigenous, global and local" and must become "adept at braiding all the traditions at [their] disposal" into the dominant cultural discourse in order to effect the slow transformation of that dominant cultural discourse (5). Barbara Christian (1995) argues that some of the most daring black, women, and third-world critics:

> have been influenced, even coopted into speaking a language and defining their discussion terms alien to and opposed to our needs and orientation. [...] For people of color have always theorized—but in forms quite different from the Western form of abstract logic. And I am inclined to say that our theorizing [...] is often in narrative forms, in the stories we create, in riddles and proverbs, in the play with language [...]. (457)

I have seen little evidence that the Internet is making great strides in promoting the sharing of wisdom in the forms of stories, riddles, proverbs, and the like.

However, I do not want to condemn or sound entirely negative regarding the possibilities for the Internet to become more culturally attuned in a postcolonial world. There are positive signs out there. One of the concepts of postcolonialism is that of hybridity, or a kind of cultural mixing, and certainly the Internet does promote such mixing, even if, at the moment, it seems to expect it to occur in a rather narrowly defined rhetorical style. Usually such cultural mixing is at least two-directional and hopefully multi-directional, so that "all elements involved in the interaction would be changed by that encounter" (Lionnet 1995: 8–9). In his work, Edward Said argues that "colonizer and colonized are now inextricably connected" (cited in Murdoch 1995: 1065), and the Internet is a forum that can help spread that realization. Postcolonials have, for example, creolized the languages imposed on them by colonizers, making new languages, new linguistic pastiches. It is entirely conceivable that stylistic pastiches could proliferate on the Internet. Lionnet argues that assimilation is not necessarily the outcome "when Western technology and education are adopted by the colonized" but instead such a melding can help all individuals see themselves in new relation to both past and present, and to admit a shift in cosmology or *Weltanschauung* (1995: 11). As Joel Swerdlow says, "technology continually assaults authority," and "free-flowing information nurtures democracy" (1995: 14). "The law of unintended consequences governs all technological revolutions," he states (5), and certainly one great boon to the diversity of the Internet is that "electronic communication provides a 'sensory expansion for the species by allowing people to experience an extraordinary array of things while staying geographically in the same spot' " (William Gibson cited in Swerdlow 1995: 6).

My challenge to Internet culture resides in the fact that Internet users are so willing to abide by regulations whose source can never be clearly located and whose values go unquestioned, and they are also so willing to punish rogue users who commit infractions against administrative apparatuses that are manifestations of deep-seated linguistic and cultural conventions and habits. This trend bears an uncomfortable resemblance to the heyday of colonialism, in which colonialist power was actually consolidated by everyday folks under the guise, for example, of giving the "natives" a proper English education. In this era in which we purport to recognize and even celebrate a multiplicity of cultures, voices, and modes of discourse, Internet culture may in some ways inhibit rather than enhance cultural expression. As we valorize the usefulness of the Internet and the World Wide Web for expanding the intellectual and cultural horizons of students of postcolonial and other literatures, so we must also examine the almost-invisible cultural assumptions underlying the Internet. Unquestioning acquiescence to those cultural assumptions is tantamount to a new form of cultural hegemony.

Note

1. Sara Suleri discusses Macaulay's "Minute on Indian Education" as a "fallacy of utilitarianism" and a treatise on "the idea of colonial blankness" (1992: 22). It may be that Macaulay's "Minute" was less relevant to the eventual decision to institutionalize English in Indian education and has been historically overrated in its relation to that decision; Macaulay did not arrive in India until 1834 and the change to English-language instruction took place in 1835.

Chapter 5

Hybrid Teaching and Learning: Pedagogy versus Pragmatism

Marjorie D. Kibby

Hybrid courses are courses where "a significant portion of the learning activities have been moved online" (Garnham & Kaleta 2002) and the time spent face-to-face in the classroom is reduced, replaced by Internet-based learning. The goal of hybrid courses is to use face-to-face time for those activities best done face-to-face, and to take advantage of the most effective instructional aspects of online learning. In such courses, students spend more of their time working either individually or collaboratively on case studies, research projects, authentic problems and assigned research, and less time getting information from their instructor; while teaching staff spend less time providing information to students, and more time guiding and interacting with students, and reviewing and responding to student work.

Although it is generally agreed that the traditional classroom is no longer a viable source of all formal learning, many critics of e-learning cite practical experience of the disadvantages of the lack of face-to-face contact with students. The drawbacks of online learning have been extensively discussed (van Shaik et al. 2003) and include the social isolation which students feel without face-to-face contact with tutors and other students; bandwidth, browser and software limitations which can restrict instructional methods, and increase student frustration; the costs that may be involved in server access, downloading and printing; the constraints on providing valid and reliable assessment; and the need for students to be self-motivated and self-directed. However, despite the disadvantages, "[o]nline education is experiencing a tremendous influx of students and is generating increased excitement and grandiose projections for the future" (Lancaster et al. 2003).

Those who have been working with both online and face-to-face learning models report that "hybrid or blended models most frequently emerge as the most effective learning strategy" (Skill & Young 2002: 24). At its best the hybrid course combines the connectedness of the classroom with the content richness and the flexibility of the virtual learning environment. Combining the strengths of both models provides highly effective learning experiences, as students are neither passively absorbing mass-oriented content nor learning in individual isolation.

Pedagogical Advantages of Hybrid Teaching/Learning

Using a hybrid mode to deliver learning activities enhances student learning in a number of ways, including making study more convenient, by allowing time shifting; improving interaction, by enabling considered responses to discussion; increasing individualized learning opportunities, through the ability to provide a menu of learning activities; providing a student-focused environment, where passive tasks such as note-taking are replaced by active experiences; developing core skills, including an ability to self- and peer-evaluate, and to apply logical, critical and creative thinking to information; and enabling support networks, from peer study groups to mentoring programs. While all of these are achievable within the fully face-to-face or completely online teaching modes, the combination of the two opens up possibilities for a greater range of learning activities more closely linked to the learning objectives.

The initial appeal to many students is increased flexibility in timetabling. Universities are seeing significant demographic changes as the number of traditional 18–20-year-old residential students decreases, and the number of students with families, jobs and outside interests increases. With the greater demand on available time, scheduling multiple classes and commuting to campus complicates managing learning time. Moving some learning activities online gives students more options in structuring their schedules, and allows them to integrate their study with downtime at work or home. Being able to undertake learning activities at the student's convenience, without the pressure of time constraints, has obvious advantages in terms of fewer missed sessions and the quality of the learning experience. The face-to-face components of the hybrid course provide incentives for completing learning tasks on time, and keep students connected with classmates and course goals. Research at the University of Central Florida found that hybrid courses have higher success rates and lower withdrawal rates than comparable face-to-face or fully online courses (UCF 2001). This research also revealed that the flexibility of not coming onto campus was the major attraction of online courses for students, with 79% of the students surveyed citing convenience as their major reason for taking an online course.

Faculty at the University of Wisconsin-Milwaukee who have used the hybrid teaching approach report an increased interaction of students with each other and with the course instructor (UWM, n.d.). The online environment offers a secure forum for students who are reticent in a face-to-face discussion. Being able to prepare before commenting, to refer to notes and to contribute without drawing attention to oneself, give a greater range of students the confidence to become actively involved in the discussion. While "students who rarely take part in classroom discussions are more likely to participate online" (Young 2002), there are indications that successfully participating in online forums increases student participation in classroom discussions. The experience of having contributions to a discussion valued, the development of an interactive environment where students discuss topics with each other rather than respond to the instructor, and the growth of a community where students offer each other information, encouragement and support, all have positive carryover effects in the face-to-face classroom. In a hybrid course traditional classroom discussions can be enlivened and invigorated by the online experience. Research into online communications suggests that "a virtual learning environment may constitute a more relaxed and stress-free atmosphere than a classroom" (Roed 2003: 155). However, there is evidence to suggest that extrovert students find online discussions less satisfying than face-to-face seminars, while students who are at all self-conscious perceive online seminars as more involving (Taylor 1997: 80). A combination of discussion modes accommodates the range of preferences.

Studies of distance education suggest that students are more likely to succeed if they are in frequent contact with their instructor (Arbaugh 2001); however, in face-to-face courses individual contact with the instructor may be limited to a quick question in the corridor after class. In a hybrid course an instructor can invite questions on the class session or an assessment item or the next week's topic and can respond to individual questions at a level of detail impossible under the situational constraints of the classroom. This has, of course, consequences for the instructor's time investment in the course, a potential problem that can be managed by having an expanded online support system that includes various kinds of instructional personnel, so that the right level of intervention is possible. Alternative staffing arrangements can include administrative staff, peer tutors or graduate course assistants who monitor forums established for specific types of questions or comments.

The possibility of individualized interaction between instructor and student is one of the great advantages of a hybrid approach. Through the careful design of the online learning activities, a student-centered approach is more likely to be achieved than in a traditional lecture/tutorial format. Drawing upon the rich resources of the Internet, students are able to follow their own interests within a topic area, and are able to accomplish personal learning goals. With the move to student-focused teaching, students become more accountable for their own learning—this involves skills that some students may need to acquire, but they are skills that will have lifelong application. The burden of providing students all of the information they require is lifted from the instructor who takes on the role of assisting students to evaluate, classify and apply the information they have gathered for themselves. Again this may necessitate the acquisition of a new set of skills, this time by the instructor, but the use of web-based learning resources, and of instructional software to deliver content, can increase students' level of engagement with course content. By combining classroom activities with individual or collaborative tasks and projects that use online resources and facilities, learning becomes much more applied as hands-on exercises punctuate information acquisition components.

A flow-on consequence of these attributes of hybrid teaching is that students have greater opportunity for the development of a number of transferable skills increasingly valued in an era of lifelong learning. Through a combination of face-to-face and online learning activities students have increased opportunity to develop or enhance the ability to manage their time, solve problems, evaluate material, think critically and communicate with clarity. Many of these are necessary skills in hybrid mode as the instructor manages student learning to a lesser degree, so students tend to acquire them or become part of the drop/withdraw/fail statistics. Where hybrid learning is organized into learning activities and debriefing sessions on those activities, there are enhanced opportunities to teach the evaluative and critical skills that can be lacking where the sum total of the students' involvement with the instructor is for delivery of content—either online or face-to-face. In addition students have a powerful incentive to become computer literate, acquiring skills in file management, web searching and computer-mediated communication. In a case of guilt by association, in contemporary universities transferable skills have acquired the negative connotations of a Quality Assurance (QA) process that seeks to standardize curriculum and pedagogy, to enable the mass production of graduates for the employment market. However, even the critics of the attempt "to transfer the factory-style QA framework to a context like higher education" (Cameron 2003: 136) recognize the need for students to develop skills in areas like "learning, speaking, writing and problem-solving" (ibid.).

Students may have greater access to support material in a hybrid course than in either face-to-face or exclusively online courses. Personal contact with the instructor provides important motivation and the early diagnosis of learning problems, while online archives of assessment guidelines, citation style guides and course bibliographies, plus auto-corrected diagnostic tests, self-paced tutorials and the opportunity to ask anonymous questions, and to raise and discuss study issues with fellow students all promote a positive learning environment. Another benefit of a hybrid approach is the ability to use online learning activities to supplement or replace activities that are problematic in the classroom. While under ideal conditions it would be preferable to remove the problems that limit the availability or effectiveness of these activities in the face-to-face classroom, virtual activities are preferable to no activities, and in some cases may offer an equivalent experience. Students can undertake virtual field trips, do dissections, conduct interviews with authors, and critique peer writing without the physical, economic and emotional constraints of the classroom.

Economics Driving Educational Change

Hybrid teaching models also have sound administrative and financial benefits. An obvious one is the maximizing of physical resources—if students spend half of their class time online, then twice as many students can be accommodated in the classroom. Increasing enrollments and constrained budgets are challenging educational institutions to provide the necessary physical space, particularly task-specific spaces such as laboratories, studios and workshops. Reducing the seat time of a course allows institutions to provide seats for more students, reducing overcrowding in classrooms, providing for over-enrolled courses and deferring expenditure on new buildings. Time shifting enabled by online activities accommodates students' off-campus commitments, such as a practicum, and allows flexibility in managing staff workloads.

Moving some learning activities online allows administrators to provide for different cohorts within the same course, allowing for larger classes and increased economies of scale. However, economies of scale and sound pedagogical practice cannot be achieved within a staffing model that sees senior faculty as solely responsible for all of the teaching and administrative functions associated with the course. Moving some activities online increases the ability to use a more hierarchal staff structure within a course, with course development being undertaken by senior staff, and the monitoring of online activities by less highly paid staff. "Not all tasks associated with a course require highly trained, expert faculty" (Twigg 2003: 2), and by replacing a single faculty member with a system of various kinds of instructional personnel the university can simultaneously "increase the person-hours devoted to the course and free faculty to concentrate on academic rather than logistical tasks" (ibid.). However, there is a risk that the benefits of scalability will lead to a situation where academic staff simply take larger and larger courses, not limited by room sizes or constrained by synchronous interaction, and attempt to provide the class members with the individualized instruction that online learning promises.

A move to a hybrid model can save on professional development costs as faculty train themselves on a needs basis. While faculty require extensive training, periods of release and financial compensation to develop fully online courses, by starting hybrid teaching with a small online component staff move toward online learning at a pace that can be incorporated into their current workloads, "In this way, the institution maximises the expertise of faculty without incurring professional development costs" (Gould 2003: 55). Instead of staff being given release time and funding to undertake training in all aspects of teaching in an online environment, they can continue with a full workload, moving small components of their teaching online as they develop specific competencies, such as uploading lecture notes, or establishing and monitoring a discussion forum. Again, however, there are risks that instead of replacing staff development release time with structured assistance and support for the gradual adoption of new information technology skills, staff development programs will be curtailed as faculty simply learn on the job. Lifelong professional development will disappear in favor of the fragmented and ad hoc development of targeted skills.

Another cost benefit is the reduction in the cost of providing resources to students. Syllabi, lecture notes, course handouts and assignment instructions can all be accessed via the web, to be read off the screen or printed at the student's expense. Set and recommended readings can be provided as links to online journal databases rather than as a course packet, with the costs of printing and distribution transferred to the student. Online journals can be used as reference materials and the need to purchase books for the library is consequently reduced.

Universities operate within an ever more corporatized discourse, adopting management models of decision-making where "the goals of higher education are increasingly fashioned in the language of debits and credits, cost analyses, and the bottom line" (Giroux 2002). The growing role that higher education plays in the economy has led to a swift commercialization of the sector. This has been accompanied by the growth of a performance-based culture within universities and an increasing impetus to turn the education of students into a recognizable, measurable and assessable product, and to manage the provision of learning in the same way as any other product in the global marketplace is managed. In addition, while "funding for higher education is decreasing or remaining flat, the number of students seeking admission will increase. We will be asked to teach more undergraduates with fewer faculty and smaller operating budgets" (Pratt 2003). Within this new economic climate, the inefficiency of the labor-intensive contact-hour attracted the close attention of university administrators who with their commercial partners saw network technology and distance education as economic saviors. Not only would the provision of web-based education give the institutions "a fashionably forward-looking image," but also it would be "a means of reducing their direct labor and plant maintenance costs—fewer teachers and classrooms" and would offer the potential for universities to become "vendors in their own right of software and content" (Noble 1998a).

However, distance learning has not proven to be a solution. The move to distance learning may open up new markets, but it also allows increased competition within those markets. E-learning requires e-teaching, but most faculty members continued to teach as they had been taught, an approach facilitated by the early introduction of course management systems that "make it almost too easy for professors to transfer their standard teaching materials to the Web" (Zemsky & Massy 2004: B6). Perhaps as a consequence, students say that while they regularly use the Internet for academic purposes, they do not see online courses as a replacement for traditional classrooms (Jones 2002). Whereas five years ago online distance education promised a "trillion-dollar market wrapped around the prospect of learning anytime, anywhere" (ibid.), those five years have seen the closure of a number of for-profit online learning institutions. When Columbia University announced the closure of its unit, Fathom, after two years, a spokesperson said: "I think we are going out on a high. We've outlasted nearly everybody." Indeed similar experiments at New York University, Temple University and the University of Maryland University College had previously failed (Carlson 2003: 1). There have, of course, been successes, such as the Open University in the United Kingdom, Jones International University and the University of Phoenix. Australia's primary involvement in the virtual university has been as part of Universitas 21, a network of institutions from primarily Commonwealth countries. Universitas 21 has been awarded the prestigious European Foundation for Management Development Certification of E-learning.

The widely reported failure of the for-profit online distance education institutions has not disillusioned university administrators, however. The enthusiasm for the apparent cost benefits of online teaching has been transferred to hybrid teaching, where the online components provide the savings and the face-to-face components mitigate the disadvantages of a remote cohort of students. UCLA has mandated the use of a course website to "facilitate the distribution of supplementary course materials, lecture notes, homework assignments, research links and electronic communication, including virtual office hours and class bulletin boards for interactive question and answer sessions" (2004). Students are charged a per-unit course materials fee, called the Instructional Enhancement fee. New Jersey's Fairleigh Dickinson University requires all students to take an online course in each year of their program. At the University of Newcastle, Australia, all courses have a Blackboard site used to at least provide an outline of the course and for announcements. In these and other examples, "the high-tech transformation of higher education is being initiated and implemented from the top down, either without any student and faculty involvement in the decision-making or despite it" (Noble 1998a).

These institutions are not alone in integrating online instruction, and a growing number of universities are developing hybrid campuses where virtual classrooms will be part of every student's experience, replacing some of the face-to-face teaching time with online learning activities. John R. Bourne, Editor of the *Journal of Asynchronous Learning Networks*, is quoted as saying that "somewhere in the 80% to 90% range of classes could sometime become hybrid," and Graham B. Spanier, as President of Pennsylvania State University, has called hybrid instruction "the single greatest unrecognised trend in higher education today" (quoted in Young 2002: A33). In the United Kingdom and Australia, universities are also mixing traditional and distance learning approaches as educational technology has come to be seen as "a way of improving the efficiency of education through productivity increases" (Rumble 2001: 75).

While different institutions give differing reasons for shifting to hybrid modes of teaching, institution-wide moves to offer reduced seat-time courses complemented by online learning components allow greater management control of a number of factors that influence the cost of course delivery. Rumble (2001: 76) outlines the factors affecting costs as:

- Course populations.
- The number of courses offered.
- The length of course lifetimes.
- The media and technologies chosen.
- The extent to which cost-inducing actions, such as the use of copyrighted materials, are avoided.
- The extent to which costs are placed on students.
- The extent to which the institution employs people on salary or on contract for a specific service.
- The extent to which the institution reduces labor costs, for example by using pre-existing materials and shared materials.
- The use of technology to increase the student–staff ratio.
- The increase in the use of academic staff for teaching at the expense of other functions such as research and community service.
- The replacement of expensive academic labor by inexpensive student and adjunct labor.

By using a hybrid teaching model, different cohorts of students can have the same course tailored to their needs, reducing the number of courses offered and increasing the course populations. Standardizing the online components within a course management system such as WebCT or Blackboard brings with it economies. Separating individual faculty from the whole course by contracting content developers and online tutors extends the lifetime of a course with consequent savings over time. Moving the information distribution of a course online allows the institution to avoid copyright clearance expenses, and transfers the cost of printing to students. Labor costs are reduced by the recycling of learning objects within and across disciplines. Online learning activities reduce timetabling constraints, allowing greater flexibility in workload allocations and an increased student–staff ratio. Student pressure on staff new to e-teaching will work to limit their involvement in research and community activity, a situation which may be made long term by administrative pressure as staff with reduced research output are given additional teaching duties. Also, once online components have been established, there may be the possibility of employing lower-level academic staff to oversee their continuance.

Yet allowing the administrative and economic benefits of hybrid teaching to drive the implementation of the model risks destroying the pedagogical benefits.

The advantages of inclusive discussion, individualized instruction and the opportunity for one-on-one contact disappear rapidly as the size of online classes and the workload of online instructors increase, while the levels of expertise and support decrease. Effective hybrid teaching and learning requires a whole course redesign that begins with an analysis of the amount and type of tasks undertaken by staff, so that a shared responsibility for course design, delivery and management maximizes the effective use of both modes. A cost–benefit approach to redesign could see a situation where student interaction is with less qualified and lower-paid adjunct staff, while the efforts of more senior staff are concentrated on scalable activities like course design and content provision. What is required is a support system consisting of a range of instructional personnel, so that, for example, senior, active researchers might lead the online discussion on course topics, but the forums where students raise administration questions or technology-related issues would be monitored by graduate assistants or peer tutors, and staff who are not research-active might have a role in developing and delivering static content. Providing hybrid learning experiences must also go beyond the expediency of replacing teaching staff with instructional software. While instructional programs and web-based learning systems can provide interactive learning opportunities and immediate feedback, self-learning machines have long been recognized as limited in their ability to engage students with the course content.

Where economic goals drive the move to hybrid teaching, the online component becomes little more than the individual study of data stored online. Instead of carefully structured online learning activities that mesh course goals with network technology, online learning in the funding-driven institution is limited to models and methods of delivery that rely on standardized, pre-packaged curricula. Even where faculty are still able and willing to prepare their own materials, standardized course management systems such as Blackboard and WebCT make it easier to upload old lecture notes and PowerPoint presentations than to design creative learning experiences. Faced with an online learning model that is little more than a do-it-yourself reading program, students are insisting that the information provided is "relevant," that is, is directly applicable to future employment possibilities. Education becomes information transfer.

Course management systems have become the dominant elements in universities' information technology capabilities for teaching and learning, operating alongside similar systems that streamline administrative and accounting functions. Course management systems such as Blackboard automate and standardize education, imposing a hierarchy on teaching practices and personnel. "Standardisation and inherent values in CMS design [...] push teaching and learning in a particular direction" (McConachie et al. 2005: 3). Course management systems "are not value neutral transmitters of facts, but instead carry the values and priorities of their producers" (ibid.). Even the organization of material under menu buttons and into folders and units creates a hierarchical structure that imposes relative values on the activities within.

As the distinction between higher education and job training breaks down and the line between democratic values and market interests becomes undefended if not indefensible, it is important to recognize that "the problems facing higher education have less to do with corporate management, efficiency and cost-effectiveness than with the erosion of democratic ideals" (Giroux 2004). The changes in Australian higher education are consistent with trends in Western education systems generally, and are a response to the context in which they operate. Nunan (2005) quotes the principal elements of this environment as: a shift to the right in political thinking; and intensification in competition, in part as a result of globalization. The Australian government's "education reform" agenda (cf. Nelson 2003) follows overseas trends in establishing a market for educational goods and regulating competition within that market. The starting point for higher education reform has been the de facto privatization of the university system through a systematic under-funding of operating costs. An immediate flow-on from changes to the funding model is an increased concern on the part of university administrators with both managing dwindling budgets and increasing income. When this is coupled with students' concerns for education-for-employment and employers' demands for job-ready graduates, then the value of a "democratic education" disappears as universities "work to provide a 'stripped down' version of the teaching and learning experience in an effort to gain market share" (Nunan 2005). The move toward hybrid modes of teaching and learning may be influenced by a strategic interest in maintaining a share of the domestic, on-campus market through ensuring that course delivery is sufficiently flexible to accommodate students who are also employed—the "earner-learner." Students who are currently on career paths are even more insistent that their education should consist of "just the facts" than students who are anticipating a place in the job market.

Democratic learning is based on fundamental principles that foster students' agency in their learning and their lives. According to Hyslop-Margison (2004: 137), these principles are as follows:

1. Respecting student rationality; that is basing curriculum design on the fact that students have the capacity to critique the subject matter.

2. Providing students with alternative viewpoints; and in doing so, enabling them to make informed critical choices.
3. Refusing to naturalize social reality; that is, allowing students to see how a socially accepted position can pass for natural fact, thereby empowering them to transform their social conditions.

Critics of technology-based learning claim that it is in opposition to democratic learning, in that it promotes uncritical acceptance of "facts" and a focus on pragmatic, individualized outcomes. Technology-based instruction is seen to promote instrumental rationality, where people do what they believe is in their own best interest, rather than linking their aims in a cooperative way. "When instrumental rationality dominates classroom instruction, it threatens democratic learning by emphasising information transfer over critical dialogue and by naturalising social reality" (Hyslop-Margison 2004: 138).

While online interactive learning has the potential to enable democratic learning, an examination of the history of distance education suggests that it has for the most part served the system. As more and more universities turn to online learning as a solution to their funding problems and as faculty translate face-to-face learning activities into an online environment, the question arises: will the decisions made enhance social learning, or will they simply make the transfer of information more efficient? "Torn between the claims of the lifeworld and the demands of the system, [distance learning] has on the whole, succumbed to system demands by precluding the interactivity that grounds communicative action" (Sumner 2000: 273). Economic pragmatism has applied the principles of rationalization to online learning, creating a marketable education product rather than providing a forum where students and teachers can engage in an open dialog, learning from each other.

Democratic Learning in the Hybrid Classroom

Since information technology is a tool for finding, storing, organizing, packaging and distributing information, it is not surprising that this would become its major use in the hybrid course. However, this does not mean that this is its only use, or that the technology necessarily privileges information delivery over critical dialog.

Instructors interested in using hybrid learning models to develop conditions supportive of communicative action may need to work around the structures imposed by course management systems and standardized presentation software; they may need to overcome administrative constraints of too-large online classes or too-disparate cohorts of students; they may have to work to mitigate the effects of little or inadequate training in information technology skills and reduced allocations of course development time; and they may have to develop strategies to minimize the effect of cost-transference to students. However, instructors who see the provision of democratic spaces within their courses as an essential part of their role will find hybrid teaching/learning a valuable tool.

In the past year, I taught three hybrid courses at the University of Newcastle, Australia. These courses were adapted from face-to-face models as difficulties or challenges arose which I found could be resolved by using Internet-based instruction. Previously, in the face-to-face version of *Communication and Culture* (CULT1100), I used a two-hour lecture to explain theories of communication and media analysis to 200 first year students, who would then apply those theories to specific texts in their tutorials, guided by set readings. In the current hybrid course, the online learning activities are: content consisting of a brief paper I have written on a type of textual analysis, plus a set reading chosen by me, and links to additional resources on the week's topic; a self-paced tutorial or an instant feedback quiz on the key points of the methodology; and a discussion forum dedicated to the week's methodology and/or type of text. The face-to-face learning activities are: a one-hour "lecture" with 200 students where I demonstrate the application of the methodology in the analysis of a particular text; and a class of 25 students where a postgraduate tutor leads students in the analysis of texts they have chosen and where the tutor addresses any areas of uncertainty revealed by the online discussion. I act as tutor for some groups, but the tutors are generally PhD students in media or cultural studies, chosen and briefed by me.

The combination of online and face-to-face discussion forums maximizes the opportunity for participation, as some students prefer the security of the asynchronous forum, while others prefer the spontaneity of the face-to-face classroom. Students document what they have learned in a journal that is assessed, and can report on their contribution to either the online or face-to-face discussions, as well as their response to the set reading, and the additional resources they accessed. The online component enables students to prepare for the face-to-face component, and facilitates students' ideas and interests being the focus of the class, rather than their responding to issues and themes raised by the tutor. The role of the tutor in the face-to-face classes becomes that of helping the group reach a consensus on what a particular text "means," and in the process exploring beliefs, value systems and experiences as well as the information gathered online and applied in the lecture. We spend less time talking about textual analysis, and more time analyzing texts.

In the face-to-face version of the course *Youth, Music and Culture* (CULT2270), I would lecture to 100 second year students on the characteristics of a particular popular music genre, and provide them with articles to read on the cultural impact of that genre. In tutorials, I would introduce specific musicians within the genre, playing limited examples of their music, leading a discussion on the genre affiliations and related cultural issues. In the hybrid version of the course now taught, students conduct individual online case studies of a musician chosen as a representative of the genre under consideration. They use links to cultural studies gateway sites, fan sites and recommended databases to locate general information and academic references including music samples and performance videos. In the face-to-face sessions with a postgraduate tutor, students discuss their chosen musician, and as a group identify the common features that constitute the genre and go on to make connections between the music and cultural issues of identity and communication. The advantage of the hybrid version of the course is that students gather information from a wide variety of sources, from academic journals to sites run by obsessed fans, from popular magazines to vested interest publications. Giving a range of information from widely differing perspectives not only enhances students' interest in the topic, but also provides them with an opportunity to critically examine the information, selecting what they will share with others. Part of the online component is a series of "infoskills" tutorials which provide self-paced instruction in information literacy. In the face-to-face sessions students negotiate a definition of a musical genre, and agree on a value system for assessing its impact on their lives and the broader culture. Points of view formed independently are shared, contested and supported until some consensus is reached. The sessions are organized as debates, round tables, party political speeches or other public speaking events, so that sometimes students need to agree on a "statement" while at other times they can agree to disagree.

Cyberculture (CULT3141), a third year course with around 50 students, was the first course that I moved to a hybrid model. In our first semester, the students and I quickly realized how ineffective it was to sit in the classroom discussing the Internet. We now meet face-to-face for the first weeks to ensure that everyone has adequate Internet access and then every four weeks to set the parameters for an "authentic" problem relating to the everyday use of the World Wide Web. Students use online resources and facilities to collaboratively undertake the task and prepare the document required by the problem scenario.

This course attracts students from a wide range of programs including economics, computer science, education and communication. For this reason, and as they are third year students, they are given advice on searching, analyzing and reporting, rather than links to information. Most have some experience of locating and using Internet material, but need to refine search and evaluation techniques. Through analytical/critical discussion using a combination of asynchronous discussion boards and synchronous collaboration sessions in Blackboard, they establish patterns of legitimacy, and reach a consensus on a solution. They collaborate online in writing the document called for by the scenario—a report, proposal or position paper. Students are given an individual mark for their participation in the process, assessed against published criteria that emphasize information literacy skills.

Students in these courses are surveyed at the beginning and end of the semester. Before starting their first hybrid course, students were (generally) apprehensive about the level of "contact" they would receive and the possibility of falling behind in their work. The first year students, in addition, were concerned that they would not have the necessary computer skills or computer access. A survey of 180 (of 207) students beginning online instruction found the major appeal was the flexibility in time management (77%), then flexibility regarding the location of instruction (15%), access to resources (5%), security to speak up (2%) and other unspecified (1%).

At the end of the courses students indicated a high level of satisfaction with the hybrid mode. A survey of 54 (of 58) students in the third year course produced these typical responses:

- I prefer the combination of online and face-to-face (76%)
- I prefer wholly face-to-face (0%)
- I prefer wholly online (8%)
- I am neutral or undecided (16%)

A forum in Blackboard that invited comments on and criticisms of the course allowed students a greater opportunity to voice opinions than did the standardized surveys; however, it is more difficult to quantify the responses. Although these comments are not valid in statistical terms, they do provide an insight into student feelings on course delivery. Noticeably, the criticisms were frequently directed at aspects of the course that were the result of administrative decisions—class sizes, and the use of the particular course management system—rather than at specific teaching/learning strategies. Looking back at six semesters across the three courses, less than one-third of the students posted comments, and of 327 messages seven were critical of an aspect of teaching and around 50 were critical of an aspect of course administration and/or delivery.

The predominant criticism was of the size of the online group. Where face-to-face tutorials have an enrollment cut-off at 25 students, the system is set up to allow 35 students to enroll in an online group. Typical of the comments addressing this issue were:

> I have to agree that this course has been a really great experience, because you have the freedom to come and go as you like, and contribute at your own pace. Like Janelle said tho[ugh], a large class equals a large amount of posts sometimes overlapping. (CULT1100)

> I found the experience overall to be an enjoyable one and i [sic] think there will be a push from some sectors of the educational institution toward this style of learning in the future. There are over some 1400 postings in this subject, so it shows that som[e]times this style can involve considerable contributions. (CULT2270)

Students at the third year level were more inclined to find fault with the course management system which is standard for our university. The university did trial a discussion board that provided a more sophisticated organization of posts, allowing, for example, all posts on a thread to be simultaneously displayed, but a decision was taken to support a single system for all online teaching. Most complaints about Blackboard related to the way that the discussion forums present just the headings of messages, and each post has to be opened separately. Recent upgrades have improved the discussion board, but the problem of having one product that is required to meet all online teaching needs still exists:

> My greatest issue is with the structure of the Blackboard forums. Having to load every response[ ], every time I visit the boards is a load my computer cannot cope with. I realise it is out of our (or your) control, but it would be much better having responses under headings. The fact the responses are not linear is also a major issue—it's a dog's breakfast, which makes it hard for conversation to flow logically. Once again, this is an issue for Blackboard. (CULT3141)

> I didn't like (and I think others have said the same thing) the mechanics of Blackboard as a forum. I am very lucky to have broadband available, but it was still cumbersome and I hate to think what dial-up speed would be like. If the messages were able to be expanded (not just from the search facility) it would be easier to read. (CULT3141)

Another frequent topic was a lack of basic computing skills. The university is addressing this in a number of ways, ranging from self-paced online tutorials to course-specific information skills workshops and competency requirements in some programs. However, it remains an impediment to effective hybrid learning. Skills development is not just an issue for students, with a few comments noting a lack of expertise among teaching staff:

> I found this course hard at first to get invl [sic] in. I am not good with computers—so was forced to try and catch up a little. I am a reasonably shy person, so found contributing online much much better. (CULT2270)

> I loved the on-line tutorial. It was so much easier to do the tut[.] on my own time as opposed to having a deadline to meet and being forced to come up with something to say in class. I wasn't really sure what to expect when coming into this on-line thing, but it turned out great. (CULT1100)

> I've also noticed a lot of lecturers aren't very computer literate either, although from my understanding the uni does offer seminars and support for staff development in regards to [B]lackboard, but maybe it should be compulsory. (CULT3141)

> Marj has been the only lecturer I have had that has used Blackboard so comprehensively. Staff need to be trained and brought up to date with the technologies that are the future. In a way they are holding back the students. (CULT3141)

In Australia, as elsewhere, we are seeing the median age of students increase, with postgraduate and overseas student numbers increasing as a share of total students. Expenses per student are increasing, while overall income stagnates. Student–staff ratios are also increasing (DEST 2004). The consequence of this statistical picture is a push to move courses online in the pursuit of economic benefits. Over half of all undergraduate courses at Australian universities contain an online component, though my area (Society and Culture) has the lowest use of the Internet (Bell et al. 2002: 15). It is anticipated that in Australia, all "university students in the future will need to use the Internet as a regular part of their university studies" and that cost factors will be a motivator in the move to online teaching and learning (Bell et al. 2002: 30). While the issue of the overall cost-effectiveness of online learning is widely debated, it is clearly apparent that there are cost savings in transferring materials to the web to be downloaded by students, rather than having that material delivered in a face-to-face class. So there is a possibility that content delivery via the web may be the predominant mode of online learning, rather than a pedagogy that uses the technology to provide a discovery-based learning experience.

Using the Internet simply as an information-clearing house can work to promote corporate ideology and instrumental learning. However, the World Wide Web in itself is not responsible for the manipulation of students toward uncritical acceptance of their world. Used as a tool to promote and foster student agency, it can provide a democratic space in which students are exposed to a range of viewpoints and have the opportunity to critique and debate these viewpoints and recognize the ways that "truth" is socially determined. Hybrid courses, which combine both online and face-to-face learning activities, seem to provide the maximum opportunity for constructing such a democratic learning space. However, if the administrative aims for introducing hybrid courses are allowed to overwhelm the pedagogical goals, then this opportunity will be lost. Rather than seeing hybrid learning as a cash cow, administrators of institutions of higher learning will need to be satisfied with modest economic benefits in order to preserve the teaching/learning advantages of the hybrid model.

Chapter 6

The New Literacy Agenda for Higher Education: Composition, Computers, and Academic Labor at US Research Universities

Robert Samuels

This chapter examines how the changing economics and politics of higher education are affecting the integration of computers and writing into contemporary universities.[1] By analyzing a national study centered on the incorporation of new media in research universities, I develop a critical model for understanding the possibilities and problems of introducing multiple literacies into undergraduate programs. Central to this analysis of the ways that computer technologies are being utilized in US universities is the connection between the teaching of writing and the new literacy agenda in higher education. Through an examination of the rhetoric of student-centered classrooms as it relates to the use of technology to teach composition skills, I show how the protection of the expertise and job security of writing faculty has often been ignored. Following this analysis of the loss of job protections in the new literacy agenda, I interpret Mark C. Taylor's Global Education Network (GEN) as an example of the problematic use of the student-centered pedagogies, the social constructionist rhetoric of information sharing, and the globalizing ideology of technological progress.

Much of this chapter is influenced by Cynthia Selfe's *Technology and Literacy in the Twenty-First Century* (1999), which represents an insightful investigation of the link between literacy and technology in new governmental and educational policies. Selfe begins her study by arguing that teachers need to be aware of a "new literacy agenda" shaping American public schools (xix). She also warns that teachers should keep in mind the continuing digital divides in our schools and the "importance of multiple literacies in our culture" (xx). As I do in my own work, Selfe seeks to avoid the current tendency to see the infusion of computer technology in education as either all bad or all good, and she motivates her readers to consider the interplay of governmental initiatives, contemporary educators, private sector businesses, and parents in the shaping of our nation's literacy agenda (xxii).

While Selfe focuses her analysis on K–12 public schools, I apply many of her concerns to the study of American research universities. This concentration on higher education is so essential because the new technology literacy agenda has often neglected to take into account how our universities and colleges have changed since the 1980s. As we shall see in my analysis of a national governmental report on introducing multiple technologies and literacies into research universities, the government, and the general public have not realized how the casualization of academic labor and the corporatization of research have worked to restructure the educational environments at most institutions of higher education (Nelson & Watt 1999; Noble 2002a; Rhoades 1998). In order to integrate concerns for literacy with concerns for academic labor, I argue that any consideration of the ability of our research universities to adapt to our new information technologies must take into account the economic, institutional, and political forces shaping contemporary higher education.

Higher Education and the Information Literacy Debate

To clarify the stakes involved in the current push to have universities integrate new technologies and literacies into undergraduate instruction, I will now turn to a recent study conducted by the National Academy of Sciences.[2] In their national report, *Preparing for the Revolution: Information Technology and the Future of the Research University* (NAS 2002), the authors point out that as of fall 1998, doctorate-granting research universities in the US enrolled over 4.24 million students (about 28% of total enrollment nationwide), and that these universities were also the recipients of over US $10 billion in federal research funding in the Financial Year 1998 (about 88% of all federal research funding for higher education institutions) (8). Due to their high level of governmental funding, and their large number of both graduate and undergraduate students, the government sees these institutions as leading the way in developing the incorporation of new communication technologies into all aspects of higher education.

Universities will have to function in a highly digital environment along with other organizations as almost every academic function will be affected, and sometimes displaced, by modern technology. The ways that universities manage their resources, relate to clients and providers, and conduct their affairs will have to be consistent not only with the nature of their own enterprise but also with the reality of "e-everything." As competitors appear, and in many cases provide more effective and less costly alternatives, universities will be forced to embrace new techniques themselves or outsource some of their functions.

In any case, the panel believes that universities should strive to become learning organizations by systematically studying the learning process and re-examining their role in the digital age. This would involve encouraging experimentation with new paradigms of education, research, and service by harvesting the best ideas, implementing them on a sufficient scale to assess their impacts, and disseminating their fruitful results (24).

Central to this governmental analysis of the role of technology in research universities is the argument that non-traditional, computer-based institutions of higher education will force "traditional" universities to either embrace new communication technologies or outsource many of their own activities (Noble 2002a). Coupled with this call for research universities to become more efficient and competitive is the emphasis on having these traditional institutions provide research and experimentation concerning the proper role of new technologies in higher education.

The potential conflict in this national agenda is that research universities are being asked to embrace simultaneously both functional and critical models of literacy. In other terms, the government wants these institutions to affirm a modern rhetoric of technological progress and cost-effectiveness at the same time that these universities provide a critical venue to explore the positive and negative aspects of the postmodern information economy.[3] In fact, the government returns to a traditional understanding of the modern research university in order to call for a deployment of non-traditional, postmodern technologies, and literacies.[4]

Learning and scholarship do require some independence from society. The research university in particular provides a relatively cloistered environment in which people can deeply investigate fundamental problems in the natural sciences, social sciences, and humanities, and can learn the art of analyzing difficult problems. But the rapid and substantial changes in store for the university—not only those related to information technology—require that academics work with the institution's many stakeholders to learn of their evolving needs, expectations, and perceptions of higher education (22).

On the one hand, the National Academy of Sciences turns to research universities to study the new information economy because these "modern" institutions are supposed to be independent from various social forces, and thus as the centers of value-free research, universities can provide a neutral and scientific understanding of technology and education. On the other hand, these same institutions are urged to give up their distance from society, and accept the new communication technologies and literacies in the greater postmodern culture. The problem with this mission is one of the fundamental problems facing all institutions of higher education: How do universities at the same time utilize new information technologies and remain critical of these same technologies (Selfe 1999)?

The variance between functional and critical literacies is rendered even more problematic by the way that this governmental report tends to affirm a false and misleading conception of our globalized world of higher education:

> We can now use powerful computers and networks to deliver educational services to anyone—any place, any time. Technology can create an open learning environment in which the student, no longer compelled to travel to a particular location in order to participate in a pedagogical process involving tightly integrated studies based mostly on lectures or seminars by local experts, is evolving into an active and demanding consumer of educational services. (7)

We can tie this globalizing rhetoric of "anyone, at any place, and any time" to the way that many representations from businesses, politicians, and popular culture tend to deny the very real digital divides in our world. Often, the government invokes these claims of global access to higher education in order to hide important disparities in access and equality concerning technology and literacy (Selfe 1999). Within the context of this national study of the roles of technology in higher education, the rhetoric of globalization is combined in a contradictory fashion with a discourse of competition and uneven development. Thus, research universities are celebrated because they are removed from normal social concerns, but they are also critiqued because they have not fully embraced the social rhetoric of globalized education.

At the heart of this contradictory representation of research universities is an unacknowledged debate over what types of values and literacies should determine the mission of our institutions of higher education (Gee 2003; Schroeder 2001). While the government wants to affirm the globalizing rhetoric of universal access to education, it also desires to place research universities in a privileged position. Our universities are therefore supposed to be both egalitarian and hierarchical, while they remain above society and central to the new social order.

These contradictory representations of research universities often work to conceal the growing corporatization (Rhoades 1998) of higher education behind a rhetoric of student-centered pedagogy and computer-mediated information sharing. For example, the following claim by this same national study calls for a radical restructuring of the teacher–student relationship:

> Yet we envision a future, enabled by information technology and driven by learner demand, in which two of the major (and taken-for-granted) ways of organizing undergraduate learning will recede in importance: the 55-minute classroom lecture and the common reading list. That digital future will challenge faculty to design technology-based experiences based primarily on interactive, collaborative learning. Although these new approaches will be quite different from traditional ones, they may be far more effective, particularly when provided through a media-rich environment. (25–26)

On one level, we can read this call to use technology to make undergraduate education more collaborative and learner-centered as a progressive affirmation of social constructivist pedagogy. However, this type of progressive claim can result in a downsizing of the expertise of teaching faculty. For example, the following argument clearly transforms the role of the teacher in higher education:

> Students may be more involved in the creation of learning environments, working shoulder to shoulder with the faculty just as they do when serving as research assistants. In that context, student and professor alike are apt to be experts, though in different domains. […] The faculty member of the twenty-first century university could thus become more of a consultant or coach than a teacher, less concerned with transmitting intellectual content directly than with inspiring, motivating, and managing an active learning process. (26)

The logic of this kind of argument will become clearer later on in this chapter when I discuss labor issues concerning different for-profit and non-profit models of computer-mediated higher education. However, for now, I want to stress the ways that this seemingly benign call for student-based learning may secretly promote the possible end of public higher education.

After all, as this report highlights, public research universities have to compete with new modes of education and technology that are driven by cost-saving and consumer-oriented priorities. According to this study, the only thing that seems to help maintain the value and purpose of research universities for many students and parents is the prestige of particular degrees and the chance to study with expert faculty members (41). Yet, we must ask what happens in a system where all expertise is shared and the teacher becomes a coach and not an important source of valued information? Does not this model of the teacher as a facilitator or coach work to downgrade the importance of the teaching faculty, and does not the field of composition display some of the results of this type of transformation of the professoriate in higher education?[5] In other terms, does the affirmation of an educational structure based on distributive knowledge systems and student-centered pedagogy work to deflate the value of the faculty members?

I believe that we must explore the ways that research universities are participating in their own devaluation by downgrading the expertise of their own teachers. Making matters even worse, progressive faculty members are unintentionally aiding this process by affirming modes of pedagogy and literacy that work to downsize their own cultural and economic capital. Central to my argument here is the claim that if faculty members do not learn how to protect their own interests by claiming a significant intellectual role in the shaping of students' multiple literacies, the academic labor system will continue to deteriorate and the value of public universities will evaporate.

For educators in the field of composition, these transformations concerning the roles of faculty members in American universities should be very apparent. Yet, I have found that many people working in this field do not understand why there is such a high reliance on non-tenured faculty to teach writing. Furthermore, I do not know of any accounts in the field of composition that have been able to explain the relation between the increase in the under-employment of writing faculty since 1980 and the increase in our field's pedagogical concern for social justice and educational democracy. In other words, what is the connection between our desire to make our classrooms more democratic and just and the growing lack of democracy and justice for faculty teaching writing?

It is important to note that according to the 2000 American Historical Association study of tenure by academic fields, 85% of the faculty teaching in free-standing writing programs are not eligible for tenure and only 64% of composition instructors in English Departments are on tenure-track. The field of composition is therefore dominated by a casualized labor force that is often void of any academic rights protected by tenure. Instead of avoiding this labor issue, I believe we must show how educational effectiveness is tied to faculty justice and demonstrate that the future of higher education is dependent on our ability to reclaim the importance of having qualified and secure faculty teach in effective educational environments.

Returning to the National Academy of Sciences' study, we see how the integration of computers into contemporary society threatens to reshape the roles of students and faculty in research universities:

> The most dramatic impacts on university education are yet to come—when learning experiences are reconceptualized to capture the power of information technology. Although the classroom is unlikely to disappear, at least as a place where students and faculty can regularly come together, the traditional lecture format of a faculty member addressing a group of relatively passive students is threatened by powerful new tools such as the simulation of physical phenomena, gaming technology, telepresence, and teleimmersion (the ability of geographically dispersed sites to collaborate in real time). Sophisticated networks and software environments can be used to break the classroom loose from the constraints of place and time to make learning available any place, any time, and to any one. The outlines of what will be possible can even now be seen in the real-time collaboration and project-management tools that are becoming common in the corporate environment. (NAS 2002: 26–27)

This passage is structured by an important conflict that is prevalent in many accounts of how technology is affecting higher education. On one level, this argument affirms that the space and time of traditional classrooms and modes of pedagogy are being replaced by electronic models of distance education and communication. Yet, this same passage wants to hold onto the idea of traditional classrooms, and the value of having teachers and students meet together in the same physical space. One obvious solution to this conflict is to call for a blended or hybrid model of education where, for example, students meet once a week with their teachers in large lecture classes and then the other class meetings are held online. However, the initial problem with this solution is that this same passage makes the important argument that new technologies are also making students desire more interactive learning environments, and thus the current use of large lecture classes will not work in this new structure.

While this report does not make a direct call for smaller classrooms and more interactive pedagogical environments, it is clear that the only way we will be able to maintain the value of undergraduate education at research universities *and* adapt to the new technologies and learning styles of contemporary students is if universities combine their investments in technology with investments in smaller classes and thus more faculty members. In fact, there is only one place in this report that the government seems to indicate its awareness of this need to consider the role of faculty funding in new technology initiatives, and we can find this labor argument in the following passage:

> The research university will face particular challenges in this regard. Although rarely acknowledged, the research university relies heavily on cross-subsidies from low-cost,

high-profit instruction in general education (e.g., large lecture courses) and low-cost professional training (such as in business administration and law) to support graduate training and research in the science and engineering fields. These high-profit programs are, not coincidentally, very attractive targets for technology-based, for-profit competitors. Their success in the higher-education marketplace could therefore undermine the current business model of the research university and imperil its core activities. This could be a politically explosive issue for some of the state universities as they try to maintain and increase public support from state legislatures. (40)

The first striking aspect of this passage is that it acknowledges that graduate and research programs are often funded out of the profits made by large undergraduate lecture classes. There is thus a counter-productive economic system at research universities that requires the wide use of educational environments that may work against our efforts to provide effective learning. Moreover, this type of mass production of education is precisely what for-profit virtual educational systems are supposed to do best (Noble 2002a). It is therefore imperative for research universities that want to maintain their role in undergraduate education to find ways of differentiating themselves from their electronic competitors by providing effective, interactive learning environments, and the use of large lecture classes is clearly working against this effort (Rose 1990). Furthermore, faculty members and university administrators are often working together to find ways to use technology to increase the use of large lecture classes and reduce the number of expert faculty teaching undergraduate courses. In other words, universities may be acting unknowingly to put themselves out of business by undermining their own value, and this act of devaluation often involves faculty denying their own expertise.

Rhetoric of Computers, Composition, and Higher Education

To further our critical understanding of the rhetoric behind many of the new technology literacy initiatives in higher education, we can examine Chris Werry's important article, "The Work of Education in the Age of ecollege" (2002b). Werry's essay provides an effective framework for understanding the discourse of democratic sharing and student-centered pedagogy that is often employed in the promotion of computer-mediated instruction.

In his insightful analysis, Werry points out that there are four major positions that structure the debate concerning online education and other modes of computer-mediated instruction: administrative, corporate, resistant, and critical (136). Starting with the role played by (university) administrators in American universities, Werry claims that the central concerns of current-traditional stakeholders are increased student enrollments, keeping up with technological advances, and cost management (ibid.). From a current-traditional administrative perspective, the turn to new modes of technology and education delivery stems from a desire to control or reduce expensive overheads caused by "human resources, security and police, counseling and career services, facilities and management, health care and utilities" (ibid.). In a totally online environment, many, if not all, of these labor-intensive functions of traditional institutions of higher education can be reduced or eliminated. Of course, this transformation of academic labor means unemployment or under-employment for many people now working at universities.

While no major universities have totally embraced this transition to online education, the National Academy of Sciences' study discussed above affirms that traditional universities are having to compete with new online universities, and many traditional institutions are moving toward an acceptance of the rhetoric and strategies of their electronic competitors. Werry posits that not only are non-online universities developing their own online courses and businesses, but these same institutions are adopting policies to shift funds from labor-intensive sectors, like tenured faculty, to technology-intensive systems of information delivery (136–137). This use of cost-cutting business models to transform the labor of education is in part derived from the growing connection between university administrators and corporations.

Werry points out that while administrators tend to speak a rhetoric of competition, rivalry, and progress, many corporate investors in higher education argue that the digitization of higher education will make these institutions "leaner, flatter, more flexible, and efficient" (137). In other words, corporations tend to circulate a modern rhetoric of technological and economic efficiency, cost-effectiveness, and flexibility (Johnson-Eilola 1997). In fact, administrators need to use these corporate principles in order to pursue their goals of being competitive and "doing more with less"; however, administrators tend to shy away from the globalizing anti-hierarchy rhetoric common among corporate sponsors of higher education.

Werry posits that in response to this linking of administrators and corporation in the quest for more computer-mediated education, many faculty members have taken on a more resistant rhetoric. Citing the work of Noble (2002a) and Nelson and Watt (1999), Werry shows how some faculty are aware of the connection between online education and the casualization of academic labor; however, Werry also affirms that these resistant faculty members choose to simply reject all technology and do not consider ways of making the incorporation of computers into higher education work in a more fair and equitable manner (137–138). In contrast to the faculty who simply want to get rid of or control new technologies in education, Werry celebrates academics like Andrew Feenberg (199) and Tim Luke who present a critical engagement with computers and education (138). According to Werry, the critical users of new technology "advocate bottom-up, faculty-driven, craft-style forms of online education that carefully adapt existing teaching practices to new technological environments" (ibid.). In this call for a blended model of electronic education, faculty retain the power over these new technologies; however, Werry does not indicate how the increase of faculty control over computer-mediated instruction will happen. In fact, everything that Werry describes in this new movement toward digitized higher education reveals that faculty will have less and less say in what technologies are purchased and how those technologies will be employed. For example, in his reference to Feenberg as a model for critical engagement, Werry relates the story of what happened when Feenberg's own institution, the California State University, engaged in a very expensive and controversial deal with several corporations in order to develop online education:

> Feenberg asked the chancellor what pedagogical model had guided the CETI project. Feenberg wrote that: "The chancellor looked at me as though I'd laid an egg, and said, 'We've got the engineering plan. It's up to you faculty to figure out what to do with it.' And off he went: subject closed!" Feenberg was surprised by this response. (143)

Here, we see how faculty members and pedagogical factors are often excluded from consideration when major deals are being brokered between university administrators and corporate leaders. Thus, even if a teacher is critically engaged in the use of technology, this does not mean that his or her university will employ technology for pedagogical and critical purposes.

In response to this potential corporate and administrative takeover of technology and higher education, Werry proposes the following solution:

> In certain respects composition specialists are well positioned to engage administrators. Composition teachers are often involved in designing computer classrooms and purchasing software, and might be able to suggest open-source and free software alternatives to administrators. The emerging open-source courseware systems, email, bulletin boards, and instructional software […] are typically free or inexpensive. This fact, if carefully used as part of an argument for a pedagogy-driven reallocation of funds (rather than an argument for mere cost cutting), could be used to help persuade administrators to invest in their use. (144)

I believe that Werry's proposed solution to these problems is a major part of the problem: faculty, like Werry, believe that the key to overcoming the power differentials at American universities is to just share more and provide better and cheaper models for effective pedagogy. Yet, this democratic ethic of sharing and service hides the fact that most composition faculty have little or no power in their institutions and that most universities are run by a series of competing power structures that are not always dedicated to improving pedagogy and education (Rhoades 1998: 173–209).

In terms of the position of composition faculty, Lisa Gerrard's argument made in 1993 still holds in 2003:

> As we well know, the practice of English, like that of other academic specialties, is built on competition and ranking. Thus, while we promote collaboration and democracy in our teaching, we are encouraged to be combative and hierarchical in other areas of our professional lives. As compositionists who use computers, we participate in a profession with contradictory values: one set for the classroom, another outside it. (23)

Gerrard here examines the central conflict between the social constructivist writing faculty who celebrate sharing, democracy, collaboration, and student-centered pedagogies and the current-traditional university that is structured by hierarchy and competition. Gerrard later extends this analysis by placing composition faculty within the larger structure of the university:

> As we interact with our colleagues, departments, and institutions, we participate in a profession that is built not on cooperation, democracy, and acceptance of divergent viewpoints, but on competition, hierarchy, and divisiveness. English departments rank their faculty, putting theorists on top, other literary specialists beneath them, and composition faculty in the basement. (27)

Following Gerrard's lead, I believe that we must begin our analysis of how we want to use computers in our writing classes by first examining the roles played by power and economics in our institutional settings. Thus, we may find that our desire to be democratic in a non-democratic structure results in a situation where our best intentions are often being used against us.

My argument here is not that we should stop trying to make our classes democratic and collaborative; rather I claim that we need to integrate this rhetoric of democracy and sharing with a call to engage power structures in an open and forceful way. Therefore, we should not only argue for more equitable classrooms, but we also must fight for more equitable institutions, and I believe the key to this fight may entail the unionization of non-tenured faculty, who have everything to gain and often very little to lose. This drive for unionization of what is becoming the majority of faculty at our institutions of higher education has to be tied to a national effort to protect the intellectual property and expertise of all teaching faculty. Only through the foundation of a strong national union will disenfranchised faculty members be able to confront the growing power of administrators and corporations in higher education.

I am not arguing here that all administrators and corporate leaders are against improving education: rather, following Werry's analysis, we need to examine how administrative and corporate interests often have very different functions and priorities in comparison to many university teachers. One of the problems facing contemporary universities is that the more these institutions become involved in research and technology, the more their administrative staffs and costs grow, and in turn, the less power and influence faculty have over technology and education issues (Nelson & Watt 1999). In this context, it is simply naïve and self-defeating to call for more faculty sharing. In fact, Werry's call for more democracy and sharing on the part of the faculty is combined with his insightful analysis of how the rhetoric of technological progress is being used to convince people to participate in processes that are not at all progressive. For example, after discussing the ways many online education corporations use a rhetoric of community in order to assure faculty that these new computer-mediated modes of instruction share the same educational concerns as progressive teachers, Werry makes the following claim:

> *Community* becomes a way of managing some of the tensions inherent in systems that
> tend to reify educational practices. The discourse of community appears strategically
> drawn on to reassure educators—to quiet their fear of automation and displacement,
> and to show that the company understands that education entails issues of culture,
> communication, and socialization. (140)

As educators, we must become aware of how this rhetoric of community, democracy, and collaboration can be used for many diverse purposes. For example, Werry examines how *The Campus Pipeline*'s advertisements for outsourcing course delivery systems proclaims that the company's educational product generates: "a community dedicated to meeting individual needs. A business streamlined for maximum efficiency. And a campus that never closes" (cited in Werry 2002b: 140). In this combination of the social constructionist rhetoric of community, the expressivist rhetoric of individual needs, and the modern rhetoric of efficiency, we see how postindustrial corporations integrate conflicting ideologies into a seamless structure. Interestingly, this combination of rhetorical strategies leaves out the profit motive, which is usually the central driving force for these educational corporations.

In analyzing the rhetoric of online education companies, Werry points to the ways that the pedagogical celebration of student-centered classrooms and democratic learning spaces is often placed within a system of economic exploitation:

> Many proponents of commercial online education stress the need to move from a traditional Fordist, mass production based model of education, to a more flexible, post-Fordist, "mass customization" model. This is sometimes allied with the language of constructivist, learner-centered approaches to education—language that stresses the importance of student-centered approaches in which knowledge is constructed within a community of learners. (139)

The key rhetorical term in Werry's analysis here is the notion of "flexibility," which is often used in academic circles as a code word for downsizing and casualizing the labor force (Readings 1996). By merging the rhetoric of flexible technologies with the discourse of flexible labor, contemporary institutions of higher education are often able to hide real economic transitions behind idealized cultural transformations. Thus, not only do faculty want to share and be democratic, but they also want to be flexible and student-centered. However, economic flexibility for administrators and corporations often means that one cannot make any permanent commitments to labor. Therefore, the rhetoric of flexibility is usually invoked when universities have to defend their high level of contingent faculty: according to this logic, the radical fluctuations in student enrollment and state funding make it necessary for universities to maintain great flexibility in their employment practices, and this often means a reduction of tenured or unionized faculty.

Since many progressive educators also call for the use of flexible and student-centered technology and educational structures, the rhetoric of these faculty members is easily used to justify the economic rhetoric of administrators and corporations. Werry shows his awareness of this manipulation of social constructivist rhetoric in the following passage:

> In some instances the connection between flexibility, mass customization, and constructivist pedagogy is thought through in a principled, sophisticated way. However, sometimes this focus on "student-centered" education seems merely a way of camouflaging shortcomings in models of online education. Some all-Internet courses offer no face-to-face interaction, and there is significant dissociation between different levels of the educational enterprise—between managers, advisors, system designers, content providers, technical assistants, and teachers. Further, the system is designed to be modular and scalable, so that teaching assistants and adjuncts can be slotted into courses as required (Irvine proposes that future models of online education will center on "reusable learning objects in customized modules with assessments for specific outcomes"). (140)

Werry argues here that in postmodern modes of communication and education, the stress on democratic discourses and student-centered media and pedagogical methods can work to hide the power of current-traditional authorities and modern systems of organization.

Central to this postmodern educational model is the emphasis on the student as reader/user/consumer of higher education. According to Werry, "[a]n impoverished notion of 'student-centered' education is often part of the argument that the technology will somehow democratize education and make student-centered learning happen by itself" (ibid.). Not only do many rhetorical celebrations of student-centered pedagogies imply a false sense of democracy, but as revealed by the following statement from Andrew Rosenfield, CEO of Unext, endorsements of student users are often coupled with attacks on teachers: "lectures are dead. They are not a good way to learn [...] People want to learn what they need to know, not what professors want them to know. You can only do that on the Internet" (cited in Werry 2002b: 140). Here, we see how central to the postmodern emphasis on student-centered individualism is an undermining of the authority of the teacher. Of course, progressive educators who proclaim the importance of student-centered classrooms also present a message that works against the authority of teacher-centered education. Thus, unknowingly, some educational theorists have played into the hands of political and corporate interests which want to do away with the expensive burden of having expert teachers in classrooms. In many ways, the extreme advocates of online education have unintentionally exposed the downgrading of teacher expertise that was going on already in American universities.

My argument here is not that we should return teachers to their rightful current-traditional place as masters, and students to their function as passive listeners; rather, I think that we need to integrate both current-traditional defenses of teacher expertise and progressive models of student-centered rhetoric. The problem is that many critical pedagogies present a polarized opposition that often works to rationalize the downsizing of faculty. Yet, very few enthusiasts of hypertextuality have questioned what this new pedagogical model will do to the employment of writing faculty and other teachers. In order to further clarify this connection among new computer technologies, the quality of university education, and the employment practices in higher education, I will end this chapter by examining Mark C. Taylor's (2001) call for a hypertextual and globalized university as presented in his book, *The Moment of Complexity: Emerging Network Culture*.

Hypertext Gone Bad

In this work, Taylor uses the notion of hypertext to argue for a new vision of higher education (234). Central to his argument is his claim that "in the future, the curriculum will look more like a constantly morphing hypertext than a fixed linear sequence of prepackaged courses" (ibid.). Due to the changing nature of the way people access information in a postmodern, networked world, Taylor envisions a growing movement toward a totally online system of higher education where "[a]nyone anywhere in the world can, in principle, sit down around the same virtual table and learn together" (ibid.). In this notion of a GEN, we find again the modern ideology of a universal system of knowledge and culture. Furthermore, by turning to the structure and logic of the hypertext, Taylor calls for the creation of a new mode of higher education patterned on the private ownership of a distributed network of interrelated information (262).

At first glance, Taylor's promotion of his GEN appears to be a progressive attempt to make higher education more responsive to our changing technological and social cultures. For instance, he begins his book by highlighting the movement from a Cold War environment based on political divisions to the postmodern globalized context of the World Wide Web, which according to Taylor is now centered on integration and the overcoming of all differences (23). Furthermore, in the first chapters of his book, Taylor concentrates on articulating the transition from the grid-oriented structure of modern society to the networked structure of postmodern culture. From his perspective, modern culture is dominated by centralized economic planning and top-down bureaucracy, while postmodern society has developed decentralized markets and bottom-up democracy (49). Moreover, Taylor posits that modern society is based on a productive economic system of manufacturing, while postmodern reproductive society is centered on "an information economy governed by new media" (66). This type of "progressive" historical narrative most often returns to a modern logic of linearity and universalized development in order to critique modern culture and celebrate contemporary society. The end result of this mode of theoretical narrativization is usually a globalized rhetoric where all social and technological changes are neutralized, naturalized, universalized, and rendered inevitable. In other words, all possibility for social change or cultural criticism is negated by the rhetorical moves that secretly posit that our particular economic, institutional, and literacy structures are natural, neutral, universal, and inevitable.

In terms of higher education, Taylor uses his notion of a global hypertext of knowledge to argue for a melding of business and educational interests. In a very revealing phrase, he states that "[i]n a networked culture, education is the currency of the realm" (234). He is quick to point out that he means that "[e]ducation, like money in the world of finance, is a currency that is also a commodity" (ibid.). Here, we find the use of hypertextuality to argue that education equals money because they both circulate in the networked global economy. Once Taylor makes this argument, it is only a small step for him to claim that all educational pursuits should be run by private corporations. In fact, Taylor's "academic" book is also an infomercial for his own product: the GEN.

Central to this advertisement for globalized online education is his strong claim that "[t]he prospect of significant profits in the educational market is, of course, the result of new technologies for providing and promoting education" (235). Thus, according to Taylor's rhetoric of inevitable technological progress, the hypertextual nature of the World Wide Web and the development of a postindustrial, globalized economy have moved us to a new networked culture, which is creating pressures on all educational systems to shift from a modern industrial notion of knowledge delivery to a postmodern, postindustrial "education industry" (236). Furthermore, employing the rhetoric of globalized inevitability, Taylor proclaims: "Just as corporations that are unable to respond to the rapidly changing economic environment cannot remain competitive, so colleges and universities that are unwilling to adapt to the new education and economic landscape cannot survive" (ibid.). In this model of universal and inevitable change, there is no space left for the public sphere or the protection of higher education from a completely business-oriented mentality. Furthermore, the radical fluctuations and disparities in today's global markets are concealed beneath a naïve celebration of contemporary business practices.

In order to gain support for his own educational product, Taylor posits that universities and colleges have turned to technology to help make them more competitive in the educational market, but these efforts have failed because the educational software programs that universities are purchasing do not come with support staffs, and the outsourcing of software development does not help the marketing of the schools' courses. Moreover, Taylor makes the important assessment that courseware developed by for-profit companies does not match each school's particular pedagogical needs (237–238). The solution, of course, is to turn to Taylor's own GEN, which will provide all of these services and will eliminate the messy conflict between not-for-profit public education institutions and for-profit businesses.

One of the reasons why hypertext plays such a prominent role in Taylor's GEN is that this connected and distributed system of knowledge storage and delivery mirrors his image of the networked, free market global economy. As a decentralized structure of linked nodes accessed by readers who are free to produce their own readings, hypertext represents the perfect model for postindustrial capitalism and postmodern education. In Taylor's own words, "[w]ith wired classrooms, the time and place of instruction are transformed: education becomes available anytime, anyplace in the world. Like networked global markets, education becomes a 24/7 business" (258). This globalized vision of education, technology, and the free market refuses to acknowledge all of the real social and economic differences that prevent much of the world's population from having any access to technology and higher education.

Another important blind spot in Taylor's argument is his claim that a hypertextual system of knowledge is necessary now because "[s]tudents are much more knowledgeable today about new media than most faculty members" (ibid.). According to this logic, which is often presented by progressive teachers and advocates of student-centered pedagogies, contemporary faculty can only facilitate the education of students because students now know more about technology than the faculty. This argument that is supposed to celebrate the students often works to downgrade the teachers and is based on a misguided notion that students' uses of new media are equivalent to their critical understanding of these new technologies.

In the field of composition, and in higher education in general, this privileging of student knowledge has often worked to undermine the degrees, expertise, and experience of faculty members. Indeed, one of the factors contributing to the continual economic exploitation of faculty in the field of composition is the development by compositionists of a whole range of practices and belief systems centered on the idea that teachers of writing should make their classes student-centered, and that, in turn, faculty members should act as facilitators and not as experts who have a particular knowledge base to which students do not yet have access. Like Taylor's model of globalized education, many writing programs are structured by the combination of a few well-paid experts with tenure, and the employment of many graduate students and part-time faculty without the same credentials and expertise. Moreover, many universities are asking their faculty to place their course material on the web, so that all of a faculty member's expertise can be shared by the other teachers. In response to this rhetoric of democratic sharing, I would warn that once one has released all of one's intellectual property into a public arena, one's employment may no longer be needed. In fact, Taylor, whose global educational model is centered on the sharing of course material across the curriculum through the generation of a communal hypertext, openly admits that his networked courses will be monitored by "a pool of qualified teaching assistants from schools throughout the world" (263). He adds that it is inevitable that tenure will be eroded by the postindustrial educational system (265) and that any faculty member who complains about this loss of academic job security is just expressing "shortsighted self-interest" (239). One has to wonder if the fact that Taylor himself already has tenure plays into his willingness to give up on the system that has protected his own employment.

At one point in his chapter on the GEN, Taylor dismisses all academic criticisms of this perfect match between commerce, education, and technology by simply stating that faculty resistance to "distributed teaching and learning [...] is often expressed in lofty educational ideals," but the real problem is that many faculty members are highly suspicious of business and technology (239). After reading Taylor's employment model for higher education, is it any wonder that some faculty members are a little afraid of this perfect marriage between business and education? The problem with most faculty members is that they are too little concerned with the growing role that businesses are playing in shaping all aspects of higher education. For the recent history of the field of composition, and other areas of higher education, has shown that the development of progressive theories of education and culture have coincided with the increased exploitation of academic labor.

Not only do faculty members ignore the concrete material forces shaping higher education, but also students are usually taught in a way that downplays the role of economic exploitation in our society. For instance, the economics of higher education is most often a taboo subject in US universities even though it shapes everything that goes on in our classrooms. Furthermore, in higher education in America, there has been a trend to detach economic factors from our discussions of technology, writing, and pedagogy. For example, when I recently asked my fellow faculty members why they never discuss the constant downsizing and outsourcing of our faculty with their students, they returned to the modern argument that education must be neutral, objective, and disinterested. Yet our world is rarely any of these things, and our desire to shelter our students from these concrete economic realities only serves to render their education abstract and unreal.

I am not arguing here that teachers should spend all of their time discussing their personal economic problems with their students, but I do feel that we need to incorporate discussions of economics with all subjects that we cover with our students. For instance, when we examine any technological system, we need to ask who profits and who does not profit. Moreover, a careful analysis of the battle between critical and functional models of literacy in higher education can aid writing faculty in expanding their students' and colleagues' notions of composition. By seeing writing as both an intellectual and pragmatic endeavor, we can help pave the way for the incorporation of new literacies into undergraduate education as we resist the types of destructive institutional policies I have examined in this chapter.

Notes

1. This chapter represents an extended version of a paper I delivered at the *2004 Computers and Writing Conference* in Manoa, Hawaii, June 2004.
2. The National Academy of Sciences is a public, non-profit organization that supplies research to the US national government.
3. For a more detailed discussion of the battle between critical and functional literacies in higher education and the corporatization of research universities, see Edmundson (1997), Minsky (2000), Nelson and Watt (1999), and Noble (2002a).
4. Throughout this chapter, I will use the term "postmodern" to refer to the contemporary stress on new media (Rifkin 2000), postindustrial economics (Baudrillard 1993), and a model of education that critiques the modern stress on universal reason.
5. I focus on composition in this chapter because the field of writing has the most highly casualized labor force in American higher education.

Chapter 7

Who Is the E-generation
and How Are They Faring in Higher Education?

Kerri-Lee Krause

In Australian universities and internationally there has been a rapid uptake of information and communication technologies (ICTs) for the purposes of developing and sharing information in research, learning, administrative and management contexts. This chapter focuses on student stakeholders and their e-learning experiences in higher education. In order to challenge prevailing generalizations regarding the e-generation and their fascination with all things technological, the argument here is for the importance of querying the one-size-fits-all approach to characterizing this generation. They are by no means a homogenous group and one characteristic which differentiates subgroups is their experiences with ICTs. To explore some of these differences, this chapter reports on a recent national study of the first year experience in Australian universities (Krause et al. 2005). Differential student e-learning experiences are reported by demographic subgroup, including students from low socioeconomic backgrounds, and mature age students (aged 25 years and older in the first year of undergraduate study).

The final section considers implications of these findings for policy. I will argue that effective higher education policy should have the following characteristics: first, it recognizes the distinct needs and experiences of student subgroups, particularly those which are disadvantaged and traditionally underrepresented in the sector; second, it takes account of, but is not solely driven by, the rapid changes and developments in ICTs and their capabilities; and third, it should assure pedagogical quality which is not sacrificed at the expense of the latest technological innovation on the market.

For the purposes of this chapter, e-learning refers to learning experiences facilitated via the electronic media, which are broadly categorized as ICTs. These experiences are not restricted to formal learning contexts and may include online interaction with peers and faculty in the broader learning community.

Who Is the E-generation in Higher Education?

Howe and Strauss (2000) describe "millennials" (i.e., 18–22 years old) as individuals who, among other things, are fascinated by new technologies. Prensky (2001) calls them "digital natives" who have grown up with technology, unlike the "digital immigrants"—the generation of students once removed as well as faculty who have migrated to technology use over time. Oblinger and Oblinger (2005) depict the "net gen" as those who have been surrounded by technology all their lives. Frand (2000: 16–22) identifies 10 attributes of the "information-age mindset," including: multitasking as a way of life; emphasis on doing rather than knowing; greater familiarity with typing rather than handwriting; the importance of staying connected; zero tolerance for delay, along with a 24 × 7 mentality; and reliance on the web as the primary source of information.

While these generalizations about the youth of the twenty-first century and their familiarity with technology are useful, they leave out of account a fundamental concern: not all have the same experiences and opportunities when it comes to ICTs in learning. Despite Frand's acknowledgment that his generalizations do not necessarily apply to all individuals, there is little recognition of the sources of difference and the widening gulf between the information haves and have-nots among the so-called e-generation. In fact, there is limited acknowledgment in the literature generally of these subgroup differences and their implications for the quality of the student experience.

Can ICTs Break Down Social Barriers?

Rheingold (2002) has written extensively on the topic of social connectedness and the possibilities of ICTs. He depicts a future made up of distributed networks of information, communication and activity which replace traditional face-to-face interactions limited by time and space. While this "social revolution" may be starting to take shape in some pockets around the globe, it is certainly not in evidence in higher education.

In a recent study of undergraduate students' use of ICTs in 13 higher education institutions across the United States (Caruso 2004), only 13% of respondents said the most valuable benefit of using ICTs in the classroom was improved learning. According to these students, the main benefit was convenience and time saving. The benefits of building community and connecting students with peers and faculty were not identified by these undergraduate respondents, although, when asked about the benefits of course management systems (CMS), just over one-third of students (39%) said that sharing materials with other students through the CMS was beneficial to their learning. However, the form which this sharing took does not appear to have been explored in any detail by the author, and no respondent comments in this regard were reported. Neither were there any details of demographic subgroup differences in this respect. Fewer than one in five students (18%) noted the benefits of online discussion in supporting their learning.

The Caruso report is aptly subtitled *Convenience, Connection, and Control.* There is, notably, no mention of "community" in this collection of descriptives. The author concludes that ICT use in higher education is primarily "for convenience and not for the higher goal of improving learning" (Caruso 2004). She acknowledges that the technology tools are not yet being used to promote higher-order learning or problem-solving skills, and the issue of community in learning is not even acknowledged. The apparent lack of community building in e-learning environments is not limited to the US higher education sector. Recent national figures representing Australian undergraduates' use of ICTs (Krause et al. 2005) point to a distinctive lack of online interaction among first year university students. The study found that just 16% of full-time first year undergraduate students made regular use of online discussion groups as a means of connecting with their university peers and faculty. While it is recognized that online discussion groups are not the only indicator of the existence of online communities, they arguably provide important insights into the extent of online discussions among groups of students and staff, as contrasted with the more unilateral asynchronous nature of email communication. Rheingold's elusive social revolution, where online communities are predicted to replace face-to-face conversations, does not appear to be in evidence if we use these data sources as a guide.

However, whether online communities currently exist in higher education is less important than whether or not we think they *should* exist and be fostered. Along with Laurillard (2002), I argue strongly in favor of the power of ICTs to enhance student engagement with learning, and with the people and places making up the broader learning community. Yet, it is not the case that technology is the panacea which many portray it to be. This panacea-like view of ICTs is illustrated by Dede (2005) who, like Rheingold, argues for the benefits of ICTs in creating community. He notes:

> At present, social groupings depend on co-presence in physical spaces. Collaboration depends on shared physical presence or cumbersome virtual mechanisms. In the future, students will participate in far-flung, loosely bounded virtual communities (independent of cohabitation, common course schedules, or enrolment at a particular campus). Interoperability, open content, and open source will enable seamless information sharing, collaborative virtual manipulation of tools and media, facile shared authoring and design, and collective critiquing. Virtual identity will be unfettered by physical attributes such as gender, race, or disabilities. (10)

This idealized future world of online communities may be on the far horizon, but what Dede fails to take into account here are three fundamental sets of questions. First, he fails to comment on the need to pose pedagogical questions such as: Are there not occasions when "shared physical presence" is to be encouraged in order to enhance students' engagement with each other? And are there learning moments which are most effectively shared face-to-face rather than online? A second set of questions which both Rheingold and Dede leave out of account in their futuristic optimism are those pertaining to the resources required to foster online communities. For instance: What happens to students in remote geographical areas for whom adequate bandwidth and hardware resources are in scarce supply? And who ensures that the faculty responsible for developing online learning communities are adequately trained, resourced and supported? Finally, futuristic notions of online communities and their value in learning typically ignore the importance of the policy-making processes so key to ensuring that such communities are not only created, where pedagogically appropriate, but that their progress is monitored and sustainable within an institution like a university.

In fairness, Dede concedes that "widespread discussion among the members of the academy [...] is important" (2005: 11). In fact, it is essential every step of the way. Dede's focus is on differential learning styles and the promise of new technologies for catering for individualized learning according to such differences. But equally important is the need to account for differences in access to and participation in ICT use across the student population. Before becoming too beguiled by the promise of the technology, we must be cautioned by the realities of the people for whom these technologies must always be servants rather than masters.

The notion of online communities in higher education settings is one which must continue to be problematized and debated on several levels. Arguably,

ICTs offer significant opportunities for connecting individuals to each other and to institutions of learning across time and space. But what makes a community distinctive is a sense of shared experiences and interests. In a world where technology is increasingly perceived as a one-stop convenience shop for information 24/7, the challenge for educators is to find creative and authentic ways to create a sense of community online. I do believe this is possible and, in many instances, can be achieved in pedagogically sound and sustainable ways so as to enhance the quality of students' learning. However, online communities will not be a reality until faculty and administrators pose the difficult questions like: Are any groups excluded from this community we are aiming to build online? Will all students benefit from an online community or should it rather be seen as one of several learning environments focused on engaging students with learning? And further, is an online community going to provide our students with optimal learning opportunities, or should we rather see the online community as a complement to the more important face-to-face interactions we strive to retain? At the moment, at least, it is clear that we cannot rely on ICTs to create the whole learning experience, nor should we. There is much more to learning than convenient access to information. The social dimension of learning is critical and evidence suggests that it simply is not being provided adequately by online technologies at present.

To further inform the debate around ICTs and their potential role in connecting individuals, building community and breaking down social barriers, I argue that we first need to understand sources of difference in the ways students currently use technologies, and plan carefully for how to best shape high-quality learning experiences with or without these technologies in the future. Of most relevance to this chapter is the question of inequities experienced by those with differential patterns of ICT access and use across demographic subgroups. When do we address the needs of those who do not meet the defining criteria of the e-generation, particularly those who are disadvantaged and fall into the information "have-nots" category? While ICTs offer enchanting promises of connectedness and empowerment through access to all manner of information, they equally have significant capacities to widen the gulf between wealthy and poor.

This chapter, and the research it reports, is based on the premise that all students deserve to be given every opportunity to succeed in higher education. It acknowledges that there are many sources of disadvantage and difference within the student body, and that these factors must be understood and their role in learning appreciated before we can begin to redress the issue of inequity. These concerns are in keeping with national higher education policy in

Australia. The Commonwealth government has identified six equity groups in higher education, including students from low socioeconomic backgrounds, and those from rural and isolated areas (DEET 1990). The objective of this policy is equitable participation for all students in higher education. This aim is clearly expressed in the title of the policy document: *A Fair Chance for All: Higher Education that's Within Everyone's Reach.*

ICTs potentially offer opportunities to expand access to higher education, to respond to diverse student learning styles, to provide vehicles for active student integration into higher education and to reduce costs (Pascarella & Terenzini 1998). However, questions remain. Are some students advantaged over others in their access to ICTs? Are ICTs creating a new information-rich/information-poor stratification in the student experience and if so, what are the implications for student learning outcomes? And, importantly, what role should institutional policy play in redressing these inequities?

The challenge for educators and policy-makers alike is to understand how the "information-age mindset" is manifested in e-learning contexts and among demographic subgroups. Are students' experiences with ICTs similar, regardless of demographic background? Or are there some fundamental differences in the ways students from diverse backgrounds engage with the technologies?

Multiple Faces of the E-generation

The following data are drawn from a national study of the first year experience in nine Australian universities. The broader study investigated several dimensions of the student experience during the first year of undergraduate study. For the purposes of this discussion, data pertain to students' use of a range of ICTs in the context of their learning experience during the first year. Two research questions guided this part of the investigation: (1) What demographic subgroup differences exist in students' use of ICTs for e-learning at university? (2) What are the institutional policy implications of these differences?

Study Design, Sample and Analysis

The First Year Experience Questionnaire© is an instrument developed by the research team for the purposes of examining a number of dimensions of the first year experience. In addition to collecting data on a wide range of demographic and enrollment information, the instrument contains Likert-scale items on student expectations, goals and study habits. It collects information on students' views of the academic aspects of their experience and perceptions of their preparedness for and overall satisfaction with the university experience.

In August 2004, the questionnaire was mailed to a 25% random sample of full-time first year commencing undergraduate students, stratified by discipline, chosen from each of the nine participating universities. Two mail outs were used and responses were anonymous. A total of 2,344 useable returns were received, with an effective response rate of 28%. Selected details of the sample relevant to the present discussion are shown in Table 7.1.

Table 7.1: Study sample

Demographic subgroups	Proportion of study sample (%)
Age	
17–19 years (young students)	61
25 years and above (mature age students)[a]	12
Gender	
Female	66
Male	34
Equity subgroups[b]	
Low SES[c] students	16
Rural students	27

[a]Students in the 19–24-year age group were omitted for the purposes of this discussion.
[b]The Australian Department of Education, Science and Training classifies these two groups as equity groups in higher education.
[c]SES: socioeconomic status.

What the Students Reported

The following section addresses the first research question: What demographic subgroup differences exist in students' use of ICTs for e-learning at university? Students were asked to indicate the frequency with which they used a range of ICTs for learning and communicating with peers and staff in the broader learning community at university. Data for each subgroup are presented and considered in light of cogent literature. Broad conclusions and implications follow in the final section of this chapter.

Age differences. As demonstrated in Table 7.2, younger students reported significantly higher satisfaction with their access to computers both at home and at university as compared with their more mature peers. Significantly more of the younger students accessed online learning materials to assist with their study, though mature age students reported using the web for study significantly more hours per week than their younger counterparts. Those in the 17–19-year age group, on the other hand, used the web for recreation much more than their more mature age peers. Surprisingly, significantly more mature age students reported emailing their peers in the course as compared with younger students.

Table 7.2: Age differences in access to and use of ICTs

Access to and use of ICTs	Young students (17–19 years) (n = 1423)	Mature age students (25 years and above) (n = 283)
Access to ICTs	*% agreement*[a]	*% agreement*[a]
Satisfactory access at university	93	78**
Satisfactory access at home	92	84**
Types of ICTs used	*% who have used*[a]	*% who have used*[a]
Online resources (e.g. course notes and materials on the web)	82	77*
Email to contact faculty	69	70
Email to contact peers in the course	55	63*
Extent of use per week	*Mean hours per week*	*Mean hours per week*
Using the web for study	3.9	4.7**
Using the web for recreation	4.4	2.0**

[a]Expressed as a proportion of the number of students in the relevant demographic subgroup.
Significant values at *p < 0.01 and **p < 0.05.

In their study of age differences in the use of e-learning resources, Hoskins and Hooff (2005) found that older students used the WebCT learning management system more than younger students. These findings, along with those of the present study, challenge the assumption that younger students are using the web more than their older peers. Indeed, a more sophisticated form of analysis is needed to determine the differential nature of web use by students across age groups. This is supported by Hoskins and Hooff who argue for the development of online learning environments which take into account the preferences and activities of a much wider student population than that which we might categorize as "traditional."

Gender differences. There were no significant gender differences in students' satisfaction with access to ICTs at home or on campus, though males were slightly more satisfied in this regard. Similarly, males and females used online course notes and web-based materials to much the same extent as each other. However, significant gender differences emerged in the use of email as a means of communication with members of the learning community, as illustrated in Table 7.3. Females typically used email to contact faculty and peers significantly more than their male peers. Males reported using the web for recreation significantly more than females sampled. The reverse was true in relation to web-for-study use, though the difference was non-significant.

Table 7.3: Gender differences in access to and use of ICTs

Access to and use of ICTs	Females (*n* = 1547)	Males (*n* = 797)
Access to ICTs	*% agreement*[a]	*% agreement*[a]
Satisfactory access at university	89	91
Satisfactory access at home	89	91
Types of ICTs used	*% who have used*[a]	*% who have used*[a]
Online resources (e.g., course notes and materials on the web)	80	81
Email to contact faculty	71	63**
Email to contact peers in the course	59	51**
Extent of use per week	*Mean hours per week*	*Mean hours per week*
Using the web for study	4.3	3.8
Using the web for recreation	3.4	5.2**

[a]Expressed as a proportion of the number of students in the relevant demographic subgroup. Significant values at **$p<0.05$.

These findings point to the fact that ICT use is by no means dominated by males. Females tend to find it a helpful means of communication. This is supported by Sullivan (2002), who points out that online experiences may be less "chilly" and more inviting for female students who value the anonymity of online exchanges as opposed to having to make verbal contributions in face-to-face classroom settings. This may be one reason for females' tendency, in this sample, to use online communication with peers and faculty more than males. Nevertheless, the male domination of the online gaming arena continues to be confirmed in the research (Colley & Comber 2003) and no doubt accounts for the significantly greater proportion of time spent by males in this sample on recreational web usage. Other uses may include surfing the web. These gender differences are worthy of closer study and bear out one of the key messages of this chapter: to understand the use of ICTs among the e-generation is to understand difference and diversity of practices.

Table 7.4: Socioeconomic differences in access to and use of ICTs

Access to and use of ICTs	Low SES[a] students (n = 375)	High SES[a] students (n = 804)
Access to ICTs	*% agreement[b]*	*% agreement[b]*
Satisfactory access at university	90	89
Satisfactory access at home	88	93**
Types of ICTs used	*% who have used[b]*	*% who have used[b]*
Online resources (e.g., course notes and materials on the web)	82	77
Email to contact faculty	70	67
Email to contact peers in the course	64	55*
Extent of use per week	*Mean hours per week*	*Mean hours per week*
Using the web for study	4.2	4.0
Using the web for recreation	3.3	4.0*

[a]Medium SES students have been omitted from analysis for this discussion.
[b]Expressed as a proportion of the number of students in the relevant demographic subgroup. Significant values at *p < 0.01 and **p < 0.05.

Socioeconomic differences. Three key points of difference emerge from the data shown in Table 7.4. First, a greater proportion of students from low socioeconomic backgrounds used email to contact peers in their course, as compared with their more economically privileged counterparts. Patterns of use of the web to download course materials were similar. A second point of difference lies in the level of satisfaction with access to ICTs at home and university. Importantly, students from lower socioeconomic status (SES) backgrounds tended to express less satisfaction with home access, but greater satisfaction with university access. Given that students of lower SES are using ICTs for email and study purposes more than their high SES peers, they are arguably faced with doing so more on campus than at home.

A third source of difference between the ICT use of students from low and high SES backgrounds is that those in higher-income brackets used the web for recreational purposes significantly more than their disadvantaged peers. While this may at first appear trivial, it becomes a serious issue if, as Dede (2005) argues, net savvy students develop important learning skills in online gaming environments and simulations. Educational technologists and researchers such as Klopfer, Squire & Jenkins (2002) and Steinkuehler (2004) advocate the use of simulations and game-based approaches in learning environments. If students are not acquainted with these skills and the culture of learning in such environments, which draw heavily on skills developed during recreational web use, then arguably they will be disadvantaged. These are matters which rarely receive airtime in discussion of the many benefits of ICT use in educational settings. The experiences of the students engaging, or not engaging, with ICTs must be acknowledged and more fully understood if we are to ensure equity and reduce disadvantage among learners in higher education.

Rural–urban differences. A fourth set of demographic subgroup differences worthy of special note is that between rural and urban Australian students in the first year of university study. Some of the key differences are shown in Table 7.5. Typically, rural students are residential students at Australian universities. They may live in college or rented accommodation, but most often they are living away from home due to the significant distances between most public universities and rural and isolated regions of Australia. Students from rural areas would generally have experienced inferior telecommunications support in their rural homes and may not have had the online experiences of many of their metropolitan peers prior to entering university (Kilpatrick & Bound 2003). Moreover, the rural students are more likely to be first generation students at university, lacking the cultural and social capital (Walpole 2003), so important for managing a range of activities in higher education, including online communication.

Table 7.5 demonstrates that Australian university students from rural backgrounds typically used online resources significantly less than their urban counterparts. They used the web for study and recreation less than their urban peers—significantly so in the case of recreational use. The difference between rural and urban students' satisfaction with home access to ICTs is approaching significance, with rural students somewhat less satisfied with their access, while the reverse was true with respect to university access to ICTs. It should be remembered, however, that the majority of these rural students would be referring to residential college accommodation as "home" for the purposes of this survey.

Table 7.5: Rural–urban differences in access to and use of ICTs

Access to and use of ICTs	Rural students (n = 633)[a]	Urban students (n = 1484)[a]
Access to ICTs	*% agreement*[b]	*% agreement*[b]
Satisfactory access at university	92	89*
Satisfactory access at home[c]	89	91
Types of ICTs used	*% who have used*[b]	*% who have used*[b]
Online resources (e.g., course notes and materials on the web)	74	84**
Email to contact faculty	65	71*
Email to contact peers in the course	50	60**
Extent of use per week	*Mean hours per week*	*Mean hours per week*
Using the web for study	3.8	4.1
Using the web for recreation	2.9	4.0**

[a]Students from international backgrounds have been omitted from the analysis for this discussion.
[b]Expressed as a proportion of the number of students in the relevant demographic subgroup.
[c]"Home" refers to place of residence during university studies.
Significant values at *p < 0.01 and **p < 0.05.

In summary, differences emerged among all four sets of demographic subgroups identified in Tables 7.2–7.5. Typically, the greatest sources of differences were time spent on the web for study and recreation, and the proportion of students using email to contact peers and faculty in the university learning community. The data show that students from rural areas had the most consistently low levels of usage of the web for study, recreation and communication purposes. Unexpectedly, students of low SES tended to use online course resources slightly more than their high SES peers and they also used email to access faculty and friends more. However, they were significantly less satisfied with their access to ICTs at home. Online communication patterns were relatively consistent among the females in the sample who tended to email peers and faculty more than their male counterparts. Males and younger students, on the other hand, were found to use the web for recreational purposes significantly more than females and older students, respectively. These findings have significant implications for policy and practice in higher education. This was the focus of the second research question, to be addressed in the next section.

Policy Implications and Conclusions

Institution-level ICT policy-making in higher education has become a challenging issue. Policy-makers struggle to keep pace with the rapid rate of change in the e-learning landscape. Nevertheless, the burden of responsibility lies increasingly with policy decision-makers and academics working together to devise policies which meet the three criteria outlined at the start of this chapter: (1) policy must recognize the needs and experiences of all students, including those underrepresented in higher education; (2) ICT policies must take account of, but not be driven by, ICT developments and innovations, and (3) the quality of the learning experience must always take priority over the imperative to innovate at all costs. The findings of this study provide an opportunity to consider policy implications using these three criteria as a guide.

The study points to some notable group differences based on such variables as age and socioeconomic background. These patterns may vary across disciplines and institutions depending on several factors, including mode of delivery and student demographics. The differences highlight the need for policy that is responsive to student diversity, and appreciative of the multidimensional nature of student engagement.

Three key policy issues emerge from these data. The first is an ongoing challenge to ask the probing and sometimes hard questions of "why?" and "how?" Why use ICTs in higher education? And if we are going to use them, how are they best used for maximum support of learning? The significant finding of Caruso (2004), that ICT use is primarily for convenience rather than improving learning, is a sobering one indeed. It is to some extent supported by this study which has found significant proportions of first year students using the web to access and download study materials. Universities must look inward at their current practices and priorities to determine if they simply plan to use ICTs as a convenience, or if they are serious about exploring ways to use them to enhance learning. If the latter is the aim, then it is now time to step in and show students how ICTs will benefit their learning, because this does not appear to be their perception currently. Policies must be put in place to determine how best to use ICTs to foster learning. In some cases, this may mean limiting the extent of material placed online for the sake of convenience alone. We will have much to answer for if we as educators and policy-makers are recorded in history as the generation who sacrificed quality learning and community for convenience.

A second policy issue pertains to computer access and provision of adequate access for all students. We know from these data that older students and those from low SES backgrounds and rural areas tend to rely on campus-based computer access since they rate their satisfaction with home access as relatively low. It is important that universities develop policies for sustainable development of spaces for these students to learn and work with ICTs. Since so much of the benefit of using ICTs involves peers (Kuh & Vesper 1997; Tinto et al. 1993), it is critical that these spaces allow for interaction and collaboration. Learning hubs or learning commons, such as the University of Guelph learning commons online (www.learningcommons.uoguelph.ca), are one such approach, but they require institution-wide planning and policy-making which is attuned to the needs of students and faculty alike.

A final policy issue emerging from these data pertains to the use of ICTs in learning contexts. As noted at the start of this chapter, it is so often the case that the current generation of university students is labeled as the net generation, comfortable with any form of technology. This assumption of homogeneity is misleading and dangerous. It means that older students who are new to higher education, for example, may be treated just the same as their younger counterparts. Even worse, however, are the more subtle differences in terms of ways in which low SES impacts on students' familiarity with the culture of the Internet which is assumed when, for example, learning depends on gaming skills. Females, also, may have different ICT experiences and skill sets compared to males in the learning environment. Rogers et al. (2001) use the marketing concept of segmentation to argue for the importance of institutions "segmenting" their learners based on demographic characteristics such as age, gender, special needs or grade point average. In this way, universities increase the likelihood of best serving the needs of their unique mix of students. False assumptions which treat all learners as part of an homogenous e-generation must be addressed in equity policies when it comes to such fundamental issues as assessing students' background skills and previous experiences with ICTs, determining assessment and learning tasks which involve online components, and building community online.

Academics, institutional leaders and policy-makers alike have a responsibility to develop proactive strategies for keeping students connected to learning communities, whether through virtual or real learning settings. In the e-learning setting, this may be achieved through creative online assessment and feedback cycles, along with active development of online learning communities through the fostering of social interactions in and around the online learning environment. Provision should be made at the institution level to ensure that faculty members receive ongoing professional development which enables them to implement the most effective pedagogical practices for promoting online engagement. Equally, however, institutions need to be active in ensuring that there are explicit policies at all levels which communicate and operationalize institutional expectations of students. The imperative for such proactivity is greater than it has ever been before as the student population becomes increasingly diverse, with a concomitant rise in the range and extent of student expectations. There is much on offer in the realm of e-learning, but with growth in curriculum offerings and options comes the need to monitor and manage the e-learning process through judicious policy-making.

In *Brave New World*, Aldous Huxley warns of the dangers of giving the state control over new and powerful technologies. The same warnings should be issued in regard to giving the quality of learning over to new and powerful technologies without considering the implications for the quality of experience of all students, particularly those who are disadvantaged and underrepresented in higher education. Wisely developed and well-informed policy can play a significant gate-keeping role in this respect, ensuring that the values and standards of higher education are maintained.

Chapter 8

Do Students Lose More than They Gain in Online Writing Classes?

Kate Kiefer

Why do we teach writing in relatively small classes? Certainly there are practical reasons having to do with workload and classroom management issues,[1] but most of our reasons flow from pedagogical and theoretical concerns. Pedagogically, we know that students are likely to learn most effectively from multiple opportunities to practice with timely feedback on their effectiveness in writing. Even more important, the most influential theories of language use and development posit the situatedness of language—how it is shaped by and shapes its users and contexts of its use. Cultural, rhetorical, and sociocognitive perspectives all emphasize the construction of meaning in context. Our goals in teaching writing explicitly include helping students become aware of writing as situated communication. The rhetorical principles embodied in most widely used writing texts consistently encourage writers to adapt to the specific writing context. Contemporary writing theory and language theory (as well as much cultural criticism) develop in even greater detail the crucial roles of language in context: for identity formation, for cultural work, and for community building. Little wonder, then, that teachers of writing insist that students are best able to learn to write most effectively when they can create and respond to specific language contexts in small groups of students (15–25 students in the class as a whole, with smaller groupings of 2–5 students working on targeted collaborative activities).

Do these theoretical assumptions about language preclude teaching writing online? Proponents of online writing courses argue that textual interactions can immerse students more fully in situated writing than face-to-face courses in which few classroom interactions involve writing. But despite what could be an advantage, online classes often fail students precisely because all interactions are textual. Unless students are sensitive to or willing to examine the different functions of text in an online class, they can be trapped by their constrained understanding of writing and finish the course with less awareness of the contexts of writing than their counterparts in a traditional classroom.

Admittedly, my view of the potential shortcomings of online writing instruction is in the minority. In 1992, Gail Hawisher summed up a prevailing positive view of electronic discourses and their extension into virtual classrooms: "As a result of our work with computers over the past decade, we can begin to imagine teaching and writing in a virtual age where a meeting of the minds might well occur without the physical presence of students and teachers." Minock and Shor (1995) discuss at length an example of a curriculum that exploits all the positive elements of computer-mediated discussion, even for students in a hybrid class which typically meets in face-to-face settings for a few sessions, and at most once per week, during the term and functions as an online course the rest of the term. Similarly, Fey (1998) reports her research on a "distance" collaboration that effectively paired college and high school students in a critical inquiry about gender roles, and Faigley (1999) offers an example of what he calls "the best possible learning environment with technology" that shows "students who use telecommunications across different geographic locations are more motivated and learn more" (138). In these instances, online textual interactions not only enhanced individual learning about substantive issues but also created opportunities for students to practice writing for specific rhetorical contexts.

Off-setting these positive results are concerns about flaming and other negative power differentials that emerge in some electronic conversations (among others, Faigley 1992; Janangelo 1991), crushing all possibility for positive student–student interactions. Furthermore, the work of Gaddis et al. (2000), who note that the online students in their study were more independent as learners and tended to value collaboration to a lesser extent than students in their on-campus classes, suggests that students may reject opportunities to interact meaningfully even when it might otherwise contribute to positive learning outcomes.

Despite this apparent lack of consensus among teachers and researchers about whether online classes can function as learning contexts equivalent to traditional classrooms for students, political and economic realities are pushing more and more students into online education. In many cases, questions about the efficacy of online education have been ignored in the face of pressures to offer a quick response to student demand and to attract the largest possible number of students to online classes. In some places, like in my state of Colorado as part of a Western Governors' initiative, legislative action is pending to reward community colleges and four-year institutions that attract large number of online students. (The clear implication is that institutions with largely on-campus instruction might well suffer in future budget allocations from the state.) Yet we do not have large-scale, objective evidence that writing teachers can maintain key instructional techniques and values in the writing classes we teach online.

Our emphasis on the situatedness of writing has long moved teachers of writing beyond the immediate classroom context. Scholars as varied in their theoretical perspectives as Miller, Moffat, Elbow, and Freire have pointed out that writing instruction cannot succeed when students do not engage in writing for at least one of several non-academic goals—personal expression, social consciousness, post-academic writing in the disciplines or in a workplace, critical literacy, or lifelong learning. More recently, pedagogies that emphasize service learning or community action have continued this trend toward focusing on writing beyond the classroom. As a profession, our history in the last 50 years has emphasized the importance of engaging students in more than individual, iterated practice of formulaic academic responses. But when we move the classroom online, are we actually expanding the boundaries of the classroom to take advantage of the larger world of varied rhetorical contexts? Or does the focus of instruction in online courses differ so greatly from that of face-to-face courses that it diminishes the richness of interactions among class members?

Deficit 1: Classroom Support Software

Anyone who has taught a distance education writing course with widely available classroom support software knows that such software, WebCT and Blackboard, was not designed with writing teachers in mind. Rather, assuming that lecture courses were the norm for higher education, most classroom support software was designed to support lecture classes. WebCT, for instance, provides a number of ways for teachers to post lecture material—as readings, notes, PowerPoint slides, or links to other textual material or websites. Materials that are created within the electronic course can be "released" to students with set starting and end dates and times so that students can be encouraged to stay on track with the syllabus. Similarly, teachers can use a test bank of questions to create randomized multiple choice quizzes and examinations that, again, are available to students for only a set amount of time. Students see only their own scores on quizzes and grades on papers or examinations. It is possible for online courses, then, to exist as individual tutorials in which students have no sense that the course exists for anyone else.

Understandably, most online course designs transferred from lecture classes feature instruction that requires almost no interaction between students. Students can retrieve the assigned materials, read and study them, take online quizzes or tests, and even write a paper without engaging other students in the course in any sustained or significant conversation. The computer in this instance not only wipes out any sense that students in the course might be "other," but also that other students in the course even exist. Students have no way of knowing how many other students are even enrolled in the same course, unless they are savvy enough to count the number of students on the class email list or pay very careful attention to discussion forum postings, should any be required.

But assume that a teacher does not want to organize the class as a "lecture" or a correspondence course with no interactions except those between the teacher and each individual student. The typical classroom support system modeled on lecture courses also includes a chat room, an asynchronous bulletin board or discussion forum, and an internal email system for communicating with all members of the course. Using the chat room requires that all students be able to log into the "classroom" website at the same time, a remarkably difficult chore given constraints on students' time (see below). And the asynchronous bulletin board is not necessarily a friendly community forum for posting messages. In WebCT, for instance, the threaded discussions on the asynchronous bulletin board are difficult to negotiate. My students have told me that they are often confused about how to read postings, and they can respond to only one posting at a time because WebCT has no option for opening two screens at the same time to view multiple texts. As it was not designed for groups of students interacting about texts, lecture-modeled classroom support software can make student dialog or other textual interactions needlessly difficult.

Furthermore, although it is possible to work around the design of WebCT to create discussion forums for smaller working groups of students, the software provides no easy way for students to exchange drafts of papers except to attach the papers to forum postings or email messages. Email at least has the advantage of being private within most classroom support software. Only the designated recipient within the class can read the email, so students who use this method of exchanging papers can comment on each other's work without worrying about who else might be reading their comments. Papers attached to bulletin board postings are available to all unless the teacher sets up privacy restrictions required for each separate bulletin board for a pair or group of students, an awkward solution at best.

Downloading from even the best classroom support software can be time consuming, moreover, if the school server is overloaded, as ours often is. Sometimes, our server is so busy that students cannot log on at the times they have available to work on a computer. At other times, the load on the server is such that any new request to the server takes a minute or more to execute (on a high-speed line on campus; access time is often tripled for students working at a distance over modems). Retrieving a paper attached to a forum posting or email can take students up to 20 minutes, often time that students do not have to sit staring at an unresponsive computer screen. So my students have tried to work outside WebCT by exchanging papers through other email programs. Almost all my students have discovered, at one time or another, that email programs have limits on the size of attached files. They try to send a draft of a paper to me or to a peer reviewer only to have the attachment deleted from the email because it exceeds size restrictions.

While it is true that some students experience stumbling blocks in our face-to-face classrooms and thus we should not assume that physical environments are all and always "student-friendly," the limitations built into lecture-modeled classroom support software make it much less welcoming than the worst physical space to students of writing. In short, many online classroom "environments" work against the notion of a writing class as a nexus of situated interactions through and about writing.

Deficit 2: Students' Time Constraints

Students' situations differ, of course, but most of my students work full-time and take one or two online courses at a time. Due to the other commitments, my students tend to work on their courses on weekends, often only on Sundays. (When I first started teaching online writing courses, I did not realize this trend until well into the first semester. I have since revised my syllabus and work plans to accommodate this student reality.) I still advise students to work in smaller chunks of time, even if they have to do the week's worth of reading and writing on the weekend, but students tell me they often only have one large block of time for completing the work on my course.

Imagine, then, the frustrations students face. First, they need to retrieve the assigned texts from their classroom management software—typically in my classes a short introduction to the week's work, several student samples, and a specific writing task, sometimes to be completed immediately and sometimes to feed into a longer paper or portfolio collection. Students log onto the classroom support system, download the texts, and either save them to read on the screen or to print later. They log off to complete the reading and any preliminary writing they need to do. At this point, they log back onto the classroom support system and post to the discussion forum or send a draft to a peer for review. Students also need to complete some writing for me every week, so they send that file to me, usually through email. If other students have posted on the bulletin board for electronic conversation, they will sometimes read those postings and sometimes not, depending on how much time they have to be online. If they do respond to each other's postings or to questions I raise in my postings, the responses are often short and unelaborated because they have little time to read online. When I respond to their postings or when a peer responds after they have logged off for the weekend, students will not read that response for another week, at which point the issue seems dead.

If, as is often the case, a student is juggling a busy family life, then multiple interruptions have also distracted her or him from the week's work of a writing class, even on a given Sunday. Add to these constraints that some of my students are borrowing computer time from a friend or using a public computer at a coffee house or library. One recent student could only check back in on the course when he was not flying missions for his military service unit. In short, many students who take online courses would not complete their education in such a haphazard format if they had a choice. But family, work, and other obligations keep them tied to places and time schedules that do not allow for frequent trips to a college campus, much less a good library. When students have to add to these constraints the lack of computer access, the chances of spending enough time online to engage in extended interactions with me or with peers about the nuances of situated texts and rhetorical responses to varied writing contexts diminish even more.

Granted, not all students fall back on the Sunday-only work pattern, and all students take away from online classes some measure of writing instruction they would not have without access to writing courses. But I am frustrated by what so many students miss in my online classes, and I have to ask if I really provide comparable instruction to my online and face-to-face students.

Deficit 3: "Market" Models of Education

Many students registering for online courses are already well established in jobs and family life. Online courses appeal to them as a way to further their education while still giving priority to 40-hour work weeks and/or family commitments. But these priorities result in students coming into hybrid or online courses with an approach that emphasizes pragmatic goals.

In my experience teaching both hybrid and online writing classes, students are most concerned with getting feedback from me as a teacher. Granted, they are focused on improving their writing, and we should applaud their willingness to engage in the hard work of a writing course. But the focus of their attention is on completing writing assignments as efficiently as possible. Two examples from one of my recent distance education courses illustrate this point.

At the beginning of the term, I asked students to introduce themselves to me and to each other by posting a short biography, including their majors and main interests, on the discussion forum. I use this task both to allow students to get to know each other and to establish a sense of who we are as a group and how our varied backgrounds can contribute to shared knowledge in the group. This activity in a face-to-face classroom almost always establishes a range of interests and shared experiences that students can use to forge connections. But of the 10 students registered in this particular online class, only two posted their biographies, and when I posted responses to these two, my questions and invitations for more biographies were ignored.

One might argue that perhaps this particular group of students resisted revealing anything about themselves, but my experiences with both hybrid and online classes have been consistent. Students typically ignore those activities that seem to them unrelated to what they perceive as the central work of the course—writing academic papers that comprise most of the graded work in the course.

And how students define what is central to the course is also a concern for me as I think of classroom interactions. Each time that I teach an online course, at least one student (and sometimes as many as half of the students registered) will get in touch with me before the beginning of the semester. Students ask what they can read in advance or how they might otherwise get a head start on the class. When a student first approached me with this question before my first offering of the online writing class, I assumed she was motivated by nervousness about taking an upper-division writing course. I have since learned from email exchanges with these students that they simply want to be able to work on the class on their own schedules. The most recent request of this sort came from a student who planned to spend her semester in Thailand with, as she puts it, "limited Internet access." When I point out that much of the course work depends on shared discussion of readings, of group activities, of peer review, the response is consistent and discouraging: "But why can't I just work on *my* writing?"

In these specific online classes, my students have been remarkably reluctant to participate in collaborative knowledge building. Discussions of readings are perfunctory at best with almost no student interest in how writers both react to and shape the writing context, and peer reviews are often disappointing, even when as a teacher I prod students to participate and critique as fully as possible.

Standard techniques—modeling good behavior, directed questions to elicit in-depth response, evaluative response—all seem ineffective in the face of students' determined pragmatic desire to improve their own writing skills without investing in community knowledge or practice. Learning from each other, then, is such a distant concern of these students that they resist most efforts to introduce genuine interaction with other students.

Of course, writing teachers do not encounter the pragmatic student only in online classes. We have all dealt with and continue to work against current models of education that emphasize the degree as a commodity. Student comments more and more often reflect the notion that the "customer is always right," and if the student is the customer of education then the teacher is at fault if the student is not satisfied with the product (the grade). When the metaphor of the marketplace becomes the model of learning, then interactions among shared knowledge builders become less and less important. Instead, students see themselves as the consumers of disposable units of education (credits) that ultimately add up to the marketable prize—the degree that will lead to a higher-paying job and financial success. Learning as an end in itself does not enter into this picture of student education, and learning that has long-term benefit (being able to understand and adapt to local literacies as parents, workers, and community members) is too removed from the immediate needs of the consumer need to be of interest or value.

These attitudes now pervade both distance and on-campus student populations, but as teachers having face-to-face contact with on-campus students, we can more effectively combat these attitudes in a physical classroom setting. We can carefully design and insist on participation in shared activities that meet our pedagogical and theoretical goals because students and teacher share the same space and time for conversations, discussions, and even in-class writing. But the distances of space and time that make online classes possible also diminish severely our chances of working effectively against a model of education that promotes pragmatic thinking and short-term goals—finishing the course as quickly as possible to check the requirement of the list of courses needed for graduation.

Summing Up the Deficits: Students Lose

Taken individually, the difficulties created by the factors above do not account for the lack of significant and sustained student–student interaction in online writing courses. We have all had moments when we question why technology, especially software, seems to distract energy away from the focus of our work as writers and teachers. We have all dealt with constraints on time and energy as students and teachers. And as teachers, we have all had students in classes who seem reluctant to participate in group activities, class discussions, or peer-review workshops, claiming that their peers have nothing of value to share with them. In a classroom setting, though, experienced teachers can deal with all of these factors and still shape a class that works more rather than less to build shared knowledge important to the class. Even if students at first only go through the motions to appear cooperative, small-group activities, peer-review workshops, and engaging full-class discussions do eventually create face-to-face classes of students who attend to the multiple functions of language in its full range of contexts. Not all face-to-face classes are equally successful in meeting these goals, but even the most dysfunctional group I worked with a few years ago developed a core of highly committed students who worked closely and productively together. In over 25 years of teaching, my students have never ended a semester unable to express in conversation and in writing more knowledge about how writing works than they began the course with.

Unfortunately, in the online writing courses I have taught, my experience has been quite different: I have not yet forged anything like a working group sharing knowledge. When only a few students complete the activities designed to help them get to know each other, those who do so feel that they have put in time on a task that does not pay off for them. When students respond perfunctorily if at all in online discussions of rhetorical contexts for writing, then their understanding of writing is seriously diminished. When students do not know each other or rhetorical principles very well, they are less likely to trust the commentary on peer reviews of drafts or to give commentary that will appreciably improve a peer's understanding of rhetorical choices. Without significant interactions about how writing works in context, students simply take much less away from online courses.

In addition, my experience and that of teachers I have talked to from several institutions and in several disciplines is equally discouraging on another point: the drop-out rate for students in distance courses averages from 30% to 50%. This high attrition rate also works as a disincentive for students in online classes: after all, why put in the extra effort to get to know or to interact with someone never seen who might drop out of the course at any moment? Two students in my class last year started to work productively together on peer reviews, but then one of those students "disappeared" for two weeks and left the other student feeling abandoned. Her sense of the advantages of working with a peer disappeared in light of her experience, and she expressed very pointedly to me that she felt her best investment of time was in working directly with me rather than waiting for peer reviews that never seemed to materialize.

Although I am sure that the students who have completed my online writing courses have learned more about writing from their interactions with me than they could have learned solely by reading a textbook or handbook, I am equally certain that they have shortchanged themselves by failing to learn from their peers. They have not had opportunities to interact with peers in small-group work on audience analysis, genre conventions, introductions, evidence, source citation—the kinds of activities, both planned and spontaneous, that fill my classroom sessions. As I teach in a networked computer classroom, I also see face-to-face students reading each other's work online, helping each other "speak" to audiences, suggesting ways to integrate visual information, and so on—all because both the students and their writing are visible in the same place at the same time. What may seem incidental to the online students is not incidental from my view. The interactions between students in a face-to-face writing class may not always result in utopian ideals of learning for learning's sake, but they do result in important learning about how writing works. And what students learn from each other about reading and writing simply cannot be replaced with tutorial instruction from the single voice of a writing teacher.

What Have We Lost? What Are We Losing?

Marilyn Cooper (1999) argues persuasively that electronic conversations can be productive in engaging students and creating shared community knowledge if we deal with them as reflective of postmodern complexity:

> Because synchronous in-class electronic discussions contain many more strands than face-to-face class discussions and move so much faster, teachers have learned that, in order to allow for the kind of reflection that is necessary to reveal complexities, problems must be re-presented to students in succeeding discussions […] Teachers can bring transcripts of electronic conversations to class and ask students to talk about what happened in them—and everyone, especially the teacher, can be enlightened about the intentions and effect of what went on. Students can also be asked to respond in writing, individually or in groups, in hard copy or in further electronic conversations, to whole or partial transcripts of electronic conversations that have taken place in class. And teachers can simply re-present in face-to-face discussions problems that arose in electronic conversations. (160)

But in all these options for dealing with the lost opportunities of electronic discourse, Cooper relies on face-to-face solutions not available for the online writing teacher trying to foster student–student interactions with no resources other than electronic discourse.

We have an obligation as writing teachers to analyze the shortcomings of our courses and to try to solve the problems that arise. Explaining the motives for certain activities will often encourage students to participate more significantly in online discussions. Exposing the flaws of current models of education can also help students to see how they might have adopted viewpoints that work against their education in both the short and long run. Even incorporating mundane solutions such as assigning points to all the writing, peer review, and discussion forums as well as informal and formal writing projects, can encourage some students to participate more fully in student–student interactions in online classes. All of these solutions have helped somewhat in my online classes, but the combination of forces mentioned above—technological impediments, time constraints, attitudes toward education—still keeps many students from learning as much about writing in my online classes as in my face-to-face classrooms.

Writing teachers value shared interactions in the classroom for a range of reasons. Writing does not happen in a vacuum, and when students recognize a learning community in the classroom they are more likely to speak to that community with rhetorical sophistication. Interaction and engagement with others in the class also imply that students will learn from each other and help each other to improve as readers and writers. The depth of conversation about writing and about texts further develops each writer's potential. And engagement with writing as rhetorically situated communication fosters richer writing skills for all classrooms, not just writing classrooms, as well as for contexts beyond the academy.

But students' preconceptions of their roles in online courses and the limitations of technology combine to work against significant interactions in online classes. As teachers of writing who believe that students learn not only by writing thoughtfully but also by reading carefully—and in particular by participating in discussions that foster original ideas and elicit well-considered responses and critiques about the situatedness of writing—we should consider the extent to which students in our online and hybrid classes are willing to participate in the exchanges of ideas and insights that we so value. And, by extension, we should question the claims of efficacy for online and hybrid classes. We must ask ourselves, finally, whether we should continue to teach writing through an instructional mode that seems so much at odds with our full range of goals for writing instruction.

Note

1. The National Council of Teachers of English Guideline, "More than a Number: Why Class Size Matters" (NCTE, n.d.), includes these practical points as well as several others that cross boundaries between pedagogical and theoretical rationales. Although a theoretical context is not explicit in the guideline, sources include key thinkers representing varied perspectives.

Chapter 9

Won't Get Googled Again: Searching for an Education

Tara Brabazon

It is difficult to determine the precise moment when the enemy crossed the barricade and pretended to be one of us. In the last five years, the techno-positivists and neophiliacs have entered schools and universities pretending that they are interested in teaching and learning, reading and writing. The money spent on proto-redundant technology and just-in-time training that invariably arrives too late is probably incalculable. There has been a seismic loss of critical thinking and the capacity to judge the appropriateness of technology for our students, colleagues and the curriculum. Instead of starting with learning goals, teachers have cut up and corroded our experience and knowledge to slot into the capabilities and strengths of software, rather than the creative potentials of wetware.

The Who, the power-chording chroniclers of the swinging sixties, critiqued the empty promises of the 1960s social "revolution." Released in 1971, "Won't Get Fooled Again" expresses anger at the promises made and the paucity of results. Over 30 years later, post-September 11, post-Bali, post-Iraq War II, we have been fooled—over and over again. The consequences for education of the systematic and structural confusion of truth and propaganda, news and entertainment, reality and reality television, needs to be tracked. My chapter investigates the relationship between information, knowledge and wisdom, asking what has happened to our standards of reading, thinking and writing in the last decade. Or, putting it another way, I ask how Google has performed our changing commitments to truth, reality, experience and education.

The marketing of information and communication technology is insidious. The type of research that is being funded by governments and the private sector aims to stress the positive correlation between Internet-mediated education and student achievement. Heather-Jane Robertson reported in October 2003 that this well-funded research has failed to show an improvement in student learning. She stated that:

> After 2 years of total and unlimited access to technology by carefully selected students whose parents had chosen the program and whose teachers enjoyed unlimited amounts of technical and instructional support, small class sizes, and half of each day to devote to preparation, the best that Apple could say about the achievement scores of ACOT [Apple Classrooms of Tomorrow] students was that they had not declined. (281)

Learning is not technologically determined. It requires a strong curriculum, experienced teachers and motivated students. Such realizations make corporations no money and will not ensure the re-election of governments. We need to ask who gains from our expensive enthusiasm for computers, the Internet and web. The answer is hardware manufacturers, software distributors, educational administrators, overworked information professionals and poor teachers. The losers are good teachers and well-trained librarians. Teachers need to explore, research and challenge the linear relationship between computers and beneficial classroom outcomes. The "research" literature about educational technologies is filled with hype, hope and faith, not research, critique and questioning. To be clear in my argument: I am not against educational technology or any innovation. I am critical of the slavish celebration of anything that is promoted without evidence and research. My favorite example of technology being the savior for all society's ills is from David Dwyer, who stated that:

> Half of America's children engage in behaviors that place them in serious risk of alienation, even death [...] technology is the only vehicle we may ride as we work to engage more children in the excitement and life-enhancing experience of learning. (1996: 31)

Compassion, empathy, discipline, good pedagogy and committed teaching are no longer mechanisms for assisting the disempowered or disenfranchised. Instead, for Dwyer, technology will solve all our problems. At a time when the public funding of education is threatened, it is too convenient to suggest that nothing beneficial emerges from teaching that does not involve technology. If we increase the machines, memory, bandwidth or technical support, social and economic inequalities will not evaporate. Teachers become puppets as we *assume* benefits, rather than *prove* benefits. While affirming interactivity and connectivity, the personal computer transforms learning into an individual and isolated activity. Now that this ideology is ubiquitous, we need to clear the decks, take a breath and determine what computers do well, and when they need to be switched off to allow other learning goals to develop.

Google Time

Google, and its naturalized mode of searching, encourages bad behavior. When confronted by an open search engine, most of us will enact the ultimate of vain acts: inserting our own name over the blinking cursor. This process now has a name: googling. A recent American survey reported that one in four of their interviewees admitted to this practice. This is a self-absorbed, rather than outward and reflexive process. It is not a search of the World Wide Web, but the construction of an Individual Narrow Portal.

It is important to be completely honest about the Internet, let alone the web, that is being searched by Google. The web is large, occasionally irrelevant, often filled with advertising; it is outdated and increasingly corporatized. It seems appropriate that Google has become ubiquitous at the moment when teachers and librarians are overworked and less available to see students. David Loertscher confirmed that:

> Search engines such as Google are so easy and immediate that many young people, faced with a research assignment, just "google" their way through the Internet rather than struggle through the hoops of a more traditional library environment. (2003: 14)

There are consequences for the proliferation of Google, which is the most popular search engine, but not the best. AltaVista has more features and search capabilities.[1] Google is also immersed in the English language (Sorgo 2003),[2] which creates a blinkered worldview. There is a reason for the limited vista of this virtual landscape.

Larry Page, one of the founders of Google, developed the technology with a doctoral candidate in engineering at Stanford. The word Google is derived from the mathematical term googol, a one followed by 100 zeros. This is important, as founding ideologies invariably frame the meaning of structures in the long term. The cultural orientation of the search engine was in engineering, not library, Internet or cultural studies. There is a suite of Google products, including the image search, a Usenet discussion service and a catalog search. In November 2003, a new software package—the Google desk bar—was released, which allowed the user to access the search engine without opening a new web browser. The software was released for free because of the exposure granted to the logo (Searching without Browser 2003).

The underpinning technology for Google is PageRank, an "objective" measurement of the importance of webpages, which works by assessing the number of links that point to them. Therefore, Google ranks its search results according to the popularity and number of links to and hits on any given site. For example, when "Tara Brabazon" is entered into Google, the number one returned link is to my homepage. That is, the site developed by me to promote my career. The sites with fewer hits, but perhaps more critical information about me, are far lower on the ranking. Even my profile on my employer's site at Murdoch University has a lower ranking. My personal webpage has so many hits because a link is presented at the bottom of each email I send from my work computer. Not surprisingly, hundreds of curious undergraduates with a bouncy index finger click to their teacher's profile. Yet this is the site that a Google search returns when a user clicks on "I'm feeling lucky." This is one example, from one person. Ponder the more serious consequences when students click onto highly ideological sites that are assessed by popularity, not importance or significance. There are many other ways that this ranking could be assembled. The assumption underpinning Google is that popularity of sites is a validation of quality. *Pop Idol*, *American Idol* and *Australian Idol* were popular. They did not promote quality singing. It is train-wreck television, where we all vicariously feed off participants' discomfort, validating our right to comment on unfortunate frock choice, fat-packed hips or a near-terminal fascination with hair gel. Google is the Internet equivalent of reality television: popular, fast and shallow. The success of Google is on such a scale that it is one of the few product names that has transformed into a verb. Googling has become a verb for surfing, following a similar path to Xeroxing and Hoovering. Like these other nouns-turned-verbs, it is a standardized response to specific problems. Photocopying requires an understanding of copyright law as much as where to insert paper into the Xerox machine. House cleaning requires time, rather than simply the purchasing of a Hoover. These nouns-turned-verbs make us forget about process, structure and obstacles. Googling is a one-size-fits all response to information sharing,[3] and assumes that a user has the literacy to utilize the search engine and the interpretative skills to handle the results.

By December 2002, Google had indexed three billion web documents, supporting 150 million searches a day. Profitable since 2001, it won the contract to be AOL's search engine and handles 75% of searching traffic (Clyde 2003: 44–45). In 2003, the Expanded Academic Database, one of the most important full-text databases for the humanities in particular, also featured a link to

Google at the top of every search page. I wish this process occurred the other way: that Google would encourage movement into more specialized databases.[4] Teachers and librarians need to encourage the arc into refereed research, stressing that Google is the start (not the entirety) of a search. There are major consequences for our students, their futures and our educational system if we are apathetic rather than proactive.

In Australia, Jacinta Squires and Lee FitzGerald, a high school teacher and teacher librarian, have been conducting some action research on the information process scaffold and the consequences for student learning outcomes (L. FitzGerald, Personal communication, January 10, 2004). They have discovered, when surveying high school history students, that they always use Google as a first search, and the Internet ahead of books. They also showed that the students never or hardly ever read the learning outcomes or marking criteria or the library catalog. Significantly, students access encyclopedias for gaining information. Squires and FitzGerald's research is timely and important, and has profound consequences when students make it to university.

Students commence first year at my university demonstrating superficial research and comprehension skills, and awkward writing modalities. They need to read diverse views and construct an argument, rather than assume that if something is written down, it must be correct. Making students think rather than assume, and read rather than cut and paste, is proving a challenge. Let me show you what was submitted to me in 2003, and some strategies I use to increase the skills and critical thinking of students. Here is an example of a bibliography submitted for a research paper at university level:

> Reference List
> http://www.beatlesagain.com/breflib.love.html
> http://www.beatesagain.com.breflib.teens.html
> http://ia_essortment.com/historyoftheb_rmdq.htm
> http://www2.canisius.edu/~dierenfb/his389.htm
> http://www.beatesagain.com/breflib/teens.html

At Murdoch University, staff provide students with a course reader of at least 100 extracts from books and articles, featuring the most relevant and important material in the subject area. This student has ignored all this material—on popular music and fandom, for example—to write a paper on the Beatles, using the Google search for "Beatles fans." My (stunned) comments on this bibliography were clear: "You must never use Internet-based sources as self-standing references" and "Where are your readings from the course?"

Another student, writing a paper on "Asian gangs," revealed the problem in an even more troubling fashion. Instead of questioning how and why Australian police place attention on Asian citizens, the student did not deploy this level of interpretation, but merely took information from highly politicized sites. Highly racist statements splattered from her bibliography, with assumptions expressed about "Asians" intrinsically being violent, tribal and insular. Once more, the student had simply inserted "Asian Gangs" into Google and these results emerged. Such bibliographies continued to be produced even after I placed the following information in study guides:

> In terms of research material, please remember that I reward a diversity of media in my marking. In other words, I will not be happy if a student constructs an essay on refugees or *Kill Bill*, taps into Google and constructs a bibliography of sites. The net is an important, diverse database but it also has major limitations. Your effort in seeking out textual diversity will be rewarded.

Students ignored this warning and utilized the most simplistic of searches, not even bothering to deploy course readings photocopied for them. Google standardizes searching at the time when there is a great diversity of both information and users.

In a fast-food, fast-data environment, the web transforms into an information drive-through. Google facilitates empty calorie searches, loaded with fat but little nutrition for knowledge building. It encourages a "type-in–download–cut–paste–submit" educational culture. A 2001 study reported that 71% of American students relied mostly on the Internet for major assignments at school. In this same study, 24% relied mostly on the library and only 4% used both the Internet and the library (Lenhart 2001). Social justice in education requires intervention, and we need to lift that 4% figure so that students are actively moving between the digital and the analog, the unrefereed web and scholarly databases. Further, we must ensure that these tools are actually used, rather than merely taught and ignored. My initial strategy has been prescriptive, rather than flexible. It has also created results. In 2002, I wrote the curriculum for a course titled *Repetitive Beat Generation*. Before writing a research essay, students were required to submit an annotated bibliography.

Annotated Bibliography

There are strict requirements on this component of the exercise. Students must include at least 30 sources. Each source is to be accompanied by a 20–50 word description, showing how is it to be used in the project. Of these 30 sources:

- At least 12 must be refereed articles and books, split evenly between the two categories. Students must therefore learn how to use databases, such as the expanded academic database. Come and see Tara, she will show you how these operate. (*Note*: These books and articles *must be* non-fiction.)
- There must be at least five references from popular music.
- There must be at least one film or television program.
- There must be at least five websites.
- There must be at least two magazine or newspaper articles.
- There must be at least two novels or collections of short stories.

This is obviously a difficult exercise, but it is important for students to increase their research capabilities, and develop analytical skills in a wide array of media.

The results from this highly regulatory assessment were innovative, considered and balanced. The essays derived from this bibliographic exercise were of the highest standard I have marked. Most of the students then went on to honors and postgraduate work. The aim is for teachers to create a scaffold for learning and to slow the research process, to create time for reflection and planning.

Google has increased the accessibility of websites, transforming the landscape of digital information into a manageable formation.[5] It also encourages sound bite solutions that are not researched or theorized. In such an environment, we have to ask how to encourage intellectual rigor in an edutainment landscape. Google makes searching for information more democratic, but it is also demeaning of the scholarship involved in considered interpretation and research. Google is the Internet equivalent of celebrity magazines and reality television. There are important questions to address about the relationship between technology, public policy and citizen activism.

Info Seek

There are consequences for relying on shortcuts for news, information and opinion. Speed searching blurs the distinction between data, information and knowledge. The human mind must shape arbitrary facts into creative and interpretative ideas. Unfortunately, life is not a giant game of Trivial Pursuit ready to be won. Attention needs to be placed on theories of knowledge and how they are built on mechanisms of classifying, organizing and storing information. Through the convergence of technology, communication and entertainment, we lose the capacity to evaluate material. There is an abundance of information, but what is scarce is the right information in an appropriate time and place. For information to be valuable, it must be placed in context.

Evaluating the quality of web and print sources requires training and skill development. Often forgotten is the rigorous refereeing process that formulates the production process for books and articles. While some material on the web is refereed, generally the pieces are short and the arguments less developed. The proliferation of homepages, where banal individual details have a potentially wide digital audience, transforms our ability to judge, rank and assess relevance and significance.

Student users must approach web searching as a process of thought and consideration. Two words in Google are not an endpoint of the research process. Before entering google.com, there is a series of issues to consider:

1. What is the most important concept, theory or thesis in the search?
2. Identify keywords emerging from this theory.
3. Ponder synonyms and plurals.
4. Read the FAQ and the instructions for the search engine.
5. Prepare a research logic.
6. Refine and redefine the search; repeat the process if necessary.

Such a process is effective and efficient. Planning for searches creates electronic and intellectual expectations, and a capacity to find the right information beyond the wayward and misleading. It also commences critical thinking and interpretation before slamming into an information glut. This rational and ordered approach to information management is distinct from the random, emotive and conversational mode of searching through Google. Finding old high school friends through Google is fine. Conducting research for high school using the same method is inappropriate. The key is not how many hits are returned from the search, but how many are relevant, relatively non-partisan, current and live sites.

While web use for academic research is increasing, the quality of sources varies tremendously. Libraries and librarians are so important because they punctuate the information landscape, theorizing and controlling enthusiasm and confusion. No search engine is an intrinsic purveyor of truth. Yet Cerise Oberman realized that:

> In today's libraries [...] the real problems seem to centre around what is almost an ideological commitment to the computer. Today it is not unusual to have students assert, to teacher and librarian alike, that the computer has given them all the

information they need. There is something subtle at work here. The nature of the computer has convinced students that all relevant information on any topic can be retrieved solely through this medium. (1996)

Students are confusing quality and quantity of information. The triviality of the material found means that we too often become enthused with access to information and do not ask why we needed access to information in the first place. The key skill that most of us need to learn, which is facilitated by the expertise of librarians, is how to manage and balance print and electronic resources. Collection management is even more important in an Internet-mediated environment than it is outside the digitized realm. Richard Sayers realized that "our challenge is to convince the techno-faddists and economic rationalists that Google is still not yet one of the seven wonders of the modern world" (2003: 410). It is rare for technologies to destroy each other. Google is a disruptive, not destructive, technology.[6] Ink jet printers, Linux and Google are the best examples of niche-marketed technologies shapeshifting into mainstream cultural formations. Newspapers, radio, television and the Internet coexist. Books did not die with the Internet. Offices and schools are not paperless. Google will only be one stop in a long journey through research and scholarship.

The Internet is not a library. This is a dangerous metaphor. The main characteristic of a library, the organization of knowledge into preservable categories, has hardly left a trace on the Internet. A catalog of accessible holdings is not a collection of numbers, but a sequence of ideas. This ordering is not an archaic relic of the analog age, but holds a social function: to allow users to search and assess information and build larger relationships to broader subjects, theories and ideas. While the web may appear to remove the physicality of information, we are yet to make this leap conceptually. The digital library will be determined as much by research training, database instruction, computer support and document delivery as the availability of search engines. Digital libraries will integrate documents, media, content and training. The expertise of librarians can support new modes of reading, writing and communicating, integrating and connecting discovery, searches, navigation and the appropriateness of diverse resources.

Divergent media encourage particular methods of accessing information. Books can be flicked through just as a hypertext link can be jumped, but electronic information encourages a smash and grab style of reading, rather than a smoother, more reflexive engagement. The key for teachers and librarians is to show students how to use divergent modes of reading and research. Through databases, students can read PDFs of documents we would never find on the shelves of a library. However, students must also learn the skill of reading, chewing, spitting out and reingesting difficult writing and monographs. Such reading is difficult to accomplish on the screen. With dense historical description and high theory, the reading must be done slowly and returned to, the reader drifting along with the sensuality of the words, so that reflexive meanings may emerge. The materiality of searching, the evocative potential of engaging with an exciting array of prospective sources, is still a significant part of an intellectual journey.

Being Literate

Information literacy is a foundation for academic success and must marinate all areas of curricula. This continuous learning environment is not determined by and through technology. Actually, some of the best modes of teaching do not begin with the presentation of information. The error of Internet-mediated teaching is the premise that education can be reduced to questions of content. Actually, we probably learn as much through the form of delivery as the content. Motivation levels for computer-based drills are frequently low. Teaching form rather than content allows students to be active participants in the academic process. The political pressures that shape our educational discourse need to be shared in an open and clear way with our students. This will create a framework for relevant and socially just information literacy pedagogy.

What lessons are we teaching our students by stressing Internet-based education as being flexible and convenient? Think about all the important lessons that we have learnt in our lives. These significant moments in our intellectual journeys were not easy or convenient and did not fit flexibly into our lifestyles. The lessons that mean the most are the ones that we worked for, the ones which were difficult, time consuming and arduous. Creating good writing, for example, is passionately troubling, precise and pedantic. It is the result of intense research, thought, care and endless drafting. It is not convenient or flexible. By cutting and pasting our way through culture, we are robbing students of skills in self-mastery: the capacity to fail, self-correct and then succeed.

As our first lesson in schools and universities, we must teach, test and re-teach how to assess the quality of all information, including Internet information. I ask that students consider five preliminary questions when selecting source material:

1. Who authored the information?
2. What expertise does the writer have to comment?
3. What evidence is used to assemble and confirm the argument?
4. What genre is the document: investigative journalism, academic paper, polemic?
5. Is the site funded by an institution? Does this funding have a consequence for their presentation of data?

Asking students to answer these questions is a way to limit the free range of searching on the Internet. They must pause, reflect and think. These questions create a recognition that finding information is not synonymous with understanding information. Without such critical pauses, the inclusion of the Internet in the school and university curriculum may ensure access to information, but does not promote the development of critical thinking, high-quality writing and innovative interpretations. Importantly, Google's popularity does not facilitate or encourage the discipline and structure that many of our students require. The technology itself is not to blame; rather, the poor funding of schools and universities, and the low credibility granted to teachers and librarians, is at fault.

The time has come for some honesty. David Garson, courageously, admitted that "outstanding lecturers will probably always outperform web-based methods of instruction when it comes to attracting and holding student interest" (1998). We need research into how the Internet has impacted—perhaps destructively—on student learning, motivation, retention, writing and reading. Instead, techno-enthusiasts such as Rob Phillips have stated that "Computer-Mediated Communications [...] create the richness of an on-campus experience for off-campus students" (2002). The computer is not equivalent to the classroom. It does not create the "richness" of the best pedagogy, but perpetuates the thickness of the information glut. The constructivist approach to learning, which is the grammar of the techno-enthusiasts, assumes that learners can build their own knowledge. However, students need to be taught how to learn, write and interpret. They require an apparatus and structure through which to develop methods of thinking, reading and writing. Cuban, in his book *Oversold and Underused*, stated the problem clearly: "there have been no advances (measured by higher academic achievement) [...] over the last decade that can be confidently attributed to broader access to computers" (2001: 178). Similarly, a four-year government-funded study in the United Kingdom found that " 'infusing' schools with technology had failed to improve student achievement" (Fielding 2003). Such a statement is no surprise to those of us who have actually taught real students in real classrooms in the last 10 years, rather than merely administering budgets. Students are reading less, writing with less fluency and are losing the capacity to interpret the words of others. Many students know about the Internet. We need to teach them what these signs and structures mean, who is left out, and what is to be gained and lost through digitization. Phrases like flexible learning suggest that students have a right to learn flexibly, rather than with discipline, motivation, respect and care. Some students do not learn best through flexibility. They need structure, enthusiasm and energy to trigger a passionate path through learning.

The skills required to evaluate retrieved information from the web must be taught. The difficulty is that information, through Google, is seen to be both abundant and cheap. The abilities required to assess this information are more difficult and costly to obtain. Too often libraries are a forgotten part of the educational experience, being sidelined as an inelegant appendage, rather than the throbbing, sparking cranium of schools, universities and civic life. In an era of ideologues claiming the terrain of truth, students and librarians require time to sort through spin and lies.

9/11: Beyond the Numbers

The seething anger of our era requires the cool, clear realization that the market is not going to save us and that a shareholding citizenry offers few entrées into social justice. Community borders of otherness and difference have calcified through the events of September 11. Our emotional responses to those burning buildings means that it is difficult to critically evaluate how these events have been represented. Three thousand people lost their lives on that dreadful day. But 250,000 lost their lives in the Bosnia conflict, and up to 1 million people were killed in 1994 during the genocide in Rwanda. Every day 24,000 people die from malnutrition and 30,000 children under five die from preventable causes (UNDP 2001: 9). However, the symbolic power of September 11—the destruction of the World Trade Centre, as the embodiment of neoliberalism, and the Pentagon, the headquarters of the US military—grants it a resonance beyond the sheer number of deaths.

News has changed since that horrifying day. During the last 20 years, foreign bureaus for news gathering have closed and the number of minutes dedicated to foreign affairs has declined. Until September 11, 2001, foreign stories in the United States occupied half the time they did in 1989 (Fleeson 2003: 33). Currently, reporters are flown into nations and cities at short notice, creating a crisis orientation to foreign affairs reportage. This lack of global content creates an inward focus to American news. Jennifer Lawson, a Washington, DC–based independent producer, stated that:

> We as a nation were so surprised by what happened with 9/11. Had we known more about how others view us and our policies, I don't think we would have been so surprised. We get very little coverage from Indonesia or the Philippines, and almost no backgrounders, even though there are links to al Qaeda-type organizations. The news is always crisis-oriented, and then it drops off the radar screen. Even our coverage of Afghanistan dropped off (Lawson in Fleeson 2003: 35)

Fox News Channel solved the problem of few foreign bureaus by reducing non-American news stories and the literacies to understand them. The station chose to be different from CNN or BBC World, being colloquial, ideological, insular and anchor heavy. Through such a filter, a preemptive war on Iraq was not only waged, but also justified.

In such a context, the Internet offers alternative sources and ideas, but also greater space for ideologues to propagate a message. It allows fast, frequently unchecked rumor to gain currency over verified and credible journalism. There are consequences for relying on research shortcuts for news and information. This sound bite culture has a major impact on the caliber of political debate and our students' ability to conduct research. In 1968, the televisual political sound bite was 43 seconds, which reduced to 9.8 seconds in 1988 and 7 seconds by 1996 (Fisher 2002: 22). The consequence of this cultural shift is that few public figures speak in full sentences anymore. A detailed argument is redundant. Slogans become facts. Ponder these phrases:

- Weapons of Mass Destruction
- Coalition of the Willing
- Regime Change
- Axis of Evil
- Asylum Seekers
- Pacific Solution
- War against Terror

Ideological baggage is carried by these phrases, so that alternative trajectories are blocked. What was the Australian problem that caused a "Pacific Solution"? If there is an Axis of Evil, is there a parallel Axis of Good? What is the Coalition willing to do? Technology has altered news values, with the World Wide Web encouraging an instantaneous proliferation of gossip. The reduction in time between information availability and the creation of a news narrative formulates a "rip and read" mentality, challenging standards of newsworthiness and accuracy. This is information that students are citing through Google searches. Living in a time of celebrities and not intellectuals creates a culture that validates Google hits ahead of scholarly citations. Speaking to people as consumers rather than citizens reforms news along commercial lines. Tabloidization transforms news into entertainment, making public relations guidelines more valuable than journalistic ethics.

The attacks on the World Trade Centre and the Pentagon changed international politics. These symbolically powerful images are seared in our minds. But how September 11 changed education is a question asked less frequently. Not only have vocabularies and literacies shifted, but also so has our capacity to interpret, debate and think. Definitions of terrorism are determined within the dictionary of the definer. Terrorism challenged the sovereignty and solidity of "us" and equally solidified "them." Great military power after "winning" the Cold War did not end vulnerability or threat. September 11 demonstrated that the primary concepts through which international relations are run—such as core and periphery, first and third worlds—no longer function. Such a demarcation of good and evil leads to slogan answers to difficult questions. The closures of language, like Axis of Evil, Operation Enduring Freedom and Freedom-Loving People, fabricate a solid enemy, rather than a vague or unsubstantiated threat to security. George W. Bush was clear on such a division. On November 6, 2001, he stated on CNN that "you are either with us or against us." The likes of al-Qaeda are anti-globalizing and transnational organizations, operating between the spaces of nations, cities and citizens. Their ideas move as freely as email, and their financing follows already established pathways of international capital. Instead of affirming good and evil, or us and them, we need more subtle approaches and methods to understand the networks of anger, resistance and hate that render binary oppositions both inadequate and redundant. Anne-Marie Slaughter stated that the war against terror is "all about language" (2002: footnote 17). Focusing on those images from September 11 and a fear for the future means that we are less likely to ask questions about the causes and context for the attacks. The discourse of terrorism as currently framed ensures that *anything* is valid or appropriate if it is countering terrorism. Terrorism organizes social relationships, creating floating and unsatisfying solutions to difficult problems. Meanings do change through time: Nelson Mandela and Menachem Begin have both been termed terrorists and later statesmen.[7] It is more productive to avoid reproducing easy definitions of terrorism. Instead, we must probe how the vocabulary, language and ideologies of terrorism function.

Hugh Mackay stated that "one of the best disguised escapes from anxiety is the escape into information" (1993: 226). We are a frightened people, scanned, surveyed, monitored and trapped. It is no surprise that we escape into Google with its transitory hits, rather than actually thinking about what has happened to celebrity and citizenship in the last five years. A major question is whether the web-based audience is more or less discriminating than television viewers. The development of 24-hour-a-day news services through cable TV means that audiences are splintering. Journalists are worried about dumbing down.[8] When journalists are worried about this, then educators and librarians need to be really concerned. The journalistic functions of filtering and synthesizing information are being sidelined. In news-gathering agencies, staff numbers are reduced, travel budgets are down and electronically sourced information has replaced that gathered through walking the beat. Investigative journalism, beyond the "Small Business Rips Off Battler" nonsense of too much current affairs programming, has almost ceased. If it happened now, Watergate would still only refer to a hotel, not the downfall of a president.

A computer is made up of hardware, software and data. It is a running system that requires a social system to give it meaning and context. Therefore, politics and ethics must be involved. Definitions of the real have real consequences. More attention should be placed on definitions. For example, one definition of the word "virtual" is "almost." Therefore, *virtual learning* is an odd combination of words. Teachers and librarians have to decide if almost is good enough for our students, our educational system and the nation.

Notes

1. AltaVista searches both the web and Usenet, but its interface is not open for the casual user. Complex searches are possible, but the options must be mastered.
2. Andrej Sorgo (2003: 315) has stated that "students who do not understand English encounter difficulties while looking for information on the Internet."
3. Russ Singletary (2003: 302) has referred to Google as facilitating "self-service Internet research."
4. Jana Ronan (2003: 46) has captured this research strategy, stated that "I often use Google for background information if I'm stumped, to help point me to the best proprietary database to search."
5. The use of manageable is intentional here. Frequently, in the research literature, the stress is on managing information, as if the Internet were an uncontrollable beast that needed to be tamed. Robert Weissberg (2003: 387) went so far as to state that "access to Google or

Yahoo can change everything—obstacles once judged too formidable to even attempt now become manageable."

6.   Tim Studt (2003: 7) described these disruptive formations as "new technologies that start off by targeting small, seemingly unprofitable market segments, but sometimes wind up taking over the entire marketplace."

7.   As Jenny Hocking suggested (2003: 361), "we need to acknowledge not only this discursive function of terrorism, but also that our understanding of terrorism is a fully mediated and constructed one."

8.   This argument runs counter to claims such as that made by Szymanski Sunal et al. (1998: 13), who stated that "inclusion of the Internet into the school curriculum will surely boost educational quality because of immediate access to information which could be readily incorporated into students' daily education."

Chapter 10

Learning through Critical Literacy: Why Google Is Not Enough

Bettina Fabos

There is a disturbing development on the information superhighway: most of the websites students now access for their projects are commercial (Ebersole 2005; Fabos 2004). This trend is exacerbated by the fact that students from junior high to university level conduct most of their research online. Students are consequently awash in commercial data, much of whose validity they do not question and much of which they plagiarize (Rainie & Hitlin 2005).

A heavily commercialized Internet, of course, is no accident. The Internet's backbone was privatized in 1995; since then, powerful business interests have continued to leverage large parts of the web toward commercial, not democratic purposes. The extensive public relations and advertising campaigns to get the Internet in schools (1995–1998) were not much more than a means to increase household connectivity and thus create a viable commercial platform (Fabos 2004; Stein unpublished). Commercial search engines, the web's most popular navigation tools, are perhaps the most egregious affront to the web's educational potential. They fly in the face of impartial knowledge gathering, which we tell our students is the goal of academic research. Due to the search engines' extraordinary and relatively recent success at generating keyword advertising sales, they (Google, Yahoo and MSN) have morphed into advertising conglomerates, bringing highly targeted audiences to their advertising clients. They are both the newest marketing strategy for advertisers, and some of the most used and trusted sites on the web. Consequently, search engines effectively betray the trust of users, most of whom still believe that the first two pages of a search's results list are the most relevant.

Meanwhile, students just want to search for "objective" information for most of their research projects. Not surprisingly they turn to commercial search engines for their ease, speed, and promise to provide "innovative, useful technologies that enable people to find, use, share, and expand knowledge" (Yahoo! Search 2005). But since commercial search engines have largely replaced libraries as a venue for college student research (Griffiths & Brophy 2005; Thompson et al. 2003), the educational promise of the web—as it is used today in our secondary and higher education classrooms—is not being realized. It should come as no surprise that commercial sites—shopping sites, corporate public relations pages, industry-supported think tanks and organizations, and even uncritical, pro-business government reports—easily find their way into students' fact-based research projects. Moreover, as search engines become more commercialized (as recent industry consolidation suggests), students will be accessing an increasingly limited array of information, not the "universe of knowledge" President Bill Clinton described in his 1997 State of the Union Address, which hyped the educational potential of the Internet.[1]

What I will argue in the next few pages is the following: if students are going to depend so much on the web, we need to go beyond teaching students how to critically evaluate web information, a typical response in the age of Internet commercialization. Students do need to understand the commercial exigencies of the web, and the fact that the medium is charged with social, political, and economic forces. But this is just the beginning. A more important move for educators is to steer students away from fact-based "objective" research projects (most often researched online) and toward projects that help students understand that all information (web-based and otherwise) is also charged with social, economic, and political contexts. To do this, educators must stop privileging the world of facts and "truth." We must teach our students ideological constructs to raise the bar on educational inquiry and information access. And we must give our students assignments that focus on the analysis of ideas, encouraging them, at the same time, to come up with their own ideas, and their own concrete ideologies.

Expand Webpage Evaluation

University educators often say they are appalled at student research: much of it plagiarized from online sources (Ercegovac & Richardson 2004; Wood 2004), much of it hapless and hurried and terrible. Block writes, "Teachers tell horror stories about students who actually believed satirical articles from *The Onion* and used them as evidence in term papers" (2002: 12). Professors and instructors typically blame student laziness and "the web" (it has replaced books!). They put plagiarism clauses in their syllabi and, if time allows (and they are adequately suspicious), they search the web for lifted paragraphs.

Educators have also begun to include webpage evaluation skills (also called information literacy) in their curriculums and requirements. This initiative has come from librarians, mostly, and to a lesser extent, high school and college English teachers as part of research paper units. In the hopes that students put more objective, trusted resources into their reports, librarians are increasingly teaching students (often during library orientations) what librarians do: judge sources (in this case websites) according to established criteria of authorship, accuracy, objectivity, currency, and coverage. By turning students into librarians, they surmise, they will enable them to weed out "untruthful" web content on a page-by-page basis. Typical teachings go like this: government sites (e.g., www.nih.gov) tend to objective; commercial sites (e.g. obesity.com) tend to want to sell you something in addition to offering often helpful information; home-built websites authored by individual people, especially those identified by a tilde (~) (e.g., www.uni.edu/~fabos), tend to be factually misleading or incredibly biased. Pages with grammatical errors, no dates, and strong opinions are especially suspected.

In this current discourse, webpage evaluation skills are often referred to as "critical thinking," an umbrella term that is loosely applied to a range of higher-order thinking skills involved in reading and producing texts. While critical thinking skills have long been applied to print texts, the general consensus among educators and librarians is that the web, with its many varied and incongruent resources, necessitates critical thinking skills above traditional research skills.

The single, dominant theory of new information literacy within this particular body of literature can thus be summarized as follows: students develop critical thinking skills by determining whether a web text is high quality and "truthful" or low quality and "not truthful." These skills, part of the liberal-humanist tradition, can then be translated to critically analyze other media. They also will lead to better student research papers, educators presume, because students will be able to select only those sources that are objective and therefore true.

As popular as these webpage evaluation strategies have recently become (and as admirable as these efforts to improve student research are), there are some immediate drawbacks. First, many students who have learned these critical thinking skills, it seems, cannot be bothered: evaluation takes too much time. Beginning in junior high, when they are looking up facts about tectonic plates and Maya Angelou, they are establishing their own evaluation shortcuts: a site is "good" depending on (a) how fast they can find the succinct fact or objective summary they are looking for, and (b) how sophisticated and accessible the design is—good design suggests time and effort were put into the site (Buschman & Warner 2005; Fabos 2004). By the time they reach college, most students are used to the idea that any fact will do so long as it *seems* correct. Indeed, fast facts, more often than not, easily satisfy the requirements of students' fact-based assignments.

Second, it appears that even students armed with webpage evaluation skills simply do not trust their ability to discern factual information on topics with which they are unfamiliar (Watson 2001). As such, they easily fall prey to the "credibility esthetic" of professionally crafted websites that appear as legitimate and objective as possible. Whether students care about the quality of their sources or not, current webpage evaluation criteria do little to prevent a student from thinking a public relations page with a well-crafted design and the esthetics of objectivity in place is valid and factual, especially when other like sites corroborate the information (Fabos 2004). Evidence also suggests that students are just fine with the results they are getting, rating their Internet research abilities highly. Meanwhile, a significant gap is appearing between their own evaluation of their research skills and the actual quality of their work (Buschman & Warner 2005).

With more classroom time spent on webpage evaluation, especially in secondary grades, most educators believe (or hope) that these drawbacks can be overcome. There is a third and even more significant drawback to webpage evaluation, however, which is drastically overlooked by current webpage evaluation practices: the entire web, at least the way students currently access it—via commercial search engines—is inherently biased from the outset. Commercial search engines stack the first two to three pages of their search results lists (the most "relevant" sites) with websites favoring commercial enterprise. Even Google, the only search engine not using paid placement strategies in its results lists (at least for now), is susceptible to commercial intrusion. As it bases its search algorithm on link relevance (the more links to a particular site, the more relevant it is), Google is a victim to the many websites that invest in schemes to increase the number of outside pages linking to them. Moreover, countless Search Engine Optimization (SEO) companies work around the clock trying (successfully) to crack and undermine Google's algorithm, a persistent problem for Google's engineers (Harmon 2004). Accordingly, students armed with webpage evaluation skills (i.e., those that choose to use them) can evaluate each particular site for its usefulness, but if they persist in seeing search engines as neutral navigation tools they are searching with blinders on, never approaching the possible breadth of a particular topic.

For these reasons, it is important to extend webpage evaluation practices to the entire web. Educators should begin to demystify search engines as the invincible tool for the information superhighway; they should show their students how search engine commercialism impedes the quest for impartial information. Critical discussions about search engines could begin by delineating the three different branches of the search engine industry, a discussion that would help students understand how small the search world really is, as follows:

1. *Directories* are often mistaken for search engines, but are nothing more than comparatively small databases that may or may not feed a search engine. Although librarians were the first to catalog sites into directories, Yahoo! developed the first commercial directory in 1994 by hiring numerous editors to compile webpages and place them into logical categories. The Yahoo! model was followed by other online directories like the Australian-based directory Looksmart, which launched in 1996. Another significant directory (especially to the search engine industry) is the Open Directory Project, which was launched in 1998. This enormous noncommercial endeavor, constructed entirely by a global army of volunteers (or as they are referred to, "net-citizens"), is by far the largest directory on the web and continues to grow in size every day. This directory is the primary database used by all search engine providers.

2. *Search engine providers* (there are only a handful—Google, Teoma, Inktomi, AlltheWeb, and AltaVista) power most searches on the web. These companies own and manage web indexes, huge databases of webpages, and have developed complicated algorithms for searching them. Such companies offer impartial searches (as opposed to commercial searches, as given below) based on their own unique formulae of site relevance. They syndicate their services to search portals.

3. *Commercial search providers* (e.g., Overture, Google Adwords) manage advertiser indexes. They broker commercial sponsorships for web search results and, like search engine providers, syndicate their services

to search portals. Their services include sponsored links (which appear on top, below, and on the sides of search results lists; paid placement links (which appear within search results lists); and paid inclusion links (which appear somewhere in every search conducted on a given search portal).

4. *Search portals* (e.g., Yahoo!, Ask Jeeves, Excite, AOL) are brand name portals powered by search engine providers *and* commercial search providers. Yahoo!, for example, is powered by both Inktomi (impartial searches) and Overture (commercial searches); CNN is powered by Google (impartial searches) and Overture (commercial searches). Sometimes search portals are search engine providers themselves, as in the case of Google and AltaVista.

Even if there are many "search portals," there are only a handful of search engine providers and commercial search providers. In fact, the search industry is similar to local radio, where dozens of stations may exist, but two or three companies are behind nearly all of them, or similar to the soda industry, where there are seemingly many soft drinks, but most of them are produced by Coke or Pepsi. Search portals mix and match between various impartial and commercial services to come up with "unique" search results, but in reality they are not unique at all.

As the search technology is currently the most profitable area of the web, it is also important to understand the recent consolidation within the industry. For example, to enter the search business, Yahoo! released its own search technology, but more significantly, purchased one of the top five search engine providers, Inktomi, in 2002 (abandoning its relationship with the syndicated search engine provider, Google). A few months later, the giant commercial search provider, Overture, bought *two* of the top five search engine providers, AlltheWeb and AltaVista. This deal enabled Overture to better influence the advertising within AlltheWeb's and AltaVista's "impartial" syndicated searches. Then Yahoo!, not to be one-upped by Overture, actually purchased Overture a month later. This purchase allowed Yahoo! ownership of *three* of the top five search engine providers (Inktomi, AlltheWeb, *and* AltaVista), as well as the top commercial search provider (Overture). With these deals, Yahoo! has become a massive media company. The only search brand in direct competition with Yahoo! is Google, which remains the most trusted search engine worldwide (and for good reason). With the recent release of its proprietary search engine provider in 2005 (after a failed attempt to acquire Google in 2003), MSN is poised to become dominant player number three.

The industry has thus experienced massive consolidation, with Yahoo!, Google, and now MSN morphing into media and advertising conglomerates. As a result of this consolidation, the number of paths students can use to access online information is minimized. Students should be aware that the commercial search engines they typically use when doing their fact-finding missions are intentionally limiting. As Roy Solomon of Yahoo! Shopping said in 2003, "Search is becoming the most efficient way for consumers to find products" (1), meaning that search engines are more concerned about consumer information than they are about gearing online information toward academic research.

If students critically evaluate the search engine industry, they should also learn about alternatives to commercial search engines, such as open source search engine development (e.g., Nutch at www.nutch.org) or subject gateways—web portals that rely on human beings to categorize and aggregate "significant" websites. Students tend to avoid subject gateways because of the extra work involved in typing key words a second time. They also do not like straying too far from the comfort of a search engine's results page (Fabos 2004). However, subject gateways, often compiled by experts within a particular topic area, can be goldmines of rich data and otherwise marginalized information. The National Science Digital Archive and INFOMINE, for example, compile and categorize comprehensive science websites. The Internet Public Library, based at the University of Michigan, has one of the best online newspaper collections on the web. And the Library of Congress has created Portals to the World (links to global resources) and has begun various digital archiving projects to put incredible primary resources online. Even more subject gateway activity, heavily funded by government initiatives, is occurring in Europe (including the United Kingdom) and Australia.

Britain's Resource Discovery Network (RDN), for example, is generously supported by the Higher Education Funding Councils for England, Scotland, and Wales. Universities throughout the United Kingdom are responsible for the growth and updating of particular subject areas: ALTIS (University of Birmingham) deals with Hospitality, Leisure, Sport, and Tourism; BIOME (University of Nottingham) covers Health and Life Sciences; EEVL (Heriot Watt University in Edinburgh) handles Engineering, Mathematics, and Computing; GEsource (the Consortium of Academic Libraries in Manchester) is concerned with Geography and Environment; Humbul (Oxford University) is taking on Humanities; PSIgate (also located within the Consortium of Academic Libraries in Manchester) manages Physical Sciences; and SOSIG (University of

Bristol) is responsible for Social Sciences, Business, and Law. Each of these university hubs is amassing thousands of "authoritative" academic web resources on its assigned subject area, with hundreds of active content experts from over 70 educational and research organizations contributing web links.

The RDN initiative is actually only a small part of the UK's larger Electronic Libraries (eLib) Programme, which is lavishing funds on academic libraries and institutions to digitize special collections, including theses and all forms of academic research. "The main remit is to provide a body of tangible, electronic resources and services for UK Higher Education," an introduction to the eLib Programme reads, "and to affect [sic] a cultural shift toward the acceptance and use of said resources and services in place of more traditional information storage and access methods" (eLib 2005). The United States has not reached this level of coordination because its universities and colleges are either state or private entities (hence more discrete), and because the various independent subject gateway initiatives are grant-, not contract-based, allowing for more creativity and innovation, perhaps, but also less consolidation and communication.

Perhaps the most exciting trend in the world of subject gateways, however, is a movement that will make subject gateways look and feel very much like search engines. The new buzzword among subject gateway developers is cross-searching: the ability to search across many subject gateway platforms at the same time. This new searching method looks and feels a lot like a search engine. Users type in key words and dynamically search (librarians like the word "harvest") across hundreds, even thousands, of different subject gateways located all over the web. If search engines crawl over an index, cross-searching tools harvest a database collective—a collective that could serve commercial or educational purposes. This technology is revolutionary because it has huge implications for the comprehensiveness and relevance of search results. In fact, a user (let us say a student) could enter a search engine-like environment, access thousands of academic sites, and not come across a single commercial entity. The OAIster project (www.oaister.org) at the University of Michigan is a good example of many content archives coming together under one searchable interface. "Our goal," project developers write, "is to create a collection of freely available, previously difficult-to-access, academically oriented digital resources that are easily searchable by anyone" (*OAIster* 2005).

Another development worth mentioning is the emergence of collaboratively built web resources. Ibiblio, for example, draws upon over 1000 volunteer contributors who tend to specialize in a particular field. As ibiblio director Paul Jones explains, "We think specialists in their fields understand what they are doing better than librarians do. We collect the best people—and their work" (Personal communication, June 13, 2003). Another example is the Merlot Project, which relies upon a community of volunteer professors to judge and advance web content. Each contributing scholar manages a subject area, and both annotates and rates selected websites. The wiki movement ("wiki" means "quick" in Hawaiian) is another fast-growing trend for online collaboration. The open source movement involves a social software that enables any user to edit and build a given webpage within a wiki site. On collaborative wiki sites, such as the citizen-built encyclopedia "Wikipedia," many different experts and interested citizens build on a plethora of topics. The volunteer contributors edit (mostly to improve) entries in an atmosphere of trust and public goodwill, and all former entries are archived so a user can see how a certain topic area has evolved. While wikis can work as interoffice collaboration tools or as online personal organization pages, these sites are also places where topic links can be stored, categorized, and harvested. In other words, they can be places where suppressed gems of information (i.e., on sites ignored by commercial search engines) can be found.

These librarian, academic, and public movements to organize and sustain valuable web information are leading to a web research environment far more eclectic and extensive than what search engines are promising for education, but only if students know about them. By 2005, the subject gateway movement, the related digital archiving movement, cross-searching tools, and collaboratively conceived public resources had not yet reached the mainstream (Willinsky 2005).

Approach Assignments Differently

It is likely that a more concrete understanding of the commercialized web, and a knowledge of other online databases and searching systems, will improve students' research projects. Another area that needs attention, however, is the very assignment that leads students to the web in the first place. In addressing student research practices, a growing number of educators (myself included) argue that the nature of information students search for is just as important as the way they do their searching. In other words, it is the assignments, not students' laziness and/or their lack of webpage evaluation skills, that are behind so much poor-quality student work; it is the fact-finding mission itself (online or not) and the constant quest for objective information (Block 2002; Salpeter 2003).

A different approach to assignments—referred to by some as "critical literacy"—asks students to work with opinions, not facts (e.g., Kapitzke 2001; Luke 2000; Semali 2000; Willinsky 1998).[2] As critical literacy scholars argue, facts are malleable, and certain facts are necessarily more privileged than others within a particular social, economic, and political context. Rather than asking students to write a paper or design a project based on "true" facts gleaned from various objective sources, critical literacy scholars suggest that students should understand why and how certain information can be advanced as truth. Thus, students can learn how to critically understand all information, whether it is the corporate press release that overwhelms an "objective" news story, or a lonely blog that rails against popular culture. In Allan Luke's (2000) words:

> The aim of critical literacy is a classroom environment where students and teachers together work to (a) see how the worlds of texts work to construct their worlds, their cultures, and their identities in powerful, often overtly ideological ways; and (b) use texts as social tools in ways that allow for a reconstruction of these same worlds. (453)

Interpreting a multiplicity of texts (ideas), valuing this multiplicity and understanding its contextual complexity, is to engage, quite literally, in democracy.

The logic for assignments that take students in this direction is quite sound: students searching for opinions, not facts, would be less likely to plagiarize. Students actively engaged in constructing a continuum, with more critical and less passive relationships with their sources, would be forming their own ideas as much as synthesizing those of others. The difficulty in having students weigh opinions, not facts, is that students have little experience at thinking ideologically and are hard pressed to place information they find on any kind of spectrum. When college students say they are apolitical (something one hears quite often in the classroom, and sees quite often in low rates of political participation) it is because, in part, they are not taught to think politically. These are typical comments from my own students, who are mostly sophomores and juniors in college, about their ideological identity (which they narrowly define as concerned with government and politics):

> I have to admit that I am not very big into politics or the workings of our government.

> I'm embarrassed to say how uninformed I am.

> I have never considered myself a political person. I can't tell you the difference in political parties in the senate, or what the senate is.

> As my first statement I would just like to say, I hate politics. I hate government. I could[n't] care less who is in office.

> My personal view on government and politics isn't very positive, nor is it a very strong viewpoint. I cannot seem to get into or even understand any part of politics no matter what I do. I know people need leaders and rules, but frankly, it all bores me.

Ideological debate to them most often means confusing arguments between the two dominant US political parties, or discussions about a vaguely present government. What it should mean, far more generally, is the open, rational discussion and consideration of all ideas, not just the ones deemed relevant by mainstream Washington, DC politics. A first step is to help students recognize what an ideological continuum is. The labels of "conservative," "liberal," "republican," and "democrat" are limiting because they have come to represent so many things that they have been rendered almost meaningless. At the same time, these terms can also elicit very strong stereotypical reactions from people. Instead, it is more helpful to get students to understand many perspectives along a broad political and economic continuum (e.g., libertarian, radical right, neoconservative, moderate republican, moderate liberal, etc.), and the influence of capitalism that shapes so much communication and information. It is also helpful to start with an issue that defies the liberal/conservative or republican/democrat dichotomy—a topic such as "obesity" or "the FCC ruling on media ownership"—and to model for students what an investigation into various ideological positions looks like.

Researching Obesity

I recently explored with my students the topic of "obesity," which has lately become a major issue both nationally and globally and, as such, a common news topic as health studies are released and new anti-obesity drugs are created. But the discourse defining *causes* of and *solutions* to obesity can be twisted into a wide range of positions about obesity, and these positions can be arranged on an ideological continuum.

I asked my students to analyze a number of documents discussing obesity. Some read excerpts from books such as *Fat Land* (Greg Critser), *Fast Food Nation* (Eric Schlosser), *Food Politics* (Marion Nestle), and *The Fat of the Land* (Michael Fumento); some read magazine articles by writer Michael Pollan. Others read a special issue on obesity in the business magazine *Forbes*. We also looked at current newspaper stories and TV documentaries, such as an ABC News special report on obesity and a *20/20* report on "healthy" fast food; TV advertisements for fast food; and public relations materials from corporations like Kraft Foods. Finally, we looked at various websites, such as those belonging to the Centers for Disease Control (a government site) and the Center for Science in the Public Interest (an advocacy group).

Then we began charting ideas—the causes for obesity, the proposed solutions to the epidemic—on a spectrum. Many texts I chose fell on the "anti-food industry" side, blaming specific practices within the fast food, soda, and snack industries for the epidemic: increasingly intense (and deceptive) advertising, marketing, and public relations campaigns, especially those geared toward children; increased portion sizes; and misleading labeling practices. Other texts targeted the larger environment created by hypercapitalism, and argued that public spaces (sidewalks, parks) and school activities (physical education and health education) have diminished in support of private enterprise, and that a general reduction of tax support in schools has led to more commercial deals promoting soft drinks and snack food, and hence more obesity. These texts also supported the idea that video games and television promote less exercise (and provide a venue for more junk food and soda advertising). Other texts presented a macro argument, blaming huge government subsidies of the corn industry since the 1960s and the massive corporate lobbying that led to these subsidies. Cheap corn, they argued, has enabled cheaper meat and sugar substitutes (corn syrup), and has allowed the fast food industry to proliferate. In general, texts that blamed the food industry or corporate enterprise called for industry regulation, taxation, lawsuits, and campaign finance reform as solutions to the obesity epidemic. While most of them did not disqualify individual responsibility as a means for curbing obesity rates, the crux of their solutions involved massive policy change.

Another set of texts, these falling on the opposite side of the spectrum, were supportive of industry, and blamed individuals—their lack of motivation, education, and their unfortunate genes—for the obesity epidemic. Many of the writers were "researchers" or physicians who advocated personal responsibility via intense exercise regimes (e.g., Jenny Craig), diet pills (e.g. Redux, Meridia, newer hormone-based drugs), and medical interventions (e.g., stomach reduction) as a solution to obesity. Regarding the condition like a treatable disease, they also advocated support networks and the need to educate society about the difficulties and discrimination faced by obese people. Some texts, often written by the formerly obese, called for a softening of public attitudes toward people with this disease. It did not take long for my students to discover that this perspective, personal responsibility, was also propagated by big business, especially the food and soft drink industries. By stressing individualism and self-reliance (values that are constantly sold to Americans through many commercial outlets) and by de-emphasizing collective action, these texts, such as the *Forbes* special issue on obesity, put the social problem of obesity squarely on the shoulders of the obese individual. They especially advocated exercise programs (i.e., exercise more, buy more processed food), diet pills and surgery—solutions that actually spawn a very profitable diet and wellness industry. Indeed, keeping people obese (and blaming them for it) is very good for corporate well-being.

Other than encouraging people to take personal responsibility for their weight gains, the business sector advocated two industry-directed solutions to the obesity "problem": flavor technology and intensified public relations and marketing efforts. Flavor technology is the science of creating foods that are fatty or sweet, but only in taste. These fat-free foods would fall under the "new and improved" label, so the industry would not have to create new brands, or significantly alter their packaging. Moreover, fatty-tasting fat-free processed foods would also encourage people to buy even more helpings because they would not feel guilty about eating too much fat, a win-win scenario. Another industry response was to suggest ways of changing people's perceptions rather than the products or other industry practices. This means public relations and marketing efforts that involve hyping the "healthy" aspects of fast food. For example, at the time we did our analysis, we watched numerous television commercials, such as those from KFC, that showed actors talking about the fast food they were eating being so healthy it caused them to lose weight. We looked at slickly produced public relations magazines sent to households by Kraft, Inc., that offered cooking tips for healthy eating—all using Kraft products. We also noted other industry public relations responses: the sponsoring of exercise programs and get-fit events, and the lobbying of public officials to make sure regulation or industry critique does not happen.

The most interesting part of our analysis occurred when we began studying "objective" news reports about the obesity epidemic. For example, we barely found any articles implicating advertising, the fast food industry, or corn subsidies in the mainstream media. Instead we collected a plethora of articles about new drugs, new surgery techniques, and the new industry strategies to highlight the "healthy" aspects of fast food. Similarly, an ABC special called *Fat Like Me* documented a family determined to lose more weight (personal responsibility) and a teenage girl who dressed up in a fat suit and tested high school students' attitudes toward her obesity. ABC's solution, exercise and be nicer to fat people, very much aligned with the industry perspective. Another high-profile obesity report, this time on *20/20*, investigated the "healthy" foods promoted by most fast food chains. The report seemed to be leading to a critique of fast food marketing deception (e.g., the salads are expensive and the dressings contain more fat than a burger), but then morphed into an endorsement of the healthy items on the menu.

Table 10.1 helped students make sense of the continuum of information about obesity.

Table 10.1: Obesity discourse: anti-industry versus pro-industry

Anti-industry	Pro-industry
Causes for obesity	
• Individuals and the environment	• Individuals
• Laziness (to a lesser extent)	• Laziness
• Genes (to a lesser extent)	• Genes
• Fast food/snack/soda industries Industrial corn production/government corn subsidies/corn syrup	
• Serving sizes	
• Advertising/marketing	
Solutions for obesity	
Personal responsibility (learn to cook)	Personal responsibility (exercise)
Exercise	Drugs/surgery
Regulation of food industry (banning advertisements aimed at children; regulating labeling)	Flavor technology Public relations
Banning of corn syrup subsidies	
Suing the fast food industry	
Increased taxes (more parks, etc.)	
Campaign finance reform	

With these kinds of examples, we were able to embark on a critique of our media system, which is supported by enormously wealthy commercial enterprise. We could easily demonstrate, through our study of this topic, that instead of well-argued accounts of the many aspects of the obesity issue, the US news media consistently framed stories in ways that did not implicate their sponsors. Students would not have been able to critique these news reports, and their obvious bias toward business, had we not outlined our obesity spectrum earlier. Indeed, we enjoyed a boisterous critique of the word "researcher" in most of the news articles we analyzed, because it was clear that these objective-sounding scientists and analysts were really paid by private enterprise to produce and examine certain drugs, flavor molecules, or surgery techniques.

By sorting through these ideas and assigning them to ideological poles, students certainly expand their educational horizons. They can appreciate how politicized a topic like obesity is, and how ineluctably tied it is to our economic system. They can understand how commercial journalism practices play into the obesity positions taken by business, and they can understand how an epidemic may be of great concern from a public perspective, but enormously profitable from a business perspective. Taxation, regulation, and even the difficult-to-digest phrase "campaign finance reform" can become clearer as a result of this kind of analysis, and this can help students understand many other issues far beyond obesity. Campbell et al. (2006) refer to this kind of discussion as the critical process, and make the distinction between information and knowledge:

> *Information* in the form of news facts, and *knowledge* about a complex social process such as a national election are not the same thing. The critical process stresses the subtle distinctions between amassing information and becoming knowledgeable, or attaining media [critical] literacy. (32)

Knowledge Is Out There
(But It Won't Be Found on a Commercial Search Engine)

To some educators (e.g., Burbules & Callister Jr. 2000; Mather 1996; Salpeter 2003), the obvious medium for this sort of ideological investigation or assignment is the World Wide Web—the "universe of knowledge," the host of "incongruent resources," the tool students turn to first for most of their college and high school projects anyway (Rainie et al. 2002). Salpeter (2003), for example, recommends that students find point-counterpoint websites to understand numerous points of view:

> you could challenge students to do their own research to find point-counterpoint sites on such topics as the effects of television viewing on children or the advantages and disadvantages of a diet high in carbohydrates—or any other controversy that ties in with a current curriculum topic. As each site is located, students can summarize the key points being made and identify which ones directly contradict what they have learned elsewhere. Then it's time to debate what is the "truth." Which point of view is more popular? Does that make it more believable? Who created each site, and what reasons

might that individual or organization have for espousing a particular point of view? Are they simply stating their opinion, or is there evidence that they are distorting or hiding information to make their case? (7)

In Burbules and Callister Jr.'s words, a critically literate assessment of Internet material uses discussions about misinformation, malinformation, messed-up information, and mostly useless information to highlight and reflect upon the procedures and criteria by which people identify information as "mis," "mal," "messed-up," or "mostly useless" (2000: 117).

But once again, if students investigate online obesity via commercial search engines, they will be given a narrow, corporate scope, not the rich material we gleaned from the variety of sources described above. Our own search on Google using the word "obesity" revealed, predictably, over 3 million hits. The first 50 websites in the search results offered what seemed to be a plethora of informed, objective resources: the American Obesity Association, the Centers for Disease Control, the National Health Institute, the International Obesity Task Force, the North American Association for the Study of Obesity, the International Journal of Obesity, and medical forums such as "Obesity Online." These sites, or pages from within these sites, accounted for 29 of the 50 leading sites on the search results lists, and demonstrated the huge amount of redundancy evident in most Internet searches. It is also important to note that of the first 50 sites on the list, 21 (nearly half) were commercial pages advertising obesity drugs, surgery options, and other "treatments" for the disease. These were most certainly the results of search engine marketing and brokered contextual links. The professional organizational and government websites would undoubtedly pass any student's objectivity radar. However, armed with the ideological foundation we were able to establish above, our search through the many articles and reports on these sites demonstrated that, as with "objective" mainstream news media reports, they hardly challenged the industry take on obesity. Personal responsibility and medical treatments loomed large as the most practical solutions (treatments) to the epidemic (disease).

Why is this? Because beyond the many commercial advertisements inundating our search results list, Google gave us the most popular views on the obesity topic. And in the world outside of Google, the most popular views typically are not the dissenting views. Indeed, Google gives us a world much like the mainstream news media, where commercially controlled and industry-sanctioned positions dominate, and dissent is marginalized. That does not mean that dissenting opinions are not valid, and they could be the best take on an issue. But if they are marginalized in the rest of the web, they will also be marginalized on Google. In our typical one-word Google search, nowhere could a student locate, for example, the webpage for the Center of Science for the Public Interest, The Commercialism in Education Research Unit, or Commercial Alert, all organizations which offer valuable dissenting opinions on the dominant obesity ideology. It is clear that the web is not the "host of so many incongruent sources" that many educators (and students) believe it to be. Google alone will not give users a full range of opinions unless they know how to search them out, and have a pretty good idea, before a search, what the range of opinions is that they are looking for. Like all mass media (and unlike public libraries) the web is a commercial medium first and an information tool second.

Perhaps the most important critical literacy lesson, then, is to reorient students to the public library and books—the source of most of the dissenting opinions we found in conducting our obesity research. Where else but in public libraries, including those in public schools and universities, can we find books and independent magazines that lead us to truly in-depth, unconventional, and controversial subject matter? Even as the future of the Internet looks more and more like commercial television, it is the noncommercial government-supported public library and the noncommercial online archives associated with education that will promote open access to the full spectrum of ideas.

Notes

1. To learn more about the public relations effort (by US government and the telecommunications industry) to get schools wired, so as to build a critical mass for the commercial Internet to thrive, refer to Fabos (2004: 30–57).
2. To clarify: "information literacy" is another way to describe the webpage evaluation skills described above. "Critical thinking" or "critical reading" extends from the liberal-humanist tradition of truth-seeking and determining authorial intent. For a good discussion about the differences between "reading" and "critical literacy," see Cervetti et al. (2001).

III: Pedagogies of Resistance

Chapter 11

Liberal Arts and Distance Education: Can Socratic Virtue (ἀρετή) and Confucius' Exemplary Person (*junzi*) Be Taught Online?*

Charles Ess

Where is the Life we have lost in living?
Where is the wisdom we have lost in knowledge?
Where is the knowledge we have lost in information?
—T.S. Eliot, *Choruses from the Rock*

Can We Educate Virtuous Human/e Beings in Cyberspace?

I begin with contemporary and classic Western accounts of the root goals of liberal arts education. These statements emphasize the educational goal of "virtue first"—that whatever our professional aspirations, our first *shared* "business" as human beings is to pursue virtue or excellence (ἀρετή) *as* human beings. Moreover, this Western injunction toward human excellence has its counterparts in numerous traditions and cultures beyond Western spheres. Here I will focus on the classical Confucian tradition and its notion of the exemplary person or *junzi*. This lets us see that, for all their important and irreducible differences, Eastern and Western traditions cohere toward a shared ethic of human excellence or virtue. In addition to these coherencies among diverse cultural ideals, I also argue that there is a strong survival value in our discerning and pursuing a globally oriented liberal arts education.

With this as background, in the second section I then raise a number of critical questions about the possibility of *fully* accomplishing the goals of a shared/global liberal arts education online. These take into account recent shifts to a more informed recognition of the costs of distance education. Moreover, I take up a number of *cultural issues* that complicate distance education, including the cultural values and communicative preferences embedded in the contemporary technologies of distance education—thus raising the danger of a "computer-mediated colonization" that might inadvertently but powerfully impose Western values and preferences on a global audience of learners. My goal in this section is not to argue against all forms of distance education for liberal arts learning—but rather, following Hubert Dreyfus in his *On the Internet*, to recognize the strengths and limits of distance education. Briefly, while the current technologies of computer-mediated communication (CMC) are demonstrably useful in the early stages of learning, I concur with Dreyfus' argument that distance education cannot achieve the highest goals of liberal arts learning—specifically, Aristotle's *phronesis* or practical wisdom.

In my final section, I return to the larger question: Can liberal arts education—an education squarely focused on human excellence as now understood in a shared, global sense and as required for global citizens—be taught completely online? My response is: clearly not. Moreover, this view is in fact shared by a number of early proponents of technology and distance learning. At the same time, I argue that a limited form of distance education— one that recognizes both what can and cannot be accomplished online—can certainly contribute to a much-needed aspect of human virtue or excellence; that is, the human characteristics and skills crucial for cross-cultural dialogue and mutual understanding.

Liberal Arts Education:
Socratic Virtue (ἀϱετυ) and the Exemplary Person (*junzi*)

We can usefully begin with "The Association of American Colleges and Universities (AACU) Statement on Liberal Learning" (1998). Allow me to highlight the following elements. To begin with, liberal arts education teaches us to:

- [a]ccept responsibility for the ethical consequences of our ideas and actions.

"Liberal" in liberal arts derives from the Latin *liber*—"free." The liberal arts are thus the arts of free persons. But, to paraphrase John Locke, liberty is not license. Rather, liberal arts education should help students recognize that their beliefs, ideas, claims, etc., have consequences—sometimes beneficent, sometimes disastrous ones. As tempting as the retreat into silence and ethical relativism may be, liberal arts education will make clear that these temptations usually serve only the interests of those who seek to make critical but responsible freedom impossible.

This understanding of the importance of our taking responsibility for our views is then facilitated by the following emphases in the AACU statement: liberal arts education is to help students acquire

- the foundations of knowledge and inquiry about nature, culture, and society;
- historical and cultural context;
- core skills of perception, analysis, and expression.

That is, the responsibility for developing one's own understanding of the world, what philosophers call *worldview*, as a chief goal of liberal arts education further requires a wide-ranging knowledge of nature, cultures, and societies, as the latter are illuminated by their often complex contexts. At the same time, such knowledge is not simply passive content: in order for it to become useful in our students' understanding of the world around them and in their developing of their own views, our students further require the active skills of "perception, analysis, and expression." (As we will see in the second section, it is especially the fact that liberal arts education is about acquiring *skills* and not just *content* that begins to demarcate the limits of online learning.)

This *active* understanding, responsive expression, and ongoing development of worldview further require the ability to make:

- *connections* among formal learning, citizenship, and service to our communities. [emphasis added]

That is, we make sense of our world and our actions in it in part as we develop a strong sense of coherency between our learning and our doing, our theory and our practice. Without making such connections, our thoughts, feelings, and actions are likely to become random, fragmented, and incoherent. By contrast, as we develop an ever-greater sense of the mutual interaction between our lives as members of communities and our ongoing development of a thoughtful and richly emotive worldview, we move toward a greater sense of meaning and wholeness—part of what Greek virtue ethics calls *eudaimonia* or a sense of well-being (cf. Aristotle, *Nicomachean Ethics*, Book VI).

Finally, as Plato's allegory of the cave in *The Republic* makes clear, these tasks cannot take place in a domain limited to just one culture and its traditions, however rich they may be. On the contrary:

- *[b]y its nature [...] liberal learning is global and pluralistic.* It embraces the diversity of ideas and experiences that characterize the social, natural, and intellectual world. [emphasis added]

That is, the liberating *liber* of the liberal arts seeks nothing less than a *world-view*—one that, in contrast with the dogmatic and authoritarian insistence on the validity of just one culture and its traditions, recognizes the legitimacy and integrity of multiple cultures and peoples. A global and pluralistic worldview, as an outcome of liberal arts education, does not seek coherency by forcing all views to fit a single model. Rather, it articulates a pluralism based precisely on the recognition that the fruitfulness and richness of our engagements with one another stem from our irreducible *differences* from one another, not simply from what we already share in common.[1]

Western roots of liberal learning. It will serve our interest in a global perspective to recall some of the primary sources of these views on liberal learning, first of all the figure of Socrates as portrayed in Plato's dialogues.[2]

In this context, I focus on a specific theme in Socrates' teaching as a foundational element of liberal learning: namely, the recognition that the pursuit of human excellence (ἀρετή) or virtue must always come first. For the hard lesson of human experience seems to be that if we allow other human interests—including the desires for wealth, honor, power, and so forth—to override our pursuit of human excellence, that pursuit is likely to be sacrificed entirely. (The recent rash of scandal in American corporations, from Enron to WorldCom, provides numerous cases in point.) Especially as Socrates argues at length in *The Republic*, the sacrifice of human excellence is ultimately self-defeating: such a life, no matter how much wealth, honor, or power might be gained, will lack the one thing all human beings seek in life, namely *eudaimonia* or well-being. By contrast, our pursuit of human excellence, Socrates argues, will certainly allow for—if indeed, it does not actively facilitate—the acquisition of at least a moderate and appropriate level of wealth, honor, and power. And in doing so, the pursuit of human excellence leads to the highest of human goods—*eudaimonia* or well-being.

While the entire argument of *The Republic* is precisely about the question as to whether the just person, as one who pursues human excellence, will enjoy greater *eudaimonia* than the perfectly unjust person (the one who pursues self-interest, wealth, and power, no matter the cost), for our purposes it will suffice to note just one place where Socrates makes his teaching clear. And in doing so, he provides a capsule description of liberal arts education as a lifelong project, one devoted to the pursuit of human excellence first. So Socrates says, toward the end of *The Republic*, that:

[…] each of us must, to the neglect of other studies, above all see to it that one is a seeker and student of that study by which one might be able to learn and find out who will give one the capacity and the knowledge to distinguish the good and the bad life, and so everywhere and always to choose the better from among those that are possible. One will take into account all the things we have just mentioned and how in combination and separately they affect the virtue [*excellence*] of a life. […] From all this one will be able to draw a conclusion and choose—in looking off toward the nature of the soul [*psyche*]—between the worse and the better life, calling worse the one that leads it toward becoming more unjust, and better the one that leads it to becoming juster. […] For in this way a human being becomes happiest [*eudaimonia*]. (618b–619a/301)[3]

As is suggested here and developed more fully elsewhere in *The Republic*, our sense of well-being depends on the nature of the *psyche* or "soul"—more specifically, on the well-attuned or harmonious functioning of its elements (reason, spirit, and appetite) in the right proportion to one another.[4] In *The Republic*, in fact, this is what justice for the individual means, and is precisely the result of the pursuit of human excellence or virtue.

It is this understanding of human nature and how we achieve *eudaimonia* or well-being, moreover, that drives Socrates' habitual challenge to others in his city of Athens. So in *The Apology* he explains:

It is God's bidding, you must understand that; and I myself believe no greater blessing has ever come to you or to your city than this service of mine to God. I have gone about doing one thing and one thing only,—exhorting all of you, young and old, not to care for your bodies or for money *above* or *beyond* your souls and their welfare, telling you that virtue does *not* come from wealth, but wealth from virtue, even as all other goods, public or private, that man can need. (29e–30b, Jowett translation; emphasis added)

Echoing the comment from *The Republic*, Socrates makes clear here the absolute priority of human excellence over all other interests if we are to achieve *eudaimonia* or well-being, and adds that the pursuit of such excellence will also lead to the other human goods that we need.

Confucian counterparts: the exemplary person (junzi). These classic roots of liberal arts education are by no means restricted to what we might think of as Western traditions. On the contrary, there are clear counterparts to a Socratic virtue ethics in classical Confucian thought.

Here we can note just three passages from the *Analects* that make these coherencies clear. To begin with, Master Kong defines the exemplary person or *junzi* as follows:

15.18 The Master said, "Having a sense of appropriate conduct (*yi*) as one's basic disposition (*zhi*), developing it in observing ritual propriety (*li*), expressing it with modesty, and consummating it in making good on one's word (*xin*): this then is an exemplary person (*junzi*)."

The exemplary person, in short, is one who has shaped his or her basic character or disposition through the practice of appropriate conduct and ritual propriety. The primary markers of such a character are then modesty and integrity.

These human excellences—the excellences or virtues that issue from what Aristotle would call the right *habits*—are in fact to be the constant focus of what we might think of as the lifelong learning program of Confucian ethics, as characterized in one of the most famous of the *Analects*:

> At fifteen my heart-and-mind was set on learning.
> At thirty my character had been formed.
> At forty I had no more perplexities.
> At fifty I realized the propensities of *tien* (*T'ian-ming*).
> At sixty I was at ease with whatever I heard.
> At seventy I could give my heart-and-mind free rein without overstepping the boundaries. (2:4)

Finally, this lifelong pursuit of excellence, of (the rarely achieved goal of) becoming an exemplary person, is to always enjoy first priority—even over wealth and honor. According to the *Analects*, Confucius anticipates Socrates in *The Republic* and *The Apology* on just this point:

> 4.5 The Master said, "Wealth and honor are what people want, but if they are the consequence of deviating from the way (*dao*), I would have no part of them. Poverty and disgrace are what people deplore, but if they are the consequence of staying on the way, I would not avoid them.[5]

In short, for both Socrates and Confucius, the pursuit of human excellence or virtue comes first—though not at the cost of other human goods, including material well-being. Rather, these important human goods are seen to follow from the pursuit of excellence. Indeed, these human goods may function as *necessary*, but not *sufficient*, conditions for the pursuit of virtue. Free persons, among other things, must be free from the constraints of material and economic necessity that would otherwise prevent them from achieving their full potentials and freedoms. Slaves are not free, Aristotle would remind us—and in more contemporary terms, "necessitous men are not free men" (Roosevelt 1936, 1944).[6]

But at the same time, putting the pursuit of wealth, honor, power, etc., *before* the pursuit of human excellence, they each warn, means the loss of that excellence. Whether we lose the possibility of *eudaimonia* (well-being), lose our attunement to the *dao*, or, in the Christian tradition, gain the whole world but lose our soul—in any case, we lose what most makes life worth living, what most gives life its authentic meaning.

A foremost goal of a *global* liberal arts education, I suggest, is precisely to consistently focus on human excellence above all else—not as a dogmatic assumption, but as the considered conclusion of a wide range of traditions and beliefs. Of course, our understanding of what excellence means and how it is to be achieved may well change over time and across cultures. Indeed, this constant reflection on the specific elements of excellence and how they are to be achieved is an intrinsic part of the *praxis* of liberal arts education and the individual and collective reflection it fosters.

Global education for global citizens. This brief comparison between Socratic and Confucian virtue ethics suggests not only that, alongside their irreducible differences, both traditions may share some agreement as to the ideals and goals of liberal arts education.[7] In addition, this agreement and coherency provide some ground for optimism that, alongside our insistence that distinctive cultural differences be preserved, respected, and enjoyed, we may also come to some agreement as to the goals of liberal arts education for citizens of the world (*cosmopolitans*), not simply citizens of one country.

Additional arguments for a global liberal arts education would include the following. To begin with, it has been common in Western countries to observe that "the world is shrinking," a phenomenon nowadays included as part of the larger complex of processes called globalization. The shrinking world or "global village" means first of all that peoples' social, economic, and political lives are more and more interwoven with one another. Today we enjoy much greater opportunities for "cultural flows," for engaging with an ever-wider range of people from an ever-wider range of cultures and traditions. This directly serves the central goal of liberal arts education: pursuing human excellence. Part of that pursuit, as Plato's allegory of the cave makes clear, is to move beyond the perspectives and views of a single culture or tradition, toward a more encompassing *worldview* that might be shared with other *cosmopolitans*—others who have likewise come to recognize that their own culture or tradition (the cave in Plato's allegory) does not necessarily provide the complete and final truth on all things. This recognition can be characterized as an *epistemological humility*; that is, precisely the understanding that one's best beliefs and views may be *limited*—in part, for example, because they are dependent on a specific context, tradition, etc., for their meaning, rather than necessarily shared as universal truths by all peoples.

This humility is both the condition and result of our encounters with others from cultures and traditions different from our own. That is, if we are engaging in dialogue and relationships with the diverse peoples and traditions of the globe, such dialogue and relationships can be fruitful only if we acknowledge the integrity, value, and legitimacy of these diverse cultures and traditions.

Such humility, resulting from our moving out of our own culture and exploring in depth the cultures and traditions of others, is high on the lists of human excellences or virtues in all traditions familiar to me. In particular, the importance of these experiences for developing such humility is a central feature of the Western model of Renaissance humanism, and is reflected in the emphasis in liberal arts education on language study and travel abroad (Ess 2002b)—an emphasis shared, perhaps not accidentally, with Confucian tradition.[8] As well, such epistemological humility is again the condition and result of the emphasis in liberal arts education on critical, especially *self*-critical, reflection; that is, the practice of articulating our most basic assumptions and views, precisely in order to critically assess and evaluate these to determine how far they may be true, not just for us, but for the larger human community.

The realities of an increasingly interconnected world thus *demand* the epistemological humility fostered by liberal arts education and (ideally) our multiple encounters with diverse peoples and cultures. Indeed, this is not simply the conclusion of an academic reflection on Socratic and Confucian virtue ethics, nor the result of recalling diverse ways in which such humility is fostered by liberal arts education. There is a simple real-world argument demonstrating the urgency and importance of our fostering such humility however we can. September 11, 2001, may be the most striking example for Americans; but there are all too many examples, in both history and the contemporary world, that make clear the bloody consequences of failing to acquire this humility.

Liberal Arts and Distance Education: Western Perspectives and Experiences

In the 1990s, at the peak of enthusiasm for distance education as the latest example of how computer technologies would "revolutionize" education, pundits confidently predicted that online learning would eliminate the traditional bricks-and-mortar universities. For a number of reasons that we can now explore, this revolutionary sentiment has been largely replaced by a much more balanced view—one that focuses more and more on *blending* the best possibilities of online education with the best practices of face-to-face teaching and learning. Here I highlight four factors that seem to me to be most important in arguing for such a turn from revolution to reformation.

From Modern/Postmodern Cartesian Dualisms to Embodiment

Briefly stated, significant research has called into question the nineties' postmodern enthusiasm for a communicative revolution, one that was supposed to be as radically transformative of individuals and cultures as the invention of the printing press, if not the discovery of fire. As but one example, *contra* early enthusiasm for "life online" and the virtual community as replacing real-life communities (including their distinctive traditions, histories, rituals, etc.), a number of commentators and researchers began to observe that the body was not so easily divorced from the mind and simply left behind at the terminal. Highlights in the development of this theme include the work of Allucquère Rosanne Stone (2000); the research on virtual communities of Nancy Baym (1995, 2002); and Katherine Hayles' arguments for a "post-postmodern" "post-human" who is marked by a rejection of the Cartesian dualisms underlying the postmodern enthusiasm for liberation in cyberspace (1999). This shift, moreover, has been accompanied by a parallel renewal of interest among philosophers in both phenomenological and hermeneutical approaches, including a thematic interest in embodiment, including the works of Barbara Becker (2000, 2001) and Albert Borgmann (1999). Indeed, two of the most prominent proponents for the electronic revolution of the 1990s (Harold Rheingold and Jay David Bolter) have taken much more guarded stances in their more recent writings, in part because of a renewed appreciation of the role of *bodies* in our experiences of learning and community (Bolter 2001; Rheingold 2000; see Ess 2002c, 2003; Lockard 2000 for further discussion).

As a final point, whatever role CMC and other forms of electronic communication may play in facilitating democratic governance, it is equally clear from the political events of the 1990s and early twenty-first century that political change likewise requires *bodies*. That is, it has ultimately been the risks of embodied beings—by the thousands and tens of thousands—in places as diverse as Yugoslavia, Indonesia, the Philippines, and Georgia that have made the difference in helping shift political power from more repressive to more democratic regimes.

Economic Realities

In sharp contrast with earlier predictions of profitability, online education has emerged as both more expensive and more difficult to implement than proponents initially recognized. In what has become an authoritative analysis of media costs, Gerald Rumble of the Open University (OU) has shown that:

print, audio-cassettes, and pre-recorded Instructional Television are the only media that are relatively low cost for courses with populations of from under 250 students a year to over 1000 students a year. […] Hülsmann, on the basis of his study of the costs of 11 courses offered by 9 different European distance teaching organisations, argues that at £350 per student learning hour print is the cheapest medium to develop. (Rumble 2001, 21f.)

By contrast, placing text on the Internet "costs at least twice that, and possibly more," with costs escalating thereafter for audio, CD-ROM, video, and television (Rumble 2001). This UK experience, moreover, is replicated in the United States (ibid.).

A central cost, perhaps not surprisingly, is the faculty labor required to create distance learning resources. Rumble summarizes several studies and estimates of the faculty time required to create online learning materials, in contrast with traditional preparation: "[a]ll the research shows that it takes more academic time to develop media that will occupy a student for one hour, than it takes to develop a one hour lecture" (26f.). Simply put, the real costs of distance education in terms of infrastructure, technical support, and faculty time and labor have led to a growing realization that distance learning will *not* serve as an economic cash cow for institutions of higher education (Carr 2001).[9]

Gender and Cultural Issues

Beyond these concerns with the real costs of distance education, genuinely global education also requires us to pay careful attention to a specific risk of using CMC technologies, at least in their current form. In contrast with the view that communication technologies may be somehow neutral or "just tools," it has become increasingly clear that our communication technologies *embed* and *foster* specific cultural values and communicative preferences.

The relevant literature, indeed, has exploded over the past few years. Here I can only highlight some striking examples.

Capitalism as culture: the commodification of CMC. There is growing concern that our uses of the Internet and the web are increasingly shaped by a consumer culture fostered by capitalism. Briefly, as "users" of these technologies spend more and more of their time as *consumers* of technology, their use of the Internet and the web may be more and more shaped by these practices of consumption—including their being extensively manipulated by the companies and corporations that seek to market goods and services to users as customers. However much individuals may "choose" to participate in these technologies as consumers—the first point is that *the more we learn how to be consumers pursuing our self-interest* vis-à-vis the seemingly limitless offerings of the web and the net, *the less we learn how to be critical students and teachers engaged in the sorts of dialogues* that help shape our self-understanding and awareness of the larger world; develop the skills of engaging with one another in real-world contexts; and foster our effective engagement in the world for the sake of greater justice, freedom, and peace.

The point here is not to demonize capitalism or to ignore the benefits of economic prosperity. It is rather to say that consumerism as the prevailing "culture of use" of CMC technologies means that, much like the men of Athens, we run the danger of putting money and prestige first—in which case, the pursuit of virtue and excellence is forgotten altogether.[10]

Moreover, consumerism represents a specific *cultural value*; that is, one largely accepted without question in the United States, but greeted with greater critical concern both in Europe and Asia. In this light, promoting consumerism, however unintentionally, thus represents a real threat to those cultures that do not emphasize consumption and consumerism as a primary good.[11]

Computer-mediated colonization: ICTs as embedding Western (male) values and preferences. A second form of "computer-mediated colonization" is threatened as the CMC technologies of distance learning, designed and (largely) used according to the communicative preferences and cultural values of their Western—indeed, initially male—sources, thus favor and foster those preferences and values over the preferences and values of multiple "Others," starting with women and minorities within the US context, for example, and extending to larger cultural contrasts, both within Europe and beyond.

To begin with, significant studies *within* the US context have shown that males and females within the same ethnic classification utilize and respond to CMC technologies in often markedly different ways (Herring 1996, 1999).[12] Moreover, Stewart et al. (2001) have documented striking differences in response to chat software use in education—including refusal to use such software at all—among Asian Americans, Native Americans, and African Americans. These findings are echoed by correlations documented between different strategies for negotiating conflict online and ethnic group membership: briefly, Anglo-Americans are more likely to seek to dominate in conflicts— while at the other end of the spectrum, Native Americans are most likely to engage in face-saving strategies that defuse conflict (Gunawardena et al. 2002; cf. Kolko et al. 2000).

Similarly, such cultural conflicts have long been encountered and discussed as significant challenges to online learning within the European context. Among the Western countries, the Open University (Milton Keynes, UK) is perhaps the premier distance learning institution: it has taken distance learning as its mission since its inception in the 1960s, and has developed the most extensive program of distance learning in Europe.

OU philosopher Ellie Chambers (2001) has helpfully identified several of the primary difficulties of cross-cultural distance education:

> [...] non-native English speakers and those from other cultures studying programmes provided in English tend to encounter significant barriers to successful study. These barriers include: linguistic competence; unfamiliarity with the social conventions governing students' interactions with their peers and teachers, and with the procedures, educational requirements and norms of the providing academy; the relative invisibility of these students' own national/cultural perspectives and values.

Not surprisingly, "[s]uch disadvantage is likely to undermine the students' performance, affecting their ability to 'make the grade', and is socio-cultural in nature." The appropriate response, according to Chambers, is to avoid a "global imperialistic stance"; that is, simply imposing the language, social conventions, and education norms of one culture upon all others. Instead, an educational pluralism is required:

> Features need to be built in to global programmes to offset cultural disadvantage; positive steps need to be taken to promote pluralism. [...] Clearly, this will require serious commitment on the providers' part (including of resources), sympathetic engagement with "other" students and some exercise of the imagination towards developing teaching–learning strategies that effectively include them.[13]

Given that cross-cultural issues have created significant problems for distance learning *within* what we ordinarily think of as Western cultures, we should expect even greater cultural differences and attendant difficulties in considering the multiple contrasts between the cultural values and communicative preferences of Western-designed information and communication technologies (ICTs), on the one hand, and indigenous and Eastern societies, on the other hand. In fact, such conflicts have been documented since the early 1990s (Ess 2001, 2005a; Ess & Sudweeks 2001). As the problems we have already seen regarding cross-cultural challenges to distance education suggest, such conflicts have led to sometimes spectacular failures in efforts to use ICTs as learning tools with indigenous peoples. As a first example, South Africa has made several efforts to establish Learning Centres that seek to help indigenous peoples learn how to use and take advantage of CMC technologies. A number of observers document, however, how these Centres repeatedly fail, primarily because of basic cultural conflicts. Louise Postma initially pointed out how the Centres reflect their designers' Western emphasis on *individual* and silent learning—the learning style associated with the technology of *literacy* and the work of the solitary learner in a traditional Western library. By contrast, as with many indigenous peoples around the world, the indigenous peoples of South Africa demonstrate strong preferences for learning as a group in *collaborative* and often noisy, *performative* ways (Postma 2001). Similar contrasts have been documented with regard to efforts to work with the Maori people of New Zealand (Duncker 2002; Keegan et al. 2004).

By the same token, finally, it is now easy to document the cultural conflicts between the *values* embedded in Western CMC technologies and the fundamental values defining South Asian cultures—first of all, as these cultures are deeply shaped by Confucian tradition. For example, Western CMC technologies, including Group Support Systems (GSS), are designed to reflect Western cultures' emphases on the positive value of individual self-expression and open and egalitarian discussion. Anonymous communication is lifted up in particular as anonymity is seen to contribute to such self-expression and open communication. By contrast, many Eastern cultures—especially as influenced by a more hierarchical and communitarian Confucian tradition—first emphasize *respect for superiors* and the importance of *face* and *saving face*. In these contexts, open questions and criticisms are rather understood as a form of insubordinate attack upon a superior's "face." So, for example, Abdat and Pervan (2000) have shown how anonymous communication channels in a GSS, as intended and valued by its Western designers, precisely encouraged its Indonesian users to raise critical questions about issues under discussion. But these Western cultural values directly conflicted with the emphasis on *face-saving* and *respect for higher authority* in Indonesian culture, as deeply shaped by Confucian tradition, resulting in considerable dissatisfaction with the GSS as originally designed. Thanasankit and Corbitt (2000) make this same point with regard to Thai culture, and reiterate the claim that these conflicts will hold for many of the cultures of Southeast Asia as deeply shaped by Confucian tradition (see especially 238f.).

In sum, contrary to the assumption that the technologies of distance education are somehow culturally and communicatively neutral tools—both the larger research on culture, technology, and communication, and specific experiences with distance education efforts in diverse cultural settings demonstrate that these technologies embed and foster specific cultural values and communicative preferences: such preferences and values may sharply contrast with those of faculty and students in diverse cultural settings, thus dramatically complicating efforts to use these technologies effectively in education. The good news is that *if* instructors and designers become aware of how gender and culture affect the design and use of ICTs, then it is quite possible to develop effective cross-cultural approaches to online education, for example, for Maori communities (Panko & Postlethwaite 2004). Doing so, however, increases costs in terms of both time and resources required for such culturally appropriate design and implementation of ICTs in distance education.

Pedagogical/Epistemological Issues:
Dreyfus and the Turn to Blended Approaches

Finally, we can examine one of the most significant, philosophically informed arguments regarding the strengths and limits of distance education, namely Hubert Dreyfus' (2001) analysis of how we learn as *embodied* beings. This analysis is of value for us for several reasons. One, it coheres with the recent (re-)turn in CMC research and philosophy more generally to *embodiment* and the recognition of the irreducible role of the body in how we come to understand our world and develop lives of meaning within it. Two, Dreyfus orients his taxonomy of the stages of learning to the liberal arts goal of acquiring *wisdom*— and thus his work is consonant with my emphasis on the development of human excellence as a central goal of liberal arts education. Finally, his analysis nicely coheres with the shift in recent years toward *blended* approaches to learning; that is, ones that combine the best possibilities of both face-to-face and computer-mediated forms of communication.

Dreyfus identifies seven stages of learning,[14] the first of which are as follows:

1. Novice
2. Advanced beginner
3. Competence

It is at this third level of competence that Dreyfus sees the limits of online education. The general point here is that while students have been equipped in the earlier stages with basic information and maxims that help them apply that information to a range of contexts—at this third level, the range of possible elements and procedures becomes overwhelming for the learner who lacks the more advanced perspectives that help sort these out in terms of what is relevant and what is not (35). In pedagogical and philosophical terms, what the student has yet to learn here is *judgment*; that is, precisely the ability to determine which rules and/or skills should be applied to a specific situation. Moreover, because we are embodied beings, our decisions and acts *make a difference*: we care about the outcomes, and oftentimes what we care about—success, avoiding failure, reputation, etc.—is *at risk* in our decisions and acts. But this only makes things more complex. Dreyfus notes that "as the competent student becomes more and more emotionally involved in his task, it becomes increasingly difficult for him to draw back and adopt the detached maxim-following stance of the advanced beginner" (37f.).

It is at this critical juncture (i.e., the competent student's inability to judge as well as his or her more experienced teacher how to proceed, juxtaposed with new levels of urgency, uncertainty, vulnerability, and risk) that the teacher's interactions with the student become especially crucial. In fact, Dreyfus argues that from here, students increasingly require the guidance and example of their teachers as *embodied* beings in real-world contexts in order to progress through the remaining stages of learning: (4) proficiency, (5) expertise, (6) mastery, and (7) practical wisdom. To begin with, *proficiency* is acquired through the practice of skills under the guidance and example of a teacher—so as to help the student move from the beginner's effort to consciously apply specific rules (which ones?) to a suite of more intuitive responses that emerge through guided experience as an embodied learner (40). As Dreyfus notes, "[a]ction becomes easier and less stressful as the learner simply sees what needs to be done rather than using a calculative procedure to select one of several possible alternatives" (40).

Such education amounts to a series of apprenticeships with embodied teachers: through these apprenticeships, the student will eventually acquire the *judgment* that marks the highest levels of expertise and mastery. It is here that Aristotle becomes an explicit component of Dreyfus' taxonomy: "What must be done, simply is done. As Aristotle says, the expert 'straightaway' does 'the appropriate thing'" (42) at the appropriate time, in the appropriate way.

In sum, while CMC technologies may well help us move through the initial levels of beginner, novice, and competence, "only emotional, involved, embodied human beings can become proficient and expert" (48).[15] So, if we are talking about certain kinds of learning—those closest by analogy to Dreyfus' favorite examples of skills (playing chess, driving a car, playing a musical instrument, practicing as a physician)—then it seems clear that distance learning can only take us so far (in his terms, competence), but not to the higher levels of mastery, expertise, and wisdom.

Nor can Dreyfus' analysis be dismissed as naïve Luddism. On the contrary, his conclusions are echoed by Andrew Lippman, founding Associate Director of the MIT Media Laboratory (2002). Dreyfus' analysis is further consistent with research on distance education. For example, Parker and Gemino (2001) found that students in a virtual seminar scored higher on the conceptual section of the final examination than place-based students.[16] At the same time, however: *Students taking the virtual seminar scored significantly lower on the technique section of the final examination than place-based students.* This finding is immediately consistent with Dreyfus' argument that learning how to *apply* rules and concepts in the specific situations we encounter as embodied beings requires teaching and learning in embodied, real-world contexts. Indeed, Parker and Gemino directly reinforce Dreyfus' point:

> Place-based seminars provide an immediate feedback and can more thoroughly handle questions about a particular case. Since the students in a place-based environment are provided with a better opportunity to develop analogs early in their learning, place-based students were expected to have higher technique scores. The results indicate that place-based students did indeed show significantly better scores in technique than virtual seminars.

In this light, it is perhaps not surprising that in the US context, there is in fact a marked shift away from an exclusive emphasis on distance learning and virtual seminars to blended or "hybrid" approaches that seek to conjoin the best possibilities of both face-to-face/embodied and CMC contexts (e.g., Young 2002).

The Future of Liberal Arts Education and Global Cosmopolitanism?

If I am correct in arguing that liberal arts education, in both Western and more global forms, must aim always first at human excellence and practical wisdom (*phronesis*) as both the goals and abilities necessary to both individual (ethical) and collective (political) human well-being; and if especially philosophical analyses of pedagogy (Dreyfus) and related lessons from the *praxis* of CMC technologies and distance education (including American and European experience) are taken seriously; then it seems clear that the central and highest goals of liberal arts education—the cultivation of human excellence and the pursuit of wisdom—can*not* be fully taught through online technologies alone, at least as they currently exist. Rather, if mastery, expertise, and practical wisdom are to be acquired by students as *embodied beings*, they will require teachers who *incarnate* the skills and wisdom that mark the highest levels of human accomplishment.

This is not to say that distance education is of no value or relevance to liberal arts education and its highest goals. On the contrary, as the shift to *blended* or "hybrid" approaches suggests, what is called for is the careful and appropriate use of distance learning. This would mean in the first instance that we take up distance learning with a realistic understanding of its full costs (including the costs of faculty labor and of design and implementation that address important gender-related and cultural differences) and of what forms of learning it appears to best facilitate, namely the acquisition of the knowledge of rules and concepts that marks the early stages of learning. Especially if we can use Dreyfus' taxonomy as an accurate description of the stages and proper trajectory of liberal learning (i.e., toward the development of real-world skills, judgment, and practical wisdom), then it would seem that liberal arts education would indeed benefit from the careful and appropriate use of the best possibilities of distance learning *in conjunction with* the best possibilities of face-to-face education. This means, roughly, that we would use—where appropriate and cost effective—distance learning approaches for the early stages of learning (i.e., the acquisition of rules and concepts) in conjunction with teaching and learning in face-to-face contexts to foster students' abilities to appropriately apply such knowledge in the multiple contexts we encounter day to day as embodied human beings. In particular, such face-to-face teaching and learning seems essential to achieving the highest goals of liberal learning, that is the cultivation of human excellence, including the pursuit of practical wisdom.

Indeed, I am optimistic that such a blended approach in liberal arts education may make a distinctive contribution to the sort of education that is needed for the *cosmopolitans* or global citizens desperately needed in our increasingly interconnected world. In particular, the Internet and the web, as they enable *cultural flows* of a previously unimagined scope and extent, can foster precisely the sorts of cultural encounters among the peoples of the globe that, at best, issue in the epistemological humility crucial for genuinely fruitful cross-cultural dialogue and understanding (M. Dahan, Personal communication, 2001; Park 2002). But if our students are to move beyond the initial levels of online competence toward expertise, mastery, and wisdom, they will do so only through multiple offline experiences with one another—guided by their teachers' examples (i.e., in embodied, real-world, face-to-face contexts).

Much more can be said about the sort of *education* needed by the *cosmopolitans* who seek precisely to develop those skills and abilities, including practical wisdom, that will make possible a global society in which the diversity of cultures is maintained through the kind of epistemological humility and familiarity with cultures beyond one's own cave that I described at the outset. In the Western context, I and others (e.g., Ess 2005b; Hamelink 2000; Mehl 2000; Ropolyi 2000) have argued for a Socratic–Aristotelian education aimed toward critical thinking, dialogue, and practical wisdom that further follows the example of Renaissance humanism to insist on embodied, real-world experience of living in cultures beyond one's own. Again, such real-world, embodied encounters with "the Other" seem to be required of human beings as embodied learners in order to most deeply appreciate (i.e., at the *embodied* level) fundamental cultural differences *and* to develop the various skills (beginning with language) and wisdom necessary to comfortably engage with "others" in ways that recognize and preserve fundamental cultural differences while simultaneously bridging them. And nicely enough, these global directions in liberal arts education are not simply the pipe-dreams of armchair philosophers. Rather, we have also seen that there are *empirical* and *praxis-oriented* examples of implementing CMC technologies in diverse cultural settings that underscore both the importance and the possibility of realizing such an education, at least as they emphasize the importance of *social context of use* of these technologies, beginning with a fundamental recognition of the primary importance of local community values as the framework within which these technologies are to be implemented.[17] Indeed, as the Thai example (Hongladarom 2000, 2001) and others make clear, these conceptions of education are not exclusively Western (e.g., Panko & Postlethwaite 2004; Park 2002). On the contrary, especially as they rest on a (re-)new(-ed) recognition of the role of *embodiment* in our identity, learning, and engagement with one another—they cohere with the nondualistic conceptions of being human and human excellence in Eastern traditions, including, as my opening remarks suggest, classical Confucian thought. (For a more extensive discussion, see Ess 2002b, 2004; Rosemont 2001).

Dialogue about and development of such a global *ethos* as the goal of a genuinely global liberal arts education are very much in the beginning stages. I am optimistic that CMC technologies in general and distance learning in particular will play fundamental roles in these dialogues and constructions. My argument has been that these roles are most effective only as we recognize both their strengths and limits as media for educating excellent human beings.

Postlude 2005

T.S. Eliot's lament suggests that my critical concerns—that our fascination with information may cause us to lose sight of the most important foci of human existence and liberal arts education, namely the acquisition of wisdom and humane excellence—are not distinctive features of only the so-called Information Age. Indeed, these concerns are at least as old as Plato, who in *The Phaedrus* famously *writes* about a character named Socrates, who in turn *tells* a story that raises critical questions about how writing, as the then new communication technology, would undermine important human capacities (e.g., memory) and work to give the *appearance* of wisdom rather than genuine wisdom ([1971] 274.D–275.B/564ff.).

At the same time, however, as Neil Postman and others have warned, the new technologies of electronic media may capture our individual and collective attention in distinctively new and powerful ways, distracting us from the central business of fostering wisdom and humane excellence, and thereby tempting us to "amuse ourselves to death" (Postman 1985).

Indeed, it is one of the supreme ironies of the Information Age that the various gurus and pundits of an ostensibly revolutionary new cyberspace appear to have forgotten the origins of "cyber" and "cybernetics," namely in Plato. Briefly, Norbert Wiener introduced the term "cybernetics" to refer to the self-correcting features of new computational technologies—a term, moreover, that has centrally *ethical* meaning in Plato and thus fitted with Wiener's focus on exploring and developing the ethical dimensions of these new technologies as well (1948). Simply put, *cybernetes* (κυβερνυτης) refers to a steersman, helmsman, or pilot—and is used in Plato's *Republic*, alongside the physician, as a primary analog of the just human being. Of central importance in these persons is their understanding and judgment of what can and cannot be done: "[…] a first-rate pilot or physician, for example, *feels* the difference between the impossibilities and possibilities in his art and attempts the one and lets the others go; and then, too, if he does happen to trip, he is equal to correcting his error" (*Republic*, 360e–361a; cf. I, 332e–c; VI, 489c). For Plato, the self-correcting capacity of the *cybernetes* is thus primarily *ethical*: the *cybernetes* thereby embodies what Aristotle will later take up as *phronesis*, the practical and ethical capacity of *judgment*—"[…] a truth-attaining rational quality, concerned with action in relation to the things that are good for human beings" ([1968] *Nicomachean Ethics VI.v.6*, 1140b20–22/339).

It would seem, then, that our collective fascination with computational technologies and the cyberspace(s) they make possible has indeed allowed us to lose sight of the centrally *ethical* and humane roots of the very term "cybernetics." In this way, our focus on information has succeeded in displacing what should have been a natural continuation of the liberal arts emphasis on seeking wisdom and humane excellence first of all.

I hope that my remarks—along with the other chapters collected in this volume—may contribute to a recovery of the *cybernetes* as an ideal of wisdom, not simply of information.

Notes

*This chapter is revised from an article by the same title that originally appeared in *Arts and Humanities in Higher Education 2*(2), June 2003, 117–137, reproduced here by kind permission. I am further grateful to Chulalongkorn University Press for permission to draw here from a keynote address given on April 3, 2002, and which appears in *Proceedings of the International Conference on Information Technology and Universities in Asia* (Bangkok, Thailand, 2003), pp. 107–137.

I also wish to acknowledge the generous assistance of my colleague, Dr. Chris Panza (Philosophy and Religion Department, Drury University). His critical review of this chapter in its earlier form, informed by his own extensive and very successful experience in developing blended approaches to teaching philosophy, has helped me considerably in seeking to sharpen the central arguments and conclusions I attempt to develop here.

Finally, this chapter has also benefited from the careful comments and criticisms of the editors, Mark Pegrum and Joe Lockard. I am very grateful indeed for their very helpful suggestions, as well as for the opportunity to revise and, I hope, thereby improve on the original.

1.   As we will see below, *pluralism* is a central concept in Western philosophy and ethics, beginning (at least) with Plato and Aristotle: see note 7 for fuller discussion.

2.   Given the rich diversity of both Western and Eastern ethical traditions, it may be helpful for me to indicate why I focus here on the figures of Socrates and Confucius.

I have chosen Socratic virtue ethics as a focal point representative of Western ethical traditions for a number of reasons. To begin with, if, as Alfred North Whitehead is famous for saying, all of Western philosophy is a series of footnotes to Plato—it is perhaps equally fair to say that Western ethical theory inevitably turns to the figure of Socrates in the Platonic dialogues as the primordial ethical philosopher: so Karl Jaspers, for example, selects Socrates alongside the Buddha, Confucius, and Jesus, as the "paradigmatic individuals" in his comprehensive account of *The Great Philosophers* ([1957] 1962). Beyond Socrates' central and foundational importance for Western ethical philosophy, the virtue ethics articulated by Socrates has enjoyed a considerable renaissance over the past 30 years or so, in part because of the emergence of feminist philosophy and its turn toward an ethics of care (see Hursthouse 2001 for a recent treatment). Finally, a number of standard treatments within the framework of comparative philosophy (most notably, Rosemont 2001) have explored and established the recognition of these indeed strong resonances between Socratic virtue ethics, feminist ethics of care, and Confucian moral thought (cf. Ess 2004).

As for Confucius: beyond Jaspers' identification of Confucius as one of the four paradigmatic individuals, Ames and Rosemont Jr. point out that Confucius is "probably the most influential thinker in human history, if influence is determined by the sheer number of people who have lived their lives, and died, in accordance with the thinker's vision of how people ought to live, and die" (1998: 1). Moreover, given the multiple resonances between Western virtue ethics and Confucian moral thought, Confucius is a critical thinker for any ethical philosophy that seeks to do justice to the multiple ethical traditions of peoples and cultures who are becoming ever-more interconnected through the forces of globalization and, most especially, through the explosive expansion of communication media, including the ICTs that daily expand the possibilities of our engagements with one another on global scales (cf. Ess 2005a).

Of course, both theories are subject to criticism—first of all, because in both traditions, critique is intrinsic to the ongoing effort to develop more comprehensive and applicable approaches to the difficulties and opportunities of developing oneself as a human/e being and thereby living a good/moral life. In this direction, no small portion of the subsequent development of ethical theory in both traditions can be read as extended critique and revision of these originary positions. Indeed, as Boss observes in her summaries of the standard criticisms of both Confucius and virtue ethics (2004: 334–336 and 416—418, respectively), both traditions are enjoying something of a renaissance in their respective cultural and historical domains—in part, I would add, precisely because their shared emphasis on continuous self-critique works to keep these traditions vital and relevant to contemporary contexts.

3. Cf. as well his earlier remark with regard to poetry—in some sense, "the last temptation" away from a primary pursuit of human excellence (608b/291).

    The first reference is the standard Stephanus page number(s); the second reference is the page number in Plato, 1991. The English translation is Bloom's—modified by the author (C.E.) in order to approach more gender-inclusive language, as justified by the inclusive pronoun *tis*, translated here as "one," and reflecting Plato's earlier arguments for gender equality precisely with regard to education, at least in respect of the guardian class: see *The Republic* 455d/134f. (My thanks to Kathleen Ess for her invaluable assistance in carefully reviewing the Greek text.)

4. This notion of harmony, drawn from Pythagorean insights regarding music and mathematics, also has its Eastern counterparts. So Confucius is quoted in the *Analects* as saying, "Exemplary persons seek harmony, not sameness" (13.2). Elberfeld (2002) explores the roles of harmony and resonance *within* Western tradition (beginning with Socrates' comments about music and education in *The Republic*, 401d) and East Asian traditions, and thereby the harmonies and resonances *between* these two traditions. Thus, notions of resonance and harmony serve as metaphors and analogs to the concepts of pluralism discussed below (note 7).

5. See also 4.11. All translations of the *Analects* are taken from Ames and Rosemont Jr. (1998).

6. Franklin Roosevelt cites this phrase in his 1944 State of the Union message, and in his 1936 speech before the Democratic Convention accepting the nomination for President: in the latter he attributes the phrase to "an old English judge" (1936: 2). I have not been able to further discover the original source.

7. It is important to stress here that such coherencies are not necessarily absolute agreements on a shared common ground or point of simple identity between two very different traditions. While such common grounds are crucial, a *pluralistic* model of the relationship between two irreducibly different worldviews, beliefs, traditions, etc., preserves the differences that distinguish and define each element alongside any notions of their coherency, connection, etc. There are any number of conceptual models for such pluralism, beginning with Plato's use of analogy in *The Republic*, that is the analogy of the line (*Republic*, Book VI, 509d–511e/190–192). Aristotle builds on this model in his development of *pros hen* and analogical equivocals; that is, terms that are neither purely univocal (marked by a single meaning) nor purely equivocal (marked by absolutely different meanings), but middle grounds that allow for irreducible difference alongside connection in the form of "pointing toward one" (*pros hen*) meaning. In the twentieth century, Wittgenstein's notion of "family resemblances" also provides a way to think about connections (resemblances) alongside irreducible differences.

    Nor are such models merely theoretical ideals of philosophers. On the contrary, such pluralisms can be seen, for example, in a basic agreement between the United States and the European Union regarding "first principles" of data privacy protection—alongside their irreducible differences in implementing those protections (i.e., in either a market-based or state-regulatory fashion, respectively; see Reidenberg 2000: 1331f.). Similar pluralisms are at work in the highly applied ethics of Internet research (Ess 2003a) and emerging conceptions of privacy and data privacy protection in both the West and Asian countries such as China, Japan, Thailand, Taiwan, and Korea (see Ess 2005a).

Such theoretical and practical (applied) pluralisms mean that we are not forced to choose between sheer agreement on only shared points of view, belief, tradition, etc. (what Barber (1995) would call "McWorld") or sheer difference that, while preserving cultural integrity and diversity, would do so at the cost of absolute, and often violent, fragmentation. Rather, pluralistic models allow us to enjoy both coherencies and agreements alongside our recognition and appreciation of the irreducible differences that distinguish and define diverse cultural traditions and identities.

For a recent and comprehensive treatment of ethical pluralism—one that includes both Western and Eastern perspectives and is focused in part precisely on the possibilities of pluralism as a way of defusing the literally explosive, religiously based conflicts in the contemporary world highlighted by Barber—see Madsen and Strong (2003).

8. Ames and Rosemont Jr.'s characterization of the *junzi* includes the observation: "He has traveled a goodly distance along the way, and lives a goodly number of roles" (1998: 62).

We will see in the second section of this chapter the central importance of *embodiment* in learning the highest skills of liberal arts education. In this light, traveling as an embodied person into the new *physical* worlds of diverse cultures, as themselves embodied in every physical artifact we encounter (beginning, perhaps, with the sound of language as well as the physical but non-verbal elements of communication between *embodied* human beings, their politeness norms, etc; from the shapes, colors, and feel of *everything*, from electrical plugs, beds, clothing, vehicles, streets, buildings, and money to the sights, sounds, and smells of the foods we eat, etc.)—in contrast with comfortably "surfing the web" in our familiar homes and offices—is an essential experience in acquiring epistemological humility.

That is, in traveling, our senses and our bodies tell us—this really *is* a different world, at every level, including the most fundamental. The physicality of this encounters issues in what philosophers call ontological shock—a challenge to our most basic beliefs, feelings, intuitions, and assumptions about *reality*, including our own identity as gendered human beings: especially as our sense of identity is shaped and reinforced by a comprehensive physical environment of specific artifacts and human relationships (as these remind us of our history, community, experiences, practices, roles, etc.). To find ourselves in a new environment marked first of all by the *absence* of those artifacts and relationships is to have our most basic assumptions and beliefs about *who we are* called into question. Such ontological shock, as part of "culture shock," seems to be a necessary condition for us to be convinced at the deepest levels of our being that our own culture and worldview are *not* the only ones in the human and humane universe. These shocks are convincing, in turn, open us up to new *bodily* experiences, for example, of new language, now made with our own mouths, tongue, and throat muscles, which in time may come to immediately express our thoughts and feelings, and thereby become our new skin and face in this different culture/setting. In these and all the other ways that are included in culture and language as a human/e *world*, we learn as embodied beings precisely the limits of our native culture(s), and the possibility of moving beyond those limits to new ways of being-in-the-world, of experiencing and living in a new *lifeworld* of a different culture.

In this light, it is interesting to note that liberal arts institutions have *not* seriously argued for the elimination of travel and study abroad experiences, to be replaced by web-based research into the diverse cultures of the world made easily accessible to us via CMC technologies. Rather to the contrary, our recognition of the life-changing importance of such travel remains undimmed in the age of the Internet. This is consistent with my larger point—that some of our most important learning experiences as humane beings require our full presence as embodied beings, not as disconnected minds surfing the web.

9.   Nor has this account of cost issues changed much. On the contrary, by 2004, Judith V. Boettcher, one of the leading authorities on costing distance learning, noted in *Syllabus* (which, as its subtitle *Technology for Higher Education* makes clear, takes a strongly pro-technology approach to education) that "the design and development of online degree programs can cost up to $25,000 per credit hour" (29). Boettcher further acknowledged that: "We have many challenges going forward in this area as the standards and metrics for costing instruction remain in flux and difficult to define—probably because the instructional mission is so integrated with an institution's multiple missions" (30).

Indeed, the most recent (March 2005) "Briefing Sheet" by infoDev, a research secretariat of the World Bank (hardly a refuge of Luddites), concludes that: "Little is known about the true costs of ICTs in education," and "[e]ven less is known about cost effectiveness," especially in less developed countries. With regard to distance education per se, the report observes that while the considerably greater up-front costs of distance education may be offset by economies of scale—the higher drop-out rates associated with some distance education programs mean that the "cost per graduate may be much higher than cost per participant."

10. Willis (2000), for example, critiques the Western conflation between democracy and consumerism as exemplified in *Wired* magazine. This commodification of democracy, one that morphs it into (and thereby subsumes it under) a primary free market model, is part of a larger pattern of commodification that Willis calls "über-consumption." Willis cites Solnit, who finds PacMan to be the symbolic metaphor of such über-consumption—its sole purpose, after all, as a disembodied head-mouth, "was to devour what is in its path as it proceeds through an invisible maze" (1995: 230f.).

I have tried to develop this critique of capitalism as culture by using the Star Trek character, "the Borg" (Ess 2000b, 2002a; see also Sy 2001).

11. Sardjiman is quoted as saying: "Most Internet sites pose a danger to our education system and our culture, in particular pornography sites and sites that promote consumerism to our students" (de Kloet 2002).

12. This now well-recognized point has rightly issued in numerous efforts to equalize access to and use of CMC technologies among women and men, including "state-sponsored feminist" projects that seek to encourage young women's pursuit of careers in ICTs (see Lagesen 2003; Gansmo 2003; Sørensen & Stewart 2002).

13. For additional studies and remarks on cross-cultural issues in online teaching in the European context, see Williams (2000).

14. Dreyfus' taxonomy is rooted specifically in the phenomenological analyses of Merleau-Ponty and is part of Dreyfus' larger critique of the project of Artificial Intelligence (e.g., Dreyfus 1992; Dreyfus & Dreyfus 1988): for an accessible account, written primarily with an eye toward cognitive science, see Dreyfus (1998).

In my view, Dreyfus' taxonomy deserves attention for several reasons, beginning with its roots in phenomenology—and thus, as I note by way of introduction, it coheres with the recent turn in philosophy toward embodiment and its role in our being human, learning, etc. Secondly, this taxonomy is a central component of Dreyfus' larger critique of Artificial Intelligence—a critique that, in my view, has largely prevailed against especially early proponents of "hard" Artificial Intelligence. Finally, his taxonomy is informed by Dreyfus' own experience as a teacher in seeking to exploit the potentials of CMC in education—an experience, moreover, that resonates with my own (Ess 2000a). It would be instructive, however, to delve into a detailed comparison between Dreyfus' taxonomy and others popular in education (e.g., Kohlberg & Gilligan in ethical development, Bloom, etc.).

15.   It is important to note that this is only half of the argument. In the following chapter, Dreyfus works through this taxonomy again, using examples of interns going on rounds with physicians, learning to play football, etc., vis-à-vis what can be conveyed through the current technologies of telepresence. From his starting point in Merleau-Ponty's phenomenological analyses of our experience as embodied beings, Dreyfus then makes the case that the perspective of embodied beings who have *control* over the perspective we take as part of our experience—in contrast with viewing the world through a screen whose inputs we do not immediately control—is a crucial element of learning, especially at the higher stages. These elements of embodied control over our perspective cannot be replicated with contemporary telepresence technologies—making them unsuited as media for these higher stages of learning.

16.   This first finding points to a larger issue: contrary to early claims that distance education would revolutionize learning by leading to superior results, a number of meta-studies of research have demonstrated the so-called "no significant difference" phenomenon. Simply put, and consistent with Parker and Gemino's first finding, there is little empirical evidence to suggest that distance education, *despite* its considerable costs in terms of infrastructure, technical support, and faculty labor, actually leads to improved outcomes in education (see Fisher 2000; Russell 1999).

      As we have seen, these findings have not changed in light of subsequent research. For example, T. Mills Kelly, Associate Director of the Center for History and New Media (George Mason University), while enthusiastic about the potential of new media for liberal learning, notes in his discussion of the multiple "tradeoffs" involved in attempting to take up new technologies, that we have yet to answer the question, "[…] when new media are added to a course, do our students learn better, more, or differently?", in *measurable* ways (2003: 30). A 2004 meta-study of learning effectiveness in distance education—in which "effectiveness" was quantitatively measured solely in terms of examination scores and grades—again drew ambiguous conclusions: "The results demonstrate little distinction between traditional and distance learning classrooms on the basis of performance" (Allen et al. 2004: 413). While some distance learning applications (most notably, foreign language ones) showed modest advantages in effectiveness, other environments showed either no difference (natural science) or negative difference, for example, in education courses, traditional methods demonstrated a slight advantage (ibid. 412). Even where distance learning showed modest advantage, the authors note that their study was unable to factor in student motivation, and observe that: "Given the extra effort perceived to be required for distance learning (mastering the technology of the course), the achievement scores of distance learning students may be the product of higher levels of motivation than traditional copresent students" (ibid. 414).

      It appears, then, that T. Mills Kelly's excellent questions, unanswered in 2003, remain unanswered in 2004 (see note 9, above).

17.   In addition to the examples we have already seen, one of the early but thereby most exemplary models of such design is provided by Harris et al. (2001).

Chapter 12

Tomorrow's Yesterdays: Teaching History in the Digital Age

T. Mills Kelly

The Roman architect Marcus Vetruvius Pollio (90–20 BCE) decreed that for a structure to be worth building, it should have three essential characteristics: commodity, firmness, and delight. Ever since, architects have measured their work against Vetruvius' standard. As educators, we would do well to use the same standards when assessing our use of digital media in the courses we offer. Does the inclusion of technology into a course, whether in a single assignment or across the entire course, have commodity—that is, does the use of technology measurably improve student learning outcomes? Can we say that our use of digital media has firmness—that is, have we decided to include these media because that decision is built upon solid scholarship and pedagogical research? Or is the technology there just because we feel like it ought to be or are impressed by the sizzle it seems to provide to our course? And, of course, do the media we use provide delight—to us and to our students? After all, learning ought to be fun, even as it is rigorous and generative.

This chapter focuses largely on the teaching and learning of history, because I am a historian and know my own field best. However, most of the questions addressed in this chapter are applicable to many other disciplines, especially because all college and university educators of my acquaintance are interested in teaching their students not only the factual content of their subject, but also the epistemologies of their discipline—the ways of knowing of chemists, nurses, or anthropologists. Moreover, teaching faculty want their students to enjoy learning. In more than 20 years of working in higher education, I have met very few professors who have no interest in whether or not their students enjoy their classes—most are actually quite interested in the results of their end-of-semester student evaluations for reasons other than the formal processes of evaluation.

As we think about ways to improve what we do in the classroom, college and university professors feel more and more pressure—whether from our students, administrators, or from within ourselves—to infuse technology into our courses. Many of us worry that if we do not "ramp up" our courses, with the inclusion of assignments using the web, the use of slideware like PowerPoint in our lecture halls, or some sort of online discussion or writing opportunities, our courses will seem outdated and even a bit moldy. This chapter argues that technology can be useful in a course, but only when it is closely tied to specific learning objectives. Technology should not be used for its own sake, especially given the often steep learning curves required to master many forms of digital media and the significant amount of time required to build websites, create and edit weblogs (blogs), and monitor students' online writing. Only when there is a clear reason for using digital media should any portion of a course be "ramped up."

Many people are surprised to hear that teaching history is quite difficult. After all, given the experience of so many former students of history, the sum total of history teaching seems to be nothing more than a ritualistic pounding of names and dates into the heads of students until they are numb enough to do reasonably well on state-mandated standardized tests. As a man from California said in a national survey of history teaching and learning, "It was just a giant data dump that we were supposed to memorize ... just numbers and names and to this day I still can't remember them." Or, as another respondent to this survey said, "My teacher was seventy years old, and she carried a blackjack" (Rosenzweig 2000: 275–276). How difficult could it be for a history teacher to recite data in a reasonably coherent narrative interspersed with some interesting or humorous anecdotes? If only history teaching were so simple.

History, as practiced by historians and as taught by more and more history teachers, is not encompassed by facts, facts, and more facts. This is not to say that historians do not care about facts—of course we do. But we care even more about what the facts *tell us* about the past. Anyone who has studied history as something more than a compendium of information knows that the facts can be assembled artfully into many competing and compelling narratives. So, rather than asking our students to memorize the date of the Treaty of Westphalia or the name of Ulysses S. Grant's Vice President, instead we demand of them that they confront history as something highly conditional, foreign to us, and difficult to make sense of.[1] As Samuel S. Wineburg puts it so eloquently: "The essence of achieving mature historical thought rests precisely on our ability to navigate the jagged landscape of history, to traverse the terrain that lies between the poles of familiarity with and distance from the past" (2001: 5).

How might the use of digital media help our students learn how to navigate this terrain? Lately, historians have begun to take seriously the notion that there is something called the "scholarship of teaching and learning" in our field and that we can learn from this scholarship how to improve our students' learning about the past as well as our teaching. Recent research on the scholarship of teaching and learning in history demonstrates that there is a substantial and persistent disconnection between the epistemological practices of historians and the ways we teach history to our students. Historians who see their work as an exercise in meaning-making too often drill their students in a factual acquisition model of historical learning foreign to our craft.[2] As part of this larger project on the teaching and learning of history, a small group of scholars, including this author, have begun to investigate the role that digital media play in that teaching and learning.

But our efforts in this regard are running up against a significant problem. Our students are deeply committed to a particular style of historical investigation—a style that is at odds with the epistemological lessons we are trying to teach them. They want firm answers to historical problems that are often inherently infirm. This desire to locate firm ground in the past generally leads them to an all too simplistic acceptance of what they find in quick searches of the sources that are available online. We want them to see the past as contentious terrain—a place where different interpretations strive with one another for our attention. Left to their own devices, our students avoid this vision of the past like the plague. Instead, they turn first (and too often only) to online sources—sources that offer seemingly definitive answers to complex questions—and stop their search for information as soon as they have located what seems to be a reasonable response to an assignment. Unfortunately, the websites they encounter first in such a search are those that the search engine they are using presents to them first according to its algorithm, not according to their merit as historical sources. This is not to say that online sources should be ignored, or that students should be banned from using them. Online resources are not the problem, nor are the search engines that call them up. It is the *process* our students most often use to access and use these sources that is the problem.

One example will suffice to demonstrate how ready access to the vast library of information and misinformation that is, the Internet has become central to our students' learning processes, and how uncritical their use of this resource can be. Recently I was evaluating the teaching of a postdoctoral fellow in my department and as part of my evaluation, I visited her class on an afternoon when the students were discussing the Holocaust of European Jewry. I arrived in the classroom 15 minutes before the class began and sat in the back-row of desks. As the students drifted in, they asked one another what answers each had arrived at for the questions their professor had posed at the end of the previous class. One young man spoke up, confidently rattling off answers from some papers he pulled from his notebook. When one of his peers asked him how he had gotten such good answers, he replied, "I Googled it up, baby. I found three pages of things to say, so I'm good to go." The students sitting around him nodded approvingly, but one asked him if he had done the assigned readings. To that question, he simply smiled, waved his sheaf of pages printed from the Internet and said, "Didn't need to. I've got all I need right here."

The fact that the young man in this example could obtain all the information he thought he needed by simply "Googling up" some answers from whatever keywords he typed into the Google search engine points to two problems. The first, and most significant, problem is the design of the assignment. If the professor in this example had constructed her questions in such a way that they were tied more explicitly to the sources she wanted her students to read, her students would have found it more difficult to Google up answers and so might have been more inclined to look for answers in the assigned readings. At the same time, no matter how well-designed the assignment, the ease with which students can access so much information online often predisposes them to seek the path of least resistance, rather than engaging in the more complicated sort of investigatory work we want them to do as novice historians.

A second problem brought on by the advent of digital media is the growing reliance of instructors on slideware (PowerPoint and other similar programs). On many campuses, mine included, slideware is rapidly becoming ubiquitous. Stroll down any campus hallway and peek into the classrooms—too often you will see students staring a little blankly at a PowerPoint slide or, worse, an instructor reading the text that appears on that slide. Edward Tufte argues in his screed against slideware, *The Cognitive Style of PowerPoint*, that "[s]lideware often reduces the analytical quality of presentations [...] usually weaken[s] verbal and spatial reasoning, and almost always corrupt[s] statistical analysis" (2003a). As much as he hates the impact of slideware on the corporate world, Tufte is even more concerned about the effect of slideware on students. Writing about K–12 education, he points out that:

> Rather than learning to write a report using sentences, children are being taught how to formulate client pitches and infomercials. Elementary school PowerPoint exercises (as seen in teacher guides and in student work posted on the Internet) typically consist of

10 to 20 words and a piece of clip art on each slide in a presentation of three to six slides—a total of perhaps 80 words (15 seconds of silent reading) for a week of work. (2003b)

Of course, given the general lack of training faculty receive in how to use presentation software, many of the slideware shows produced by teaching faculty are little better, simply reinforcing their students' belief that learning happens when information is transcribed from a screen to a notebook page. And yet, across the United States (and I suspect elsewhere), faculty are *strongly encouraged* to start using this technology with grants, release time, or simply hints and nudges about the amount of money spent to install projectors in classrooms, and our students' "visual learning styles."

This is not all to say that the arrival of digital media in the teaching and learning of history is a bad thing. On the contrary, *carefully constructed* digital media can give our students access to immediate multimedia experiences that conventional teaching cannot provide—encounters with still and moving images, music, data, and text more or less simultaneously. Common sense tells us that these media have the *potential* to change both teaching and learning in substantial ways. This prospect alone offers a genuinely revolutionary possibility for the teaching and learning of history, especially if students might actually be pursuing different lines of inquiry simultaneously and interactively in an increasingly networked environment. What we still lack is enough research to substantiate what our common sense tells us is likely to happen (cf. Kelly 2000).

I would submit that one reason it is likely that student learning is being transformed is that the use of networked information transfers control over the exploratory aspect of learning from the instructor to the student. When our students pursue their own lines of reasoning, rather than just trying to answer a question posed by their professor, it is *possible* that they will arrive at new insights that neither they nor we anticipate. This result is only *possible*, because my own research on student use of the Internet indicates that a substantial majority of students in the freshman history survey,[3] despite encouragement from their professor, do not embark on what George Landow calls their own "unmediated intellectual quest" (1997: 183). Instead, like the young man in the example cited earlier, they call up a search engine such as Google, type in some likely keywords for their search, peruse the first websites that appear in the Google rankings without much critical analysis of those websites, select some reasonable sounding information that seems to answer their question, and then move on to the next assignment. In the analog world, this pattern of behavior would be like walking into the library, asking the librarian where books on the independence movements in Africa are shelved, going into the stacks, pulling down the first few books with interesting looking spines, going to the copier and making copies of the first few pages in each book. By way of demonstrating how problematic this approach to research can be, a recent Google search on "Latin American history" and "primary sources" turned up 3,130 hits when the terms were delimited, and 2,530,000 when no delimiters were used. The good news is that one of the first sites to come up in such a search is the Modern History Sourcebook—a reasonable, albeit imperfect choice. The bad news is that the rest of the top 10 possibilities are all library sites offering useful links (often to more sites with links, which provide more sites with links to more sites with links).

A diligent student will move beyond the first 10 results of such a search, but as we have all experienced, even the most diligent student often ends up at a site of questionable quality. For example, if one types "Adolf Hitler" into the Google search engine, the third website to appear in the rankings is the *Hitler Historical Museum*. This website can seem like a reasonable choice for research. After all, it appears in the third position in the Google rankings, its production values are fair, and the site offers visitors:

> a non-biased, non-profit museum devoted to the study and preservation of the world history related to Adolf Hitler and the National Socialist Party. True to its role as an educational museum, these exhibits allow for visitors to understand and examine historical documents and information for themselves […] No biased judgments, slanderous labels or childish name calling exist here as they do in most of the writings on this topic. (www.hitler.org)

Only a careful reading of the website indicates that it is clearly a production of those who believe that Hitler was on the right track and has gotten a bad rap over the years. And it is no surprise that our students get taken in by this sort of thing when even teachers point them to such sites.[4] Students (and teachers) visiting this site should be concerned that it offers no information about its creators, but few students have either the skill or the motivation to ask such a question about a website. This simple example demonstrates how desperately we need to train our students how to use the resources that are available to them on the Internet. At the same time, it must also be said that a minority of our students are doing very interesting work in the vast online archive we are creating for them, producing essays, multimedia presentations, weblogs, and other results that are quite impressive. For the present though, these students remain in the minority.

Given the many challenges and opportunities we face in bringing digital media to our classrooms, I believe there are three important issues that will guide what we do in the coming five years or so. We know that our students are very sophisticated *users* of technology, but we know very little about how they *learn* with technology at the post-secondary level. Until we know more about how the actual learning takes place online, we need to be very explicit in designing resources for our students that promote the kinds of skills with technology that we think are essential to their success in our courses. In the same way that a generation ago we gave our students library skills-building assignments, we now need to create similar exercises that take advantage of what the technology offers us.

A second important issue that must be addressed if we are to tap the full potential of digital media is the training of faculty. As far as I know, nationwide, only my department at George Mason University includes mandatory new media courses in our training for history doctoral students. Only a tiny minority of historians has the skills necessary to produce sophisticated digital media materials and this situation is not going to change much in the coming decades unless there is a significant investment in such training by other PhD programs. The pressures of professional practice are already such that only a few historians will ever have the time or energy to devote to learning how to produce Flash movies or write MySQL/PHP code. Instead, what is more important is that our colleagues be trained in how to *use* the resources that already exist in ways that maximize learning.

Most of us are pretty adept by now at searching for information online and are more critical consumers than our students of the information we locate. Now we need training in how to teach our students to engage in historical research and analysis online. At present, such training is largely non-existent. Not one of the many National Endowment for the Humanities-funded summer seminars for faculty in 2005 offered this sort of training. Each year this problem grows more acute. In the American history survey course, the number of syllabi posted online doubled each year between 1997 and 2004, but we are doing next to nothing to teach our colleagues how to make appropriate use of the materials to which they direct their students. As evidence of how reluctant faculty teaching history survey courses are to use online resources, Daniel J. Cohen's analysis of US history syllabi posted online shows that only 6% of 2004 syllabi posted online included links to online resources other than the website associated with the course's textbook (Cohen 2005).[5] At a moment when our students' *first* (and often only) inclination is to seek additional information online, Cohen's data speak to a clear disconnect between students and their professors.

The third issue remaining to be addressed on our campuses is the continuing lack of sufficient technology infrastructure for those faculty who do want to make full use of digital media to do so without having to cart their own projectors and laptops with them from class to class, or for their students to have sufficient Internet access in the classroom. Despite a massive investment in infrastructure, most campuses in the United States still have only a few classrooms, relative to the total number on campus, that are fully enabled for students and faculty to maximize their experience with new media. In addition, the share of new students on our campuses who come from economically and educationally disadvantaged backgrounds continues to grow, and many of these students find it difficult to access technologically enhanced learning opportunities in the same ways that their more advantaged peers can. These are familiar challenges, all of which are primarily administrative in nature and all of which can be overcome by increased investment in curricular change, technology infrastructure, and the equalization of student access to technology.

Thus far this chapter has sounded like a lot of bad news. Fortunately, there is a lot of good news to balance the bad. Most encouraging is the growing number of high-quality websites that provide researchers, whether students or faculty, with sophisticated access to large libraries of primary source material. As more and more of these websites place their source materials into databases rather than folders of flat HTML files, powerful search software makes it possible for visitors to locate information through keyword and other searches. The two largest examples in my own field are the American Memory Project at the Library of Congress, which has placed more than seven million primary sources online, and the Archivo General de Indias in Seville, Spain, which has placed more than 11 million pages of historical documents online. Databases such as these allow students to create and pursue their own lines of inquiry and to engage in the kind of research previously reserved for advanced graduate students and faculty. Seven years ago Randy Bass and Brett Eynon (1998) wrote about these "novices in the archive" to describe what the availability of a vast library of primary source materials online meant for our students. Access to large collections of primary sources is a potentially wonderful thing, Bass and Eynon wrote, but having access to the sources is not the same thing as being able to work with those sources effectively. Thus, one important agenda for the coming years is the use of technology to make visible to novice learners the often mysterious cognitive processes of expert learners.

One example of how new media can address this need is from a project I co-direct with my colleagues Roy Rosenzweig and Kelly Schrum at the Center for History and New Media at George Mason University in Fairfax, Virginia. Among its many resources, *World History Matters* provides students with multimedia case studies of scholars describing how they analyze a particular primary source, and it gives them specific guidance on how they can engage in the same kind of sophisticated analysis of sources.[6] For example, in one of these case studies, Smith College art historian Dana Leibsohn walks students through the analysis of two complicated images: a post-conquest map of Mexico City by an Aztec artist and the painting *The Mulatto Gentlemen of Esmeraldas* by Andrés Sánchez Gallque. Leibsohn tells students how she decodes each image, giving detailed instructions on how they too can decode images they find in their research.[7] By the conclusion of the module, students have learned something about how an expert learner learns and have acquired some tools they can use in future research situations.

This project also addresses the problem of students not finding appropriate websites for their own research. *World History Matters* contains a database of 200 website reviews written by teaching historians, each of which includes suggestions for students and teachers as to how best to use the resources found at these sites. Students who begin their research in this database, rather than with Google, will start at the best websites, rather than blundering around on the web looking for something worth using.[8] This database of reviewed websites also provides a model for how one might teach students to pay closer attention to the websites they find as they "Google around" on the web. Two years ago, I created a database for students to use in my survey course. This "Webography Project" requires students to locate websites containing primary sources, write reviews of those websites using a standard rubric, and then deposit those reviews into the project database, thereby making their thinking visible for all students in the class. The most important result of this simple teaching intervention is that my students no longer turn in essays citing strange or simply bad websites as sources. More than 40 teaching historians in North America and Europe now use this project in their courses and the project database contains more than 700 (500 of which are public) student reviews of websites ranging from those deemed to be excellent sites to those to be avoided.[9]

This database also offers very interesting insights into the ways students assess the quality of a website they review. Because the student reviewers must all fill out the same rubric when completing their reviews, it is possible to examine the ways different students evaluate the same website. For instance, Paul Halsall's various Sourcebook websites are currently reviewed 35 times in the database. Each review is assigned a score between 5 and 30, and the scoring of Halsall's sites ranges from a low of 18 to a high of 30 (with an average of 26). The student who was the most critical of the site correctly pointed out that "The material is very good, but the website itself is not very up to date," while the students most enamored of the site tended to laud it for the large amount of information available. In this simple example, we see the difference between critical and uncritical analysis, and evidence that students can be taught to look very carefully at the websites they are using.

Digital media are also transforming the way that students write about the past and participate in collective knowledge production. Since the late 1990s, various forms of the discussion forum—WebCT, Blackboard, and others— have become common on college and university campuses. Already we see evidence that these "older" forms of online collaboration are being pushed aside by the expanding blogosphere. Where once students had websites of their own and used discussion forums and chatrooms to exchange information, now they link their lives, personal and academic, through weblogs, "live journals," and other forms of digital diaries. The website *LiveJournal.com* alone counts more than 2.5 million active users, most of whom are between the ages of 15 and 23 years and more than two-thirds of whom are female.[10] This one example demonstrates how comfortable our students are expressing themselves and exposing their lives online. At the same time, the online environment is transforming the way they write. Catherine Smith argues that students "take real-world writing more seriously when it is done on the web, where it might actually be seen and used" (2000: 241). My own research on student writing in my survey course validates Smith's conclusions. In addition to taking more care with their writing when it is posted online, my students show increasing signs of integrating new ideas from other students' and scholars' work into their own. I and other researchers have seen evidence that this sort of integration of ideas occurs more often in weblog writing than it does in postings to discussion forums, such as those in WebCT or Blackboard, but none of us can yet say why this is so. For the development of historical thinking skills, which rely so heavily on students being able to think across time and space to draw together examples from disparate cultures, this integrative style of writing seems especially important.

The final big question when we think about the integration of digital media into our courses is perhaps the most difficult to answer. When these media are added to a course, do our students learn better, more, or differently? In other words, is there some sort of *measurable* beneficial outcome from all the time and money invested in ramping up a course? After all, if we cannot point to improved or different learning, then it seems to me that we have wasted both our time and our students'. Fortunately, a growing number of researchers spread across a range of disciplines are inching toward answers to this vexing question, and their answers are rooted in their own epistemologies, rather than being solely the property of cognitive psychologists and schools of education. Historians, literary theorists, chemists, mathematicians, and many others are engaging in more and more assessment of the impact of technology on learning in their courses. While some of this research is being conducted by individuals working in isolation, a substantial portion of the inquiry into what is really different about teaching and learning with new media is occurring in collaborative endeavors like the Carnegie Academy for the Scholarship of Teaching and Learning (CASTL) and the Visible Knowledge Project (VKP) based at Georgetown University.[11]

As a participant in both of these efforts over the past several years, I can say that the researchers affiliated with the two projects have made some significant progress in the framing of the right questions to ask about technology and learning, and some have even begun to offer interesting, albeit tentative conclusions. In my own case, I have been able to demonstrate that web-based assignments can induce greater recursive reading of sources. Similarly, Sherry Linkon's students at Youngstown State University have demonstrated a deeper understanding of the interdisciplinary concepts central to American Studies as a result of certain exercises in new media that she created for them (Linkon, n.d.). In both cases, and in most I am familiar with, these small successes were not the result of the general adoption of technology in a course. Rather, they were the result of carefully designed assignments that were rooted in specific learning objectives and were also the result of several trials (with accompanying errors along the way) spread over multiple semesters. What has not appeared from any of these efforts, individual or collaborative, is a consensus about what we *know*, as opposed to hope or suspect, about the real impact of digital technology on student learning. Much more research is needed before such a consensus will emerge.

I believe that we are on the brink of something genuinely different when it comes to teaching and learning at the post-secondary level. Since digital media have such promise, and because they are so readily adopted by our students, we have many opportunities before us to transform what we are doing in our courses. At the same time, taking full advantage of these opportunities is not going to be inexpensive. It remains to be seen if our institutions will invest sufficiently in the infrastructure and training that will make it possible for us to harness digital media to our learning goals, or whether we will continue to nibble around the fringes of what is possible.

Notes

1. The correct answers are 1648 and Schuyler Colfax. The answers to these and just about any other "who" or "when" questions dealing with the years 1000–1999 can be obtained from H-Bot at chnm.gmu.edu/tools/h-bot/

2. For a concise overview of the scholarship of teaching and learning as it applies to the teaching and learning of history, see Pace (2004) and Calder et al. (2002).

3. In the United States, first year college courses in the disciplines are often taught as "survey" courses in which instructors attempt to introduce students to the essential information under the rubric of the course title. Thus in the course "Western Civilization," students generally receive a synthetic overview of the history of "the West" from Plato to NATO in either one or two semesters.

4. Among the websites linking to the Hitler Historical Museum is one called *TeacherNet: The Net's Educational Resource Center* (members.aol.com/TeacherNet/Holocaust.html, accessed February 10, 2005). Among the many Holocaust links provided is one to the Hitler Historical Museum, presented to visitors without comment by the website's author. The large Holocaust site, www.remember.org, similarly points visitors to this website, restating the site's claims to be non-biased and a non-profit museum, neither of which can be substantiated. If the creators of these websites are putting forward such a website as a good source of information, it is no wonder students often use it as a source for the papers that they write. When I point out to my students that a large number of the sites linking to this website are white supremacist sites like www.stormfront.org, they finally begin to question their choice of sources.

5. My thanks to Prof. Cohen for sharing the penultimate version of this chapter with me in advance of publication. See Cohen (2005).

6. See *World History Matters*. Accessed February 10, 2005, at chnm.gmu.edu/worldhistorymatters/

7. See "Analyzing documents: material culture/images" in *World History Matters*. Accessed February 10, 2005, at chnm.gmu.edu/whm/analyzing/mcimages/analyzingimgintro.html

8. See "Finding World History" in *World History Matters*. Accessed February 10, 2005, at chnm.gmu.edu/whm/whmfinding.php

9. See *Western Civilization Webography Project*. Accessed May 25, 2005, at chnm.gmu.edu/webography/

10. See *LiveJournal.com*. Accessed February 2, 2005, at www.livejournal.com/stats.bml

11. See the *CASTL* website, accessed February 10, 2005, at www.carnegiefoundation.org/CASTL/index.htm; and the *VKP* website, accessed February 10, 2005, at crossroads.georgetown.edu/vkp

Chapter 13

The Technical Codes of Online Education

Edward Hamilton and Andrew Feenberg

A Deterministic Politics of Online Education

Online education was invented by academics, and at its origin reflected their values and pedagogical conceptions. But they lacked resources for imposing their innovation on a wide scale. University computer centers were often uncooperative, administrations indifferent, and business prospects as yet unimagined. Individual faculty might gain support for small experiments, but online education seemed more a hobby of a few odd champions than a significant advance.

All this changed in the late 1990s, when university administrations realized they faced insoluble budgetary challenges in serving the coming generation of students and meeting the mounting demands from government and industry for a highly educated workforce. In this context, online education was called upon to solve some of the deepest economic, pedagogical, and organizational problems of the university. In solving these problems, however, online education was also expected to transform higher education in a way that would leave no corner of the institution untouched.

Computer and software companies saw a market in this transformation and suddenly online education was on the front page of the newspapers as the Next Big Thing. Those who had worked quietly in the field for the previous 15 years were generally ignored in the rush toward a technological revolution that, it became rapidly clear, was all about money—money to be saved by substituting capital for labor on campus along lines familiar from many earlier de-skillings of crafts and professions—with only secondary consideration given to the pedagogical and professional concerns that guided early experimentation and innovation.

In the late 1990s, online education thus emerged as an object of considerable political contention in the university. It became embedded in a rhetoric of reform which tended to set traditional structures and practices in fundamental opposition to the next evolutionary stage in higher education. The "virtual university" stood as a technological destiny, the logical replacement for the cumbersome, rigid, and anachronistic "traditional" institution.

In such evangelical discourses, online education was often represented as an inevitable challenge and a transformative force. In the stronger version of this rhetoric, brick-and-mortar universities would vanish, no doubt in a puff of pipe smoke and a rustle of tweeds, to be replaced by the effervescent movement of digital information in global telecommunication networks. The structural transformation of academic labor and the academic profession was depicted as both a necessary prerequisite for and an inevitable consequence of the increasing technological mediation of higher education.

The zeal with which this evangelical vision was professed is perhaps difficult to remember in a more sober age.[1] Nevertheless, it was not so very many years ago that encomiums on the "death of the traditional university" were being uttered with little caution by university administrators, corporate CEOs, the heads of research organizations, government officials, and even some faculty. Peter Drucker's prediction that traditional universities would become "relics" in the early decades of the twenty-first century (Drucker 1997) was only an inflated version of a claim being made in calmer tones elsewhere. According to some, the virtualization of the university would mean the replacement of "physical processes with new processes that can be accomplished over networks" (Katz & Oblinger 2000: 2). For others, the technology heralded the "unbundling of higher education services" with "different providers carrying out different functions: curricular development, delivery of instructional modules, provision of student services, student evaluation, and awarding credentials" (Wallhaus 2000: 22). The intensified division of labor made possible by breaking the faculty's monopoly on education would demote professors to deprofessionalized "content experts," or at least allow universities to "rationalize" their labor practices. One university professor, commenting on and offering admonishment to faculty resistant to online education, stated that:

> [u]niversities are in the information business, and the information railroad is coming
> [...] we would be wise to ask whether the particularly quaint way that we manufacture,

distribute and deliver that education will survive the arrival of the information railroad. (Wulf 1998: 1–2)

It is this type of rhetoric that early critics of online education responded to and came to equate with the real developmental trajectories of the field despite the wide diversity of actual practice. For critics, the dissolution of the university into digital networks would make possible the further dissolution of the traditional social and professional structures in which higher education had been embedded for close to a millennium. Thus, online education became a major focus of debate over the future of higher education. The debate, however, was one in which the question of online education as an actually existing socio-technical movement with a complex history became inseparable from the simplistic rhetoric surrounding the technology underlying it. Once "online education" had been solidified as a rhetorical or discursive figure, the debate could be carried out with little detailed examination of ongoing socio-technical developments in the field, specifically the way in which the technology itself actually embodied and supported the vision depicted in the evangelical discourse. Its "nature" was fixed, and conflictual interests polarized around it.

Online education thus appears in one of two registers in debates over educational reform in the late 1990s. One side presents a story of the progressive development of technology as it is applied to the organization of higher education, leading to pedagogical advances and to the new forms of administration required for the realization of the technology's full potentials, both pedagogical and economic. Peter Drucker's famous claim, mentioned above, is a much-cited, if extreme, instance of this view, though it has had more recent and more sober-minded proponents as well: "[Universities] will need to transform [to take advantage of online education] or they will die" (Bates 2004).[2] Here, online education is understood as a concatenation of tools that impose certain adaptations and structural adjustments. The alignment of these changes with particular economic interests is regarded as merely incidental.[3] Online education is neutralized to the point where any suggestion of a political context disappears behind a façade of technical inevitability.

The other side presents a socio-political account of the dynamics of corporate power in the contemporary university. Online education is seen as a lever of neoliberal reform, an extension to the university of a capitalism which is now digital, global, and knowledge-based. Information technology has supplied capital with a powerful means of integrating and transforming a site of social practice previously independent of markets and economic production. In David Noble's words, "[…] here as elsewhere technology is but a vehicle and a disarming disguise" (2002b: 26).[4] In this view, online education is reified around political–economic interests which it is claimed, unequivocally, to represent. Commodification, commercialization, and corporatization are understood as fundamental dimensions of the technology and its consequences for higher education and the university.

Both sides of the debate pay particular attention to the way in which technology will, for better or worse, transform the professional structure and pedagogical practices of university teaching. What one group conceives as a search for greater efficiency and accountability, the other sees as the increasing deprofessionalization (even the automation) of academic labor. What one side praises as greater flexibility for students, the other condemns as an extension of managerial control over instructors. What one side sees as a means of integrating higher education into a rapidly changing information society, the other regards as the death of the critical university and its subordination to commercial interests. What one side interprets as a pedagogical advance, the other criticizes as an attempt to wrestle profit out of an expensive and recalcitrant institution through the commodification of learning.

The problem with these accounts is not that their claims, taken individually, are entirely incorrect, nor that they point to insignificant trends in the university. The problem is the general philosophy of technology underlying *both* versions of the story. On each side, technology emerges as a *fait accompli* with which the university must comply or which it must reject out of hand in defense of traditional academic values and priorities. Educational technologies are supposedly uniquely compatible with neoliberalism, which supplies their ultimate meaning and supports the growth of online education as an instance of pure technical development. Both views, then, are based on essentially deterministic assumptions, drawing on a perspective which has been rigorously criticized in both philosophical and empirical studies of technology.[5]

This has led to an unfortunate situation in which each account, while sharing an identical spontaneous philosophy of technology, appears exclusive of the other; they are divided between priorities and values which are imagined to be irreconcilable. One side tends to ignore or dismiss the political–economic climate within which online education has developed, externalizing critical claims, while the other depicts technology as a static given, intrinsically biased in favor of capitalism and unresponsive to social pressures and choices. While some recent research has begun to note and respond to this situation,[6] the debate largely continues to reproduce these polarized and reified terms.

This impasse is in need of redressing from within an alternative philosophical orientation that can widen the scope of critical debate over online education and the restructuring of the university. Critical theory of technology supplies such an orientation in its emphasis on the dynamics of technological design and development as social and political processes. In order to resituate technology in the politics of the contemporary university, we will examine the case of an early experiment in educational computer conferencing. In the final sections of this chapter, we will draw some conclusions from this case regarding methodology and policy in the online education debate.

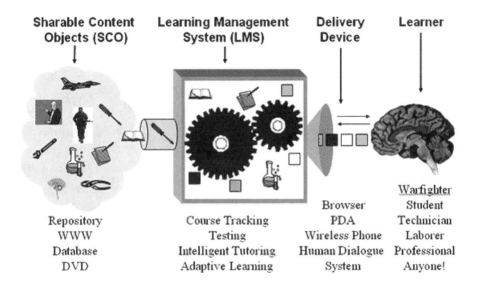

Figure 13.1: A graphical illustration of automated online education, reproduced courtesy of the Advanced Distributed Learning Initiative of the Office of the US Secretary of Defense.[7]

From Commodification to Communication:
Differing Socio-technical Paradigms

Critical observers of the potential "impacts" of the computer in higher education have, from early on, envisaged it in terms of the commodification of knowledge, the automation—or at least de-skilling—of instruction, and the subordination of education to economic ends (Figure 13.1). Lyotard (1984), for example, sees the computer reducing knowledge to "quantities of information," and as "rigorously [externalizing knowledge] with respect to the knower" (13). Aronowitz (2000) concurs: in computer-mediated education the student "responds to packaged material," which is prepared by star academics but delivered by a casualized labor force (155). In a rather dystopian projection depicted by Klass (2000), this casualized labor force is replaced by actors, presumably because once adequately standardized content is supplied, its delivery is best handled by experts in performance and persuasion. Noble (2002b) also follows this line, depicting online education as successor to the commodified educational products and Taylorized labor process of early twentieth century correspondence schools. The critics agree: computer mediation means a reduction of education to information, of faculty to deprofessionalized "content providers," and of the university to a site of commercial information production.

Were these conclusions based on thorough empirical study, they could be challenged only by equally thorough studies. Indeed, the empirical reality of online education is a great deal more heterogeneous than the critical discourse, in its fear of a monolithic technical juggernaut, has allowed. Unfortunately, critiques of online education have largely failed to capture the real situation. Rather, they have tended to argue from the numerous historical precedents for the process they believe themselves to be observing. Indeed, similar critiques have appeared throughout the history of educational technologies and media, from Plato's attack on writing to the fear in the 1950s that TV would usher in the era of "the automatic student and the robot professor" (Plato 1973; Smith 1958).

What Plato has to say about writing is not much different in substance from later critics of educational broadcasting and computing, centering as it does on the way in which the new medium offers a static embodiment of knowledge and a vehicle for distributing it independent of social relations, contexts, and structures. Plato was clearly thinking of the educational application of the computer, or perhaps the Internet, when he prophesied that "students will receive a quantity of information without proper instruction" (1973: 96). "Proper" instruction requires dynamic contexts of co-presence. As Lyotard later approaches the computer, so Plato approaches writing as a means of "externalizing knowledge from the knower." Both critiques are rooted in a formal conception of how writing or the computer act on information—the technologies are conceived as essentially *representational* in nature, and it is as such that they are understood to relate to and remodel the education process according to a narrow pedagogy of information delivery and acquisition (Blake & Standish 2000; Robins & Webster 2002).

Early educational applications of the computer, such as computer-assisted instruction (CAI), clearly reflect just such a reduction of education, and support both the commodification of content and an agenda of automation. Designed as basic drill-and-practice tools, CAI systems draw upon the affordances granted by the pre-network era computer as a stand-alone information processor—its capacity to record, store, analyze, represent, and organize information. The system presents a specific content and the student "interacts" with the technology by responding to prompts that cue movement through it. The system regulates the student's progress by intermittently evaluating performance on standardized quizzes (Distefano et al. 2004; Hiltz 1994). The social relations of education are here broken down along functional lines. Social interaction is replaced by interaction with technology and the static content it delivers, and the producers of knowledge are separated from the learners they traditionally encounter in the classroom.

This configuration of the computer in the education process is not limited to "classic" CAI, though the latter represents the most clearly automated form of computer-mediated education. The CD-ROM courseware disparaged by Noble (2002b) reproduces a similar model, and offers education in a similarly commodified form alienated from human interaction and dialog. Contemporary learning management systems (LMS) such as WebCT, while they are not designed to support full automation, can and sometimes have been appropriated for deprofessionalized forms of computer-mediated education on the basis of an interpretation of the Internet as a means of distributing computerized representations of knowledge. In that context, the computer is configured as an information-delivery device, and the educational process is divided into discrete production tasks. The work of the teacher is partly delegated to the system, and the remaining human tasks, such as information gathering, performance evaluation, and certification, can be handled by low-paid clerical employees or part-time tutors.

It is easy to see why critics might disparage this version of computer-mediated education as a commodified pedagogy of information delivery. Reduced to information, education seemingly no longer requires its traditional social mediations—the physical classroom, the university as an institution, or the professional teacher. It can be organized like a process of industrial production of commodified goods consumed by isolated individual learners. It is also easy to imagine who might find such a redefinition of education attractive. It is a short step from a pedagogical model of information delivery to an industrial model of information production, and a commercial model of information marketing and consumption. The transformation of education into a product promises a new revenue stream for economically beleaguered universities. In economic terms this product resembles CDs or software, the marginal cost of which declines rapidly with the number of units produced. A popular "brand," such as MIT, might become a sort of educational Britney Spears, milking "platinum" courseware for big profits. The university finally has a "business model." University administrators eager to cut costs can find common ground here with commercial interests seeking access to the multi-billion dollar education market.

An economic logic which views education as simply another variety of "e-commerce," with knowledge as a commodity to be packaged, marketed, and sold, appropriates the available technologies as a system for distributed representation. If these technologies can divest higher education of a need for classrooms, physical plant, and teachers, they can also reduce the operating costs of serving a fast-growing student population. While often disguised with claims of improved quality, accessibility, and a more flexible "student-centered" approach, the economic motives behind this pedagogical model are strong enough to tar educational technologies irredeemably with the brush of Mammon. On the university's economic ledger pedagogical niceties are incidental to cost-efficient delivery of prepackaged, standardized courseware, and access to globally dispersed learner markets (cf. Galan 2001: 18–21).

A pedagogy based on commodified, automated, decontextualized information delivery, the technologies of distance education and the prevalence of an economic discourse of higher education have been so tightly interwoven as to enable a critique of the one to imply, even stand in for, a critique of the others. Even where networked educational technologies are concerned— technologies that can and do support human interaction—the tendency has been to understand them in terms of the representational capacities of the computer rather than as redefining or resituating these capacities in the context of new forms of mediated communication.

But it is precisely this latter potential that opens the computer up for appropriation within pedagogical (and political) frameworks other than the delivery of information commodities, and so raises the possibility of directing the technology, and online education as a movement, away from a formal replication of teacher functions in a strategy of automation and deprofessionalization. Networked learning can be based on the computer's *relational* rather than its *representational* capacities. The assumption that online education is equivalent to the organization, presentation, and delivery of information ignores a vital impact of the convergence of telecommunication and computing, namely, the creation of an environment for social interaction between geographically and temporally distant users. While this might seem an obvious point, it has great significance for the politics of online education. A historical case may serve to clarify this significance.

Computer Conferencing at WBSI[8]

In the early 1980s, while CAI was still the dominant mode of educational computing, a number of academically based experiments tested educational applications of asynchronous, text-based computer conferencing. Successful online discussion groups of a more general, voluntary, and sometimes random sort had emerged prior to this on such services as The Source and CompuServe. Educators critical of the information-delivery model of CAI hoped to draw upon the capacity of conferencing systems to support group communication in order to realize a model of online education based on a dialogic pedagogy (Feenberg 1993; Kerr & Hiltz 1982; Mason & Kaye 1989). Among the early experiments were a series of teacher training courses at the New Jersey Institute of Technology (NJIT), some Adult and Continuing Education courses at the New York Institute of Technology, the Connected Education program at the New School for Social Research in New York City, and an experiment in mass education using computer conferencing at the Open University in the United Kingdom. The first organized online education program, however, was the School of Management and Strategic Studies (SMSS), which opened in January 1982 at the Western Behavioral Sciences Institute (WBSI) in La Jolla, California.

The SMSS was a two-year executive education program dedicated to fostering critical humanistic dialog around issues and problems of information societies in a rapidly globalizing economy. Participants came together at week-long biannual meetings at the Institute, but otherwise their only link with the program and one another was the Electronic Information Exchange System (EIES)—the conferencing system employed in the SMSS. The program was divided into four semester-long courses, bracketed by the face-to-face meetings, with each course broken down into month-long seminars moderated by university faculty from all over the United States. There were no assignments, no grades, and no certification—and yet despite the lack of the usual external motivations for study, the SMSS grew from a program with eight initial participants, all but one in the United States, to over 150 participants from two dozen countries around the world. So successful was the SMSS that it was ranked in Harvard Business School's top five executive education programs (Gottschalk 1983; Meeks 1987).[9] While the success of an asynchronous, globally distributed online education program might appear in hindsight merely to confirm what everybody already knew about the "impacts" of new communication technologies on education—increased access and quality, user enthusiasm, and the potentials of "virtualization"—the SMSS owed less to the abstract properties of new technologies than to the way in which their affordances and limitations were interpreted through specific pedagogical and social values, and actively appropriated. WBSI's faculty and staff realized from the start that computer conferencing was not a means of information delivery but a context for social interaction, communication, and dialog. However, since the medium was untried in education, no models for conducting an educational computer conference existed. Moreover, conferencing systems had not been designed with specifically educational applications in mind, but according to generic definitions of the communication process (Hiltz 1994; WBSI 1987). Faculty, staff, and participants in the SMSS had to invent online education as they went along, negotiating between various notions of alternative pedagogy and the affordances and constraints of the conferencing medium.

Distributed, asynchronous, text-based communication is the primary mode of interaction afforded by computer conferencing. Today there is a standard discourse for describing the advantages of this mode of interaction: flexible anytime/anywhere learning, increased time for formulating considered contributions, egalitarian communication in the absence of visible status markers, and so on. But in the practical contexts of the early experiments, these features of computer conferencing bore an ambivalent relationship to the education process. Distribution and asynchronicity also meant the absence of a ready-made physical context for learning, and the devaluation of passive forms of participation that are perfectly legitimate in such contexts, where visible co-presence enables the easy flow of tacit communication. The verbal cues and situational norms that contextualize interaction in face-to-face settings are absent in text-based communication, making it awkwardly opaque and even intimidating for new users (Feenberg 1989). The ambivalence of these formal features of the technology raised a number of pedagogical challenges for faculty, staff, and participants alike.

In CAI, learning is coded in the prescriptive structure of the system itself as a shell for organizing a content and for evaluating student performance. Most contemporary LMS similarly provide a structure for the representation and acquisition of content and the configuration of tools and applications. In computer conferencing, by contrast, there are no predetermined prescriptions for learning at all. The system provides a structure for interaction and basic tools to facilitate communication, but no more. Conferencing systems do not replicate teaching functions, nor do they supply an explicit pattern for focused, cumulative, or directed engagement with content—central elements of learning. There is no content, as far as the system is concerned, apart from the participants' messages. However, regardless of the pure potential of the systems, interaction is by no means a given in the absence of technical prescriptions or social norms of participation.

Where a limited type of human–machine interaction is simply imposed by CAI, human-to-human interaction is a very real *problem* in computer conferencing. Since it is not predetermined or prescribed technically, it has to be actively achieved. And, as was quickly discovered at WBSI, it had to be achieved in the absence of precedents: at first neither teachers nor students had ever been in an online classroom before. How do you achieve interaction, participation, and focused dialog—in a word, education—in an environment in which there are no explicit social norms, in which visual cues are absent, and in which none of the participants are together in the moment of interaction? Whereas CAI systems answered these questions by delegating teaching functions and roles to the machine, at WBSI they were answered by communicative strategies. These strategies focused primarily on the development of techniques of moderating online discussion.

Arriving at these techniques was not an easy process. Two pedagogical approaches were tried in the early weeks of the first session of the SMSS. One approach was rooted in a belief that the open communication structure of computer conferencing required a "low-impact" moderator. It was presumed that student interest, independent of the conferencing context itself, would drive discussion as it had in other non-educational online forums, and that the provision of a space for communication would suffice to generate focused and meaningful interaction. Students, having completed a reading assignment, were asked to respond to the readings on the basis of very general questions. The questions were accompanied by a fleeting formal introduction to the course, the extent of which was: "Greetings! Here we go." No context or background was supplied through which participants could understand how they might engage substantively in discussion. No norms were proposed through which the participants could understand their roles and responsibilities in this strange environment. And in the absence of the pressures of co-presence, there was no particular compulsion to engage at all. Understandably, little participation resulted.

The other approach came from the opposite direction, assuming that the "emptiness" of the computer conferencing environment needed to be filled with content to which students could react. A series of lengthy introductory messages, analogous to a lecture, was sent out detailing the substantive focus of the seminar, and followed up by a set of challenging and thought-provoking problems to which participants were invited to respond. Whereas the "low-impact" approach did little to defuse the anxiety provoked by the blank computer screen, this "high-impact" approach increased the presence of the moderator to such an extent that it left little room for engagement and participation. As a consequence, it inadvertently transformed the conferencing system into yet another vehicle for delivering content rather than facilitating discussion. Again, little active participation followed from this approach.

Unlike interest-based discussion forums, educational computer conferencing begged for the strong, active presence of a live teacher employing a self-conscious pedagogy. Participation was a function of the moderator's ability to achieve and invite presence, to maintain coherence and direction, and to contextualize, both intellectually and socially, a highly ambiguous communication environment. The moderator had to take on contextualizing, prompting, synthesizing, and facilitating functions and an active leadership role, in such a way as to provide enough structure to engage participants and ensure enough openness to admit them into dialog (Feenberg 1989; Kerr 1984). Providing context and background, establishing the norms and expectations for interaction, outlining a program and a set of goals, and monitoring the progress of participants—standard dimensions of teaching in the offline world—were thus reinterpreted in the conferencing medium as a means of facilitating and sustaining educational interaction.

But contrary to a familiar division between "process" and "content," the moderator could not carry out these organizational functions without being an expert in a particular field of study. Prompt responses to student questions and contributions were necessary in order to sustain the flow and coherence of dialog in a context which tended toward fragmentation. But in the SMSS, the dialog itself consisted of humanistic inquiry into philosophical, social, and political–economic issues, as well as the historical and cultural backgrounds of emerging information societies. This called for an ability on the part of the moderator to evaluate and synthesize abstract concepts, provide historical background and contexts, and survey arguments within a field of inquiry.[10]

WBSI faculty soon realized, however, that here expertise bore a different relation to the educational process than in their classrooms. In order to maintain a coherent and directed flow of dialog and a high level of participation, the synthetic, contextualizing, and reflective activity of the moderator had to be more "punctual" than persistent, but no less incisive than in traditional educational contexts. Perceptions of the limitations of the technology for active, dialogic pedagogy served to contextualize how subject expertise was brought to bear. The moderator needed to guide discussion based on the contributions of the participants themselves, providing background and delineating the scope of a problem to be explored. Expertise took on a quality of responsiveness in conferencing that it does not have in information-delivery models of computer-mediated education. With the computer in charge rather than a teacher, expert knowledge is programmed in before the educational process actually begins and students simply respond to it as an unalterable context. Far from playing out an agenda of automation and commodification, however, WBSI's model of online education innovated an active social role for the instructor in response to the specific constraints and affordances of the conferencing medium.

So far our discussion of the communicative functions of computer conferencing at WBSI seems to reinscribe the traditional antinomy of human and machine. But this cliché does not in fact describe the evolution of the WBSI experiment. It soon became obvious to the group that created the SMSS that they would also have to reinvent computer conferencing if their enterprise was to succeed—to engage directly, that is, in the process of technical innovation. The communicative functions of moderating needed to be accompanied by the development of technical features that could support both the functions themselves and WBSI's pedagogical model. This recognition arose from the problems encountered in using a generic communication technology for specifically educational purposes.

The generic interpretation of communication in conferencing systems failed to take account of how communication differs across social settings. Communication within educational contexts is clearly conducted with different purposes, expectations, roles, values, and norms than dinner table conversation within the family, debates at political meetings, or discussions among hobbyists about their hobbies. At the very least, CAI came with a model, however impoverished, of how education took place, assigning roles, norms, and expectations in a coherent manner. Conferencing did not. The social and pedagogical functions of moderating at WBSI answered to, and in part derived from, this situation. But they also acted as a framework within which certain design features became desirable, and on the basis of which additional features could be innovated.

These features could be as simple as an ability to track individual participants' progress through the conference, allowing the moderator to better facilitate the conversation on the basis of a clear view of everybody's location within it (WBSI 1987). They could be as complex as a subject indexing feature enabling both participants and moderators to follow different thematic threads and to weave these threads together at appropriate moments in summary comments useful for keeping the conversation on track (Feenberg 1989). Experiments at WBSI with this latter feature failed for lack of sufficient computing power, but subsequently inspired the TextWeaver project discussed in a later section of this chapter. Social roles and practices did not develop out of the prior presence of these features. Rather the features were seen as desirable from within the purview of a particular social practice and pedagogical model.

Another major problem with early conferencing was the complexity of the user interface. It required a page of instructions just to sign on to EIES; and once online, the user was faced with lengthy sets of commands for operations as simple and taken-for-granted as writing, editing, quoting, sending and receiving, reading messages, printing, and attaching documents. The so-called "quick reference card" for EIES was 16 pages long (NJIT 1986). The complexity of the system, however, was of a piece with its flexibility—in order to achieve as open and generic a communication environment as possible, designers merely added menus and command strings, to the point where flexibility seemed to reflect the needs and competences of a narrow stratum of technical designers and what came to be called "computer geeks," rather than students and teachers. The memorization of non-intuitive command codes for the performance of intuitive social acts sets a high bar for communication.

WBSI addressed this situation through the development of an original software application: a user interface for educational computer conferencing called Passkey (WBSI 1986, 1987). Similar to web browsers, Passkey was designed as a simplified command interface layered over the more complex communication structure supplied by the conferencing system. Its effect, like the web browser's for the Internet, was to make the process of online communication more accessible to lay users, obviating the need to rely upon an abstruse set of commands. Designed with the experience of both moderators and participants in the SMSS conferences in mind, Passkey represented a technical expression of the social, pedagogical, and programmatic framework developed over the first four years of the program. Once again, the case exhibits not acquiescence to a set of given technical prescriptions, but the adaptation of technology to the needs of a specific user group.

The desire to enact a dialogic pedagogy, the development of social rather than technical delegations in response to technical constraints, and the undertaking of technological development in response and deference to local social values and expectations tells a much different story of online education than is often portrayed in mainstream debates today. One reason for this difference lies in the proximity of both programmatic and technological development to the contexts of actual educational practice. Automation and commodification did not play as agendas in the SMSS, not only because the technology could not easily support them, but because the interests of instructors were directly present in the design and development contexts. The automation of certain moderating functions was suggested at NJIT, and implemented as yet another menu option, on the assumption that participation could most easily be achieved by building in technical features that would require it (Hiltz 1982). If taken in that direction, the technology might have developed to support an agenda similar to information-delivery oriented CAI systems. But it was in providing an alternative to those systems that WBSI largely understood its work.

All in all, dynamic processes of negotiation and development between technical and social factors not only yielded an alternative model of online education, but in the present context they also open up a range of questions for the critical politics of online education, questions that need to be addressed less in terms of the formal properties of technologies as causative agents, and more in terms of the impact of social contexts of design, development, and pedagogical practice.

A Revised Politics of Online Education

Educational technologies only gain definition, functionality, and value in the framework of the pedagogical models they instantiate, the forms of social relationship they construct, and the educational goals they are applied to achieve. The technology only "works" within that model, those relationships, and those goals, which supply a set of guidelines for what education in general is. On an abstract, formal level, of course, it could be said that technologies like CAI, CD-ROM courseware, or content-based online education "transform" education according to a pedagogical model they in a sense "possess." However, this model itself has its origins not in some abstracted technical realm, but at the point where pedagogical, social, and institutional values articulate with design principles, processes, and parameters—the point at which social values and choices come to be translated into technically rational design features.[11] Indeed, the design of technologies is predicated on a prior definition of the situation to which the technologies are to apply. Education must be defined in a functional, social, and organizational sense before a technology can be developed to support it. The technology may embody a pedagogical model that carries certain political implications for society or career consequences for professional educators, but it only does so through an iterative process in which pedagogical assumptions, values, and roles are delegated to technical systems.

Critical theory of technology calls this background of values, assumptions, definitions, and roles that guides technological design the "technical code" (Feenberg 1991, 2002). Technical codes define a framework of technical decision-making within which certain choices appear rational. These codes are a function of the delineation and circumscription of technological development and design by particular social groups to which the ultimate form of the technology is relative. The technical code of online education is relative, then, to the interests, assumptions, and values of the actors who are engaged in the design and development process, and who are thus positioned as powerful interpreters of the technology and the social forms it mediates.

CAI, for example, is not simply a logical derivation from the abstract properties of the computer. It is the product of an interpretation of education which valorizes the representational affordances of the computer and directs development toward automated and commodified forms. Computer conferencing, as the WBSI case shows, opened a completely different interpretive field for computer-mediated education in highlighting the functionality of the computer as a communication device. The alternative pedagogy developed at WBSI was not so much the result of the formal properties of computer conferencing as an appropriation of those properties. Conferencing's formal ambivalences with respect to education were addressed at WBSI through both social and technical adaptations aimed at realizing an active, dialogic online pedagogy. Automation was never an option, not only because technical limitations at that early date precluded it, but also because it was never a value for the developers of the SMSS program. It was incompatible with the technical code out of which WBSI's model of online education emerged.

Computer conferencing and CAI, then, are not just two different uses of the same technology, but supply two completely different paths for the educational appropriation of the computer. They draw upon and support two completely different pedagogical models. They delegate interaction in education in completely different ways. And they operate on two completely different dimensions of the social process of education. Automation and commodification, far from being inevitable consequences of online education, must be understood as contingent outcomes whose realization depends on a particular configuration of the technology and a particular set of pedagogical choices. Here, as elsewhere, the crucial philosophical and political questions to be asked are: what does the technology stand in for in the educational process, how is it involved in delegating functions across that process, and how is a field of social interests delineated to encourage one iteration over other possible ones?

In information-centric iterations of computer-mediated education such as CAI, the technology is designed to stand in for the teacher, to enable the technical performance of the functions of human professionals. It is this that aligns it with a program of automation. Communication-centered models of computer-mediated education present a very different scenario. Here the technology stands in for the classroom as an environment for interaction, dialog, and the formation of community. Rather than taking on a functional role within the educational process, it provides a more or less flexible structure for the negotiation of familiar social roles. Functional delegations are not simply built into the technology, but are actively configured out of a combination of social and technical options that, as in the case of the SMSS, include a role for the professional teacher.

Technologies, educational or otherwise, do not autonomously transform the social contexts into which they are introduced, though their influence in giving shape and substance to those contexts is considerable. Certainly writing transformed the process of learning, but it did not replace dynamic interaction with static information-gathering, as Plato predicted. Over the centuries, educators and students have managed to devise ways of situating writing within interactive social processes. Writing has added its capacities as an information technology to the communicative processes of teaching and learning in ways now so obvious and taken-for-granted that they are barely noted. Networked computing also provides a powerful means of organizing, representing, and transmitting information, but to limit it to these capacities is to sub-optimize its potential as a communication medium. The integration of the technology into education is, however, ongoing, and its ultimate form is not yet decided. There is still time for intervention and redirection in accordance with academic interests and values. Whether a positive evolution of the technology will emerge will depend, in part, on the ability of academics themselves to move beyond the static oppositions and absolute positions that have characterized debates in the field.

Questions of Educational Technology

What are the implications of this analysis for technical design? The "interpretative flexibility" of computer networking is very great. It was easy for new actors with different goals to take over the original project of online education and to redefine it to mean something new. Very quickly, this new conception of the field was reflected in the design of the new "LMS" which have spread across North American campuses. Online education was finally successful but in a form unrecognizable to its original inventors.

These LMS generally emphasize the representational rather than the relational potential of networked computers. Often, but not always, a web forum, equivalent to the computer conferences of old, is included in the product but given little attention by trainers preparing instructors to use the new technology. The interpretation of online education resisted by Noble and others was effectively inscribed in its technical code to the extent that this was technically and politically feasible. In response, resistance to online education has tended to accept this code as inevitable, mistaking a particular social design for the nature of the technology itself.

The WBSI case takes on its full significance against this background. True, it never achieved the widespread usage of the current systems. But it represents an existence proof of the alternative. It demonstrates the possibility of another line of development that would emphasize relational potentials rooted in traditional pedagogical conceptions shared by most faculty rather than the budgetary concerns of administrations and commercial strategists. The single most important constraint that flows from this alternative line of development is small classes, manageable by a living professor, rather than huge audiences or markets for semi-automated educational "products." In this form online education must defend its value on a pedagogical basis because it cannot significantly contribute to cheapening education or selling educational products. There is no "business model" for learning as traditionally conceived, even when the classroom is virtual.

This line of development, too, is inscribed in a technical code. Insofar as the movement for open source educational software depends primarily on faculty input and support, this technical code is likely to emerge as its agenda. To illustrate this point, we will briefly describe two initiatives in this field.

The primitive web forums in most LMS have no educational features but are simple copies of old newsgroup software. Andrew Feenberg, one of the founders of the SMSS, has developed an open source alternative called TextWeaver.[12] This is a conferencing application that includes features specifically designed for education, which enhance online discourse by facilitating quotation from multiple messages, and which enable students and teachers to create and assign their own individual keywords for organizing the discussion archive. These features serve particular pedagogical goals, such as encouraging student-to-student interaction and periodic summations by the teacher.

On a much larger scale, the Sakai Project[13] is a US $6.8 million community source software development project founded by the University of Michigan, Indiana University, MIT, Stanford, the uPortal Consortium, and the Open Knowledge Initiative, with the support of the Andrew W. Mellon Foundation. Sakai is, among other things, creating an open source LMS, the first version of which was released in July 2004. In addition to providing open source online education tools and applications, Sakai is also developing a "Tool Portability Protocol" which will provide a framework for universities to develop and share software. While the open source license of Sakai does not prevent the commercialization of its software, it ensures that the knowledge base upon which such developments are made remains open and sharable. Universities are thus able to retain a much greater level of control over development, adoption, support, and implementation than is possible with commercial systems. This project is perhaps the largest and most promising effort to free online education software development from commercial control, both for cost savings and, more importantly, to ensure that faculty have significant input into the design of the software environments they will employ in their work.

The current state of online education is deeply ambiguous. Administrations have had to temper their ambitions as they discovered that the technology was not capable of delivering on the promise of cost-effectiveness without severely degrading educational quality. This was a prospect resisted by both faculty and students, notably in the California State University System, where demonstrations at the state legislature and resolutions by faculty senates blocked a corporate-sponsored attempt to "wire" the campuses. But before this realization had sunk in, universities invested millions in the infrastructure of online education. The basic software acquired in this context and used now on most campuses retains the representational emphasis reflecting the automating agenda of the commercial vendors who originally drove this process with unrealistic promises.

Meanwhile, faculty often, if not always, appropriate the available systems for a familiar pedagogical practice that combines representation of content, the online equivalent of the textbook, with the active use of a web forum, the online equivalent of classroom discussion. This is precisely the sort of thing envisaged at WBSI 20 years ago. But these practices are not often supported by corresponding reductions in teaching loads and class sizes to render the interactive online pedagogy truly comparable with classroom teaching in terms of burden and effort. This confusing state of affairs may slowly give way to a satisfactory synthesis if open source initiatives are successful and faculty organizations aggressive. This is the outcome toward which we should work rather than resisting online education as such.

Conclusion: Policy and Design

The essential question to ask in a revised politics of online education is whether educational technologies and online programs will work to facilitate the transmission of static information, fostering standardized modes of interaction between human users, machines and commodified knowledge, or whether they can be rooted in an essentially social ideal of education, extending and enabling new forms of mediated interaction. Technology could potentially support either one of these outcomes. But, as outcomes, they are in no sense given prior to specific appropriations within particular social settings.

Struggles over technological change take place in social contexts that have their own historical dynamics, and that provide their own affordances for action, authority, and intervention. The university is no exception. It is a complex social institution organized around an administrative core whose relative power and independence of action have increased significantly over the past half century, but in which there is still a strong tradition of professional self-governance, relative academic autonomy, and participatory decision-making.[14] Despite the growing discretionary power of both administrative bodies and state/corporate interests, faculty and students still have some authority in the institution and can intervene in institutional change. Community-based interventions are crucial sites for the enactment and also the analysis of an alternative critical politics of online education.

One of the most powerful examples of this in recent days was faculty and student intervention into administrative–corporate initiatives in online education at York University, well known from Noble's *Digital Diploma Mills* series. This intervention took place in the context of the largest faculty strike in Canadian history, situating online education as a matter of "the classroom versus the boardroom" (Noble 1998a). While the strike involved more than educational technologies, of concern to striking faculty were initiatives put forward unilaterally by the York administration, which proposed to use online course offerings as leverage for corporate advertising revenue. The university administration was attempting to appropriate the technology under a horizon of commercial/economic values. Online education thus appeared to be a top-down project of university administrators whose motives stemmed not from any particular pedagogical goal, but rather from economic imperatives.

Unsurprisingly, the administrative appropriation of the technology provoked opposition from some faculty and students.

What is significant in this, from the standpoint of a critical theory of technology, is the use of the administrative prerogative for policy formation to give a specific form, shape, and substance to online learning within the university. The York administration was doing what university administrators generally do—shape policy. In doing so, it established a framework within which online education was to be understood to interact with existing structures in higher education. By manipulating the incentive and promotion structure within the university to encourage the articulation of online education within a set of economic relations and goals, the York administration contributed to defining the code under which online education would emerge.

Faculty countered the administrative initiative in a similar way, not by waging a successful struggle against technology, but by negotiating a new contract with the university; that is, by intervening in the institutional appropriation of technology by contributing to defining the parameters within which it would be implemented into both educational practices and institutional structures. The new contract instituted provisions which give faculty "direct and unambiguous control over all decisions relating to the automation of instruction, including veto power" (Noble 1998a). Such control extends both to use of technology for classroom enhancement as well as online delivery as an alternative method, and is designed to ensure that all technology-based initiatives are consistent with principles and values of the academic community. Contract negotiation and policy formation—familiar arenas of the timeless struggle between university faculty and administration—can thus be understood as significant sites for the determination of the technical code of online education, as well as important sites for the enactment of a critical politics of online education. This example demonstrates that faculty can draw upon the traditional structures of self-governance to redirect online education in a manner that reflects their interests.

Similarly, though in less extreme circumstances, California State University System faculty and students, as mentioned above, managed to block a corporate-sponsored attempt to "wire" the campuses. San Diego State University's faculty senate then developed a comprehensive distance education policy which addresses the issues of automation, de-skilling, and commercialization.[15] The policy grounds the development of distance education in the traditional mission, governance and decision-making structures, and value frameworks of the university. It mandates that distance education technologies be evaluated according to traditional pedagogical and professional principles, and that relationships with external organizations providing courseware and technology be open to scrutiny by faculty committees. Most importantly, the policy requires that both educational technologies and distance programs be organized in a way that respects faculty autonomy, academic freedom, and intellectual property. The policy also contains guidelines for employment of adjunct and part-time non-tenured faculty, and thus engages directly and proactively with one of the main points of political contention in debates over online education, its role in the deprofessionalization of university teaching.

Noble (1998b) depicts the faculty and student action at York as evidence that "the bloom is off the rose"—that the promise of educational technologies as imagined by university managers, corporate developers, and marketing consultants has failed.[16] But, perhaps more lastingly and significantly, Noble has also participated in defining the technical code of online education for faculty— ironically making his own positive contribution to the field of educational technology. Read in this way, Noble's critical writing and the struggles of faculty and students against a particular program do not slay the dragon of online education, but (more powerfully) add to the general framework of development, implementation, and design out of which educational technologies and online programs will subsequently emerge. The struggles of critical constituents within the university can, in instances such as this, lead to the incorporation of such concerns as guidelines for designing and adopting technologies. Critical engagement rather than critical opposition must inform a revised critical politics of online education, and contribute to the furtherance of a technical code that is palatable to faculty.

Policy developments with respect to educational technologies and distance education show that critical academic concerns are becoming part of the assumptive background of online education within the university. Dramatic actions such as that at York are not, however, the only means of establishing a context for critical intervention. Local, regional, and national faculty associations have been quick to establish guidelines for the framing of faculty concerns around online education, and some universities have formulated implementation, development, and use policies that reflect such concerns. Faculty association guidelines and university policies have thus acted for the incorporation of faculty interests into online education—the shifting of the technical code to admit of the critical concerns that have been voiced by faculty and students.

The American Association of University Professors (AAUP) and the Canadian Association of University Teachers (CAUT) have issued position statements on online and distance education that act as an important basis for local faculty intervention in the appropriation of educational technologies.[17] In the case of CAUT, these statements address issues of commercialization, privatization, and deprofessionalization. By framing its position with respect to particular social issues, CAUT establishes a framework through which faculty can actively intervene in and contribute to the formation of technical codes of online education, and direct an alternative course of development. What this framework promotes is critical engagement by local institutions in the appropriation of educational technologies, allowing the possibility that faculty concerns can be realized as constitutive elements of design.

The AAUP statement on distance education is framed in terms of the disjuncture between academic policies governing more traditional means of distance education and the novel affordances of networked technologies. Recognition that the new technologies have the capacity to support a fundamentally different pedagogy than that of the correspondence school model and CAI suggests that they ought to be designed to better conform with basic academic values and priorities. Academic freedom, free access to information, freedom of teaching, intellectual property rights, and so on are central to the position statement and outline clearly the need to embed new technologies and online programs in traditional professional and institutional interests and structures. The responsibility for developing online education is situated within the academic community as a whole, with recognition that new technologies must be integrated into education through the normal academic channels.

Do these position statements have any impact on local policy? We have not surveyed the broad spectrum of institutions adopting the new technologies nor the full range of policies and implementation strategies developed in them, but the community-based initiatives at York and San Diego State provide significant examples of the sort of developments we hope are widespread. The general frameworks for action provided by CAUT and AAUP can certainly act as guidelines for local faculty associations in efforts to ensure that online education emerges in extension rather than opposition to their professional interests and pedagogical concerns.

What is most significant for a revised critical politics of online education is that these policies and position statements provide a framework for the development and implementation of online education and educational technologies *within* the context of the values, norms, and expectations that typify universities as professional organizations. They strengthen the alternative technical code of online education worked out in early computer conferencing by placing that code within the larger institutional and organizational frameworks of universities and professional associations. And they address the concerns of online education's most vehement critics, appropriating critical discourse into socio-technical decision-making.

In the wake of the general disappointment with the exaggerated claims made for online education, there is wide latitude for faculty intervention and participation in shaping the terms on which it will impact the academic labor process, the division of academic labor, and ownership of intellectual resources. It is now clear that online education will not destroy the university as we know it. What it will become will be determined ultimately by the politics of the very institution and the political engagement of the professional academics it promised to replace only a few years ago.

Notes

1. Contrast this evangelism with the contemporary language of "blended learning" or "instructional enhancement."
2. It is ironic that when in the mid-1980s, the Western Behavioral Sciences Institute invited Peter Drucker to speak to the first online educational program, he had his secretary send back a preprinted card declining the invitation. Apparently, it took a while for this futurologist to see the future and even then his vision turned out to be pretty fuzzy.
3. Cf. Bates (2000), Duderstadt (1999), Inglis et al. (2002), Katz and Oblinger (2000), Naidu (2003), Smith (2002), and Steeples and Jones (2002).
4. Cf. Aronowitz (2000), Levidow (2002), Moll (1997, 2001), Robins and Webster (1999), and Schiller (1999).
5. Cf. Callon and Latour (1981), Latour (1991, 1995, 1999), Pinch and Bijker (1989), and Winner (1977, 1986).
6. Cf. Cornford and Pollock (2003), Feenberg (1993, 1999a, 2002), Gunawardena and McIsaac (2004), and Robins and Webster (2002).
7. See Slosser (2001). A more recent iteration of this model is available at cordra.lsal.cmu.edu/cordra/information/presentations/2005/nime/global20050509.ppt.
8. Documentary material for this section was obtained from the WBSI archive in the Applied Communication and Technology Lab at Simon Fraser University, Vancouver, Canada.
9. For a more detailed account of the structure and legacy of the SMSS program, see Feenberg (1993, 1999a).
10. For an account of the relation of communicative and intellectual functions in educational conferencing, see Xin (2003).
11. See Feenberg (1995, 1999c, 2002), Latour (1995), and Callon and Latour (1981).
12. The website for the TextWeaver project can be found at www.textweaver.org
13. The website for the Sakai Project can be found at www.sakaiproject.org
14. Clark Kerr's famous account of increasing administrative autonomy in the "multiversity" (Kerr 2001) tends to be confirmed by more recent studies of the growth and development of university management and managerial strategies; cf. Bruneau and Savage (2002), Collins (2002), Delanty (2001), and Reed and Deem (2002).

15. The policy is posted on Andrew Feenberg's homepage, to be found at www-rohan.sdsu.edu/faculty/feenberg/sdsudisted.html

16. It should be noted that educational technologies also raised questions of the "virtual" crossing of picket lines in a later strike at York—this one involving the union for teaching assistants, graduate assistants, and contract lecturers; see Lotherington (2001).

17. See www.aaup.org; www.caut.ca/english/

Chapter 14

Braving the Body:
Embodiment and (Cyber-)Texts

Tina S. Kazan

While rhetorical situations operate on two levels—the discursive and the corporeal—popular culture reinforces the notion that online communication occurs without bodies and that face-to-face communication is not only a distinctly physical act but one that portrays a drastically different persona from the selves people create online.[1] In other words, it seems that who we are online is not who we are "in real life." It is not only that we are "different" selves in each of these forums, but also that the media want to valorize one of these selves as the "real" self. Dean (1999) discusses the many fears the public has about the Internet, such as the spread of viruses and the presence of predators who prey on children and women. She argues, we "fear that new communication technologies threaten to destroy reality" and what is at stake is authority: "the need to fix the real, to find that place where it cannot be refuted, where it must be conceded, is rooted in an apparent need to ground authority" (1069).

In rhetorical theory, one's authority derives from one's *ethos*, the Greek word for "moral character" and the root for "ethics." Though "ethos is generally defined as the good character and the consequent credibility of the rhetor," where such authority resides is debatable. Aristotle located authority in the text, which was to "demonstrate that the rhetor is a person of good sense (*phronesis*), virtue (*arete*), and good will (*eunoia*)." Others, like Cicero and Quintilian, argued that nondiscursive elements such as the rhetor's "actions and examples in life" factored into one's ethos (Covino & Jolliffe 1995: 15). For Aristotle, "discourse becomes an active construction of character—or, rather, of an image, a representation of character—and Aristotelian theory seeks to outline the means whereby such imagemaking is achieved" (Baumlin & Baumlin 1994: xv). The speaker is thus positioned within the text, "no longer simply its origin (and thus a consciousness standing outside the text) but rather a signifier standing *inside* an expanded text. The rhetor's physical presence and appearance, his gestures, inflections, and accents of style, are all involved in acts of signification" (Baumlin & Baumlin 1994: xvi).

In textually oriented forums like email and listservs, one constructs oneself discursively.[2] Yet, nonlinguistic elements also contribute to one's ethos. If one's screen name designates one's institutional affiliation, for example, the rhetor may garner prestige (or derision, as the case might be). How one is reacted to by other participants and with what frequency, for instance, on a listserv, might suggest that one is considered an "expert," or worthy of attention. Although such information may be evidenced only through text, these responses nevertheless reveal information about one's (nondiscursive) reputation. When we interact in cyberspace, we construct an online ethos and this ethos shifts depending on our audience and depending on the "self" we want to create. I am thinking here of what Eva Bednarowicz (2002) calls "*persona*-bility," describing how online tutors must create personas appropriate to the context and must be both personal and personable to be effective. So is it with other kinds of online participants: those who can create a range of personas are the more successful communicators.

According to Baumlin (1994), if one takes:

> an incarnationist perspective, one might argue that all discourse, in its essence, is oriented toward (or proceeds from) the body; there is *ethos* precisely *because* there is a body, because there is a material presence that "stands before" the texts that it speaks or writes. (xxiii–xxiv)

Yet, ethos, according to Baumlin, can be approached "only within a set of paradoxes and downright contradictions" (Baumlin 1994: xxvi). These paradoxes and contradictions are perhaps why some people fear the Internet and why popular media seem obsessed with locating the "real self" online. This chapter looks at the body's relationship to online communication, how the body gets (dis-)embodied online, and how ethos and ethics factor into the "selves" writers and readers forge in cyberspace.

As hyper-readers,[3] we are what Bakhtin (1981) would call "concrete listener[s]." Rhetoric, in Bakhtin's conception, "oriented toward the listener and his answer," relies on a concrete listener "who actively answers and reacts" (280). This listener offers a "surplus" integral to the rhetorical act. In other words, meaning does not reside in the typed body, or utterance, but in the interaction(s) between the various speakers and listeners, with the position of listener an active and dialogic one.

This chapter is primarily confined to textually oriented spaces, such as email, interactive discussions, and discussion boards, but its main argument—that we create embodied personas online and that very creation involves ethical choices—holds true for other forms of electronic communication and might be particularly relevant for e-classrooms, spaces in which teachers and students never meet face-to-face. In email and (a-)synchronous discussions, we communicate as *typed* bodies. These uniform utterances suggest a homogenized body, because in cyberspace, we seem to take on an undifferentiated identity. Physically, each interaction looks the same. Yet, hyper-readers must listen beyond these typing bodies. They must look beyond appearances to the discursive and corporeal substance of the exchange, from diction, grammar and syntax to disclosure and desire.

The challenge of presenting a "self" or "selves" online is a formidable task for both writers and readers. Writers strive not only to represent themselves, but also to decide which "self" or "selves" to present. Hyper-readers struggle with interpretation and determining what they believe or reject. More importantly, they operate in a forum that invites response. Hyper-readers, bombarded by cybertext, have the difficult task of making judgments, formulating responses, and asking questions. This must be done *in text*, and in most pedagogical cases these replies are documented.

"You've Got No Body": Cultural Notions of Computer Technology

I begin my discussion with two popular movies, Nora Ephron's *You've Got Mail* (1998) and Irwin Winkler's *The Net* (1995), to show how prevailing cultural texts want to fix the "real." In the first example, I uncover how *You've Got Mail* denies fluidity between online and offline personas. The movie tries to excuse the "real life" unethical actions of Joe Fox (Tom Hanks) and locates his "real" self online. In this case, "the online self" is equivalent to one's expression of feelings. The second example, *The Net*, invokes the popular fear that computers can erase one's identity. The movie suggests that Angela Bennett (Sandra Bullock) *is* her computer identity, again locating the "real" self online, but in this case, "the online self" is information rather than emotion. Nevertheless, the embodied Angela Bennett is able to subvert this discursive construction. The contradictory relationships between disembodiment and embodiment in these two films mirror the same tension hyper-readers and writers encounter. Indeed, this movie analysis is followed with two teaching examples in which students make specific choices about their online embodiments. Hollywood's (mis-)conceptions influence students' as well as teachers' understanding of electronic communication and technology in general.

In *You've Got Mail*, as soon as her boyfriend leaves for work and is safely out of view, Kathleen Kelly (Meg Ryan) runs to her laptop to continue her online correspondence with "NY 152." When she logs on as "Shopgirl," her AOL account tells her, "You've got mail." As film viewers, we quickly learn that "NY 152" is Joe Fox (Tom Hanks) and that, like Kathleen, he has a partner from whom he conceals his online dialogs. More importantly, Joe Fox hails from the family that owns *Fox Books* Superstore, the corporate bookstore that will put Kathleen's *The Shop Around the Corner* (the name of the 1940 film which inspired this remake) out of business.

Kathleen and Joe meet face-to-face for the first time when Joe brings his much younger relatives to Kathleen's children's bookstore. When Kathleen introduces herself as the owner of the shop, Joe identifies himself as "Joe," for he does not want her to know that he is Joe Fox, responsible for the superstore that is being built around the corner from Kathleen's bookstore. Kathleen cannot identify him on either level—as Joe Fox, her business adversary, or as "NY 152," her online "affair." Joe knows that his store will compete with Kathleen's children's bookstore, but he, too, is unaware that she is the "Shopgirl" with whom he is infatuated. The movie continues to exploit the differences between the online selves of these characters and their face-to-face selves.[4] It is only in the final scene of the film that Kathleen learns what we know—that NY 152, the man with whom she has fallen in love online, is in fact Joe Fox, the man whose company has put her out of business and who subsequently tries to woo her. Of course, the two leads must fall in love according to the romantic comedy formula.

But the movie wants to have it both ways. Joe says, "If I hadn't been *Fox Books* and you hadn't been *The Shop Around the Corner* and we'd just met ... ." He pauses, wondering what might have been. But Joe and Kathleen *are Fox Books* and *The Shop Around the Corner*. And they are the identities they reveal online. Otherwise, why would we want them to eventually come together? At the same time, we are to "forgive" the fact that Joe's super bookstore has put Kathleen's independent bookstore out of business. The film suggests that the "real" identity of the two characters is expressed online and that some of the more complicated aspects of their material lives will vanish or should not matter. In the celluloid world, love conquers all, including bankruptcy, but the important point for my analysis is that the film deliberately exaggerates the differences between the online and face-to-face personas of these characters. The film depends on our being able simultaneously to sustain a belief in these differences while desiring them to be reconciled so the love plot can culminate.[5] The film exalts the cyber persona as the "true" self. In real life, which is much messier, the characters exchange barbs, encounter work challenges, fall ill, and even cry. The characters are not "more" themselves "in real life" than in cyberspace; rather, it is a false dichotomy to pretend that when Joe Fox goes online he is no longer the owner of a bookstore conglomerate. However the film may subvert these boundaries by the conclusion, it depends on our believing they exist in the first place.

We see similar distinctions in *The Net*, a thriller involving Angela Bennett (Sandra Bullock), a program systems analyst who telecommutes. Film critic Roger Ebert (1995) describes Bennett as "a shy, reclusive intellectual who, in the old days, would have been a librarian or a schoolmarm," and maybe a bookstore owner is another contemporary parallel. Like most thrillers, *The Net* involves a number of betrayals and misreadings, as Angela Bennett tries to discover why some cyber-terrorist group wants her killed. The film revolves around Bennett's identity—both online and offline, and this identity confusion is played out in a number of ways. For example, Bennett's mother has Alzheimer's disease and thus never recognizes Angela when she comes to visit. Even after Angela reminds her that "No, Mom, my name's Angela," her mother believes Angela must be one of her former students, thus misreading her.

Even the tagline used to advertise the film captures the fear that many people have of the Internet: *Her driver's license. Her credit cards. Her bank accounts. Her identity. DELETED.* The film suggests that Angela's identity *can* easily be deleted. Moszkowicz (1999) describes how Bennett:

> is then set up by an adversary from the world of computer networks, who deletes her files from all public records and secures her re-emergence in cyberspace, not as Angela Bennett at all, but as a more dubious character by the name Ruth Marx. Her dislocation within cyberspace is a focus for anxiety, contributing to the film's success as a thriller by working on popular fears of technology. (214–215)

Everything about Bennett's identity is taken away, from her social security number to her home; even her corporeal identity has been assumed by an imposter who establishes herself as Angela Bennett at the corporation. Moszkowicz (1999) outlines the plot as concerning "a woman on-the-run from an assassin who wants to cause her physical harm and who uses new technology to bring about her virtual death before an actual one" (210). Both an expert on—and now victim of—technology, Bennett must outwit her pursuer, Jack Devlin (Jeremy Northam), a representative of the cyber-terrorist group infiltrating US institutions like Wall Street and LAX.

The Net contains the same tension between embodiment and disembodiment that we see in *You've Got Mail*, a cultural trend of exaggerating the differences between online and offline identities, while desiring to establish the "real" self.[6] Is Angela Bennett her online self, someone who can be reduced to a screen name, a social security number and government records? Or is she a woman who, in several physical confrontations, must defend herself against Jack Devlin? If she *were* only data, then why would Devlin need to pursue her? The film erases her discursively, but also bodily, by putting another woman in Bennett's job. Using the film's own logic, why would someone need to kill Angela Bennett if her "identity" had already been destroyed?

Of course, the film subverts its own premise. If Angela's identity were in fact "deleted," viewers would not need to watch an entire film of the "bad guys" tailing her and trying to kill her. If she could be reduced to a cyber-identity, her physical self would no longer remain a threat. Indeed, we would *have* no thriller if identifying data corresponded to identity, if we were only our discursive selves and not our corporeal selves. The film seems to locate the "real self" more fully online than "in real life," but nonetheless the bodily self must be eliminated. As in *You've Got Mail*, the movie rests on a dichotomy that must ultimately be subverted in order for the film to exist: physical self versus cyberself. In this case, an embodied Angela versus her personal records. However *The Net* may erase Angela's textual identity, it cannot reduce her to a pile of information. Moszkowicz (1999) observes that "experiences of the social—of the film itself—suggest the body still provides fundamental clues to meaning and identity" (225).

Creating an "Other" Body: Identity Online

Movies like *You've Got Mail* and *The Net* unnecessarily divorce bodies from technology. Some readers may find themselves sympathetic to the contradictions that Hollywood embellishes. On the one hand, the lack of identifying markers and corporeal text in cyberspace offers endless possibility; on the other hand, the dominance of discursive text threatens to obliterate the body, leaving readers searching for clues. The following teaching scenario helps clarify these tensions. In it, a student uses computer-mediated communication to create a "self" online.

During the first few weeks of one fall semester, while I was teaching business writing at the University of Illinois at Chicago, a public research university, I received emails regularly from Mike Johnson.[7] These emails asked specific questions about assignments and class discussions from the business communications course I was teaching at the time. Since no "Mike Johnson" appeared on my rosters, I wasn't sure what to make of this correspondence. Because the university had a two-week drop/add period, I assumed that maybe this Mike Johnson had added the course and his name would surface on an updated roster. Nevertheless, each time I went into class, no Mike Johnson came to talk to me. No Mike Johnson signed the attendance book. Mike Johnson seemed to exist only in my email inbox. Yet, he knew all the details of the course and had substantial questions online about class activities and homework.

In week three of the semester, a student waited to talk to me after class. Manuel Rodriguez was a Latino male who sat in the very back of the class. He was slightly older than the 20–25 year olds who populated the course. He asked if I had received the email that he had sent that morning. I quickly responded "no" and that I would check again and get back to him. It didn't occur to me until I read my email that afternoon that Manuel Rodriguez in class was Mike Johnson online. As the semester progressed, reading notes from Manuel Rodriguez signed "Mike Johnson" became less unsettling, since I now knew the person with whom I was interacting. I did wonder why this student opted to erase the identity that bodies and names *embody* and instead create the rather generic persona of a Mike Johnson. I was curious as to why Manuel Rodriguez selected a name that would be read differently, a name less likely to be read as "ethnic" by the dominant culture. What online ethos was he crafting in choosing a screen name and persona that encouraged a different reading than did his given name and "offline self"?

By removing the physical markers of participants, cyberspace alters the rhetorical situation. How writers choose to construct themselves in that space is telling. For instance, in many ways, online communication allows one to exploit the gaps between the culturally read body and one's identity. While many identities cannot be read on our bodies, society nonetheless conflates bodies and identities, interpreting them through what Roof and Wiegman (1995) call an "already culturally determined matrix" (193–194). A person with a body that is not "read" as African American, for instance, in a face-to-face encounter, might have a difficult time being believed or accepted by some people as embodying that racial identity. Indeed, some African Americans "pass" as white whether they mean to do so or not. Nevertheless, the written or oral text can be used to reveal chosen identities that the body does not, and computer-mediated communication makes such disclosure particularly easy. Language continues to dominate online communication (though this is slowly changing as graphics become easier to download). When one reveals an identity online, the corporeal text is not always readily available and so does not compete with the textual identity for meaning.

In his ethnographic work at the University of Hawaii, Warschauer (2000) found that a computer-intensive language course in Hawaiian permitted multiracial students to use discursive text that seemed to conflict with their culturally read corporeal texts. Cyberspace, according to Warschauer, gave these students "an opportunity to fully engage in their Hawaiian selves." Warschauer focuses on one student, Onaona, who was primarily of European ancestry but had a great-grandparent who was Hawaiian. In contrast to the popular notion that cyberlife and "real" life are not connected, Onaona's webpages "allowed her to project herself as a Hawaiian not only online, but 'in real life' as well" (161). I read this "new image" as a new "self" that Onaona has crafted; she has a new corporeal text, one that she can choose to divulge or disguise.

Onaona used cybertext and the "real life text" of her body together, as each supplemented the other. She actually showed coworkers her website, despite the fact that the language was unintelligible to them. The existence of the cybertext prompted a rereading of Onaona, who used her website to re-code her culturally coded body, adding credibility to a reading that her body alone lacked. Through these webpages, she augmented her undisclosed ethnic identity and did so in a public way—in the form of a website and by introducing her friends to this representation of herself. Onaona's experience puts "an interesting twist on the example of 'race-passing' " (Warschauer 2000: 162). Manuel Rodriguez used a screen name that resisted ethnic coding; Onaona chose cyberspace to display her ethnicity. Warschauer does not attribute Onaona's experience, which he notes was similar to the experiences of many of the other students, solely to Internet communication. The teacher used the technology in ways that Warschauer deems "culturally appropriate." In this particular case, the technology was used in ways consistent with Hawaiian values. He cites "informal interaction, community networking, and multimedia learning" and believes "the email exchange and the web publishing project gave students a sense that they were doing something of benefit for the broader Hawaiian community" (163).

Onaona's website used language as the primary form of representation. She crafted an identity rooted in language and one that allowed her to make this identity more explicit in her everyday life. Warschauer (2000) observes that while language is "deeply rooted in personal and social history," it:

> allows a greater flexibility than race and ethnicity, with a person able to consciously or unconsciously express dual identities by the linguistic choices they make—even in a single sentence (e.g., through code-switching; see Blom and Gumperz 1972). (155)

These language choices and dialect options allow "people [to] constantly make and remake who they are. A Yugoslav becomes a Croatian, a Soviet becomes a Lithuanian, and an American emphasizes his African American linguistic and cultural heritage" (ibid.). Language thus has more versatility than some other identity markers and it can display this versatility via the *typing body*.

Cyberspace in particular facilitates both disclosure and concealment. In her ethnographic work, Markham (1998) surmises that users "enjoy the capacity to control the presentation and performance of self in online contexts [...] to control the conditions of interaction and to control the extent to which people online have access to the self" (20). Nearly all the people in Markham's study identified "control" as "a significant and meaningful benefit of online communication" (ibid.). When Manuel Rodriguez goes online as Mike Johnson, he is proposing a certain version of himself that conceals some things and reveals others. Of course, presenting a "self" and being *read* as that self are not the same thing. Markham explains that "whether that self is interpreted by you to be the same (as the) self I presented is unclear, and unlikely" (123–124). Nevertheless, she continues, "I *believe* that I control what others see, read, and therefore know about me, and the channels available to them to think otherwise are limited or nonexistent" (124). This chapter will return to the necessity for interpretation, for an "other" who reads this "self," in the concluding section. For now, I underscore the ability to use language to highlight certain "selves" and the *perceived* control over disclosure that cyberspace seems to allow us.[8]

The next section looks at specific instances of corporeal identity to discuss how cyberspace both reveals and conceals identities. The concluding section returns to a more thorough application of Bakhtin's concrete listener and the surplus this listener offers. As the typed body appears to be *no* body or can be unquestioningly assimilated by the reading body, we must read thoughtfully in cyberspace, query carefully, and pursue the "not said."

(Hand-)Writing and (Type-)Writers: Is the Text the Body?

[E]very teacher tends to grade up students who resemble him the most. If your own writing shows neat penmanship you regard that more important in a student than if it doesn't.
—Phaedrus in Robert M. Pirsig's *Zen and the Art of Motorcycle Maintenance*

Any act of reading involves the *body* of the text. How thought gets embodied in writing—through various fonts, colors, and materials—affects our ways of reading. If we have failed to watch how we read these manifestations, then a student like Manuel Rodriguez *does* inadvertently become a Mike Johnson, or is interchangeable with any other student. In other words, without Manuel's corporeal text, and however he may represent himself online—the language he sends via computer is conveyed in uniform, typed characters. It imparts the same *physicality*, the same visual rhetoric, as an email from any student. Handwriting "seems" more "bodily" than computer-generated text—more physical than typing, more closely related to one's identity, and even a better determinant of one's ethos. But is it?

Jones (2000) argues that writing bodies are disciplined by teachers and students through the physical act of writing. Jones maintains that the teacher uses a student's handwriting to evaluate a number of categories, including the inculcation of institutional norms. If we think of handwriting as not only the embodiment of a writer's ideas, but as the corporeal presence of the absent writer, we can see how pleasure and pain are inextricably linked when teachers discipline writing bodies. Young students are punished for producing "incorrect" handwriting. Their bodies of writing are rejected for not representing a sufficiently linear, clean, neat material body to read. At the same time, Jones notes the pleasures of producing words. Jones recalls writing with fountain pens and ink and laments that "the post-fountain pen era offers other less fluid pleasures: cheap, mass produced ballpoint pens" (153). On the contrary, the erotics of writing are not diminished with new technologies. Different computer keyboards produce different "clicking" sounds and feel differently under one's fingers. Monitors restrain and release visuals, colors, sizes and sounds. Indeed, typing on a computer keyboard involves more sensory experiences, since computers offer a wider range of colors, sounds, and graphics than ruled white paper does. It is dangerous to consider writing with a fountain pen any more (or less) "bodily" than typing at a computer. Building on Jones' argument that teachers conflate the written word and the writing body, I posit that by conflating the two, teachers are trying to stabilize the student, to get a handle on the student's "real" self and therefore to get a more "accurate" reading of the student.

Recalling her experiences in grade school, Jones says that beyond content, teachers read her " 'beautiful neat' shapes, significant evidence of my being a 'good' student [...] Neat writing came to be, for some girls like myself, the signal of our superiority and capitulation" (ibid.). To (mis-)quote Quintilian, the good rhetor is the one with good handwriting. Jones contends that teachers read the corporeal body into the written word. By extension, then, all readers, not only teachers, seek bodily clues in text, as well as making (non-)corporeal judgments about the writers of these texts. Indeed, when we think about these issues in light of computer text, the very uniformity of typed text leaves hyper-readers perplexed and pleasured. If readers, however erroneously, conflate content and appearance, what happens when hyper-readers have even fewer physical clues? *Whose* body is the typing body?

In exploring this relationship between identity and reading, I failed to mention the *other* physicality of writing—word choice, syntax, sentences, and paragraphs. Jones comments on how "typewritten or word-processed assignments" do not make:

> the student body […] entirely invisible, however; it is still there, its signs evident in the production of the printed text, the order or disorder of the words' arrangement on the page, the evenness of the margins and spaces, the choices of font and point size. (156)

Not only the individual letters that one writes or types, but also what letters (and words) one chooses to use allow readers to formulate opinions. If readers were only studying handwriting, then they would be doing a simple handwriting analysis. A focus on the discourse itself, on the other hand, involves an examination of word choice, syntax, and rhetorical strategies. Writers further embody their texts through the ideas they pose and their perspectives on those ideas. Thus language, handwritten or typed, embodies a particular "self." Jones maintains that because of "the absent student body," equivalent to what I am calling the typed body, "the teacher suffers a loss" (ibid.). However, I disagree. Typing bodies do *not* create an "absence of shared interactions with a real person which offer affective texture" (ibid.). The affective texture is inscribed in the typed text, just as it is inscribed in the handwritten text. Handwritten text or typed text does not allow readers a transparent vision of the writer's "real" self. But both kinds of writing deceive us into thinking that they do. Handwriting seems to offer endless idiosyncrasies and therefore a particular subjectivity; word-processed text presents readers with an imagined "blank slate" onto which to project themselves. While writing and typing may produce different products, both are *meant* to be uniform—the ways in which handwriting is *not* uniform are "mistakes." In its appearance of objectivity, typed text encourages readers to inscribe their own subjectivity. The typed text, however uniform it might be among users, is not any less material than handwritten text and is not any less embodied; in both cases, writers construct a self through their discursive choices.

Rather than a disembodied forum, online communication, because of its uniformity such as in emails and listservs, deludes hyper-readers into thinking other participants are "just like me." The assumption seems to be not that the interaction is disembodied but that the embodied act is parallel for all participants, though it is possible certain marginalized bodies realize the other cyber participants may not be like them. Those users might create personas with the intent of "appearing" like the others. It is possible that Manuel Rodriguez, for instance, used "Mike Johnson" in order to enter what he assumed to be the mainstream. Research shows computer-mediated communication, however romanticized it has been as a forum for unlimited social transformation, is actually a strong norming device (Addison & Hilligoss 1999; Stone 1995). In cyberspace, readers are much more likely to read in a "standardized" manner, especially because corporeal texts are not evident. First, the anonymity leads to a kind of "blind" reading. Second, the lack of physical clues mitigates against the expression of "other" identities. In both these cases, hyper-readers must ask fundamental questions about the typing body.

On the one hand, the norming forces of computer-mediated communication and the unified typing exert pressure that homogenizes and depersonalizes cyberspace, similar to what Bakhtin (1981) calls "unifying, centralizing, centripetal forces of verbal-ideological life" (272–273), though his analysis is of the novel and not cyberspace. Simultaneously, however, the centrifugal forces ("decentralizing tendencies," according to Bakhtin) in cyberspace, notably discourse, disclosure and desire, disrupt the centripetal forces. These centrifugal forces make the space personal and individualized. How students make use of technology, how they envision the technology in relation to their bodies, as well as the technology in relation to their literacy, may be highly distinctive, despite the norming forces of computer-mediated communication. In fact, the popular notion we see in *You've Got Mail* is of online dialog as *more* intimate than its face-to-face counterpart. Such exchanges can exert centrifugal forces against standardization and homogenization.

As a cautionary point, I want to add that computer-mediated education must not (and cannot) become a way to *avoid* the body or the intimacy of the pedagogical act (cf. Ess, this volume). We must question institutions' motive(s) for promoting the use of technology and the move toward distance education.[9] McWilliam and Palmer (1996) observe:

> Increasingly, academic managers of the new corporate universities deem material bodies to be stumbling blocks in terms of the temporal and spatial dimensions of university campuses. Without them, the pedagogical process becomes faster, potentially cheaper, and more accessible. Furthermore, keeping bodies away from each other has the added benefit of militating against charges of abusive pedagogy as overt sexual misconduct. In pedagogical terms, the "virtual" space created by technology is also a *virtuous* space (Angel 1995), devoid of fleshly bodies that could distract the mind. (165)

Technology ostensibly enables institutions to avoid the "messier" aspects of pedagogy.[10]

Given that teaching is a social relationship between teachers and students, between bodies, then a move toward distance education motivated by a desire to eliminate bodies is not only a naïve one, but also a sinister one. Such actions may encourage the Manuel Rodriguezes of the world to masquerade as Mike Johnsons and to do so without critical reflection. "Unmarked" cyberbodies, as it were, seem to be safer bodies. More significantly, to pretend that cyberspace erases sexuality and power relationships is a damaging assumption that reinforces the (false) dichotomy between "online" and "real life." Even in cyberspace, we are in the realm of the physical. Argyle and Shields (1996) describe how "the screen, keyboard and monitor are physically in contact with the user, with the flesh up against barrier after barrier" (68). In affirming "a multiplicity, multiple layers of being, a way to be in the body at all times, to express the whole of the person so there can be no separations," they ask, "[…] how can we eliminate the physical at all?" (ibid.). We cannot eliminate the physical nor can we disregard the power differentials between the participants. Students might explore their otherness (as Onaona did), play with the classroom dynamic, dispute the teacher's authority, or engage in other centrifugal activities that unmask the power structure. It is more likely, however, that students will react like Manuel Rodriguez, trying to assimilate themselves to unmarked forms, thereby increasing the centripetal effect of the interaction and the institution, a probability "the new corporate universities" would embrace.

As teachers, our challenge is to help students see online participation as embodied practice that requires not only the production of text, but also the production of "selves." The challenge, as we incorporate technology into our classrooms, is to find ways to embody our texts online and explore various constructions of "selves," selves which may act centrifugally and centripetally in the academy and the larger society. While we might aim to teach students many things, one primary goal should be to teach students to consciously *embody* their texts, creating a presence through their typing/typed bodies. I see this objective operating on several levels—that we want to "hear" our students in their texts; that we want them to understand writing as decision-making, as they must make choices about *what* they write and *how* they write; and finally, that those choices are ethical ones that they are held accountable for and that impact "real life." Creating an embodied ethos seems especially important in e-spaces, in light of Markham's (1998) observation:

> To be present in cyberspace is to learn how to be embodied there. To be embodied there is to participate. To participate is to know enough about the rules for interaction and movement so that movement and interaction with and within this space is possible. Although this may not be so different than what we experience whenever we enter any

strange context, it seems very blatant in cyberspace, perhaps because this process
cannot be ignored, and because movement and interaction create embodied presence,
not simply accompany it. (23–24)

To teach effectively is to engage in teaching as a situated, embodied practice.
How dull it would be if our students disappeared into their texts, whether
onscreen or on printed paper. The challenge we face as educators holds true
whether we are in a traditional classroom or using computers—helping students
bridge their personal voices with their academic voices, their personal interests
with a particular assignment, course, and field. To be effective rhetors, students
must learn a range of strategies to create persuasive online and offline selves. Or
more accurately, they must learn to construct a particular ethos for the
particular audience(s) they hope to persuade.

Recognizing that e-spaces are rife with societal prejudices does not mean we
should avoid these spaces, but rather that we should engage in them critically.
These spaces are permeated with the same social demarcations, assumptions,
and codes as "real life." Online communication offers an opportunity for critical
awareness that is less readily available when classrooms meet face-to-face. Julier
et al. (1999) note that email provides "*visual* representation" of communicative
acts and thus it is a medium that makes interactions accessible "for re-
examination and scrutiny and analysis" (318), making it particularly useful for
examining the relationship between written text, the body, identity, and social
change. Within cyberspace, writers have flexibility in how they construct a self
and the more strategies they acquire, the more flexibility they have. Less
experienced writers might not be using these tools critically, unaware of how
their discursive choices and hyper-reading could be better informed by a
sensitivity to embodiment and an awareness of cyberspace's constraints and
possibilities. As students learn and explore, they can make informed rhetorical
decisions. Some writers may work against societal norms while others may bow
to them, using the discursive text as an act of resistance or assimilation.

Bakhtin's Addressive Surplus:
Listening for/to "Other" (Written) Bodies

In the novel *Written on the Body*, Winterson (1992) tells the story of a nameless
and genderless narrator who loses a lover to cancer. Critics like Burns (1998)
praise Winterson's technique for not asking readers "to interpret the language of
love in a gendered manner" (385), whereas reviewers like Kendrick (1993)
consider this genderless narrator a "distraction, turning the reader into a
reluctant sleuth in search of gender giveaways (I found none)" (131). As hyper-

readers, we might be positioned like Kendrick. On the other hand, what kind of sleuths we are (reluctant? enthusiastic?) will probably be closely linked with our own identities and assumptions. When asked whether she wanted the narrator in *Written on the Body* to have an ambiguous gender, Winterson replied:

> Well, no, I just couldn't be bothered. I didn't want to pin it down. I thought, There is no need to do so, so I won't do so. If I put in a gender then it weights my story in a way that I don't want it to be weighted. So I didn't. I didn't expect that a huge furor would arise. I must say that took me totally by surprise. (Bilger 1998: 106)

How our online communication gets "weighted" has as much to do with readers as it does with writers. Kendrick was a reader for whom gender mattered. Indeed, he had difficulty getting beyond that "omission" in the novel, whereas Winterson saw "no need" to assign a gender. As readers, we might choose not to believe either Kendrick or Winterson. Maybe Kendrick was looking for Winterson to make a mistake that would indeed reveal the narrator's gender, perhaps a pronoun or two that would repudiate the novel's premise. And maybe Winterson assumed readers would be eager to know the narrator's gender and that part of continuing to read was to read for gender, while she lured readers toward her larger point about love and commitment. In an e-space, Kendrick might ask a participant to reveal his or her gender. Such a question raises even more questions: Why does one need to know? When and why should we reveal certain identities online? What are the risks of self-disclosure? What are the risks of concealment? And, like Winterson, will there be times when we just can't "be bothered"—when we think the discussion should really be about something else?

In approaching the role of embodied writing and hyper-reading, I advocate what Morson and Emerson (1990) term Bakhtin's "addressive surplus"—"the surplus of the good listener [...] Without trying to finalize the other or define him once and for all, one uses one's 'outsideness' and experience to ask the right sort of questions" (242). In the novel, "addressive surplus" is how characters interact with one another, but it is a concept that works equally well "in real life." Morson and Emerson insist that "we may use it in everyday life, and, Bakhtin intimates, would be wise to do so more often" (ibid.). Bakhtin (1984) describes this surplus as "simply an active (not a duplicating) understanding, a willingness to listen," as "an open and honest surplus, dialogically revealed to the other person, a surplus expressed by the addressed and not by the secondhand word" (299). The two interactions one must *not* engage in are: (1) to attempt to finalize the other, thus furnishing a stable and static identity and (2) to merge with the other, thus negating the possibility of either surplus or dialog (Morson & Emerson 1990). These two warnings serve us well when we engage in online communication. Given the fluidity and complexity of identity, we must avoid making limiting assumptions about the "typed body" on our computer screens and must resist filling in cyberspace with our corporeal norms. We must contemplate what we might learn about someone's corporeal text that we do not have access to online and reflect upon whether asking about this text(s) is "the right sort of question." Addressive surplus reminds us that there is always more than what we see on the screen, more than can be contained in those typed words. As Faigley (1992) puts it, "electronic discussions" contain "an excess of meaning that defies the effort to dig out an underlying meaning" (197).

An "addressive" surplus reinforces the idea that as we communicate, we are addressing (an-)other person. This principle holds true whether I am talking face-to-face or posting to a listserv. My utterance, according to Bakhtin, anticipates a response. The idea of "response" is an important corrective to the belief that we can "control" who we are in cyberspace. The respondent, who brings an addressive surplus to the act, helps create the meaning. All utterances, electronic or otherwise, are "drenched in social factors [...] on the border between what is said and what is not said" (Holquist 1990: 61). The "not said," perhaps especially in e-spaces, may suggest that the typed body is Every *Man's* Body. Or worse, no body at all.

Similar to mentioning ethos, to invoke Bakhtin is to raise the issue of ethics. As we project utterances into cyberspace, we answer others and are answerable to them. We must listen carefully to what is said and to what goes unsaid, especially given the tendency of e-spaces to be normative spaces, as Addison and Hilligoss (1999) and Stone (1995) maintain. To speak of "ethics" is not an appeal to a norm or a universal truth. A discussion of rhetoric and ethics is not, as Faigley (1992) reminds us, "a matter of collapsing spectacular diversity into universal truth" (239). Using Lyotard's work, Faigley characterizes ethics as "accepting the responsibility for judgment. It is a pausing to reflect on the limits of understanding. It is respect for diversity and unassimilated otherness. It is finding the spaces to listen" (ibid.). Hyper-readers must listen attentively for the "silences" of cyberspace. It is oftentimes within these silences that the body resides. Turkle (1995) says we must ask:

> What is the nature of my relationships? What are the limits of my responsibility? And even more basic: Who and what am I? What is the connection between my physical and virtual bodies? And is it different in different cyberspaces? These questions are framed to interrogate an individual, but with minor modifications, they are equally central for thinking about community. What is the nature of our social ties? What kind of

accountability do we have for our actions in real life and in cyberspace? What kind of society or societies are we creating, both on and off the screen? (231)

Some of these ethical questions are ones Bakhtin could not have anticipated, and all are equally applicable to what the present volume terms "brave new classrooms." Turkle contends that we need to see our personas online as part of who we are offline and vice versa.[11] Similarly, we need to see our academic personas as part of who we are "in real life" and vice versa. We must communicate ethically as the embodied beings we are.

If we are aware of ourselves as embodied beings, then we will better understand the fluidity between e-space and "real" space. We will use e-spaces in exploratory ways in the hope that these experiences will enrich our lives and the wider culture. We will experiment with other "selves," foster discussions about how corporeal texts may alter the rhetorical decisions writers make, and help students construct online personas that are rhetorically persuasive. The process is one of both construction and deconstruction, as we interrogate the realities we and others create with rhetoric. Manuel Rodriguez may indeed opt to be "Mike Johnson" online, but he (and his classmates) should be aware of the benefits and risks. He can begin to anticipate what hyper-readers, who possess an addressive surplus, might assume and what "right sort of questions" they might ask. Or, conversely, what questions they might fail to ask about "Mike Johnson" that they might have otherwise asked Manuel Rodriguez and *why*.

As technology progresses, we must judge how to employ these resources. Manuel Rodriguez has the liberty to create a name for himself online, a freedom not as easily accomplished "in real life." Fortunately, electronic communication facilitates the analysis of the concomitant ethical complexities. Recall Julier's observation that email provides a "*visual* representation" of our exchanges. Such a medium is necessary to correct some of the shortcomings of Bakhtin's concept of "surplus." Bakhtin's use of a visual and spatial metaphor necessitates, according to Farmer (2001), "a temporal dimension." Otherwise, Farmer insists, "we would have no way of disputing whatever outside perspective we encounter" (97). That is, we would need time to lapse in order to be able to address this "other's" perspective. Various forms of electronic discourse, such as bulletin boards and email, allow us both the space and time to revisit utterances and to respond to others. Such forums more readily allow us to "take account of all the relevant factors, not merely a single factor," as Huxley (1965: 318) advises us to do when approaching "any complex human situation."

New technologies bring new pedagogies and possibilities. We have many technological options and pedagogical decisions, and both continue to proliferate, as we teach in cyberspace. To conceptualize e-pedagogy as any less personal, as any less passionate, as any less complicated, or as any less embodied than face-to-face pedagogy is to seriously misunderstand the nature of our pedagogical relationships, of rhetoric, and of our relationship to any technology—from papyrus to cyberspace.[12] We should absolutely be concerned with the interconnections among technologies and bodies. We must develop our "addressive surplus," asking the questions *we* feel are relevant and exploring why those questions matter to us. To debate the advantages and disadvantages of being "Mike Johnson," to contest computers as liberatory, or to scrutinize the move toward distance education is not to reject technology. As the narrator in *Written on the Body* explains, "Luddite? No, I don't want to smash the machines but neither do I want the machines to smash me" (Winterson 1992: 98). When we communicate in cyberspace, we bring an "addressive surplus" that exceeds what the text "says" and that extends our bodies, as we can communicate irrespective of time and distance. "Listening" in cyberspace reminds us to be conscious of our bodily senses as we click away at the keyboard, to be aware of the interaction as one that involves "others," and to heed how the rhetoric we create online (de-)constructs our (cyber-)bodies.

Notes

I am indebted to Jim Sosnoski for his encouragement on early drafts, and thank Joe Lockard and Mark Pegrum for their tireless support of this collection.

1. I follow Markham's (1998) lead and do not differentiate between various phrases like online correspondence, computer-mediated communication, cyberspace, etc. As Markham explains, "online communication encompasses many forms of computer-mediated communication," and "because the meanings of these terms—and the experiences they imply—are still up for debate, I do not want to stabilize them either, or to provide you with a singular meaning" (21).

2. I acknowledge that the web is filled with a range of visuals and people use colors and images to embody themselves online. Still, I focus here primarily on what has traditionally been textually oriented space, like email and bulletin boards, while recognizing that those spaces are increasingly becoming supplemented by images.

3. I am using Sosnoski's (1999) term "hyper-readers" to refer to readers in cyberspace, taking into account the full range of computer-assisted reading that people engage in. Although Sosnoski does not use the term hyper-readers to suggest "hyperactivity," I employ it to imply that cyber-reading is a kind of "overactive" traditional reading, as the process is interactive, and the forum is animated.

4. In fact, other forms of technology are involved as well. For instance, when Joe sees Kathleen on the evening news, in a story about her bookstore's struggle with the big chain, Joe says, "She's not as nice as she seems on television." It seems that technology, whether computers or television, radically transforms our identity and offers false appearances.

5. To some extent, *You've Got Mail* plays with dichotomies by blurring the line between the personal and the public, and distinctions between home and work. We see both characters in these settings and we see how the failure of Kathleen's bookstore affects her intimately. But the drama of the movie—the way it can sustain itself—is to play with the idea that Kathleen and Joe are in love online, but detest each other "in real life."

6. Perhaps this exaggeration is a US cultural trend, given that *You've Got Mail* and *The Net* are mainstream Hollywood movies.

7. Names have been changed to maintain confidentiality. This project was reviewed and granted exemption by the University of Illinois at Chicago Office for the Protection of Human Subjects under Protocol #H-98–1028.

8. Computer-mediated communication may not give us more distributive control. Email, for instance, can be forwarded to any number of recipients. However, experienced users *do* have methods to control distribution. They can encrypt, prevent copying, and even enforce timed deletions.

9. Faigley (1999) sees economics as a motive for distance education. The logic informing "higher education on the cheap [...] is economy of scale. What can be taught to 10 can be taught to 100. What can be taught to 100 can be taught to 1000. What can be taught to 1000 can be taught to an infinite number" (137). This notion of online learning as a cheap alternative—which was certainly a motivating factor—has been shown to be false. Jewett and Henderson (2003), who take a positive stance toward online teaching, nonetheless conclude that "mediated instruction can be less expensive than classroom instruction provided that course enrollments are sufficiently large" and estimate the requisite number at 60 students in the case study they examine using data from Washington State University (24). Furthermore, many scholars note the increased demands on their time in online education courses. At Christopher Newport University, Vachris (1999) says that "compared with delivering a traditional course in the classroom, most on-line faculty spend two to three times the amount of time delivering an on-line course (excluding development time) [...] this interaction is more costly in terms of instructor time than is the case of a traditional classroom section" (302).

10. Part of the institution's desire (no pun intended) is to eliminate issues of sexual harassment. In their preface to *Academic Keywords*, Nelson and Watt (1999) note, "a few decades ago [...] no one would have thought an entry for *sexual harassment* should appear in such a book; indeed, until the 1970s the term was essentially unknown, though you could find discussions of male chauvinism as early as the 1930s. But no one would now argue about whether sexual harassment is one of the defining issues in academic life" (ix). Nelson and Watt devote 26 pages to discussing "sexual harassment," the longest entry in the book.

11. According to Turkle (1995), "Without a deep understanding of the many selves that we express in the virtual we cannot use our experiences there to enrich the real. If we cultivate our awareness of what stands behind our screen personae, we are more likely to succeed in using virtual experience for personal transformation" (269).

12. This is the subtitle to O'Donnell's (1998) *Avatars of the Word: From Papyrus to Cyberspace*.

Chapter 15

The Question of Education
in Technological Society*

Darin Barney

Among the great challenges facing the prospect of citizenship today, two can be singled out as particularly serious: the challenge of difference and the challenge of technology. To say that "these are challenges for citizenship" is also to say that "they are challenges for education," at least to the extent that it is still sensible to believe that education bears some responsibility for the cultivation of citizenship. The challenge of difference—the challenge of establishing a viable conception and practice of citizenship in the context of radical cultural pluralism and heterogeneity—is one that has received considerable critical attention in recent years (Isin 2002; Kymlicka 2002). The challenge of technology has received less attention, perhaps because the modern inclination is to view technology as either neutral or unambiguously beneficial with regard to citizenship: as I will suggest below, our public culture predisposes us toward recognizing technology primarily as an opportunity, and not especially as a challenge. Against this view, I will elaborate a fairly simple set of claims: that technology presents a challenge for citizenship; that this challenge has implications for education; and that our collective response to this challenge in the sphere of formal education has been less than adequate.

Citizenship

There are several conceptions of citizenship that could serve as a normative ideal in relation to technology. One could adopt a classical liberal conception, in which citizenship names the individual possession of rights and establishes the boundaries of membership in a political community. Or, one could opt for a model of social citizenship, which emphasizes the distribution of social and material resources that allow people to act on otherwise abstract liberties. Finally, there is the conception of citizenship as a regulatory or disciplinary category central to the operation of social reproduction and cultural transmission. Each of these can raise productive questions about the politics of technology. That being said, to get at the heart of the problem of citizenship in technological societies, I recommend a fourth, more demanding model of citizenship—the republican model.

The republican conception of citizenship is rooted in ancient political philosophy and taken up, to varying degrees, in modern theories of strong, deliberative, participatory democracy. As Ronald Beiner (1992: 104) defines it, republican citizenship consists in:

> active participation in a dialogue that weighs the substantive merit of competing conceptions of the good and that aims at transforming social arrangements in the direction of what is judged, in this active public dialogue, as the best possible (individual and collective) good.

Citizenship is here defined in terms of an active practice of public judgment about collective ends and the means to achieve them, through engagement in the public sphere among public-spirited fellows, animated by common concern for what is good and just.[1] Whereas liberal conceptions of citizenship define citizenship in terms of *membership*, and social citizenship is defined in terms of the *distribution* of material resources, republican citizenship is defined in terms of a particular, distinctive, *practice*. The question raised by liberal conceptions of citizenship is who gets *in*; the question raised by social citizenship is who gets *what*; the question raised by republican citizenship is what people *do*. It is a theory of citizenship that is concerned not just with "a more *extensive* civic membership," or even a more *equitable* distribution of civic resources, but also, or perhaps rather, with "a more *intensive* civic experience" (Beiner 1992: 114; Pettit 1997).

Republican citizenship is, of course, fraught with a theoretical legacy, and a practical history, of elitism and exclusion, a history that raises serious doubts about the possibility of a citizenship that is both republican and democratic at the same time. Any thoroughgoing defense of the republican model of citizenship would have to reckon with this history and provide a persuasive account of how republican citizenship could be anything other than aristocratic, gendered and racist (Maynor 2003; Pettit 1997). My purpose here is rather just to shine a light on the challenge that technology poses for citizenship, a challenge that becomes most visible in the demanding practical light of republican citizenship, despite its liabilities. Furthermore, it is something like republican citizenship—a citizenship defined by participation in public judgment about ends and means—that is most greatly challenged by the material facts of technology, and by the affordances of contemporary technological societies.

Technology

What is the challenge that technology poses for citizenship? The answer is far from self-evident, not least because the cultural dispensation of modern technological society inclines toward a view that technology sets before citizenship not a challenge but rather an opportunity. The instrumentalist approach to technology, in which technology is understood to be nothing but an indifferent set of instruments whose proliferation and perfection pave the way for the progress of freedom and prosperity, does not conceive of technology as a problem at all. In this view, which still prevails in our public culture, the presumed material benefits of technological advance are understood as a condition and confirmation of democracy, citizenship's greatest security, and not its greatest problem. Nowhere is the tenacity of this conviction more evident than in relation to new information and communication technologies which, like basically every technology of mass communication that preceded them, have been equated in the popular mind with either the salvation or extension of democratic citizenship (Mosco 2004).

Fortunately, the twentieth century has provided for us not only a formidable set of technological instruments, but also a formidable body of critical theory that reveals this instrumentalist view to be ideological. The list of thinkers who, despite their variety of approaches and significant differences, have put paid to the notion that technology and democracy are necessary or uncomplicated allies, is a long one, stretching from the likes of Heidegger, Horkheimer, Marcuse, Habermas, Ellul and Mumford at one end to Winner, Feenberg, Haraway, Latour and Borgmann at the other. If there is one thing that critical theorists of technology seem to agree upon despite their many differences, it is that the relationship between modern technology (whether in its essential characteristics, or as it has been socially constructed in the context of liberal capitalism) and citizenship is ambiguous, at best (Melzer et al. 1993).

Assuming there are theoretically justifiable grounds for asking after the challenge technology poses for citizenship, it remains necessary to disaggregate the specific ways in which technology bears on citizenship, of which I believe there are three: as potential *means*, as a potential *object* and as a *setting*.

As potential *means* of citizenship, technological instruments can be used as tools of citizenship practice, a possibility that is most obvious with regard to mass media and communication technologies, and which has been raised to high relief by the Internet. Citizenship as engagement in public judgment about ends and means is necessarily a communicative practice, and there is no reason to assume that technological mediation of communication, even on a mass scale, cannot be, or has not sometimes been, configured to support rather than to undermine this practice. Television has become an instrument by which people are "demoralized in the shortest possible time on the largest possible scale at the cheapest possible price," as Kierkegaard (1967, Vol. 2, No. 489) once said of the daily press, but it could just as easily be configured to elevate and inform public judgment, as it sometimes does, in some contexts. And the Internet, already a medium of everything *but* citizenship—entertainment, personal correspondence, labor, consumption and surveillance—is only *predominantly*, and not exclusively, so. One would have to harbor a quite irrational animus against technology to deny the significant citizenship activity presently mediated by the Internet, or to dismiss the likelihood of its persistence, however marginal it might be in the present scheme of things, and however strongly the political economy of contemporary capitalism militates against it. In short, technology, especially communication technology, is almost always a potential means of citizenship, and it is well not to lose sight of this, perhaps *especially* because this potential has been so seldom, and only ever marginally, realized (McCaughey & Ayers 2003; Wilhelm 2000).

Technology (and here we move well beyond the confines of communication technology) is also potentially an *object* of citizenship, which is to say that technology comprises not just a medium through which we might engage in public judgment about common ends and the means to achieve them, but also that technological artifacts and systems *constitute* ends and means in relation to which we might reasonably expect to exercise public judgment. In a social world in which technology often seems to appear as if by magic, and to be non-negotiable in its outcomes, it perhaps seems fantastic to suggest that technology is properly an object of citizenship, but this is precisely what the very best democratic critiques of technology have taught us. Technology must be understood as an object of citizenship because, as Andrew Feenberg (1999b) has argued, it is "legislative"; because "artifacts," as Langdon Winner (1986) has taught us, "have politics"; because "code," as Lawrence Lessig (1999) has written, "is law." Technology is properly an object of citizenship because it is intimately bound up in the establishment and enforcement of prohibitions and permissions, the distribution of power and resources, and the structure of human practices and relationships. So many of our ends (whether genuinely common or not) and the means for achieving them are realized technologically that denying technology as an object of citizenship prejudicially depoliticizes a massive portion of contemporary social existence (Winner 1995).

Technology should be considered an object of citizenship not only because it *has* political outcomes, but also because it *is* a political outcome. The sociology of technology has taught us that technological artifacts and systems are not *just* objects; they do not emerge automatically from the rational, disinterested, objective progress of science. Like legislation, technologies are the product of complex institutional arrangements, and equally complex sets of assumptions, priorities, relationships and contests (Bijker & Law 1992; Bijker et al. 1989; MacKenzie & Wajcman 1999). Were this is not the case—where there is no contingency in technological outcomes—to speak of technology as a potential object of citizenship would be to speak in vain. Technologies are not *just* objects, but technology can be made *an object of citizenship* precisely because it remains open to political intervention.

It is possible to imagine citizenship exercised upon the object of technology in a number of ways. We could imagine, for example, citizens exercising political judgment in the selection, design and development of technological artifacts and systems. We could also imagine a role for citizens in the regulation and governance of technologies that are already in place. Of course, the fact that we have to *imagine* such roles is instructive: in their current configuration, most societies in which technology figures centrally exhibit a paucity of meaningful opportunities for citizenship in relation to technology itself. In these societies, political judgment about technology, whether at the point of design or governance, is typically reserved for some combination of scientists, engineers, businessmen and technocrats who, while they are certainly citizens as well, do not necessarily bring the disposition and concerns of a citizen to bear in their professional determinations (Noble 1977). Most people encounter technology as consumers or users, not as citizens. This absence of institutional opportunities for citizenship means that whatever political agency people retain in relation to technology is exceptional and subversive, exercised sporadically through what Feenberg (1999b) has called "democratic rationalization" (130) of otherwise undemocratic instruments and systems.

Citizenship is also challenged by technology because technological *societies* do not provide a *setting* that is necessarily hospitable to its practice. A technological society is one that is saturated by complex technological devices and systems, and which experiences perpetual technological dynamism; it is one in which material life, and in particular the economy, is bound up tightly with technological activity; one in which security, prosperity, freedom and progress are identified culturally with technological development; and one in which the instrumental rationality characteristic of technology, in which the question of ends is subsumed under the optimization of means, penetrates otherwise non-technological spheres of interest and activity.[2]

Technological societies truncate the possibilities of citizenship because the question of the good life is fundamentally answered in the very fabric of their material constitution. This is why technology comports so well with liberal conceptions of citizenship. Whereas technology and liberal democracy are characteristically presented as neutral as to possible ends, both, in fact, embody a substantive view of the good life as self-realization and mastery, achieved through individual choice-making unfettered by any restraint other than those for which we freely volunteer. The Canadian philosopher George Grant (1969) has characterized the relationship between technology and liberal democracy in precisely this manner, seeing both, along with capitalism, as expressions of the modern conviction that the human essence is freedom (114). This is not to say that liberalism, capitalism or technology have actually *delivered* on the promise of freedom; it was not so long ago, after all, that the Frankfurt School characterized technology as capitalist domination materialized and liberalism as its apology (Horkheimer 1990; Horkheimer & Adorno 2002). In any case, the point is that the affinity of technology, capitalism and liberalism derives not from their abstinence on the question of ends, but from their common conviction that a certain kind of freedom is the only possible answer to that question. As Albert Borgmann (1984) writes:

> Liberal democracy is enacted as technology. It does not leave the question of the good life open, but answers it along technological lines [...] when we promote a just society along liberal democratic lines we also advance the technological society and its specific and dubious notion of the good life. (93–94)

Technological society, then, is itself a decisive, if often unspoken, answer to the question about ends, one which obviates, rather than invites, the practice of public judgment that defines citizenship, at least in its more demanding forms. Having reached hegemonic proportions, technological society's promise of the good life leaves little room for political judgment. Indeed, in a technological society that is also a liberal (and capitalist) society, citizenship—as a practice in which ends and means, including technology itself, are subjected to public judgment—can only get in the way of realizing that version of prosperity about which there can be no question.

Education

To review, technology challenges citizenship in three ways: as a potential means, as a potential object and as a necessary (because practically unavoidable) setting. There is the challenge to optimize technologies (such as, for example, the Internet) as effective means of political participation and judgment; the challenge to enforce the political judgment of citizens upon technological design, development and governance; and the challenge to recover ground in technological society for public judgment as to ends, including the end of technology itself.

Whether citizenship will rise or succumb to these challenges depends on a variety of factors, only one of which is education—though education is, arguably, a crucial one. The notion that education is central to the possibility of citizenship is so well-worn that it hardly needs mentioning. This is perhaps especially true in relation to the more demanding, republican conception of citizenship I have emphasized here: liberal citizens are typically born into their rights, or acquire them either through due process as immigrants or struggle as revolutionaries; citizens with the inclination, capacities and habits of participation in political judgment must be cultivated, and education is a primary means of cultivation.[3]

Nevertheless, to speak of education as the cultivation of citizenship is to assume a certain risk. We should not forget the history of the use of education by states and churches in order to "civilize" various troublesome populations. Citizenship education can take, and has taken, several unacceptable forms: "civics" education aimed at legitimation and depoliticization of the status quo; cultural, religious and linguistic unification of diverse populations along national lines, typically with violence to difference and history; transmission of the dominant ideology; and reproduction of, and habituation to, social regimes of discipline and normalization that maintain prevailing distributions of socioeconomic power. In my own country of Canada, for example, aboriginal children were forcibly taken from their parents and their homes, and incarcerated in residential schools, where they were denied access to their heritage, their language and their culture, and often physically abused, all in the name of making "good citizens" of them (Fournier & Crey 1997). Thus, the terrain is dangerous, but it cannot be avoided. The fact is that formal education exists, and it cultivates us as subjects whether we like it or not (Bourdieu 1977).

The only question is what sort of subjectivity it cultivates, or fails to cultivate. If we are to hold out hope for citizenship in technological society, it seems unavoidable that we think through the contribution formal education might make to this outcome, not *despite* the fact that citizenship education has sometimes gone so horribly wrong, but rather *because* it has.

Technology challenges citizenship as a potential means. For that potential to be realized—for example, in relation to communication technologies—a number of structural changes in the political and cultural economy of mass commercial media would have to occur, changes aimed at extricating mass media from the grip of capitalist corporations and redirecting them toward the service of democratic communication (McChesney 1999). Assuming these structural changes, what would citizens need in order to make the most of this potential, and to appropriate these technologies as means of public deliberation and judgment on a significant scale? At a minimum, they would require *facility* with these technologies, the capacity to use them creatively, with relative ease, for political purposes—which is to say in order to inform themselves and others, and to participate in deliberation and dialog pursuant to public judgment on matters of common concern. Many people already enjoy such facility; too many do not. An educational program aimed at cultivating citizens capable of rising to the challenge of technology as a potential means of citizenship would seek to promote this facility. This is not a particularly demanding expectation in the current context; as I will suggest below, contemporary education systems are *already* oriented significantly in this direction.

Technology also challenges citizenship as a potential object. Meeting this challenge would require a fundamental structural reform of the institutional basis of technology design, implementation and governance. As mentioned above, participation in decision-making regarding technology is more or less reserved for scientists, engineers, corporate executives and technocrats, who tend to equate the public good with some combination of efficiency, productivity and economic growth. Citizens are typically invited to the table primarily as consumers, whose sole choice with regard to technology is whether to buy or not. To make technology properly an object of citizenship, institutional regimes of technological design, implementation and governance would have to be systematically reconfigured to place citizens and their deliberations at their center. Assuming this was accomplished, what would citizens need in order to engage in public deliberation and judgment about technology and technological issues? At a minimum, they would require the disposition and habits of citizenship *in relation to technology*. Beyond this, they would need a certain degree of *literacy* with respect to technology and the issues arising from it, including an awareness of the possibilities of technological reform and restraint. An educational program aimed at cultivating citizens capable of rising to the challenge of technology as an object of citizenship would have to actively incline students to approach technology *as a political issue*, and habituate them to engagement in public deliberation and judgment about technology. It would also seek to equip students with the literacy necessary to do so critically and autonomously, not necessarily as experts, but as citizens able to evaluate the claims that experts make.

It must be kept in mind that literacy can serve hegemonic, as well as critical, purposes. Reading can enroll us in the dominant culture just as easily as it enables us to critique it. In some accounts, technological literacy amounts to little more than an uncritical appreciation of "where things come from" and "how things work," a sort of "know-how" aimed at reproducing technological society rather than provoking critical engagement with it. For example, in 1999, the Committee on Information Technology Literacy of the National Academy of the United States wrote that technological literacy demands:

> that persons understand information technology broadly enough to be able to apply it productively at work and in their everyday lives, to recognize when information technology would assist or impede the achievement of a goal, and to continually adapt to the changes in and advancement of information technology.

There is little or no room in this conception of literacy for a reading of technology that might call into question its basic assumptions and operation. This is why it is necessary to specify that the sort of literacy citizens need in order to rise to the challenge of technology as an object of citizenship is *critical* technological literacy: the sort that equips citizens to read through the ideology and operation of technology, and into its historicity, its situation in the political economy of capitalism, its affordances and its denials. The expectation of critical technological literacy demands more from contemporary education than does mere technological facility—but it is still, I think, well within the horizon of technological society.[4]

It is not clear that the same can be said about the recommended educational response to the third challenge technology poses for citizenship, that in which technological society constitutes the material, epistemological and ontological setting in which the possibility of citizenship is situated. Citizenship, as I have argued, centers on political judgment and public deliberation about ends, and the best means to achieve them. The challenge that technological society poses for citizenship is that, at a fundamental level, it constitutes a decisive answer to the question of ends, the question of the good life. The answer is freedom as self-realization, expressed in and through the proliferation and extension of technology. It is an answer that discourages alternatives, makes the question itself seem redundant and, in so doing, erodes the ground of citizenship. Indeed, the consensus around this end is such that technological societies are able to devote almost all their political energy to squabbles over means. The only conceivable response to this challenge, aside from either nihilist abandon or apolitical passivity, is to recover and restore the ground of citizenship, by sustaining the possibility of thinking—*publicly*, not just privately—about ends other than that of self-realization by means of technology.

What contribution can education make to this effort? To say that citizenship demands the possibility of thinking about a plurality of ends is to say that it requires sustaining the possibility of humanity against the dominant culture of technology (Borgmann 1984, 1992). There is a clue in this phrasing. It suggests that the best hope for citizenship in technological society lies in an education that cultivates the human capacity for judgment as to ends, an education rooted in the humanities, for it is only in the humanities—in history, in art, in music, in literature, in philosophy, in the study of religion—that the question of ends is regularly raised for consideration (Grant 1969). It is only in the humanities that the question of ends has not been shunted aside by the assumption that it has already been answered. Humanities education is not a denial of the reality of technological society, but rather a recognition of the depth of the challenge such a society poses for citizenship. It is not an escape from technological society, but a practical response to its basic character.

Two qualifications are necessary here. The suggestion is not that we look to the humanities for *instruction*: Hamlet cannot instruct us as to the relative merits of private vengeance and public justice. Immersion in the humanities will not tell us what our ends should be; it will habituate us to a practice in which the question of ends is publicly present, open and routinely engaged, rather than absent, closed and systematically evaded. By bringing the question of ends forward into beauty, the humanities *accustom* us to precisely that aspect of citizenship that is missing in technological society.

When the humanities are instrumentalized as means of ideological transmission and "civilization," they are reduced to mere counterfeit, which brings me to the second qualification. To call for an education in the humanities that develops the habits of engagement with a plurality of possible ends is necessarily to reject an education that confines itself to reproducing *one* tradition, *one* vocabulary, and *one* account of what it is to be human. The only humanities education worth its name is one that affirms rather than denies the plurality of possible ends, one which not only recognizes but also celebrates that literature means literatures, history histories and philosophy philosophies. In this manner, the point of a humanities education is not so much cultural as ethical. It is not about the generalization of a common vocabulary; it is about a generalized habit of engaging with the question of ends, a question that can be asked using many possible vocabularies, including subversive ones.

These, then, are the educational responses I would propose in response to the challenge posed to citizenship by technology as means, object and setting: technological facility, critical technological literacy and the humanities, in all their pluralism. These responses exhibit escalating levels of difficulty. Technological facility beyond that required for proletarian labor and consumption is at least imaginable within the current horizons of education in a "knowledge-based society," as is technological literacy, perhaps even the critical variant. The prospects for the humanities, at least as a systemic educational commitment, are less certain within these horizons. There is only so much we can do. One wonders whether, as a practical matter, an education system committed to technological facility and literacy could *also* be committed to the humanities, or vice versa. The problem of the epistemological fit between these three proposals is even more vexing than the practical one. For wouldn't a commitment to technological facility and technological literacy imply agreement with the answer given by technology to the question of ends? And wouldn't an education centered upon technological facility and literacy amount to precisely that overriding attention to means, that is the *problem* humanities education is supposed to correct? Does it make any sense at all to endorse each of these three at the same time?

This is a considerable dilemma. Still, an education geared to only *one* of *either* the technical *or* the ethical priorities I have discussed would leave us only half-equipped to meet the challenges of citizenship in a technological society. Technology is not about to disappear—one might argue that our recent experience with digital networks is but a gentle prelude to the dynamism to come with nano-, bio- and genetic technology. We will be unable to deal with technology as a means and object of citizenship if we are not equipped with technological facility and critical technological literacy. But we will also be unable to recover the very *ground* of citizenship, a ground defined by engagement in public judgment as to ends, without an education that habituates us to asking the question of ends, against the apparent monism of liberal, capitalist, technological society (Grant 1969: 114). For this we need the humanities as well. And so, I would argue, what appears to be a practical and epistemological contradiction might nevertheless be a political necessity.

Attention to this necessity has been less than fulsome. In general, affluent capitalist democracies have been keener to orient their educational systems to the demands of capital accumulation in the context of so-called "information," "knowledge" or "network" society than to the ongoing challenge to citizenship posed by technology (Noble 2002b; Robins & Webster 1999; Sears 2003). This orientation has several features:

- Investment in education as the foundation for a competitive economy based on innovation.
- Emphasis on the commercialization of research, including support for public–private partnerships and closer integration of universities and the private sector.
- Vocational orientation to the demands of post-Fordism, including the generation of both highly skilled and highly "flexible" workers.
- Stress on perpetual training and skills development, euphemized as "lifelong learning."
- Support for integration of technological infrastructure in educational settings.

At the level of institutions, priorities have included the following:

- Expansion of access to new technologies and network infrastructure.
- Development of platforms and pedagogies for technologically enhanced and mediated learning, including distance learning.
- Use of technology to realize efficiencies/flexibilities in information and education delivery, including administration and instructional labor.
- Digitization of instructional materials, including library resources.
- Development of students' and educators' technology skills and competencies.

These things are not necessarily bad. In their hegemonic applications under the auspices of contemporary neoliberalism, such measures are politically and pedagogically suspect, and should be resisted in the name of democratic education. However, practices such as distance education or online learning are also open to appropriation for decidedly democratic purposes, and good educators everywhere are working hard to develop and deploy tools and pedagogies conducive to this outcome (cf. Hamilton & Feenberg, this volume; Pegrum, this volume). Which of these models will prevail is not a foregone conclusion, and prejudicial dismissal of the progressive possibilities of technologically mediated teaching and learning serves only to guarantee an unhappy result. It is also true that two of the responses advocated above—technological facility and technological literacy—do appear. In most cases, these are specific to digital media, and it is not yet clear whether the literacy models popping up in some jurisdictions are oriented to enrollment in technological society or to critical citizenship. Nevertheless, they do arise, though this should come as no surprise given how comfortably at least certain versions of facility and literacy sit within the horizon of technological society.

It is not that the current agenda is uniformly or necessarily opposed to citizenship, but rather that citizenship *as a special challenge in technological contexts* does not figure highly in the present imagination of the place of education in relation to technology. Where citizenship does appear, it is in the form of active and productive membership in the highly competitive knowledge economy, or as a category of entitlement to equal access to technologically mediated benefits and services. These are not insignificant things: they are also not all there is to citizenship. There is also the matter of public engagement in political judgment, including judgment about technology itself, not just as a means but also as an end. Citizenship of this sort runs counter to the current of contemporary technological society and also, it would seem, to current priorities for an education system designed to serve that society. This is a serious political problem, one that calls for an equally serious political effort on behalf of the priority of citizenship in the educational agenda of technological societies.

Notes

*An abbreviated version of this chapter was delivered at the Common Ground Conference on Technology, Knowledge and Society at the University of California, Berkeley on February 19, 2005.

1.   The politicization of the good *and* the just distinguishes republicanism from most versions of liberal democracy. In the latter, politics is comprised of the contest, within neutral institutions and procedures, over just outcomes, in light of a background conception of the good that is presumed to be shared. In most liberal models, politicizing the good life is a recipe for unjust outcomes or, worse, perfectionism leading to domination and subordination, especially in contexts where cultural pluralism is an irreducible fact of life. Republicanism, by contrast, assumes that questions of the good life are always in play and ought, therefore, to be part of political deliberation. It is for this reason that republicanism and liberalism are often posited as incompatible (Kymlicka 2002: 294–299).

2. Obviously, this substantivist conception of technological society owes a great deal to the accounts given by Martin Heidegger (1977), Herbert Marcuse (1964) and Jacques Ellul (1964).

3. Classic statements on education and republican citizenship include Aristotle (1967) and Niccolo Machiavelli (1970). For contemporary treatments of the theme, see Pettit (1997) and Maynor (2003).

4. The Committee on Technological Literacy of the National Academy of Engineering of the United States—an association devoted to technological progress—has endorsed quite a robust conception of technological literacy. See Committee on Technological Literacy (National Academy of Engineering, National Research Council) (2002). Perhaps the horizons of engineers are broader than those of physical scientists and mathematicians after all.

Chapter 16

Manifesto for Democratic Education and the Internet

Joe Lockard

An IBM television commercial broadcast in the United States frames the Internet education myth: in an indeterminate space, a small Chinese girl approaches a wise-looking, sternly avuncular US black man seated behind a desk. She tells him how much she wants to learn about many things, especially about dinosaurs. But she cannot: she lives in a small village in China. He invites her into the infinitely expandable space of the virtual classroom, where she can learn together with children throughout the world.

We challenge the now-commonplace mythography underlying that IBM television spot. Untenable educational assumptions and corporate marketing underpin the vision of education being sold in this commercial, one that reflects much of the policy surrounding online education. The commercial echoes those assumptions and avoids the obvious questions: how do a Chinese-speaking student and an English-speaking teacher communicate, and how do they come to speak English as a unifying global language? How does a Chinese girl in a rural Chinese village go online where her family does not possess the economic means for computer purchase, online access fees, or where there is no telephone, cable or wireless access in the village? What is the "virtual classroom" into whose student community the teacher invites her? Do such classrooms—or disembodied classroom teachers—even exist? Or are the appealing figures of this commercial the social camouflage adopted by high-tech corporations building new profit centers through the commodification of education? And crucially, what is the political economy of the "virtual classroom" vision that this commercial proposes?

Critics asking questions like these, along with many other questions about the nature, quality, and goals of online education, have not been dominant voices in the development of online education. Asking basic questions such as "is the shift from in-classroom to online education more effective as pedagogy, or are we losing more than we gain?" marginalizes the inquirer. Observing that a momentous shift from classroom to online education has proceeded almost entirely without educational research, unlike the vast research that preceded and accompanied racial desegregation in schools and challenged gender stereotypes, is to become the proverbial child pointing out that the king is naked.[1] Frequently such questions and observations come from front-line teaching faculty with first-hand practical knowledge of the problems and distortions inherent in online education, but who are not academic decision-makers and have less and less power to shape the learning environment. Line teaching faculty in the United States, three-quarters of whom are now contingent hires without job security (Entin 2005: 27), often adopt online technologies because these have become a necessity of ensuring that their skills conform to marketplace demand. Even if they disbelieve the efficacy of their own mode of electronic pedagogy, adoption provides employment and its prospective continuation. For contingent faculty reliant on short-term hiring, voicing dissatisfaction with, alienation from, or refusal to adopt computer-mediated or online teaching is a quick route to unemployment. Allowable questions are those concerning how to make technology function better, not whether students and teachers need educational technology and computer-mediated learning in the first place.

This extreme disincentive to dissent among teachers represents one of the basic features of electronic education. Whereas until the last decade of the twentieth-century teachers could by-and-large shape their physical classrooms, even under strict supervisory regimes, the virtual classroom comes configured by software engineers. A virtual classroom mode is at best a set of elective options, as in Blackboard software. Teachers either adopt pre-configured modes of electronic education or do not: in the virtual classroom, teachers have lost control of the means of production. To dissent and rebel against this new means of educational production frequently results in administrators and conforming instructors labeling rebels as contemporary Luddites, those whose opinions can be safely dismissed. But to equate rebellion against the modes, usages, appropriateness, or prevalence of electronic education confuses dissent with rejection. We need to remember that the original late eighteenth- and early nineteenth-century (in England, particularly 1811–1816) frame-breakers were protesting against economic injustice, impoverishment, and communal dislocation created by machines, and that the term "Luddite" is a badge of honor.[2] Like the original Luddites, present-day critics of educational technology are demanding that working people exercise control over machines, not the opposite; it is to their credit that they oppose the use of educational technology to serve capital's relentless search for profit. Too many teachers with humanistic values have become rejectionist Luddites in order to uphold those values: they should never be forced to choose between humanism and technology.

There are other visions and other voices that seek reconciliation and adaptation, who recognize both the limits and value of electronic pedagogies. These are the visions and voices of teachers who work daily with technology yet understand that there is a time and place for technology: where technology illegitimately invades and monopolizes teaching and learning, we must become Luddites in order to teach well. The purpose of creating the present volume has been to dissent strongly against many practices and developments in electronic education: teachers experienced with electronic pedagogies rarely reject them since there is little sense in rejecting advantages even if there are many pedagogical disadvantages, inappropriate uses, and low- or no-quality online coursework, coupled with blatant servicing of for-profit corporate educational ventures to the detriment of student needs. Instead, these teachers become educational reform advocates and electronic activists, creating better and more appropriate uses, emphasizing development of offline–online hybrid courses, constructing international educational collaborations via the Internet, and integrating simple do-it-yourself (DIY) electronic technologies (e.g., blogging) into teaching and learning. They recognize that improving computer-mediated education is not just purchasing more up-to-date computers, plugging more bandwidth into classrooms, or building more sophisticated websites. In short, they become creative dissenters.

Dismissive association of critics and dissenters on electronic pedagogy with technological ignorance or techno-phobia is false; it serves the interests of both professional self-promotion for educational technophiles and that of social censorship.[3] Critics of electronic education almost uniformly have significant personal experience in computer-mediated and online teaching, and have lived professional careers in academic contexts where electronic education has and will continue to expand. Those who develop critical electronic pedagogies are exercising the "creative maladjustment" that inheres in good educational practice (Kohl 1994).

Anti-technology rejectionism is not only futile where global economies and information-driven citizenship create a new reliance on technology, but such rejection is counter-productive to contemporary education. Since the nineteenth-century development of national education systems, education toward democratic citizenship has been a normative feature of most Western public education systems.[4] The advent of information-based economies has transformed concepts of citizenship toward substantially more recognition of regional and global interconnection, and education toward citizenship is transforming itself in parallel. Absolute rejection refuses to recognize such change and demands that information technologies remain outside a traditional core education, even as the content of primary, secondary, and tertiary educations are being revolutionized by the same technologies. Such a separation between offline "education" and online "technology" is not only unreasonable, but also impossible. However, other and more nuanced rejections are not only feasible, but also necessary in order to ensure that education both contributes to democratic citizenship and promotes critical thought. It is the indiscriminate attempts to merge technology with learning itself, as witnessed in Nicolas Negroponte's techno-triumphalist claim that "Digital is the means through which children learn learning" (Twist 2005), that must be rejected.

After examining objections and rejections, the real questions lie in positive visions for electronic education. How can the learner-affirmative and liberating potential of electronic pedagogies and Internet-conscious education be achieved? How will students and teachers contest social forces that seek to employ the Internet as a means of mechanistic education and social discipline, rather than an instrument through which to oppose market-defined social values, education-as-capital, and alienation of labor? Can Internet-based education function to overcome rather than reinforce class barriers to educational provision? Can the Internet expand access to high-quality free public education rather than become a co-opted vehicle for privatization, commodity delivery, capital accumulation, and corporate profit? In short, if we recognize in the Internet a means of social oppression, both potential and real, how can that realization function to transform electronic education into a controversial, subversive, anti-authoritarian, democratic, collaborative, and emancipatory site of humanistic culture?

Opposition to the misuse of online education affirms utopianism located in the material world; it locates its politics within the daily existence and interaction of physical communities that constitute humanity's irreplaceable home. This is an opposition that rejects the subordination of classroom learning to technological triumphalism, while simultaneously realizing the advantages of electronic pedagogies where advantage can be obtained. The first section of this manifesto outlines principles of electronic education that take learning as a communitarian process based in physical classrooms, with each principle rooted in a critique of technological ideologies, electronic education commodification, labor practices, and class issues. The second section expands these principles to address ways social democracy can be developed in educational systems. If the initial section appears harsh and negative in its criticism, the following section contributes a more positive vision toward a possible future for electronic education.

Democracy in the Electronic Classroom

- *Reject electronic pedagogies and information technologies that seek to displace and supplant the physical communities of classrooms with communication networks and immaterial assemblies. Affirm electronic pedagogies that link people, educational spaces, and learning cultures in new and imaginative ways.*

A social gathering in a physically present, shared common learning space is a foundation of educational practice. That space of socialization is as crucial as the content of education, and is intrinsic to educational content. Social articulations of learning spaces, places that include the broadest possible range of architectures as well as outdoor sites, are inseparable from education. These social articulations that translate space into learning places range from large cosmopolitan universities through tin-roof huts and open nature. Materiality provides the basis for assembled communities that can engage in both abstract and concrete labor.

"Virtual space" is pseudo-space and a delusory claim: it does not exist as three-dimensional space and cannot translate into place. A "virtual classroom" participates in this false illusion of space and place, providing an imitative substitute that equates immateriality with materiality. A "virtual community," the parent concept of virtual classrooms, is a terminological and conceptual sleight-of-hand, one whose tendentious claim to commensurability with real community should be refused (Lockard 1997: 224–226, 2000: 172–174). Any "virtual community" represents an invitation to join a credulous hallucination based on acceptance of an implicit belief that community resides within a metaphysical nexus created by a server, or that electronic communications can represent the full breadth of physical community. This does not enter a sociological debate over what constitutes a community; rather, it asserts that either a "classroom" or a "community" exists as a tangible social place.[5] Such terminological shifts do more than provide computer-mediated communications with a saleable metaphor, much as re-branding can change a product into a more marketable item. As Charles Ess argues earlier in this volume (Chapter 11), this disembodiment operates to the profound detriment of humanities education and dialogic ideals. The appropriative politics here are dark, for as Tina Kazan also points out (Chapter 14), "Given that teaching is a social relationship between teachers and students, between bodies, then a move toward distance education motivated by a desire to eliminate bodies is not only a naïve one, but a sinister one."

This sinister move has identifiable social forms. During a period when human services budget reductions have led to severe cuts or relative funding declines imposed against public education systems in the United States and many other countries, the "virtual classroom" has become a bait-and-switch tactic to replace investment in physical infrastructure with technological promises of a new and better learning space. Schools and colleges need wired or wireless buildings with computers, not computers without school buildings. The shift of capitalization expenses onto students and their families through mandated from-home participation in virtual classes, common in some US high schools, relieves public education budgets of responsibility for bricks-and-mortar construction to mitigate over-crowding and to provide more teachers. It marks part of a continued global neoliberal shift toward the privatization of educational costs, one that increases burdens on low-income families and expands class inequalities in educational provision.

Although online education is not necessarily less expensive than in-class provision, "virtual classrooms" are being marketed for their ability to reduce the costs of educational delivery in physical settings. Palaces of virtual learning—a phrase that echoes of Father Matteo Ricci's sixteenth-century "memory palaces" (Spence 1984: 10)—have been constructed online with a promise to entirely replace the need for physical delivery, with corresponding savings on capital investment. However, this is an educational vision that switches investment from buildings with many decades (or centuries) of potential durability toward hardware that will be out-of-date in less than five years, served by software which will date even more quickly. When reduced to communication and "virtual campuses," education is a short-term investment dissociated from a stable teaching labor force and presence in a physical community. It markets to potential students a boundlessly optimistic vision of education as painless consumption leading to increased income potential, while ensuring educational capital of tuition cash-flow, unorganized and under-paid teaching labor, minimized campus capitalization, excellent return on investment, and flexibility in market positioning. A "virtual campus" is an educational scam in progress.

Online education here is no different than many other commodities whose consumption purports to facilitate beneficial changes in social identity. The Internet assists a diffuse but deep market penetration by educational myth-sellers whose ultimate achievement can only be intensified social frustration among gullible buyers who do not succeed in transforming themselves through purchase of "education," which is by nature a long-term process. The real product innovation in online education lies in the virtual de-territorialization as a means of marketing identity change through education, an innovation that aligns educational commodities with the practices of contemporary global capitalism (Grzinic 2004: 177–180). By participating in processes of de-territorialization and re-territorialization via the Internet, the "distance education industry" joins the classic work of Western capitalism that reproduces and increases capital by creating new definitions of territory and its possession in order to profit from them. A "virtual classroom," whose electronic production re-defines both territory and ownership control, is a new New World frontier that bases itself on the displacement, expropriation, and elimination of our physical classroom communities and their learning spaces. In its more virulent and aggressive forms, electronic education is no less than a means of technological colonization in the service of capital. The work of reclaiming shared common spaces in public education, together with inventing non-exploitative modes of electronic education controlled by students and teachers, is the work of progressive educators.

- *Equivalence between in-class and online learning is a fallacy. Use online learning and hybrid pedagogies as empowering complements to in-class learning, not as substitutes.*

In-class and online learning are not and cannot be equal: they are different types of learning and their effectiveness depends on educational context, student groups, subject materials, and learning needs. There is no authoritative research that allows their equation or privileges electronic education as a superior method.[6] Rather, the equation and inter-substitution of these two types of learning provide conceptual and administrative foundations for accreditation and the legitimization of unequal educational provision.[7] Institutions credit and participate in online education despite this fallacy because, among other reasons, it represents the promise of technological progress driving educational progress and the threat of becoming outmoded by competing institutions if they do not participate.

Larger social questions than individual institutional marketplace advantage must govern educational policy-making. Social and educational policy should link the physical and virtual domains of education through licensing and accreditation in order to ensure proximate equivalence. In the case of many online courses and degree programs, legislation or accreditation credentialing requiring demonstrable equivalence between online and in-class learning would end or strip accreditation from online offerings. Choosing only one example, a US community college that offers a complete B.Ed. with state teacher's license certification entirely online, except for a final-year on-site practicum course, is engaged in still legally protected educational fraud that must end. In this type of education, learning from group settings and undergoing educational socialization, together with evaluation of a student's self-presentation, are central to becoming a good teacher. Such experience is not obtainable via the Internet but US institutions are graduating more and more under-trained or "fast track" teachers on the basis of patently inadequate online coursework. The logic of educational commodification fulfills itself: if there is a market, no greater rationale is needed for selling, even if the product cannot possibly fill the learning need.

To oppose such exploitative practice, demands for credit-to-credit learning equivalence between online and in-class education, if and where that is possible, must become a cornerstone of progressive educational policy. Although the present US social climate makes increased government regulation very difficult to obtain, consumer protection regulation of online education is needed for the benefit of both students and society.

With current technology, the advantages electronic pedagogy offers arrive largely via hybrid courses that combine both in-class learning and online support. It takes advantage of each mode to employ classrooms as a center for discussion between students and teachers, and online services for assignments that add to the robustness of in-class learning. Electronic pedagogies and their advocates must respect place-centered learning by recognizing learning advantages and disadvantages, rather than attempting to convert all classrooms into wired, technology-filled "smart classrooms" and appropriate ever-expanding proportions of institutional budgets. Unless specifically germane to learning or teaching a subject, fully computerized classrooms are more trouble than assistance to instructors, frequently create architectural barriers to open classroom space, and distract students. As experienced teachers realize, it can be sufficiently challenging to build and sustain an intense classroom discussion; to compete with open laptop computers—and particularly their entertainment or wireless communications options—destroys good teaching.

A classroom is an irreplaceable space for ideas and discussion, not another domain for machines. There is an intrinsic sterility where electronic education refuses to recognize pedagogical limitations and appropriateness; that sterility derives from a reductiveness that cannot distinguish between information and learning, or between broadcasting and communication. The power of education, whether online or face-to-face, lies in acquiring social abilities to convert information into learning. Confusing or distorting that relationship serves the purposes of disempowerment through education; it helps maintain or increase social inequalities, and configures educational ideology and practices toward exploitation of students and teachers. Seen in this negative light, the totalizing expansion of electronic education engenders attempts to shift toward a false equation of information and learning, deprive students of means of critique and abstract labor, weaken participatory democracy, and create new terms of social exploitation. By refusing to accept this false substitution and employing electronic education in active and hybrid terms, students and teachers can begin to confront the passive practices and disintegrative work of much electronic education.

Good education and good technology are not synonymous; a good education is not an electronic deliverable. After a generation online, more people than ever recognize a balance of advantages and disadvantages in electronic education. The movement toward critical electronic education is already today finding creative ground in pedagogies that refuse such fallacious equations, emphasize collaborative and face-to-face learning, and employ in-class and electronic settings together to their best hybrid advantage. It is a movement that must and will continue.

- *There are no teachers on the Internet, only data streams. Teach to the student, not to the electronic avatar.*

This simple and radical proposition results from an affirmation of physicality and material communities as the basis of education. If there are no communities on the Internet, neither are there teachers: both exist in the physically present world. What the Internet (or televised, radio, and correspondence instruction) can provide is the *representation* of teachers and teaching. These are icon-teachers, capable of communication to a greater or lesser extent depending on the medium.

This distinction between substance and image is crucial: the entire predicate of online teaching lies in the equal substitutability of in-class and online instruction. Some proponents of electronic education take the argument of equal substitution a stage further by claiming that online delivery is superior because it can provide a broadcast forum for great teachers. Both arguments of substitutability and superiority fail due to a fallacy of equivalence: a representation of reality is never reality. Online teaching activity is not in-class teaching; a streaming video of a teacher is not a teacher. Virtual production in education operates through reproduction of persona, settings, or pedagogical strategies from in-class teaching, and that serial iteration of virtual workers, workplaces, and work is key to the economic viability of online learning. Yet material and immaterial teaching role fulfillment are different activities, ones where immaterial versions imitate material versions. As students and teachers, we have a right to real-time, real-place education: a data stream is not enough.

Teachers do not exist on the Internet, but teaching labor does. Electronic education is as perfect a means as any yet invented to recycle teaching labor, using websites as a device to capture, store, and repeatedly deliver teaching labor to successive students. It is no longer teaching per se that has value, but rather recyclable images (e.g., streaming video), digital materials (e.g., Blackboard documents), and instructional programs that acquire value. When commodification of teaching labor increases through technological progress and the educational post-Fordism of mass just-in-time delivery upon demand, the separation of teaching from its immanent physical–social meaning increases simultaneously. The responsive immanence and spontaneous communication that has characterized good teaching practice is now an image or sub-routine; even live interactive classroom broadcasts suffer from absent vitality. This transformation via electronic representation from physical teachers into immaterial and service-based teaching is a process that strips teaching labor's surplus value and converts it into a manageable product, a form of pedagogical industrialization.

This same process converts online students into avatars, student-semblances that an instructor must continually work to locate as entire personalities. Where students and teachers never meet physically, teaching work frequently becomes a failed effort to bridge between the rational and phenomenal. Students and teachers become textual beings searching for rational expression, rather than unified and embodied beings for whom expression lies in a range of emotive features. It is that reduction of students and teachers into a mutually dependent set of dematerialized avatars that creates a profound obstacle to democratic education based on human holism where personality is a visible attribute. A mechanistic relationship between teachers and their students based on exploitative exchange contradicts the human care, as opposed to use-value, that is at the heart of meaningful democratic practice.

One of the most valuable sources of opposition to this de-humanization via electronic education lies in reversing the process by using electronic means to personalize and humanize interaction, and to create opportunities to meet in physical settings to embody ourselves. A data stream that reveals our humanity and inseparability as students and teachers can engage and enlarge us.

- *Electronic pedagogies are not an appropriate solution to all questions and problems: resist imposition of inappropriate electronic pedagogies. Electronic education must not serve as a market gateway.*

There are many educational situations where technology constitutes positive, even obliterating, interference to engagement with a text or problem. To pursue a critical interpretation of a poem, to work through the terms of an equation, or to practice verb conjugation in solitude are activities where educational technologies have functioned frequently as more hindrance than help. Solitariness, retreat, and reflection are learning practices as much as sociality, companionship, and engaged discussion. The practices of intellectual wrestling with a problem in individual isolation, without mechanical assistance, constitute a necessary passage and continuing requirement for intellectual development. Equally, learning activities that rely on intense personal interaction and close attention—for example, remedial writing courses are notoriously difficult and ineffective in online settings—are inappropriate for distance learning. Individual responsibility for learning cannot be substituted by computer mediation; such mediation precisely relieves both students and teachers of full engagement with learning and its responsibilities.

Yet on-screen or other forms of mediated sensory engagement provide an irreplaceable core for electronic learning (e-learning). Online mimesis of solitary work responsibility replaces the simplicity (and cheapness) of offline contemplation and self-reliance in expression and problem-solving. Artificial intelligence or mediated human presences provide a formative and inescapable environment in online education, one that insists on attention and distracts from independent imagination or deeper conceptual engagement. Effective education lies in a cultivated ability to throw off distraction, to focus on the question or text at hand, and to engage in its discussion. This ability, crucial to participation in one's own education, is inimical to an active electronic format.[8] Criteria for the evaluation of e-learning do not even contemplate this domain of reflective thought (Schank 2002: 215–225) or propose mechanistic benchmarks for process quality necessarily based on "a relative paucity of true, original research dedicated to explaining or predicting phenomena related to distance learning" (Phipps & Merisotis 1999: 2).

Some online courses, whose formats most frequently defeat prolonged contemplation, derive their appeal from the condensation, brevity, and packaging of information within a rapidly changing series of presentations. Thoreau's "pastures of the imagination," where learning emerges from an absence of noise and disturbance, have no electronic equivalent. Data streams replace brook streams; reliance on pseudo-teaching replaces direct experience; and knowledge management replaces an aware, self-controlled consciousness. We become acclimatized to the white noise of a virtual classroom, one engineered into the software applications, control configurations, and content data selections. User-friendly software options provide students with choices whose alternatives create distractions from any immanent realization of the moment.

The anti-intellectual reductionism endemic to online coursework can specify rationalized frameworks of specific facts, but more essential facts lie outside these frames. A profoundly perverse social imitation of knowledge substitutes information technologies and their products for imagination itself, rather than recognizing the fallibility and limitations of knowledge where "I know not the first letter of the alphabet" (Thoreau 1993: 93). Under new electronic paradigms fostered by the intensification of knowledge utility as an educational value, imagination falls beneath commercial colonization. Unknown means unprofitable, rather than a beginning point for exploration. An epistemological understanding of knowledge as ambiguous or susceptible to open interpretation needs to be discarded or suppressed in such reductive electronic schema.

Electronic pedagogies commonly function by re-inventing educational wheels that do not need re-invention, or by presenting information technology as an all-problem solver. This mechanistic educational worldview treats the educational system as set of discrete markets—primary, secondary, and higher education, with multiple sub-markets at each level—that can be provided with electronic solutions that will expand learning opportunities and increase student success rates. For educational information technology vendors, it is not only content and pedagogical methods that need to be rendered into electronic solutions, but also it is equally educational systems that must be altered to adopt a constant flow of new electronic products (Schiller 1999: especially 143–202). They have become transformative centers of market creation, both in the consumption and production of knowledge. The model employed for this transformation was the corporation; the new values especially promoted by this model included competitiveness, innovation skills, and a proprietary relationship with culture. Such values are antithetical to the equality, cooperation, and free sharing that most concepts of democratic education seek to encourage. Modes of electronic education that envision or treat classrooms as gateway markets accept market values as legitimate social determination; they accept commodification, privatization, and market exchange as normative conditions. Educational democracy embodies a resistance to privatization and market values as universal norms through its emphasis on education as universal entitlement and human right.

- *Use appropriate electronic pedagogy and DIY with free or cheap software. Learn electronic self-reliance.*

DIY technology infusion into humanities curricula responds to many needs with simple and readily available computer tools. Too often the "new model" of electronic pedagogy comes bound together with special development budgets and technical assistance for faculties who do not have computer skills or time to spend acquiring them. Internet-based courses with high-quality designs and streaming video downloads typically require sufficient projected revenue streams to justify a team of support personnel, in addition to the course instructor. DIY hybrid courses use easy-to-master computer skills and bundled software to enable individual instructors, with only occasional need to ask for technical help, to enhance their teaching.

DIY approaches to bringing technology into humanities courses emphasize a Freirean method in computer literacy, a refusal to accept the dictates of "superior" cultural, or technological, knowledge in creating a learning environment that responds to social needs. A hands-on approach to information technology, where teachers assume responsibility for translating their own teaching ideas into electronic form, is insubordination turned practical. Mass delivery of pre-packaged humanities and social sciences courses via the Internet, a highly problematic development in what Langdon Winner calls "technoglobalism's assault on education" (Winner 1997), creates the very real prospect of submerging humanistic educational initiatives. Abdication from effective response, or teaching without acknowledging how computerization has and continues to change contemporary discourse, surrenders education to the social forces of capitalism seeking to "re-engineer" humanistic education as market-driven vocational training while simultaneously creating an in-school market for electronics product consumption. The struggle for humanistic education needs to develop DIY competencies among teachers in order to recognize the quasi-monopolistic practices of the major software and hardware firms, and to identify open-source and other solutions to avoid the draining of education budgets by Microsoft and Windows-reliant computing (McNaughton 2005). DIY open-source computing is electronic prophylaxis in action.

Course design in US public higher education too often emerges against the background of a political environment that places ever-increasing emphasis on the visibility of educational technology, and where educational "value" lies in promoting technology even if this does nothing to promote critical reading and argument. Surfing through university course websites, one encounters too many websites that are Potemkin Village affairs that do not involve students and have no living relationship to daily teaching. They have no actual pedagogical use and remain unchanged throughout the semester: these are display windows, no more. The same information as appears on the website gets handed out as a first-day syllabus. Why have a visible teaching website if it is not used to teach? The DIY approach emphasizes that if teachers are going to the time and trouble to build a course website, they should be prepared to use it to actually teach, deliver course content, hold discussions, and provide review materials. The satisfaction of hands-on hybrid teaching lies in taking control, in making a course website come alive, in refusing to become one more Internet-delivered "knowledge commodity."

The real technological limitation in a contemporary US university environment is less likely to be student access to sufficient bandwidth and more likely to be instructor willingness to enter into increasingly sophisticated technologies (e.g., streaming video) without convincing pedagogical rationales, learning pay-off, and available equipment and technical support. A DIY electronic pedagogy does not mean turning teachers' offices into production studios; it means making rational choices among commonly available, easy-to-use, and relatively inexpensive computer technologies. Cheap and simple DIY technologies, like free blogging software, can be adapted to far better effect than indulging expensive technical obsessions to the detriment of engaging in face-to-face discussions of a subject.

Social Democracy and Electronic Education

- *Class defines both online and in-class education: use both modes to overcome and eliminate class privilege.*

Education in the United States, Europe, and elsewhere historically constituted an extension, reiteration, and reification of dominant class structures.

Universities in early modern Europe were established through royal or ecclesiastical charter; their internal governance and pedagogies were faithful to their sponsors. Until well into the twentieth century, relatively few European students obtained academic high school matriculation certificates; fewer still had opportunities for university-level education. The US educational system, nominally more democratic, provided educational access and content delimited by race, gender, and class hierarchies. Large minority populations in the United States—blacks and Hispanics in segregated schools, native peoples in federal boarding schools—received low-quality, service-oriented education. These limitations on educational access began to ease under post–World War II reform governments in Western Europe and communist governments in Eastern Europe, and the legal and political changes created by the civil rights movement in the United States.

The effective advent of electronic education came in the late twentieth century, after neoliberal movements had assumed new prominence and power in the United States and Europe. Neoliberal concepts of citizenship emphasized individual achievement over collective social justice; effectively re-solidified race and class lines through heightened discrimination in access and provision; and privileged capital creation as a central task of education. Under both conservative statist and neoliberal social paradigms, corporate capital and profit enhancement shape and frame education: private benefit replaces public good. This shift has become clearly visible in the social and legal re-definition of public education as a private benefit. In the United States, educational policy-making has increasingly regarded education as primarily an individual asset, such as creates career mobility, rather than a collective public responsibility and trust, such as creates a better society. Successful arguments for educational change, whether for expanded daycare systems or increased public investment in research universities, emphasize economic utility and quantifiable return to investment. As O'Sullivan and Palaskas argued earlier in this volume (Chapter 2), "Within hegemonic neoliberalism the [knowledge-based economy] has become the master economic narrative driving changes in Western societies and gaining resonance in [...] the reorganization of higher educational institutions."

Online education promised, however hypothetically, to produce monitored deliverables, meet measurable financial criteria, and achieve such a reorganization in a way that offline bricks-and-mortar educational settings never could. Hamilton and Feenberg (Chapter 13) have discussed how the administrators of corporate universities have sought to employ this promise to redesign the fundamental structure of higher education. Through online education and similar allied initiatives demanding accountability for investment, education would remodel itself as a mode of production rather than as a service. This was a new–old ideological regime, for much of this "reform" rhetoric derived from nineteenth-century arguments toward creating "well-trained mechanics" to fuel the Industrial Revolution. According to these early nationalist advocacies for an improved education system, the expansion of public education served both to accommodate the labor market and to create an "enlightened"—that is, ideologically compliant—citizenry. The dual task of education under twentieth-century US-style late capitalism became creation of a knowledge-based high-tech economy through development of human capital, and the establishment of norms of capitalism (intense competition, individual merit, differential reward) as self-realizing, immanent, and unchallenged values within the educational system.[9] The standards movement of the late twentieth and early twenty-first centuries has provided a new means for verifying, quality-checking, and quantifying educational achievement—or in post-industrial terms, the creation and delivery of knowledge. This transformation of education from social entitlement into a post-industrial product has relied upon similar means of disciplinary surveillance and control as applied toward commodity production. The pedagogical phylogeny of online education recapitulates its capitalism-defined ontogeny.

Electronic education rose upon and attracted its continuing infrastructure investment through adapting itself to politics that evaluated public education budgets in terms of training workforces for corporate employment or subsidizing corporations via laboratory research, public–private corporate park environments, or the creation of relocation magnets. In higher education, policy emphases on suffusing information technology throughout university curricula provided continuing impetus to these educational politics. Electronic education became the thin edge of a corporate wedge and an optimization tool, one that adapted students to the requirements of post-industrial and global production modes before they joined corporate workforces. This construction of education as a series of optimization processes for individual workers emphasized the creation and reinforcement of electronic skills as a guarantee of middle-class status.

The rising tide of electronic education demanded an incorporation of ideological compliance, even as many instructors and administrators recognized and personally opposed the terms of the system they were building. However, it would have been a suicidal professional contradiction to advocate for critical electronic education that would recognize and oppose its function as a corporate training ground, its participation in a repressive mode of production, and its reproduction of managerial-employee class relations. Indeed, the sometimes explicit, sometimes implied promise of information technology to students in higher education is that it will provide them with a means of technological self-reliance and economic independence. But this is a false promise based on hopeful belief in technology as providing individual exemption from class and exchange inequalities. Essentially the role demanded of teachers employing electronic education is to become participants in a lie that technology use by itself will change class structures.

An ideology of pseudo-classlessness has arisen among both teachers and students, one premised on such promises of individual autonomy linked to market demand for advanced technical knowledge. In a "knowledge economy," online classes supposedly create economic winners and class becomes an irrelevant anachronism. But like all modern education systems, online education articulates principles of a class system based on control of the means of production, the appropriation of labor's surplus value, and unequal social exchange supported by legal systems that protect capital. Despite its rhetoric of classlessness and techno-equality, online education manifests a class morphology like any other mode of education. Recognizing and critiquing class structures incorporated into electronic pedagogies is a crucial intellectual step for both students and teachers toward gaining control over their learning and teaching.

- *Electronic education is a central tool in the corporatization of higher education; it helps shape universities into preparatory schools for servicing capital. Resist commercialization, social control, and discipline via electronic education. Re-invent electronic education as a means of self-realization, collaborative labor, and anti-capitalist work.*

The mainstream vision that has driven electronic education centers on realization of economic utility value in learning. According to one representative corporate-oriented voice, the future is corporate: "The line between corporate education and university education will begin to blur" and "There won't be 1000 different economics courses to choose from. Eventually the field of economics, rather than the individual universities at which economists happen to work, will control the content of economics courses" (Schank 2002: 256). These themes of corporatization and standardization are common in the visionary literature of electronic education. They support another theme of corporation–university synergy: corporations and higher education institutions will meld in their cultures and purposes. As Marc J. Rosenberg, another corporate-oriented writer, states, "Today, organizations are investing in corporate universities [...] They're appointing 'chief learning officers' or 'chief knowledge officers' " whose purposes are "to demonstrate a clear linkage between learning investments and business strategy, and to create and maintain a knowledge-creating and knowledge-sharing culture" (Rosenberg 2001). In this vision of synergy between education and commerce, there will be a seamless flow between knowledge and skills acquisition in university settings and the needs of the regional, national, and global-corporate economy. An e-learning university will function both to accomplish corporate research agendas and to shape students into trained, high-value labor within corporations.

In the late 1970s, Lyotard was already arguing that this synergy between electronic education and the production demands of capital was a feature of a postmodern economy. If the only goal of education was utilitarian attainment, not legitimating narratives of self-realization or human emancipation, then computer-mediated education might serve equally as well as real teachers. He wrote that in higher education:

> limiting ourselves to a narrowly functionalist point of view, an organized stock of knowledge is the essential thing to be transmitted [...] To the extent that learning is translatable into computer language and the traditional teacher is replaceable by memory banks, didactics can be entrusted to machines linking traditional memory banks (libraries, etc.) and computer data banks to intelligent terminals placed at the students' disposal. (Lyotard 1984: 51)

While Lyotard identified databanks as "nature" for postmodern humanity, he argued that decisive advantage accrued not to perfect information (i.e., knowledge management) and skills reproduction, but rather to innovation and interdisciplinarity. The conceptually impoverished students who emerged from functionalist education systems "have at their disposal no metalanguage or metanarrative in which to formulate the final goal and correct use of that machinery" (52).

What Lyotard viewed as a deficit, neoliberal corporate culture views as either a redundant irrelevancy or outright advantage. A non-ideological labor force fully engaged in knowledge management represents ideal compliance with corporate focus on productivity, competitiveness, and profitability. Humanistic and philosophical meta-narratives originating from universities interfere with realization of surplus value in an information economy, and functionalist views of the university emphasize its role as a site for production of human capital. Insofar as the orthodox social constructionist version of electronic education presents itself as a non-ideological vehicle for achievement of potential profitability within the corporate-university synergy, administrators will encourage its adoption and diffusion. With its promise to re-invent classrooms, electronic education offers an opportunity to de-ideologize these classrooms in their new form as "virtual classrooms." This development parallels network culture where, as Jeremy Valentine argues, it is no longer regarded as realistic "to talk about ideology at all if this means a systematically distorted view of the world produced by capital in order that people misunderstand their place in it" (Valentine 2004: 68).

Non-ideology is a self-delusory state, but claims of excessive classroom "ideology" sign resistance by non-conformist teachers to a pre-ordained "natural" and organic order of education subordinated to the service of capital.[10] This is an organicism characteristic of bourgeois economic relations and its reliance on educational systems to transmit, reinforce, and replicate those relations. The open introduction of social ideology into course content and academic work via electronic means only specifies what bourgeois anti- and non-ideological approaches refuse to enunciate. There is real discontent within line electronic teaching faculty ranks today, a discontent that creates non-conformist, humanistic, and pro-democracy e-Luddites. Rebellious e-Luddites have the capacity to re-ideologize the electronic teaching sphere, creating transformation instead of surrender to naturalized hierarchies of knowledge and power.

That transformation will not be easy. To voice or enact oppositional politics through electronic education invites surveillance, discipline, and control. Online and interactive software platforms provide new opportunities for administrators to enter electronic educational fora to supervise classes and instructors. During the New York University (NYU) graduate students unionization strike in November 2005, deans and administrators added themselves as unannounced "instructors" to Blackboard course shells in order to monitor teaching activities and retaliate by firing strikers. In reaction, the NYU faculty senate passed a resolution condemning administrative abuse of Blackboard accounts; a group of 225 teachers, calling themselves Faculty Democracy, condemned the intrusions and asked for assurances against their repetition; and some university teachers now refuse to use online education tools (Leonard 2005a, b; Loeb 2005).

The events at NYU were no more than a small demonstration of the global potential of the systemic electronic surveillance that has proliferated in both education and the public sphere. What happened within this university-wide system was only a large-scale exhibition of the same surveillance potential that is commonly available to electronic classroom instructors who can quietly examine a student's log-in data or what currently appears on multiple student screens. Electronic education provides abundant opportunities for real-time surveillance and control over both students and teachers. Moreover, given Patriot Act prohibitions against revealing information demands by government investigators, it would be illegal for a teacher to inform a student that he/she was being monitored in an electronic classroom (or equally, for administrators to notify a teacher of eavesdropping by government authorities). Electronic education lends itself readily to surveillance regimes that Henry Giroux links to rising authoritarianism in US culture and use of education to reinforce passive acceptance of authority.

The targets of surveillance—non-productivity, alienation from work, and labor revolts—are all manifestations of narratives that differ from those of capital. Corporate universities are learning to apply the techniques and lessons of contemporary executive government and industrial production, supported by a monoculture of consensus surrounding its use of electronic education. In refusing to recognize that electronic education incorporates ideologies other than progress, or in framing it as a non-ideological instrument in its own right, the corporate university assumes the task of training a compliant workforce accustomed to the look-and-feel of electronic workplaces.

Democratic education is concerned with realization of individual freedom and social equality, together with the responsibilities of participatory citizenship. Electronic surveillance and control in order to remodel critical education as a vocational training ground or to discipline the teaching labor force is antithetical to democratic education. This is not the necessary conclusion of electronic education, even if it does represent a potential that requires constant awareness of possibilities toward abuse.[11]

Collaborative and cooperative electronic education looks in another direction, away from commodity production, hierarchies, surveillance, and disciplinary control. It looks toward a critique of self-commodification as the immanent purpose of education. It opposes the totalization of the human persona, the center of education, within economic utility and production. If electronic education is to be no more than yet another technological extension of the spiraling and environmentally devastating cycle of commodity production, exchange, and profit, then virtual classrooms will be no more than virtual holding cells. If electronic education stands between these two contradictory possibilities of commodification and emancipation, this constitutes a measure of both its negative and positive potentials.

- *Unionize the electronic teaching commons: support labor organizing among distance education faculty and throughout educational systems.*

The commodification of education through electronic technologies has proceeded through privileging of capital and corporate interests, use of educational systems as new markets, privatization of public resources and services, re-direction of public budgets for corporate profit, and support for technological monopolism—all in the name of educational innovation and progress. The subordination of labor inherent within these developments is antithetical to democratic education, one of whose foundational principles is respect for and fair treatment of teachers and allied staff as co-equal partners in education.

The sum value of labor represented by the Internet is incomparably greater than the value of its fixed capital assets. This truism underlies the emergence of a labor-reliant electronic global commons, albeit one deeply flawed by meager or absent Internet service and resources due to global mal-distribution of wealth. Whether in hybrid or online teaching models, building learning resources, or doing administrative work, educational labor constitutes a major share of human labor invested into the Internet. A technology-conscious and unionized educational labor force represents one of the largest sources of potential opposition to the increasing control of capital over educational systems via Internet-based provision. The labor power that built and continues to build the Internet needs to find expression in educational politics through union organizing.

Labor organizing on campuses—particularly among graduate students and contingent faculty who provide the bulk of electronic education—can contribute heavily toward raising the quality of distance education. Issues of appropriate in-class versus online curriculum, hybrid/online course and electronic resource development, pedagogical decision-making, workload, compensation, teacher training, and evaluation are all issues where labor should take the lead in achieving quality electronic education. The current prevailing concept that technology decisions and budget are administrative affairs, not within the scope of decision-making by labor, reproduces corporate hierarchy within educational organizations. Democratic education emphasizes that decisions within educational institutions are open to collective or representative participation, which must include the use, nature, and extent of technology, and control over the work conditions technology creates. These decisions include the right of teachers to decide not to adopt hybrid or online pedagogies, or online learning platforms; this is a right that must be defended as intrinsic to the work autonomy of teachers. Current practice in educational administration has so naturalized administrative claims to decision-making authority over technology adoption and use that it seems barely conceivable to administrators to grant teachers substantive decision-making powers in this domain. This hierarchical mode of top-down control is not only antithetical to educational democracy, but also to network culture with its autonomous and distributive decision-making.

Technology decision-making power in education will not be relinquished voluntarily: it must be seized. Labor organizing in US higher education has been notoriously weak during the past decade, although there have been signal successes on some public and private university campuses. Campus-based distance education is equally subject to these adverse organizing conditions; further, given the comparative invisibility of distance education and its reliance on a permanent, un-represented underclass of academic teachers, distance education instructors are even more vulnerable to exploitation than in-class instructors. Off-campus, at-home instructors have the least bargaining power among online faculty. Major online institutions such as the University of Phoenix recruit among such home-based, part-time instructors with few options on the academic employment market and no effective negotiating power. Commercial online education providers like Thompson Learning's "Education to Go" division[12] market their courses through community college catalogs and displace regional teaching labor pools with distance-delivered, standardized "instructor-facilitated" courses, turning cooperating local educational institutions into marketing platforms with reduced teaching labor needs. Whether they work in classrooms or online, teachers share common labor issues demanding post-industrial models of labor organization. Organizing this emergent, populous, heavily fragmented, low-paid, and disempowered "virtual labor market" is one of the most pressing challenges for democratizing electronic education.[13]

- *High-quality, accessible, and free public education at all levels is a global human right and civic good. Electronic education should serve to advance our right to education and other human rights.*

Under current neoliberal paradigms, social forces advocating commodification, market creation, and privatization shape the dominant trends in education. Neoliberal globalization has led to the increasing privatization of education as a service, complementing another trend toward diminishing state guarantees of universal free education due to social budget cuts. The result has been a new global order for education where a conflict has arisen between international human rights law which defines education as a right,[14] whereas international trade law defines it as a service (Tomasevski 2005: 1). In the United States, the international human rights legal dimension of education remains commonly ignored (Gross 2001), largely due to widespread cultural ambivalence or hostility toward international human rights norms and treaty responsibilities. Human rights discourse on the complementary rights to education and participation in an information-based society (UN 2003a: Section A, 1–18) remains alien in the United States, where the emphasis lies on maintaining US economic competitiveness. Instead of recognizing a collective ethical and legal obligation to provide an adequate budget for high-quality public education for all, with particular attention to equity for less-advantaged populations, US society has increasingly defined education as an individual and family benefit and financial responsibility.

Internationally, the human rights-based promise of free education has been undermined in many countries by for-fee provision of public schooling or reversion to a variety of private-tuition systems. These developments have fostered the creation of a global export market in educational services and reinforced the position of a select set of international cosmopolitan centers whose world-class institutions provide education to multinational elites. Such shifts away from human rights-based and equalitarian educational provision into privatized, consumption-based educational systems result in mass deprivation of educational opportunity, radically foreshortened schooling, declining levels of educational achievement, and the creation of a permanently impoverished and unskilled global labor force available for exploitation. The social damage done by the commodification of education is incalculable; it contributes to human tragedy on an immense scale.

Electronic education is not the primary solution to remedying this global educational tragedy; indeed, in its current formation it aids and abets commodification of teaching and learning. The central solutions to this catastrophe lie in fundamental democratic reforms; social control over capital; re-orientation of national budgets toward human services; emphasis on gender equality in education; development of teacher education; and public investment in primary, secondary, and university physical plants. Basic issues of capitalization and maintenance costs, technical infrastructure, and intellectual property regimes (Vadén 2003) today constitute formidable barriers to e-learning in even mid-tier national economies, let alone poor economies. Pay-to-play neoliberal politics and "the extremes of e-stratification driven by a pure digital market" (Dyer-Witheford 2002: 149) currently frame electronic education and its marketing, not human rights politics or the massive expansion of social budgets.

A hundred or a thousand more idealistic new e-learning schemes for Third World countries will make no difference if the terms of economic exploitation under neoliberal globalization remain unaltered. More to the point, such Internet learning schemes and cheap gear for faraway poor students of color are neocolonial philanthropy at work. Nothing changes, but concerned First World citizens feel better about themselves and the Internet remains a safe tool for capital. Whether in poor or rich countries, technology in education has no inherent powers of liberation. Rather, educational technology demands a politics of self-reliance in order to achieve its social potential. In opposing global capitalism nearly a quarter-century ago, before the Internet, Armand Mattelart emphasized the necessity of a self-reliance policy toward achieving democracy: "Self-reliance refuses to take the state and its administrative apparatuses as the only social subject. It is the multiplicity of organized interlocutors that characterizes a social self-reliance situation" (Mattelart 1983: 151).

Technology can be one of those actors helping achieve collective educational self-reliance. Mode of delivery does not pre-determine the politics of electronic educational projects; technology can either advance or obstruct the realization of education as a human right. Where these projects participate in opening the electronic commons, in challenging market commodification, and in enabling students and teachers to oppose the subjugation of education to the demands of capital, then they contribute to the work of practical utopianism. Both information and education resist ownership: we own the power for democratic change in our education.

Notes

1. Small-scale research studies of online distance learning began emerging in the United States during the late 1980s. Careful review of the Education Resources Information Center (ERIC) database indicates that during 1995–2005, over 3,000 articles and research documents addressed the evaluation of distance learning. Nearly all evaluation research studies are limited, self-descriptive, single-institution reports; there are no identifiable large-scale (1,000+ subjects) or authoritative studies. There is a clear tendency by evaluators to assume, as does the author of one inventory study of online education in Florida, that "any technology in the classroom is good" (Sandiford 2001). Distance learning evaluations have been undertaken largely by those with a vested interest in proving the usefulness of educational technology, not by neutral parties willing to consider seriously alternate cases of non-usefulness, comparative inadequacy, or poor return on investment. Outside the United States, there is far less educational research literature on electronic pedagogies. In Great Britain, the British Educational Communications and Technology Agency (BECTA), the government's primary partner for e-learning development, is substantially more forthright.

It states, "Little comprehensive national data is available about the use of [information and communications technology] to support assessment in schools and colleges" (2005).

2. See Thomas Pynchon's (1984) argument that Luddism centered on protest against technological degradation of human life, not against technology itself.

3. In a characteristic example of this ad hominem argument, Susan Ko and Steve Rossen (2001: 291) write that "certain faculty members [...] often express the idea that online education has nothing to offer pedagogically and that online education will undermine face-to-face interaction between student and instructor. Many of them have no experience in an online classroom, either as student or as teacher. In this sense they resemble an anthropologist of Bali who undertakes all his field research without leaving his apartment in Manhattan."

4. The term "democratic education" has a heavily disputed history. I employ it here to refer to the body of theories emphasizing development of free public education under political control through representative democracy, and democratic self-management within classrooms and schools. For discussion of the term, see Guttman (1987: 6–16).

5. For a slightly dated sociological review of this issue, see Wellman and Gulia (1999). Although they admit a lack of comparative data between "virtual" and physical communities, Wellman and Gulia argue that critics "confuse the pastoralist myth of community" for a reality where communities in Western cities are weak and diffuse (187). This does not address the issue of terminological confusion of shadow for substance.

6. See note 1. In the United States, this absence has not prevented claims from distance learning advocates that research substantiates such statements. Typically, these claims base themselves on literature reviews of non-comparable small-sample studies or qualitative reports produced by non-expert or interested parties. For an excellent discussion of the methodological problems of distance learning evaluation studies, see Phipps and Merisotis (1999). For a six-college case study of distance learning quality benchmarks, sponsored by the National Education Association and Blackboard, Inc., see Phipps and Merisotis (2000).

7. Equally critical as the non-existence of authoritative studies, as of current writing, negligible education research has been done concerning comparative learning outcome measures between online and in-class coursework in secondary and higher education to support the equal substitutability of credit hours between the two modes. Since online coursework typically covers substantially less material at a lower level and with less instructional support than in-class coursework, this absence of a foundation work of educational research represents an empirical Achilles heel. Academic administrators rely on equal substitution between in-class and online credit hours, without empirical basis. This absence of evidence raises substantial questions about the accreditation of online coursework, questions that accreditation bodies have not yet addressed effectively. A 2004 US General Accounting Office (GAO) report on post-secondary distance education found that only one of seven accreditation agencies assessed whether post-secondary institutions had measurable goals for distance learning program outcomes, strategies to meet these goals, and provided public disclosure of results (GAO 2004: 3). Also see Cavanaugh (2004) for a recent review of distance learning accreditation. To the negligible extent that quality assessment for accreditation is an issue in US distance learning, it concerns restrictions on the percentage of courses a school can offer and still qualify for federal student aid. The ability of the distance learning industry to expand has been hampered by this 50% restriction and concerns over educational loan fraud and abuse if, as the industry wants, the restriction is altered or ended altogether.

8. For on-point observations about the counter-productive distractions of "smart classrooms," see Allitt (2005). He refers to himself as an "old geezer" who may be slightly nostalgic, but

his calls for "Professors, stop your engines. Take to class only with your wits" and to "discover the pleasure of learning as a communal activity" emphasize that whatever possibly divergent social perceptions of electronic education, a variety of electronic classroom observers simply find them to be sites of consistently poor and inappropriate teaching practice.

9. For a summary of prevailing trends during the late twentieth century in the merger of capitalistic practice and tertiary-level education in four countries, see Slaughter and Leslie (1997: 208–245).

10. The term "organic" is employed here in the sense used by Eagleton, not Gramsci. This sense denotes "symmetrically integrated systems characterized by the harmonious interdependence of their component elements" (Eagleton 1975: 103, footnote 4).

11. Such abuse has grown together with the Internet and search machine surveillance. Amitava Kumar (1997) records that in the early 1990s in now-defunct gopherspace his students were publishing writing assignments via a gopher server. He writes that this method served as a means to "reconfigure the local academic course as a public site of interaction and intervention" and as a means of "making the intellectual work of the course [...] more publicly accountable" (173). In the pre-boom World Wide Web, transparent public course sites were common; today they are far less common and the vast bulk of online coursework occurs in closed webspace of courseware. This transformation underlines not only technological change, but also an ideological shift away from public transparency and toward electronic enclosure, prompted both by security issues and surveillance concerns of teachers. There is an almost historical sense of early Internet idealism where Kumar writes that the public "virtual spaces created by computer networks constitute a landscape in which the traditional power relations between student and teacher can be significantly altered, in which students and teachers alike can speak from, critique, and explore various subject positions" (174).

12. See *Chandler-Gilbert Community College: Continuing Education*. Accessed January 26, 2006, at www.ed2go.com/cgc

13. No effective attempts have yet been made to organize unions of online teachers, and no systematic information is yet available about labor issues of online teaching in the United States. Even the approximate number and distribution of online instructors in the United States is currently a matter of haphazard estimate. For one recent study of labor issues at four online educational institutions, see Gen and Glahn (2002).

14. Universal Declaration of Human Rights, art. 26 (adopted 1948); International Covenant on Economic, Social and Cultural Rights, art. 13 (adopted 1966; entered into force 1976); Convention on the Rights of the Child, arts. 28 and 29 (adopted 1989; entered into force 1990) (see also UN 1999). The proposed European Union (EU) constitution, one currently unlikely to be ratified, adopts a human rights-centered approach to education (section 5, art. III-282), based on the European Convention on Human Rights, Protocol 1 (1952), art. 2. Interestingly, the proposed EU constitution includes a specific clause on "encouraging the development of distance education" (section 5, art. III-282, 1f). See *Europa: Consitution. Section 5: Education, Youth, Sport and Vocational Training*. Accessed January 26, 2006, at europa.eu.int/constitution/en/ptoc61_en.htm#a355

Bibliography

AACU (The Association of American Colleges and Universities) (1998). Statement on liberal learning. (Adopted by the Board of Directors of the Association of American Colleges & Universities, October 1998.) Accessed June 18, 2006 at www.aacu.edu.org/About/statements/liberal_learning.cfm

AAUP (The Association of American University Presses) (1999). Statement on distance education. (Special Committee on Distance Education and Intellectual Property Issues.) Accessed December 13, 2004, at www.aaup.org/statements/Redbook/StDistEd.HTM

AAUP (The Association of American University Presses) (2004). Academic freedom and electronic communications (revised version). (Committee on Academic Freedom and Tenure.) Accessed January 12, 2005, at www.aaup.org/statements/REPORTS/04AFelec.htm

Abdat, S., & Pervan, G.P. (2000). Reducing the negative effects of power distance during asynchronous pre-meeting without using anonymity in Indonesian culture. In F. Sudweeks & C. Ess (Eds.), *Proceedings: Cultural attitudes towards technology and communication 2000* (pp. 209–215). Perth, Australia: Murdoch University.

Addison, J., & Hilligoss, S. (1999). Technological fronts: Lesbian lives "on-the-line." In K. Blair & P. Takayoshi (Eds.), *Feminist cyberscapes: Mapping gendered academic spaces* (pp. 21–40). Stamford, CT: Ablex.

Allen, M. (2002, January 1). Discovery learning: Repurposing an old paradigm. How to make learning active and student-centered. *Learning and Training Innovations*. Accessed December 16, 2005, at www.ltimagazine.com/ltimagazine/article/articleDetail.jsp?id=6709

Allen, M., et al. (2004). Evaluating the effectiveness of distance learning: A comparison using meta-analysis. *Journal of Communication, 54*, 402–420.

Allitt, P. (2005, June 24). Professors, stop your microchips. *Chronicle of Higher Education, 51*, B38.

Altbach, P. (1995). Literary colonialism: Books in the third world. In B. Ashcroft, G. Griffiths, & H. Tiffin (Eds.), *The post-colonial studies reader* (pp.485–490). New York: Routledge.

The American Historical Association (1999, Fall). Who is teaching in US college classrooms? A collaborative study of undergraduate faculty. Accessed November 5, 2005, at www.theaha.org/caw

Ames, R., & Rosemont Jr., H. (1998). *The analects of Confucius: A philosophical translation*. New York: Ballantine.

Apple, M. (1986). *Teachers and texts: A political economy of class and gender relations in education*. New York: Routledge & Kegan Paul.

Apple, M. (1995). *Education and power* (2nd ed.). New York: Routledge.

Arbaugh, J.B. (2001). How instructor immediacy behaviors affect student satisfaction and learning in web-based courses. *Business Communication Quarterly, 64*(4), 42–54.

Argyle, K., & Shields, R. (1996). Is there a body in the net? In R. Shields (Ed.), *Cultures of Internet: Virtual spaces, real histories, living bodies* (pp.58–69). London: Sage.

Aristotle (1967). *Politics* (E. Barker, Trans.). Oxford: Oxford University Press.

Aristotle (1968). *Nicomachean ethics* (H. Rackham, Trans.). Cambridge, MA: Harvard University Press.

Arnold, J.M., & Jayne, E.A. (1998). Dangling by a slender thread: The lessons and implications of teaching the World Wide Web to freshmen. *The Journal of Academic Librarianship, 24*(1), 43–52.

Aronowitz, S. (2000). *The knowledge factory: Dismantling the corporate university and creating true higher learning.* Boston, MA: Beacon Press.

Aronowitz, S., & Giroux, H. (1985). *Education under siege.* South Hadley, MA: Bergin & Garvey.

Aronowitz, S., & Giroux, H. (1991). *Postmodern education: Politics, culture, and social criticism.* Minneapolis, MN: University of Minnesota Press.

Ashcroft, B., Griffiths, G., & Tiffin, H. (1989). *The empire writes back: Theory and practice in post-colonial literature.* New York: Routledge.

Aston, L., & Bekhradnia, B. (2005). Non-completion at the University of North London and London Guildhall University: A case study. Higher Education Policy Institute Publications. Accessed November 3, 2005, at www.hepi.ac.uk/pubdetail.asp?ID=168&DOC=reportsS

Azevedo, A. (1998). Computers don't teach—people teach: The Socrates online method. Accessed December 16, 2005, at ist-socrates.berkeley.edu/~americ/essays/teaching.htm

Bakhtin, M.M. (1981). Discourse in the novel. In M. Holquist (Ed.), *The dialogic imagination: Four essays by M.M. Bakhtin* (pp.259–422). Austin, TX: University of Texas Press.

Bakhtin, M.M. (1984). Toward a reworking of the Dostoevsky book. In C. Emerson (Ed.), *Problems of Dostoevsky's poetics* (pp.283–302). Minneapolis, MN: University of Minnesota Press.

Balraj, L., et al. (1999, November 15). Usage guidelines for LIBREF-L. Message posted to LIBREF-L Listserv.

Barber, B. (1995). *Jihad versus McWorld.* New York: Times Books.

Bass, R., & Eynon, B. (1998). Teaching culture, learning culture, and new media technologies: An introduction and framework. *Works and Days, 16,* 1–2.

Bates, A.W. (2000). *Managing technological change: Strategies for university leaders.* San Francisco, CA: Jossey-Bass.

Bates, A.W. (2004, June 9). Why universities must change: The challenge of eLearning. Paper delivered at *Learning and Instructional Development Centre,* Simon Fraser University, Burnaby, Canada.

Bates, A.W., & Poole, G. (2003). *Effective teaching with technology in higher education: Foundations for success.* San Francisco, CA: Jossey-Bass.

Baudrillard, J. (1993). *The transparency of evil.* New York: Verso.

Baumlin, J.S., & Baumlin, T.F. (1994). "Introduction: Positioning ethos in historical and contemporary theory," *Ethos: New essays in rhetorical and critical theory* (pp.xi–xxxi). Dallas, TX: Southern Methodist University Press.

Baym, N.K. (1995). The emergence of community in computer-mediated communication. In S.G. Jones (Ed.), *CyberSociety: Computer-mediated communication and community* (pp.138–163). Thousand Oaks, CA: Sage.

Baym, N.K. (2002). Interpersonal life online. In L. Lievrouw, & S. Livingstone (Eds.), *Handbook of new media* (pp.62–76). London: Sage.

Becker, B. (2000). Cyborg, agents and transhumanists. *Leonardo, 33*(5), 361–365.

Becker, B. (2001). Sinn und Sinnlichkeit: Anmerkungen zur Eigendynamik und Fremdheit des eigenen Leibe. In L. Jäger (Ed.), *Mentalität und Medialität* (pp.35–46). München, Germany: Fink Verlag.

BECTA (British Educational Communications and Technology Agency) (2005). *The Becta review 2005: Evidence on the progress of ICT in education.* Coventry, UK: BECTA. Accessed December 16, 2005, at www.becta.org.uk

Bednarowicz, E.K. (2002). *The revisionary writing center: The rhetoric of a moo tutorial.* Unpublished doctoral dissertation, University of Illinois, Chicago, IL.

Beiner, R. (1992). *What's the matter with liberalism?* Berkeley, CA: University of California Press.

Bekhradnia, B. (2005, July 14). A case of flying pigs and impossible targets. *The Independent.* Accessed November 3, 2005, at education.independent.co.uk/higher/article298981.ece

Belanger, F., & Jordan, D.H. (2000). *Evaluation and implementation of distance learning: Technologies, tools and techniques.* Hershey, PA: Idea Group.

Bell, M., et al. (2002). *Universities online: A survey of online education and services in Australia.* Canberra, Australia: Department of Education, Science and Training. Accessed October 11, 2004, at www.dest.gov.au/highered/occpaper/02a/02_a.pdf

Bijker, W., Hughes, T., & Pinch, T. (Eds.) (1989). *The social construction of technological systems.* Cambridge, MA: MIT Press.

Bijker, W., & Law, J. (Eds.) (1992). *Shaping technology/building society.* Cambridge, MA: MIT Press.

Bilger, A. (1998). The art of fiction CL: Jeannette Winterson (Interview). *Paris Review, 44*(2), 68–112.

Blake, N., & Standish, P. (2000). *Enquiries at the interface: Philosophical problems of online education.* Oxford: Blackwell.

Bloch, R.H., & Hesse, C. (1993). Introduction. *Representations, 42,* 1–12.

Block, Marylaine (2002). Gullible's travels. *Library Journal, 48* (5), 12–15.

Bloom, A. (1988). *The closing of the American mind: How higher education has failed democracy and impoverished the souls of today's students.* Harmondsworth, UK: Penguin.

Bloom, B., et al. (1956). *Taxonomy of educational objectives: The classification of educational goals. Handbook 1: Cognitive domain.* London: Longmans, Green & Co.

Boettcher, J.V. (2004). Online course development: What does it cost? *Syllabus: Technology for Higher Education, 17*(12), 26–30.

Bollag, B. (1996, June 28). Better Internet access sought for researchers around the world: Industrialized nations push for faster connections and uniform regulations. *Chronicle of Higher Education,* A14–A16.

Bolter, J.D. (1991). *Writing space: The computer, hypertext, and the history of writing.* Hillsdale, NJ: Lawrence Erlbaum.

Bolter, J.D. (2001). Identity. In T. Swiss (Ed.), *Unspun* (pp.17–29). New York: New York University Press.

Bonal, X. (2003). The neoliberal educational agenda and the legitimation crisis: Old and new state strategies. *British Journal of Sociology of Education, 24*(2), 159–175.

Bonk, C.J. (2004). The perfect e-storm: Emerging technology, enormous learner demand, enhanced pedagogy, and erased budgets. *The Observatory on Borderless Higher Education.* Accessed November 3, 2005, at www.obhe.ac.uk/products/reports/pdf/Bonk.pdf

Borgmann, A. (1984). *Technology and the character of contemporary life.* Chicago, IL: University of Chicago Press.

Borgmann, A. (1992). *Crossing the postmodern divide.* Chicago, IL: University of Chicago Press.

Borgmann, A. (1999). *Holding on to reality: The nature of information at the turn of the millennium.* Chicago, IL: University of Chicago Press.

Boshier, R., & Onn, C.N. (2000). Distance constructions of web learning and education. *Journal of Distance Education, 15*(2), 1–16.

Boss, J. (2004). *Ethics for life: A text with readings.* Boston, MA: McGraw Hill.

Bourdieu, P. (1977). *Outline of a theory of practice.* Cambridge: Cambridge University Press.

Bourdieu, P. (1998). *Acts of resistance: Against the tyranny of the market* (R. Nice, Trans.). New York: New Press.

Bourdieu, P., & Passeron, J.C. (1990). *Reproduction in education, society and culture* (2nd ed.). London: Sage.

Brabazon, T. (2002). *Digital hemlock: Internet education and the poisoning of teaching.* Sydney, Australia: University of New South Wales Press.

Bransford, J., Brown, A.L., & Cocking, R.R. (2000). *How people learn: Brain, mind, experience, and school.* Washington, DC: National Academy Press.

BrightIdeas (2005). Socrates is alive and living in Hove! Accessed January 20, 2006, at www.bright-wave.co.uk/01_01_11.htm

Brown, J.S. (2001). Learning in the digital age. *The Internet and the University: 2001 Forum* (Forum for the Future of Higher Education/Educause) (pp.65–86). Accessed January 20, 2006, at www.educause.edu/ir/library/pdf/ffpiu015.pdf

Brown, J.S., & Duguid, P. (1996). Universities in the digital age. *Change, 26*(4), 10–20.

Bruneau, W., & Savage, D.C. (2002). *Counting out the scholars: The case against performance indicators in higher education.* Toronto, Ont.: James Lorimer.

Bullen, M. (1998). Participation and critical thinking in online university distance education. *Journal of Distance Education/Revue de l'enseignement à distance, 13*(2). Accessed November 3, 2005, at cade.icaap.org/vol13.2/bullen.html

Burbules, N.C., & Callister Jr., T.A. (2000). *Watch it: The risks and promises of information technologies for education.* Boulder, CO: Westview Press.

Burbules, N.C., & Rice, S. (1991). Dialogue across differences: Continuing the conversation. *Harvard Educational Review, 61*(4), 393–416.

Burniske, R.W., & Monke, L. (2001). *Breaking down the digital walls: Learning to teach in a post-modern world.* Albany, NY: SUNY Press.

Burns, C.L. (1998). Powerful differences: Critique and *eros* in Jeanette Winterson and Virginia Woolf. *Modern Fiction Studies, 44*(2), 364–392.

Buschman, J., & Warner, D.A. (2005). Researching and shaping information literacy initiatives in relation to the web: Some framework problems and needs. *Journal of Academic Librarianship, 31*(1), 12–18.

Calder, L., Cutler, W.T., & Kelly, T.M. (2002). History lessons: Historians and the scholarship of teaching and learning. In M.T. Huber & S.P. Morreale (Eds.), *Disciplinary styles in the scholarship of teaching and learning* (pp.45–68). Washington, DC: American Association of Higher Education.

Callon, M., & Latour, B. (1981). Unscrewing the big leviathan: How actors macro-structure reality and how sociologists help them to do so. In K. Knorr-Cetina & A.V. Cicourel (Eds.), *Advances in social theory and methodology: Toward an integration of micro- and macro-sociologies* (pp.277–303). London: Routledge & Kegan Paul.

Cameron, D. (2002). Globalization and the teaching of "communication skills." In D. Block & D. Cameron (Eds.), *Globalization and language teaching* (pp.67–82). London: Routledge.

Cameron, D. (2003). Doing exactly what it says on the tin: Some thoughts on the future of higher education. *Changing English, 10*(2), 133–141.

Campbell, R., Martin, C.R., & Fabos, B. (2006). *Media and culture: An introduction to mass communication* (5th ed.). New York: Bedford/St. Martins.

Carlson, S. (2003). After losing millions, Columbia U will close online-learning venture. *Chronicle of Higher Education, 49*(19), 1.

Carnoy, M. (1999). *Globalisation and educational reform: What planners need to know.* Paris: UNESCO/International Institute for Educational Planning.

Carr, S. (2001, February 16). Is anyone making money on distance education? *Chronicle of Higher Education,* A41.

Carr, V.H. (2002). Technology adoption and diffusion. Accessed February 4, 2005, at www.au.af.mil/au/awc/awcgate/innovation/adoptiondiffusion.htm

Caruso, J.B. (2004). *ECAR study of students and information technology, 2004: Convenience, connection, and control.* Madison, WI: Educause Center for Applied Research.

Castells, M. (2000). *The information age: Economy, society, and culture. Vol. I: The rise of the network society.* Oxford: Blackwell.

CAUT (Canadian Association of University Teachers) (2004a). Policy statement on academic freedom. (Academic Freedom and Tenure Committee.) Accessed December 13, 2004, at www.caut.ca/en/policies/academicfreedom.asp

CAUT (Canadian Association of University Teachers) (2004b). Policy statement on distance education. Accessed December 13, 2004, at www.caut.ca/en/policies/distance_education .asp

Cavanaugh, C. (2004). Distance learning success factors in the RPR cycle and virtual school accreditation. In C. Cavanaugh (Ed.), *Development and management of virtual schools: Issues and trends* (pp.69–83). Hershey, PA: Idea Group.

Cervetti, G., Pardales, M.J., & Damico, J.S. (2001). A tale of differences: Comparing traditions, perspectives, and educational goals of critical reading and critical literacy. *Reading Online, 4*(9). Accessed November 5, 2005, at www.readingonline.org/articles/art_index.asp?HREF=/articles/cervetti/index.html

Chambers, E. (2001, July). Cultural imperialism or pluralism? Approaches to cross-cultural electronic teaching. Keynote paper delivered at *Tertiary Teaching and Learning: Dealing with Diversity*, Northern Territory University, Darwin, Australia.

Chapman, A. (2001–2004). Demographics classification. Accessed November 3, 2005, at www.businessballs.com/demographicsclassifications.htm.

Childers, J., & Hentzi, G. (Eds.) (1995). *The Columbia dictionary of modern literary and cultural criticism.* New York: Columbia University Press.

Christian, B. (1995). The race for theory. In B. Ashcroft, G. Griffiths, & H. Tiffin (Eds.), *The postcolonial studies reader* (pp.457–460). New York: Routledge.

Clyde, L. (2003). Search engines are improving—but they still can't find everything. *Teacher Librarian, 30*, 44–45.

Coates, H., James, R., & Baldwin, G. (2005). A critical examination of the effects of learning management systems on university teaching and learning. *Tertiary Education and Management, 11*, 19–36.

Cohen, D. (2005, March). By the book: Assessing the place of textbooks in US survey courses. *Journal of American History.* Accessed June 21, 2006, at www.historycooperative.org/journals/jah/91.4/cohen.html

Colley, A., & Comber, C. (2003). Age and gender differences in computer use and attitudes among secondary school students: What has changed? *Educational Research, 45*(2), 155–165.

Collins, D.J. (2002). New business models for higher education. In S. Brint (Ed.), *The future of the city of intellect: The changing American University* (pp.181–202). Stanford, CA: Stanford University Press.

Committee on Information Technology Literacy (Computer Science and Telecommunications Board, Commission on Physical Sciences, Mathematics, and Applications, National Research Council) (US) (1999). *Being fluent with information technology.* Washington, DC: National Academy Press. Accessed April 19, 2005, at www.nap.edu/html/beingfluent/

Committee on Technological Literacy (National Academy of Engineering, National Research Council) (US) (2002). *Technically speaking: Why all Americans need to know more about technology.* Washington, DC: National Academy Press.

Considine, M., Marginson, S., Sheehan, P., & Kumnick, M. (2001). The comparative performance of Australia as a knowledge nation. Chifley Research Centre. Accessed November 15, 2005, at www.cfses.com/documents/knowledge_nation_chifley_2001.pdf

Coomey, M., & Stephenson, J. (2001). Online learning: It is all about dialogue, involvement, support and control—according to the research. In J. Stephenson (Ed.), *Teaching and learning online: Pedagogies for new technologies* (pp.37–52). London: Kogan Page.

Cooper, M. (1999). Postmodern possibilities in electronic conversations. In G. Hawisher & C. Selfe (Eds.), *Passions, pedagogies, and 21st-century technologies* (pp.140–160). Logan, UT & Urbana, IL: Utah State University Press & NCTE.

Coppola, N.W., Hiltz, S.R., & Rotter, N.G. (2002). Becoming a virtual professor: Pedagogical roles and asynchronous learning networks. *Journal of Management Information Systems, 18*(4), 169–189.

Cornford, J., & Pollock, N. (2003). *Putting the university online: Information technology and organizational change.* Philadelphia, PA: Society for Research into Higher Education and Open University Press.

Covino, W.A., & Jolliffe, D.A. (Eds.) (1995). *Rhetoric: Concepts, definitions, boundaries.* Boston, MA: Allyn & Bacon.

Cuban, L. (2001). *Oversold and underused: Computers in the classroom.* Cambridge, MA: Harvard University Press.

Curran, C. (2001). Universities and the challenge of e-learning: What lessons from the European open universities? Paper delivered at *E-Learning as E-Business*, University of California, Berkeley, CA. Accessed November 3, 2005, at ishi.lib.berkeley.edu/cshe/projects/university/

Currie, J. (2005). Organisational culture of Australian universities: Community or corporate? *Research and Development in Higher Education, 28* (Special issue: "Higher education in a changing world" (A. Brew, & C. Asmar, Eds.)), 5–16.

Daniels, J. (1996). *Mega-universities and knowledge media.* London: Kogan Page.

Daniels, J. (1998). Knowledge media for mega-universities: Scaling up new technology at the Open University. Paper delivered at *Shanghai Open and Distance Education Symposium.* Accessed November 3, 2005, at www.open.ac.uk/johndanielspeeches/chinatlk.html

Davies, D. (1998). Towards a learning society. In R. Teare, D. Davies, & E. Sandelands (Eds.), *The virtual university: An action paradigm and process for workplace learning* (pp.17–26). London: Cassell.

Davis, N. (1999, Autumn/Winter). The globalisation of education though teacher education with new technologies: A view informed by research. *Educational Technology Review,* 9–12.

Dean, J. (1999). Virtual fears. *Signs: Journal of Women in Culture and Society, 24*(4), 1069–1078.

Decoo, W. (2001). On the mortality of language learning methods. Paper delivered as *James L. Barker Lecture at Brigham Young University,* USA. Accessed November 8, 2005, at www.didascalia.be/mortality.htm

Dede, C. (2005). Planning for neomillennial learning styles. *Educause Quarterly, 1,* 7–12.

DEET (Department of Employment, Education and Training) (Australia) (1990). *A fair chance for all: Higher education that's within everyone's reach.* Canberra, Australia: AGPS.

de Kloet, J. (2002). *Internet, development and education: An exploratory study of Internet usage at higher education institutions in Asia.* International Institute of Infonomics. Accessed October 27, 2005, at www.infonomics.nl.

Delanty, G. (2001). *Challenging knowledge: The university in the knowledge society.* Philadelphia, PA: Society for Research into Higher Education; Open UP.

Deleuze, G. (1973). Pensée nomade. In *Nietzsche aujourd'hui?* (Vol. 1, pp.159–190). Paris: UGE.

Derrida, J. (1995, Summer). Archive fever: A Freudian impression. *Diacritics, 25,* 9–63.

DEST (Department of Education, Science and Training) (Australia) (2004). *Characteristics and performance indicators of higher education institutions.* Commonwealth Department of Education, Science and Training. Accessed October 11, 2004, at www.dest.gov.au/archive/highered/statistics/contents.htm

DfES (Department for Education and Skills) (UK) (2003). *The future of higher education.* Accessed November 3, 2005, at www.dfes.gov.uk/hegateway/uploads/White%20Pape.pdf

DfES (Department for Education and Skills) (UK) (1998). *A renaissance for a New Britain.* Accessed June 13, 2006, at http://www.lifelonglearning.co.uk/greepaper/

Dikshit, H.P., Garg, S., Panda, S., & Vijayshri (2002). *Access and equity: Challenges for open and distance education.* New Delhi: Kogan Page.

Distefano, A., Rudestam, K.E., & Silverman, R.J. (Eds.) (2004). *Encyclopaedia of distributed learning.* Thousand Oaks, CA: Sage.

Docker, J. (1995). The neocolonial assumption in university teaching of English. In B. Ashcroft, G. Griffiths, & H. Tiffin (Eds.), *The post-colonial studies reader* (pp.443–446). New York: Routledge.

Doherty, P.B. (1998). Learner control in asynchronous learning environments. *Asynchronous Learning Networks Magazine, 2*(2). Accessed January 20, 2006, at www.aln.org/publications/magazine/v2n2/doherty.asp

Dreyfus, H. (1992). *What computers (still) can't do* (3rd ed.). Cambridge, MA: MIT Press.

Dreyfus, H. (1998). Merleau-Ponty's critique of mental representation: The relevance of phenomenology to scientific explanation. Intelligence without representation. Accessed August 11, 2005, at www.hfac.uh.edu/cogsci/dreyfus.html

Dreyfus, H. (2001). *On the Internet.* New York: Routledge.

Dreyfus, H., & Dreyfus, S.E. (1988). *Mind over machine*. New York: Free Press.

Drucker, P. (1997, March 10). Seeing things as they really are (Interview with R. Lenzner & S.S. Johnson). *Forbes*. Accessed Oct. 4, 2004, at http://www.forbes.com/forbes/1997/0310/5905122a.html

Duderstadt, J.J. (1999). Can colleges and universities survive in the information age? In Katz, R.N., & Associates (Eds.), *Dancing with the devil: Information technology and the new competition in higher education* (pp.1–25). San Francisco, CA: Jossey-Bass, Educause & PricewaterhouseCoopers.

Duderstadt, J.J. (2000). *A university for the 21st century*. Ann Arbor, MI: University of Michigan Press.

Duncker, E. (2002). Cross-cultural usability of computing metaphors: Do we colonize the minds of indigenous web users? In F. Sudweeks & C. Ess (Eds.), *Proceedings: Cultural attitudes towards technology and communication 2002* (pp.217–236). Perth, Australia: Murdoch University.

Durst, R. (1999). *Collision course: Conflict, negotiation, and learning in college composition*. Urbana, IL: National Council of Teachers of English.

Dwyer, D. (1996). The imperative to change our schools. In C. Fisher, D. Dwyer, & K. Yocam (Eds.), *Education and technology* (pp.15–33). San Francisco, CA: Jossey-Bass.

Dyer-Witheford, N. (2002). E-capital and the many-headed hydra. In G. Elmer (Ed.), *Critical perspectives on the Internet* (pp.129–163). Lanham, MD: Rowman & Littlefield.

Eagleton, T. (1975). *Criticism and ideology: A study in Marxist literary theory*. London: Verso.

Ebersole, S. (2000). Uses and gratifications of the web among students. *Journal of Computer-Mediated Communication, 6*(1). Accessed November 5, 2005, at www.ascusc.org/jcmc/vol6/issue1/ebersole.html

Ebersole, Samuel E. (2005). On their own: Students' academic use of the commercialized Web. *Library Trends, 53* (4) 530–538.

Ebert, R. (1995). Review of 'The Net'. Accessed December 11, 2004, at www.suntimes.com/ebert/ebert_reviews/1995/07/989964.html

Edmundson, M. (1997, September). On the uses of a liberal education. *Harper's Magazine*, 39–49.

Edwards, R., & Usher, R. (2000). *Globalisation and pedagogy: Space, place and identity*. London & New York: Routledge Falmer.

Elberfeld, R. (2002). Resonanz als Grundmotiv ostasiatischer Ethik. In R. Elberfeld, & G. Wohlfart (Eds.), *Komparative Ethik: Das gute Leben zwischen den Kulturen* (pp.131–141). Cologne, Germany: Edition Chora.

eLib (2005). eLib: The Electronic Libraries Programme. Accessed January 27, 2006, at www.ukoln.ac.uk/services/elib/

Ellsworth, E. (1989). Why doesn't this feel empowering? Working through the repressive myths of critical pedagogy. *Harvard Educational Review, 59*(3), 297–324.

Ellul, J. (1964). *The technological society*. New York: Vintage.

Entin, J. (2005). Contingent teaching, corporate universities, and the academic labor movement. *Radical Teacher, 73*, 26–32.

Ercegovac, Z., & Richardson, J. (2004). Academic dishonesty, plagiarism included, in the digital age: A literature review. *College and Research Libraries, 65*(4), 301–318.

Ess, C. (2000a). Wag the dog? Online conferencing and teaching. *Computers and the Humanities, 34*(3), 297–309.

Ess, C. (2000b, Fall). We are the Borg: The web as agent of assimilation or cultural renaissance? *Ephilosopher*. Accessed November 1, 2005, at 24.86.132.253/archives/philtech/philtech.htm

Ess, C. (2001). What's culture got to do with it? Cultural collisions in the electronic global village, creative interferences, and the rise of culturally-mediated computing. In C. Ess & F. Sudweeks (Eds.), *Culture, technology, communication: Towards an intercultural global village* (pp.1–50). Albany, NY: SUNY Press.

Ess, C. (2002a). Borgmann and the Borg: *Consumerism vs. Holding on to Reality.* A review essay on Albert Borgmann's *Holding on to Reality. Techne* (Special issue, P. Mullins, Ed.). Accessed October 26, 2005, at scholar.lib.vt.edu/ejournals/SPT/v6n1/ess.html

Ess, C. (2002b). Computer-mediated colonization, the renaissance, and educational imperatives for an intercultural global village. *Ethics and Information Technology, 4,* 11–22.

Ess, C. (2002c). Cultures in collision: Philosophical lessons from computer-mediated communication. *Metaphilosophy, 33*(1/2), 229–253.

Ess, C. (2003a). The cathedral or the bazaar? The AoIR document on Internet research ethics as an exercise in open source ethics. In M. Consalvo, et al. (Eds.), *Internet research annual. Vol. 1: Selected papers from the Association of Internet Researchers Conferences 2000–2002* (pp.95–103). New York: Peter Lang.

Ess, C. (2003b). Computer-mediated communication and human–computer interaction. In L. Floridi (Ed.), *The Blackwell guide to the philosophy of computing and information* (pp.76–91). Oxford: Blackwell.

Ess, C. (2004). Beyond *contemptus mundi* and Cartesian dualism: Western resurrection of the BodySubject and (re)New(ed) coherencies with Eastern approaches to life/death. In G. Wohlfart & H.-G. Moeller (Eds.), *Philosophie des Todes: Death philosophy east and west* (pp.15–36). Munich, Germany: Chora Verlag.

Ess, C. (2005a). "Lost in translation"? Intercultural dialogues on privacy and information ethics. (Introduction to special issue on Privacy and Data Privacy Protection in Asia.). *Ethics and Information Technology, 7*(1), 1–6.

Ess, C. (2005b). Computer-mediated colonization, the Renaissance, and educational imperatives for an intercultural global village. In R. Cavalier (Ed.), *The Internet and Our Moral Lives* (pp.161-193). Albany, NY: SUNY Press.

Ess, C., & Sudweeks, F. (2001). On the edge: Cultural barriers and catalysts to IT diffusion among remote and marginalized communities. (Introduction to special issue.) *New Media and Society, 3*(3), 259–269.

Fabos, B. (2004). *Wrong turn on the information superhighway: Education and the commercialism of the Internet.* New York: Teachers College Press.

Faigley, L. (1992). *Fragments of rationality: Postmodernity and the subject of composition* (pp.30–57). Pittsburgh, PA: University of Pittsburgh Press.

Faigley, L. (1999). Beyond imagination: The Internet and global digital literacy. In G. E. Hawisher & C. Selfe (Eds.), *Passions, pedagogies, and 21st-century technologies* (pp.129–139). Logan, UT & Urbana, IL: Utah State University Press & NCTE.

Farmer, F. (2001). *Saying and silence: Listening to composition with Bakhtin.* Logan, UT: Utah State University Press.

Farrell, G. (Ed.) (1999). The development of virtual education: A global perspective. *The Commonwealth of Learning.* Accessed November 3, 2005, at www.col.org/virtualed/index.htm

Fay, M. (2002). Knowing what you're doing: The skills agenda and the language degree. In M. Fay (Ed.), *Learning from languages.* Preston: TransLang/University of Central Lancashire. Accessed January 19, 2006, at web.apu.ac.uk/languages/translang/Knowing.html

Feenberg, A. (1989). The written world: On the theory and practice of computer conferencing. In R. Mason & A. Kaye (Eds.), *Mindweave: Communication, computers and distance education* (pp.22–39). Oxford: Pergamon Press.

Feenberg, A. (1991). *Critical theory of technology.* Oxford: Oxford University Press.

Feenberg, A. (1993). Building a global network: The WBSI experience. In L. Harasim (Ed.), *Global networks: Computers and international communication* (pp.185–197). Cambridge, MA: MIT Press.

Feenberg, A. (1995). *Alternative modernity: The technical turn in philosophy and social theory.* Berkeley, CA: University of California Press.

Feenberg, A. (1999a, Winter). Distance learning: Promise or threat? *Crosstalk.* Accessed June 2, 2002, at www-rohan.sdsu.edu/faculty/feenberg/

Feenberg, A. (1999b). *Questioning technology.* New York: Routledge.

Feenberg, A. (1999c). Whither educational technology? *Peer Review, 1*(4). Accessed June 2, 2002, at www-rohan.sdsu.edu/faculty/feenberg/peer4.html

Feenberg, A. (2002). *Transforming technology: A critical theory revisited*. Oxford: Oxford University Press.

Fey, M. (1998). Critical literacy in school–college collaboration through computer networking: A feminist research project. *Journal of Literacy Research, 30*(1), 85–117.

Fielding, R. (2003, January 15). IT in schools fails to raise standards. *VNU Business Publications*. Accessed December 27, 2003, at www.vnunet.com

Filmer, P. (1997). Disinterestedness and the modern university. In A. Smith & F. Webster (Eds.), *The postmodern university? Contested visions of higher education in society* (pp.48–58). Buckingham, UK: Society for Research into Higher Education and Open University Press.

Fisher, M. (2002, November). The metamorphosis. *American Journalism Review*, 20–29.

Fisher, S. (2000, August 11). Medium, method, and message: Why we *can* measure the pedagogical effectiveness of instructional technology. Paper delivered at *15th Annual Computing and Philosophy Conference*, Carnegie Mellon University, Pittsburgh, PA.

Fleeson, L. (2003, October/November). Bureau of missing bureaus. *American Journalism Review*, 32–39.

Foucault, M. (1972). *The archaeology of knowledge; and the discourse on language*. New York: Pantheon Books.

Foucault, M. (1976). *Histoire de la sexualité. Vol. 1: La volonté de savoir*. Paris: Gallimard.

Foucault, M. (1991). Politics and the study of discourse. In G. Burchell, C. Gordon, & P. Miller (Eds.), *The Foucault effect: Studies in governmentality* (pp.53–72). Chicago, IL: Chicago University Press.

Fournier, S., & Crey, E. (1997). *Stolen from our embrace: The abduction of first nations children and restoration of aboriginal communities*. Vancouver: Douglas & McIntyre.

Frand, J.L. (2000, September/October). The information-age mindset: Changes in students and implications for higher education. *Educause*, 15–24.

Freire, P. (1996). *Pedagogy of the oppressed* (M. Bergman Ramos, Trans.). Harmondsworth, UK: Penguin.

Gaddis, B., Napierkowski, H., Guzman, N., & Muth, R. (2000, October). A comparison of collaborative learning and audience awareness in two computer-mediated writing environments. *Annual proceedings of selected research and development papers presented at the 23rd national convention of the Association for Educational Communications and Technology*, Denver, CO.

Gagné, R.M., Briggs, L.J., & Wager, W.W. (1988). *Principles of instructional design* (3rd ed.). Chicago, IL: Holt, Rinehart & Winston.

Galan, N.V. (2001). Throwing down the gauntlet: The rise of the for-profit education industry. In B. Lewis, R. Smith, & C. Massey (Eds.), *The tower under siege: Technology, power, and education* (pp.11–28). Montreal/Kingston: McGill-Queen's University Press.

Galbreath, J. (1999). Preparing the 21st century worker: The link between computer-based technology and future skill sets. *Educational Technology, 39*(6), 14–22.

Gallop, D. (1999). Introduction. In Plato, *Defence of Socrates-Euthyphro-Crito* (D. Gallop, Trans., pp.vii–xxxiv). Oxford: Oxford University Press.

Gansmo, H. (2003). Limits of state feminism. In M. Lie (Ed.), *He, she and IT revisited: New perspectives on gender in the information society* (pp.135–172). Oslo, Norway: Gyldendal Akademisk.

GAO (General Accounting Office) (US) (2004, February). *Distance education: Improved data on program costs and guidelines on quality assessments needed to inform federal policy*. GAO-04-279. Accessed December 20, 2005, at www.gao.gov/new.items/d04279.pdf

Gappa, J., & Leslie, D. (1993). *The invisible faculty: Improving the status of part-timers in higher education*. San Francisco, CA: Jossey-Bass.

Gardner, H. (1983). *Frames of mind: The theory of multiple intelligences*. New York: Basic Books.

Gardner, H. (1999). *Intelligence reframed: Multiple intelligences for the 21st century*. New York: Basic Books.

Gardner, S., Benham, H., & Newell, B.M. (1999). Oh, what a tangled web we've woven! Helping students evaluate web sources. *English Journal, 89*(1), 39–44.

Garnham, C., & Kaleta, R. (2002). Introduction to hybrid courses. *Teaching with Technology Today, 8*(6). Accessed October 11, 2004, at www.uwsa.edu/ttt/articles/garnham.htm

Garrett, R. (2004). The global education index 2004. Part 2: Public companies—relationships with non-profit higher education. *The Observatory on Borderless Higher Education.* Accessed November 3, 2005, at www.obhe.ac.uk/products/reports/pdf/May2004.pdf

Garrison, D.R., & Anderson, T. (2003). *E-learning in the 21st century: A framework for research and practice.* London: Routledge Falmer.

Garson, D. (1998). Evaluating implementation of web-based teaching in political science. *Political Science and Politics,* 31 (September) 585–590.

Gee, J.P. (2000). Teenagers in new times: A new literacy studies perspective. *Journal of Adolescent and Adult Literacy, 43*(5), 412–420.

Gee, J.P. (2003). *What video games have to teach us about learning and literacy.* New York: Palgrave.

Gee, J.P., Hull, G., & Lankshear, C. (1996). *The new work order: Behind the language of the new capitalism.* Boulder, CO: Westview.

Geiger, J. (2004). Special relationships: British higher education and the global marketplace. *Publications of the Modern Language Association of America, 119*(1), 58–68.

Gen, R.M., & Glahn, R. (2002). *Teaching in the next millennium: The implications of an organization's human resource management infrastructure on the adoption of online education practices.* Unpublished doctoral dissertation, Pepperdine University, Malibu, CA.

Gergen, K. (1991). *The saturated self: Dilemmas of identity in contemporary life.* New York: Basic Books.

Gerrard, L. (1991). Computers and compositionists: A view from the floating bottom. *Computers and Composition, 8*(2), 5–15.

Gerrard, L. (1993). Computers and composition: Rethinking our values. *Computers and Composition, 10*(2), 23–34.

Gibbons, M. (1998, October). Higher education relevance in the 21st century. Paper delivered at the *UNESCO World Conference on Higher Education,* Paris.

Ginsburg, M., Espinoza, O., Popa, S., & Terano, M. (2003). Privatisation, domestic marketisation and international commercialisation of higher education: Vulnerabilities and opportunities for Chile and Romania within the framework of WTO/GATS [1]. *Globalisation, Societies and Education, 1*(3), 413–445.

Giroux, H.A. (1997). *Pedagogy and the politics of hope: Theory, culture, and schooling. A critical reader.* Boulder, CO: Westview Press.

Giroux, H.A. (2002). The corporate war against higher education. *Workplace, 5*(1). Accessed October 11, 2004, at www.louisville.edu/journal/workplace/issue5p1/giroux.html

Giroux, H.A. (2003). Public pedagogy and the politics of resistance: Notes on a critical theory of educational struggle. *Educational Philosophy and Theory, 35*(1), 5–16.

Giroux, H.A. (2004, January 26). Higher education is more than a corporate logo. *Dissident Voice.* Accessed October 11, 2004, at www.dissidentvoice.org

Giroux, H.A., & Myrsiades, K. (2001). *Beyond the corporate university.* Lanham, MD: Rowman & Littlefield.

Goodfellow, R. (2001). Credit where it's due: assessing students' contributions to collaborative online learning. In D. Murphy, R. Walker, & G. Webb (Eds.), *Online learning and teaching with technology: Case studies, experience and practice.* London: Kogan Page. Accessed December 16, 2005, at iet.open.ac.uk/pp/r.goodfellow/H802Research/credit.htm

Goodfellow, R. (2003a, September 5). Literacies, technologies, and learning communities—Speaking and writing in the virtual classroom. Paper delivered at *EuroCALL 03,* Limerick, Ireland. Accessed December 16, 2005, at iet.open.ac.uk/pp/r.goodfellow/Euroc03/talk.htm

Goodfellow, R. (2003b, September 24). Online literacies and learning—Cultural and critical dimensions in a virtual power struggle. Paper delivered at *AILA Literacy 03,* Ghent, Belgium. Accessed December 16, 2005, at iet.open.ac.uk/pp/r.goodfellow/ghent2003.htm

Goodfellow, R., Lea, M., Gonzalez, P., & Mason, R. (2001). Opportunity and e-quality—Intercultural and linguistic issues in global online learning. *Distance Education, 22*(1), 65–84.

Goodman, D. (1995, November/December). Education and the Internet: The coming challenge to Internet culture. *Syllabus, 9*, 10–12.

Goodyear, P. (1999, June). Pedagogical frameworks and action research in open and distance learning. *European Journal of Open and Distance Learning*, 1–12.

Gorard, S., Selwyn, N., Madden, L., & Furlong, J. (2002, July). Technology and lifelong learning: Are we cutting IT? Paper delivered at the *All-Wales Education Research Conference*, University of Wales Conference Centre, Gregynog, Wales. Accessed November 3, 2005, at www.leeds.ac.uk/educol/documents/00002117.htm

Gordon, C. (1991). Governmental rationality: An introduction. In G. Burchell, C. Gordon, & P. Miller (Eds.), *The Foucault effect: Studies in governmentality* (pp.1–51). Chicago, IL: Chicago University Press.

Gorra, M. (1994). Rudyard Kipling to Salman Rushdie: Imperialism to post-colonialism. In John Richetti, et al. (Eds.), *The Columbia history of the British novel* (pp.631–657). New York: Columbia University Press.

Gottschalk, E.C. (1983, February 10). California Institute uses "teleconferences" to teach business strategy, computer use. *The Wall Street Journal*, 33.

Gould, T. (2003, June). Hybrid classes: Maximizing institutional resources and student learning. *Proceedings of the 2003 ASCUE Conference*, Myrtle Beach, SC. Accessed October 11, 2004, at fits.depauw.edu/ascue/Proceedings/2003/p54.pdf

Gourley, B. (2004). *The Geoffrey Hubbard lecture for the National Extension College.* Accessed November 3, 2005, at www.nec.ac.uk/download/files/4909/GHLecture04.pdf

Graddol, D. (1989). Some CMC discourse properties and their educational significance. In R. Mason & A. Kaye (Eds.), *Mindweave: Communication, computers and distance education* (pp.236–241). Oxford: Pergamon Press.

Graham, D.W. (1996). Socrates and Plato. In W.J. Prior (Ed.), *Socrates: Critical assessments. Vol. 1: The Socratic problem and Socratic ignorance* (pp.179–201). London: Routledge.

Grant, G. (1969). *Technology and empire: Perspectives on North America.* Toronto, Ont.: Anansi.

Greener, I., & Perriton, L. (2005). The political economy of networked learning communities in higher education. *Studies in Higher Education, 30*(1), 67–79.

Greenwald, S.R., & Rosner, D.J. (2003). Are we distance educating our students to death? Some reflections on the educational assumptions of distance learning. *Radical Pedagogy, 5*(1). Accessed December 15, 2005, at radicalpedagogy.icaap.org/content/issue5_1/04_greenwald-rosner.html

Griffiths, J.T., & Brophy, P. (2005). Student searching behaviour and the web: Use of academic resources and Google. *Library Trends, 53*(4), 539–554.

Gross, J.A. (2001). A human rights perspective on US education: Only some children matter. *Catholic University Law Review, 50*, 919–956.

Grzinic, M. (2004). Flexible colonisation. In G. Cox, J. Krysa, & A. Lewin (Eds.), *Data Browser 01. Economising Culture: On "the (Digital) Culture Industry"* (pp.171–184). New York: Autonomedia.

Gunawardena, C., et al. (2002). Negotiating "face" in a non-face-to-face learning environment. In F. Sudweeks & C. Ess (Eds.), *Proceedings: Cultural attitudes towards technology and communication 2002* (pp.89–106). Perth, Australia: Murdoch University.

Gunawardena, C.N. & McIsaac, M.S. (2004). Distance education. In D.H. Jonassen (Ed.). *Handbook of research on educational communication and technology* (pp.355–395). Mahwah, NJ: Lawrence Erlbaum.

Gupta, R.K. (1995). English in a postcolonial situation: The example of India. In P. Franklin (Ed.), *Profession 95* (pp.73–78). New York: Modern Language Association.

Guthrie, W.K.C. (1956). Introduction. In Plato, *Protagoras and Meno* (W.K.C. Guthrie, Trans., pp.7–25). Harmondsworth, UK: Penguin.

Guttman, A. (1987). *Democratic education.* Princeton, NJ: Princeton University Press.

Hackforth, R. (1996). Socrates. In W.J. Prior (Ed.), *Socrates: Critical assessments. Vol. 1: The Socratic problem and Socratic ignorance* (pp.1–13). London: Routledge.

Hall, J.W. (1995). The revolution in electronic technology and the modern university: The convergence of means. *Educom Review, 30*(4), 42–45.

Hall, M. (1999). Virtual colonization. *Journal of Material Culture, 4*(1), 39–55.

Hamelink, C. (2000). *The ethics of cyberspace.* London: Sage.

Harasim, L. (1989). On-line education: A new domain. In R. Mason & A. Kaye (Eds.), *Mindweave: Communication, computers and distance education* (pp.50–62). Oxford: Pergamon Press.

Harasim, L., et al. (1995). *Learning networks: A field guide to teaching and learning online.* Cambridge, MA: MIT Press.

Hardaway, F. (2005). Is your child learning what he/she needs to know? *Always On.* Accessed June 28, 2005, at www.alwayson-network.com/comments.php?id=10962_0_5_0_C

Hardin, K. (2004). Teach them to fly: Strategies for encouraging active online learning. *Turkish Online Journal of Distance Education, 5*(2). Accessed December 16, 2005, at tojde.anadolu.edu.tr/tojde14/notes_for_editor/hardin.htm

Hardt, M., & Negri, A. (2004). *Multitude.* New York: Penguin.

Harmon, A. (2004, May 2). Is a do-gooder company a good thing? *The New York Times,* Week in Review Section, 12.

Harris, D. (1987). *Openness and closure in distance education.* Basingstoke, UK: Falmer.

Harris, R., et al. (2001). Challenges and opportunities in introducing information and communication technologies to the Kelabit Community of North Central Borneo. *New Media and Society, 3*(3), 271–296.

Hawisher, G.E. (1992). Electronic meetings of the minds: Research, electronic conferences, and composition studies. In G.E. Hawisher & P. LeBlanc (Eds.), *Reimagining computers and composition: Teaching and research in the virtual age* (pp.81–101). Portsmouth, NH: Boynton-Cook.

Hawkes, T. (1989). General Editor's Preface. In B. Ashcroft, G. Griffiths, & H. Tiffin (Eds.), *The empire writes back: Theory and practice in post-colonial literature* (pp.vii–viii). New York: Routledge.

Hayles, K. (1999). *How we became posthuman.* Chicago, IL: University of Chicago Press.

Heidegger, M. (1977). *The question concerning technology and other essays.* New York: Harper & Row.

Helleiner, E. (2003). Economic liberalism and its critics: the past as prologue? *Review of International Political Economy, 10*(4), 685–696.

Herring, S. (1996). Posting in a different voice: Gender and ethics in computer-mediated communication. In C. Ess (Ed.), *Philosophical perspectives on computer-mediated communication* (pp.115–145). Albany, NY: SUNY Press.

Herring, S. (1999). The rhetorical dynamics of gender harassment on-line. *The Information Society, 15*(3), 151–167.

Hiltz, S.R. (1982, February 21). Comment CC14. In E. Kerr (Ed.), *Computers in education.* Unpublished computer conference transcript, New Jersey Institute of Technology, Newark, NJ.

Hiltz, S.R. (1994). *The virtual classroom: Learning without limits via computer networks.* Norwood, NJ: Ablex.

Hirsch, E.D. (1987). *Cultural literacy: What every American needs to know* [with an Appendix: "What literate Americans know," co-authored with J. Kett, & J. Trefil]. Boston, MA: Houghton Mifflin.

Hocking, J. (2003). Counter-terrorism and the criminalization of politics. *Australian Journal of Politics and History, 49*, 355–371.

Holquist, M. (1990). *Dialogism: Bakhtin and his world.* London: Routledge.

Hongladarom, S. (2000). Negotiating the global and the local: How Thai culture coopts the Internet. *First Monday, 5*(8). Accessed October 27, 2005, at firstmonday.org/issues/issue5_8/hongladarom/index.html

Hongladarom, S. (2001). Global culture, local cultures and the Internet: The Thai example. In C. Ess & F. Sudweeks (Eds.), *Culture, technology, communication: Towards an intercultural global village* (pp.307–324). Albany, NY: SUNY Press.

Horkheimer, M. (1990). The end of reason. In A. Arato & E. Gebhardt (Eds.), *The essential Frankfurt school reader* (pp.26–48). New York: Continuum.

Horkheimer, M., & Adorno, T. (2002). *Dialectic of enlightenment* (E. Jephcott, Trans.). Stanford, CA: Stanford University Press.

Hoskins, S.L., & Hooff, J.C. (2005). Motivation and ability: Which students use online learning and what influence does it have on their achievement? *British Journal of Educational Technology, 36*(2), 177–193.

Howe, N., & Strauss, W. (2000). *Millennials rising: The next great generation.* New York: Vintage Books.

Huisman, J., Maassen, P., & Neave, G. (2001). *Higher education and the nation state.* New York: Pergamon.

Human Rights Watch (2001). *Freedom of expression and the Internet in China: A Human Rights Watch backgrounder.* Accessed October 31, 2005, at www.hrw.org/backgrounder/asia/china-bck-0701.htm

Hursthouse, R. (2001). *On virtue ethics.* Oxford: Oxford University Press.

Huxley, A. (1965). *Brave new world and brave new world revisited.* New York: Harper Perennial.

Hyslop-Margison, E. (2004). Technology, human agency and Dewey's constructivism: Opening democratic spaces in virtual classrooms. *Australasian Journal of Educational Technology, 20*(2), 137–148.

IGNOU (Indira Gandhi National Open University) (1985). *Handbook Section 3.* Accessed November 3, 2005, at www.ignou.ac.in/stridehandbook2/section3.pdf

infoDev (World Bank) (2005). *Knowledge map on information and communication technologies in education. Topic: Costs.* Accessed January 27, 2006, at www.infodev.org/section/programs/mainstreaming_icts/education/knowledgemaps_education/km_costs

Inglis, A., Ling, P., & Joosten, V. (2002). *Delivering digitally: Managing the transition to the knowledge media* (2nd ed.). London: Kogan Page.

Internet Society (2005). *ISOC@WSIS: Commentary from ISOC delegates at WSIS.* Accessed October 16, 2005, at geneva.isoc.org/blogs/wsis/

"Is an E-Toy by Another Name the Same?" (1999, December 13). Narr. Madeleine Brand. *Morning Edition.* National Public Radio. Indianapolis, IN: WFYI.

Isin, E.F. (2002). *Being political: Genealogies of citizenship.* Minneapolis, MN: University of Minnesota Press.

Jakupec, V. (2000). The politics of flexible learning: Opportunities and challenges in a globalised world. In V. Jakupec & J. Garrick (Eds.), *Flexible learning, human resource and organisational development* (pp.67–84). London & New York: Routledge Falmer.

Janangelo, J. (1991). Technopower and technoppression: Some abuses of power and control in computer-assisted writing environments. *Computers and Composition, 9*(1), 46–64.

Jaspers, K. (1962). *Socrates, Buddha, Confucius, Jesus: The paradigmatic individuals.* New York: Harcourt, Brace & World.

Jessop, B. (2002). *The future of the capitalist state.* Cambridge: Polity Press.

Jessop, B. (2004). Critical semiotic analysis and cultural political economy. *Critical Discourse Studies, 1*(2), 159–174.

Jewett, W., & Henderson, F. (2003). Interpreting instructional cost data. *Planning for Higher Education, 32*(1), 15–27.

Johnson-Eilola, J. (1997). *Nostalgic angels.* Norwood, NJ: Ablex.

Jonassen, D.H. (1994). *Technology as cognitive tools: Learners as designers.* Accessed November 4, 2002, at it.coe.uga.edu/itforum/paper1/paper1.html

Jonassen, D.H. (Ed.) (1996). *Handbook of research for educational communications and technology: A project of the Association for Educational Communications and Technology.* New York: Simon & Schuster Macmillan.

Jones, A. (2000). Surveillance and student handwriting: Tracing the body. In C. O'Farrell, D. Meadmore, E. McWilliam, & C. Symes (Eds.), *Taught bodies* (pp.151–164). New York: Peter Lang.

Jones, S. (2002). The Internet goes to college. *Pew Internet and American Life Project.* Accessed October 11, 2004, at www.pewinternet.org

Julier, L., Gillespie, P., & Yancey, K.B. (1999). Voicing the landscape: A discourse of their own. In K. Blair, & P. Takayoshi (Eds.), *Feminist cyberscapes: Mapping gendered academic spaces* (pp.297–325). Stamford, CT: Ablex.

Kapitzke, C. (2001). Information literacy: The changing library. *Journal of Adolescent and Adult Literacy, 44*(5), 450–456.

Katz, R.N., & Oblinger, D.G. (Eds.) (2000). *The "e" is for everything: E-commerce, e-business and e-learning in the future of higher education.* San Francisco, CA: Jossey-Bass, Educause & PricewaterhouseCoopers.

Katz, S.N. (2000). Don't confuse a tool with a goal: Making information technology serve higher education, rather than the other way around. *The Internet and the University: 2001 Forum* (Forum for the Future of Higher Education/Educause) (pp.29–43). Accessed December 16, 2005, at www.educause.edu/ir/library/pdf/ffpiu0002.pdf

Kaye, T. (1987, November 12–14). Computer conferencing for distance education. Paper delivered at *Nuove tecnologia e vita quotidiana in Europa,* Bologna.

Keegan, D. (1986). *The foundations of distance education* (2nd ed.). London: Routledge.

Keegan, T., Lewis, R., Roa, T., & Tarnowska, J. (2004). Indigenous language in an e-learning interface: Translation of PLACE™ into the Māori language. In F. Sudweeks & C. Ess (Eds.), *Proceedings: Cultural attitudes towards technology and communication 2004* (pp.250–254). Perth, Australia: Murdoch University.

Kelly, T.M. (2000). For better or worse? The marriage of web and the history classroom. *Journal of the Association for History and Computing, 3*(2). Accessed May 25, 2005, at mcel.pacificu.edu/JAHC/JAHCIII2/ARTICLES/kelly/kelly.html

Kelly, T.M. (2003, January/February). Remaking liberal education: The challenges of new media. *Academe,* 28–31. Accessed January 25, 2005, at www.aaup.org/publications/Academe/2003/03jf/03jfkel.htm

Kember, D. (1995). *Open learning courses for adults: A model of student progress.* Englewood Cliffs, NJ: Educational Technology Publications.

Kendrick, W. (1993). Fiction in review. *Yale Review, 81*(4), 124–137.

Kerr, C. (2001). *The uses of the university.* 5th ed. Cambridge, MA: Harvard UP.

Kerr, E.B. (1984). *Moderating online conferences.* Computerized Conferencing and Communications Center Research Report 20. Newark, NJ: New Jersey Institute of Technology.

Kerr, E.B., & Hiltz, S.R. (1982). *Computer-mediated communication systems: Status and evaluation.* New York: Academic Press.

Kettner-Polley, R.B. (1999). The making of a virtual professor. *Asynchronous Learning Networks Magazine, 3*(1). Accessed January 20, 2006, at www.aln.org/publications/magazine/v3n1/kettner.asp

Kierkegaard, S. (1967). *Journals and papers* (Vol. 2) (H.V. Hong & E.H. Hong, Eds. & Trans.). Bloomington, IN: Indiana University Press.

Kilpatrick, S., & Bound, H. (2003). *Learning online: Benefits and barriers in regional Australia.* Leabrook, Australia: National Centre for Vocational Education Research.

Kim, K.J., & Bonk, C.J. (2002). Cross-cultural comparisons of online collaboration. *Journal of Computer-Mediated Communication, 8*(1). Accessed November 3, 2005, at www.ascusc.org/jcmc/vol8/issue1/kimandbonk.htm

King, R. (2003). The rise and regulation of for-profit higher education. *The Observatory on Borderless Higher Education.* Accessed November 3, 2005, at www.obhe.ac.uk/products/reports/pdf/November2003.pdf

Klass, G. (2000). Plato as distance education pioneer: Status and quality threats of distance education. *First Monday, 5*(7). Accessed March 22, 2004, at www.firstmonday.dk/issues/issue5_7/klass/index.html

Kleinman, S.S. (1998). Membership has its benefits: Computer-mediated communication and social identification in an online discussion group for women in science and engineering. *Dissertation Abstracts International Section A: Humanities and Social Sciences, 59,* 4-A, 0996.

Klopfer, E., Squire, K., & Jenkins, H. (2002). Environmental detectives: PDAs as a window into a virtual simulated world. Paper presented at the IEEE International Workshop on Wireless and Mobile Technologies in Education, Växjö, Sweden, August 29–30, 2002.

Ko, S., & Rossen, S. (2001). *Teaching online: A practical guide.* Boston, MA: Houghton Mifflin.

Kohl, H. (1994). *"I won't learn from you": And other thoughts on creative maladjustment.* New York: New Press.

Kolko, B., Nakamura, L., & Rodman, G. (Eds.) (2000). *Race in cyberspace.* New York: Routledge.

Krause, K., Hartley, R., James, R., & McInnis, C. (2005). *The first year experience in Australian universities: Findings from a decade of national studies.* Canberra, Australia: Department of Education, Science and Training.

Kuh, G.D., & Vesper, N. (1997). A comparison of student experiences with good practices in undergraduate education between 1990 and 1994. *The Review of Higher Education, 21,* 43–61.

Kumar, A. (1997). *Class issues: Pedagogy, cultural studies, and the public sphere.* New York: New York University Press.

Kumaravadivelu, B. (2001). Toward a postmethod pedagogy. *TESOL Quarterly, 35*(4), 537–560.

Kumaravadivelu, B. (2003). *Beyond methods: Macrostrategies for language teaching.* New Haven, CT: Yale University Press.

Kymlicka, W. (2002). *Contemporary political philosophy* (2nd ed.). Oxford: Oxford University Press.

Labour Party Manifesto (1964). Accessed November 3, 2005, at www.labour-party.org.uk/manifestos/1964/1964-labour-manifesto.shtml

Lagesen, V. (2003). Advertising computer science to women (or was it the other way around?). In M. Lie (Ed.), *He, she and IT revisited: New perspectives on gender in the information society* (pp.69–102). Oslo, Norway: Gyldendal Akademisk.

Lancaster, S., Yen, D., & Wang, J.C. (2003, October). Online education in the USA: Overview of a modern avenue for education delivery. *Industry and Higher Education,* 365–374.

Landow, G.P. (1997). *Hypertext 2.0: The convergence of contemporary critical theory and technology.* Baltimore, MD: Johns Hopkins University Press.

Lapadat, J.C. (2002). Written interaction: A key component in online learning. *Journal of Computer-Mediated Communication, 7*(4). Accessed January 18, 2006, at jcmc.indiana.edu/vol7/issue4/lapadat.html

Latour, B. (1991). Technology is society made durable. In J. Law (Ed.), *A sociology of monsters* (pp.103–131). London: Routledge.

Latour, B. (1995). Mixing humans and nonhumans together: The sociology of a door closer. In S.L. Star (Ed.), *Ecologies of knowledge: Work and practices in science and technology* (pp.257–277). Albany, NY: SUNY Press.

Latour, B. (1999). On recalling ANT. In J. Law, & J. Hassard (Eds.), *Actor network theory and after* (pp.15–25). Boston, MA: Blackwell.

Laurillard, D. (2002). *Rethinking university teaching: A conversational framework for the effective use of learning technologies* (2nd ed.). Abingdon: Routledge Falmer.

Lauzon, A.C. (1999). Situating cognition and crossing borders: Resisting the hegemony of mediated education. *British Journal of Educational Technology, 30*(3), 261–276.

Lee, D. (2003). Translator's introduction. In Plato, *The Republic* (D. Lee, Trans., 2nd ed., pp.xiii–lviii). London: Penguin.

Lenderman, H., & Sandelands, E. (2002). Learning for a purpose: Building a corporate university. *International Journal of Contemporary Hospitality Management, 14*(7), 382–384. Accessed August 15, 2005, at www.emeraldinsight.com/0959-6119.htm

Lenhart, A. (2001). *The Internet and education: Findings of the Pew Internet and American Life Project.* Accessed January 15, 2004, at www.pewtrusts.com/pubs/pubs.item.cfm?image=img5&content_item_id=729&content_type_id=8&page=p1

Leonard, B. (2005a, November 10). Administrators access class Blackboard sites. *Washington Square News.* Accessed January 25, 2006, at www.nyunews.com/vnews/display.v/ART/2005/11/10/4372f5ee4a129?in_archive=1

Leonard, B. (2005b, November 30). Faculty strike concerns unanswered. *Washington Square News.* Accessed January 27, 2006, at www.nyunews.com/vnews/display.v/ART/2005/11/30/438d3eb97e474?in_archive=1

Lesher, J.H. (1996). Socrates' disavowal of knowledge. In W.J. Prior (Ed.), *Socrates: Critical assessments. Vol. 1: The Socratic problem and Socratic ignorance* (pp.261–274). London: Routledge.

Lessig, L. (1999). *Code and other laws of cyberspace.* New York: Basic Books.

Levidow, L. (2002). Marketising higher education: Neoliberal strategies and counter-strategies. *The Commoner, 3.* Accessed March 31, 2002, at www.thecommoner.org.uk

Levin, J.S. (2002). Global culture and the community college. *Community College Journal of Research and Practice, 26*, 121–145.

Lewis, B., Smith, R., & Massey, C. (2001). *The tower under siege: Technology, power, and education.* Montreal/Kingston: McGill-Queen's University Press.

Linkon, S. (n.d.). *Learning interdisciplinarity: A course portfolio.* Accessed November 10, 2005, at www.as.ysu.edu/%7Eamerst/CoursePortfolioHome.htm

Lionnet, F. (1995). *Postcolonial representations: Women, literature, identity.* Ithaca, NY: Cornell University Press.

Lippman, A. (2002). Lippman on learning: Fundamental changes. *Syllabus, 13*, 12–13.

Lockard, J. (1997). Progressive politics, electronic individualism, and the myth of virtual community. In D. Porter (Ed.), *Internet culture* (pp.219–231). New York: Routledge.

Lockard, J. (2000). Babel machines and electronic universalism. In B.E. Kolko, L. Nakamura, & G.B. Rodman (Eds.), *Race in cyberspace* (pp.171–189). New York: Routledge.

Lockwood, F. (2002). Access and equity in distance education: Revisiting previously identified trends and directions. In H.P. Dikshit, et al. (Eds.), *Access and equity: Challenges for open and distance education* (pp.3–12). New Delhi: Kogan Page.

Loeb, E. (2005, November 15). Spying not civil discourse. *Washington Square News.* Accessed January 27, 2006, at www.nyunews.com/vnews/display.v/ART/2005/11/15/43795d2d87ff2

Loertscher, D. (2003). The digital school library. *Teacher Librarian, 30*, 14–24.

Lotherington, H. (2001, July). Going virtual: Lessons learned during a strike at York University. Paper presented at the *8th International Literacy and Educational Research Network Conference,* Spetses, Greece. Accessed October 11, 2004, at www.yorku.ca/irlt/reports/Learning.htm

Luke, A. (2000). Critical literacy in Australia: A matter of context and standpoint. *Journal of Adolescent and Adult Literacy, 43*(5), 448–459.

Lyotard, J.-F. (1976). Petite mise en perspective de la décadence et de quelques combats minoritaires à y mener. In D. Grisoni (Ed.), *Politiques de la philosophie* (pp.121–153). Paris: Grasset.

Lyotard, J.-F. (1984). *The postmodern condition: A report on knowledge* (G. Bennington & B. Massumi, Trans.) Minneapolis, MN: University of Minnesota Press.

Macaulay, T. (1972). Minute on Indian education. In J. Clive & T. Pinney (Eds.), *Thomas Babington Macaulay: Selected writings* (pp.235–251). Chicago, IL: University of Chicago Press.

Machiavelli, N. (1970). *The discourses* (L. Walker, Trans.). Harmondsworth, UK: Penguin.

Mackay, H. (1993). *Reinventing Australia: The mind and mood of Australia in the 90s.* Sydney: Angus & Robertson.

MacKenzie, D., & Wajcman, J. (Eds.) (1999). *The social shaping of technology.* Buckingham, UK: Open University Press.

Madsen, R., & Strong, T. (2003). *The many and the one: Religious and secular perspectives on ethical pluralism in the modern world.* Princeton, NJ: Princeton University Press.

Maeroff, G.I. (2003). *A classroom of one: How online learning is changing our schools and colleges.* New York: Palgrave Macmillan.

Magee, B. (1987). Plato (Dialogue with M. Burnyeat). *The great philosophers: An introduction to Western philosophy* (pp.12–30). London: BBC Books.

Marcuse, H. (1964). *One-dimensional man.* Boston, MA: Beacon Press.

Marginson, S. (1997). *Markets in education.* St. Leonards, NSW: Allen & Unwin.

Marginson, S., & Considine, M. (2000). *The enterprise university.* Cambridge: Cambridge University Press.

Markham, A.N. (1998). *Life online: Researching real experience in virtual space.* Walnut Creek, CA: AltaMira Press.

Mason, R., & Kaye, A. (Eds.) (1989). *Mindweave: Communication, computers and distance education.* Oxford: Pergamon Press.

Mather, P. (1996, December 11). Critical literacy: The WWW's great potential. *WWW: Beyond the basics.* Accessed November 6, 2005, at ei.cs.vt.edu/%7Ewwwbtb/book/chap6/critical.html

Mathison, S., & Ross, E.W. (2002). The hegemony of accountability in schools and universities. *Workplace, 5*(1). Accessed January 14, 2006, at www.louisville.edu/journal/workplace/issue5p1/mathison.html

Mattelart, A. (1983). *Transnationals and the third world.* South Hadley, MA: Bergin & Garvey.

Mavor, S., & Traynor, B. (2003). Exclusion in international online learning communities. In S. Reisman, J. Flores, & D. Edge (Eds.), *Electronic learning communities: Issues and practices* (pp.457–488). Greenwich, CT: Information Age Publishing.

Maynor, J.W. (2003). *Republicanism in the modern world.* Cambridge: Polity Press.

McCaughey, M., & Ayers, M. (Eds.) (2003). *Cyberactivism: Online activism in theory and practice.* New York: Routledge.

McChesney, R. (1999). *Rich media, poor democracy: Communication politics in dubious times.* Urbana, IL: University of Illinois Press.

McConachie, J., Danaher, P.A., Luck, J., & Jones, D. (2005). Central Queensland University's course management systems: Accelerator or brake in engaging change? *International Review of Research in Open and Distance Learning, 6*(1). Accessed October 8, 2005, at www.irrodl.org/content/v6.1/mcconachie.html

McIsaac, M.S., & Gunawardena, C.N. (1996). Distance education. In D.H. Jonassen (Ed.), *Handbook of research for educational communications and technology: A project of the Association for Educational Communications and Technology* (pp.403–437). New York: Simon & Schuster Macmillan. Accessed November 3, 2005, at seamonkey.ed.asu.edu/~mcisaac/dechapter/index.html

McLaren, P. (2003). Critical pedagogy and class struggle in the age of neoliberal globalization: Notes from history's underside. *Democracy and Nature, 9*(1), 65–90.

McNaughton, J. (2005, May 15). Lesson number one: Get rid of Microsoft. *The Observer.* Accessed January 26, 2006, at education.guardian.co.uk/elearning/comment/0,1484113,00.html

McWilliam, E., & Palmer, P. (1996). Pedagogues, tech(no)bods: Re-inventing postgraduate pedagogy. In E. McWilliam, & P.G. Taylor (Eds.), *Pedagogy, technology and the body* (pp.163–170). New York: Peter Lang.

Meeks, B. (1987, February). The quiet revolution: Online education becomes a real alternative. *Byte*, 183–190.

Mehl, J.V. (2000). Drawing parallels with the renaissance: Late-modernism, postmodernism, and the possibility of historical layering. *The Midwest Quarterly: A Journal of Contemporary Thought, 41*(4), 401–415.

Melzer, A.M., Weinberger, J., & Zinman, R. (Eds.) (1993). *Technology in the Western political tradition.* Ithaca, NY: Cornell University Press.

Minock, M., & Shor, F. (1995). Crisscrossing *Grand Canyon*: Bridging the gaps with computer conferencing. *Computers and Composition, 12*(3), 355–365.

Minsky, L. (2000). Dead souls: The aftermath of Bayh-Dole. In G. White, et al. (Eds.), *Campus, Inc.: Corporate power in the ivory tower.* New York: Prometheus Books.

MIT (Massachusetts Institute of Technology) Media Lab (n.d.). *$100 Dollar Laptop.* Accessed November 27, 2005, at laptop.media.mit.edu

Miyoshi, M. (1996). A borderless world? From colonialism to transnationalism and the decline of the nation-state. *Global/local: Cultural production and the transnational imaginary* (pp.78–106). Durham, NC: Duke University Press.

Miyoshi, M. (1998). "Globalization," culture, and the university. In F. Jameson & M. Miyoshi (Eds.), *The cultures of globalization* (pp.247–270). Durham, NC: Duke University Press.

Moll, M. (Ed.) (1997). *Tech high: Globalisation and the future of Canadian education.* Ottawa, Ont.: Canadian Centre for Policy Alternatives and Fernwood Publishing.

Moll, M. (Ed.) (2001). *But it's only a tool! The politics of technology and education reform.* Ottawa, Ont.: Canadian Centre for Policy Alternatives.

Morgan, M.C. (2000, November). Guiding online discussions: A social argument framework. Paper delivered at *TOHE 2000.* Accessed October 31, 2004, at cal.bemidji.msus.edu/english/morgan/docs/TOHE/tohePresentation.html

Morrell, K.S. (2000). Now that students have wings. *The Internet and the University: 2000 Forum* (Forum for the Future of Higher Education/Educause) (pp.61–78). Accessed January 20, 2006, at www.educause.edu/ir/library/pdf/ffpiu0004.pdf

Morson, G.S., & Emerson, C. (1990). *Mikhail Bakhtin: Creation of a prosaics.* Stanford, CA: Stanford University Press.

Mosco, V. (2004). *The digital sublime: Myth, power and cyberspace.* Cambridge, MA: MIT Press.

Moszkowicz, J. (1999). The girls can't hack it: The changing status of the female body in representations of new technology. In J. Arthurs & J. Grimshaw (Eds.), *Women's bodies: Discipline and transgression* (pp.208–231). London: Cassell.

Muirhead, B. (2001). Interactivity research studies. *Educational Technology and Society, 4*(3), 108–112. Accessed August 1, 2005, at ifets.ieee.org/periodical/vol-3-2001/murihead.pdf

Murdoch, D. (1995). The riches of empire: Postcolonialism in literature and criticism. *Choice, 32,* 1059–1071.

Murphy, D., Wei-yuan, Z., & Perris, K. (2003). Online learning in Asian Open Universities: Resisting "content imperialism"? *The Observatory on Borderless Higher Education.* Accessed November 3, 2005, at www.obhe.ac.uk/products/reports/pdf/June2003.pdf

Naidu, S. (Ed.) (2003). *Learning and teaching with technology: Principles and practices.* London: Kogan Page.

NAS (National Academy of Sciences) (US) (2002). *Preparing for the revolution: Information technology and the future of the research university.* Accessed November 5, 2005, at books.nap.edu/books/030908640X/html/3.html

NCTE (National Council of Teachers of English) (US) (n.d.). More than a number: Why class size matters. Accessed December 16, 2005, at www.ncte.org/about/over/positions/category/class/107620.htm?source=gs

Nelson, B. (2003). *Our universities: Backing Australia's future.* Canberra, Australia: Commonwealth of Australia.

Nelson, C., & Watt, S. (1999). *Academic keywords: A devil's dictionary for higher education.* New York: Routledge.

The New London Group (2000). A pedagogy of multiliteracies: Designing social futures. In B. Cope, & M. Kalantzis (Eds.), *Multiliteracies: Literacy learning and the design of social futures* (pp.9–37). London: Routledge.

NJIT (New Jersey Institute of Technology) (US) (1986). *EIES quick reference card*. Unpublished computer conference transcript, Newark, NJ.

Noble, D.F. (1977). *America by design: Science, technology, and the rise of corporate capitalism*. New York: Knopf.

Noble, D.F. (1998a). Digital diploma mills: The automation of higher education. *First Monday, 3*(1). Accessed October 11, 2004, at www.firstmonday.org/issues/issue3_1/noble/

Noble, D.F. (1998b). Digital diploma mills. Part III: The bloom is off the rose. Accessed July 8, 1999, at communication.ucsd.edu/dl/ddm3.html

Noble, D.F. (2002a). *Digital diploma mills: The automation of higher education*. New York: Monthly Review Press.

Noble, D.F. (2002b). *Digital diploma mills: The automation of higher education*. Toronto, Ont.: Between the Lines.

Nunan, T. (2005). Markets, distance education, and Australian higher education. *International Review of Research in Open and Distance Learning, 6*(1). Accessed October 8, 2005, at www.irrodl.org/content/v6.1/nunan.html

OAIster (2005). Homepage. Accessed December 16, 2005, at www.oaister.org/o/oaister/

Oberman, C. (1996). Library instruction: Concepts and pedagogy in the electronic environment. *RQ, 35 (3)*, 315–323.

Oblinger, D.G., & Oblinger, J. (2005). Is it age or IT: First steps toward understanding the net generation. In D.G. Oblinger & J. Oblinger (Eds.), *Educating the net generation*. Educause. Accessed October 12, 2005, at www.educause.edu/educatingthenetgen/

O'Donnell, J.J. (1998). *Avatars of the word: From papyrus to cyberspace*. Cambridge, MA: Harvard University Press.

Open Universiteit Nederland (2004). Objectives. Accessed online November 3, 2004, at www.ou.nl/info-alg-english-introduction/index.htm#objectives

O'Tuathail, G., & McCormack, D. (1998). The technoliteracy challenge: Teaching globalization using the Internet. *Journal of Geography in Higher Education, 22*(3), 347–361.

OU (Open University) (UK) (2004a). *Charter and statutes*. Accessed November 12, 2005, at www.open.ac.uk/foi-docs/charter.doc

OU (Open University) (UK) (2004b). *Factsheets*. Accessed November 3, 2004, at www3.open.ac.uk/media/factsheets/index.asp

OU (Open University) (UK) (2004c). *OU futures. The Open University's strategic priorities 2004–2008*. Accessed November 12, 2005, at www.open.ac.uk/planning/futures/pics/d26585.pdf

OU (Open University) (UK) (n.d.). *About the OU: Our mission*. Accessed November 12, 2005, at www.open.ac.uk/about/ou/p2.shtml

The OU then and now (2003, June 23). *BBC News*. Accessed November 3, 2005, at news.bbc.co.uk/2/hi/uk_news/education/3012754.stm

Pace, D. (2004). The amateur in the operating room: History and the scholarship of teaching and learning. *American Historical Review, 109*(4), 1171–1192.

Palloff, R.M., & Pratt, K. (1999). *Building learning communities in cyberspace*. San Francisco, CA: Jossey-Bass.

Palloff, R.M., & Pratt, K. (2001). *Lessons from the cyberspace classroom: The realities of online teaching*. San Francisco, CA: Jossey-Bass.

Palmquist, M. (2003). A brief history of computer support for writing centers and writing across the curriculum programs. *Computers and Composition, 20*(4), 395–413.

Panko, M., & Postlethwaite, M. (2004). Online discussion and *Ako* in Aotearoa, New Zealand. In F. Sudweeks & C. Ess (Eds.), *Proceedings: Cultural attitudes towards technology and communication 2004* (pp.524–527). Perth, Australia: Murdoch University.

Park, K.J. (2002, April 3). On the KW Cross-Cultural Distance Learning Project and its significance in English education. Keynote address at *Information Technologies and the Universities of Asia (ITUA) Conference*, Bangkok, Thailand.

Parker, D., & Gemino, A. (2001). Inside online learning: Comparing conceptual and technique learning performance in place-based and ALN format. *Journal of Asynchronous Learning Networks, 5*(2). Accessed October 26, 2005, at www.sloan-c.org/publications/jaln/v5n2/ v5n2_parkergemino.asp

Parker, S. (1997). *Reflective teaching in the postmodern world: A manifesto for education in postmodernity.* Buckingham, UK: Open University Press.

Pascarella, E., & Terenzini, P. (1998). Studying college students in the 21st century: Meeting new challenges. *The Review of Higher Education, 21*(2), 151–165.

Pegrum, M. (2004). And on the eighth day: The struggle for linguistic organization. *Bad Subjects, 65.* Accessed December 16, 2005, at eserver.org/bs/65/pegrum.html

Pegrum, M., & Cook, B. (2003, September 5). Learning together: Fostering collaborative approaches among individualistic students in an online environment. Paper delivered at *EuroCALL 03,* Limerick, Ireland.

Pegrum, M., & Spöring, M. (2004, July 1). Virtual learning and virtual teaching: Challenging learner and teacher identities in a distance learning professional development programme. Paper delivered at *Navigating the New Landscape for Languages (CILT),* London, UK. Accessed December 16, 2005, at www.llas.ac.uk/resources/paper.aspx?resourceid=2531

Pennycook, A. (2001). *Critical applied linguistics: A critical introduction.* Mahwah, NJ: Lawrence Erlbaum.

Perraton, H. (2000). *Open and distance learning in the developing world.* London: Routledge.

Perry, W. (1976). *Open University: A personal account by the first Vice-Chancellor.* Milton Keynes, UK: The Open University Press.

Peters, M., & Roberts, P. (2000). Universities, futurology and globalisation. *Discourse studies in the cultural politics of education, 21*(2), 125–139.

Pettit, P. (1997). *Republicanism: A theory of freedom and government.* Oxford: Clarendon Press.

Phillips, R. (2002). *What is the most appropriate way to use the Internet for teaching and learning?* Accessed January 4, 2005, at www.ocln.cmctafe.wa.edu.au/aset/phillips.htm

Phipps, R., & Merisotis, J. (1999). *What's the difference?* Washington, DC: Institute for Higher Education Policy.

Phipps, R., & Merisotis, J. (2000). *Quality on the line: Benchmarks for success in Internet-based distance education.* Washington, DC: Institute for Higher Education Policy.

Pinch, T., & Bijker, W. (1989). The social construction of facts and artefacts: Or how the sociology of science and the sociology of technology might benefit each other. In W.E. Bijker, T.P. Hughes, & T. Pinch (Eds.), *The social construction of technological systems: New directions in the sociology and history of technology* (pp.17–50). Cambridge, MA: MIT Press.

Pirsig, R.M. (1974). *Zen and the art of motorcycle maintenance: An inquiry into values.* New York: Bantam.

Plato (1971). *Plato in twelve volumes. Vol. I: Euthyphro, Apology, Crito, Phaedo, Phaedrus* (H.N. Fowler, Trans.). Cambridge, MA: Harvard University Press.

Plato (1973). *Phaedrus and Letters VII and VIII* (W. Hamilton, Trans.). London: Penguin.

Plato (1991). *The Republic of Plato* (A. Bloom, Trans.). New York: Basic Books.

Plato (1997). *Complete works* (J.M. Cooper with D.S. Hutchinson, Eds.). Indianapolis, IN: Hackett Publishing.

Popper, K.R. (1966). *The open society and its enemies. Vol. 1: The spell of Plato.* London: Routledge & Kegan Paul.

Postcolonial Archive (1995, September/October). University of Virginia. Accessed December 13, 1999, at gopher://lists.village.virginia.edu:70/00/pubs/listservs/spoons/postcolonial.archive/postco_ 1995/postco_Sep.95.ind, and gopher:lsist.village.virginia.edu:70/00/pubs/listservs/spoons/ postcolonial.archive/postco_1995/postco_Oct.95.ind

Postma, L. (2001). A theoretical argumentation and evaluation of South African learners' orientation towards and perceptions of the empowering use of information: A calculated prediction of computerized learning for the marginalized. *New Media and Society, 3*(3), 313–326.

Postman, N. (1985). *Amusing ourselves to death: Public discourse in the age of show business*. New York: Penguin.

Power, K. (2002). Access and equity in Indian higher education. In H.P. Dikshit, et al. (Eds.), *Access and equity: Challenges for open and distance education* (pp.52–61). New Delhi: Kogan Page.

Pratt, L.R. (2003). Will budget troubles restructure higher education? *Academe, 89*(1). Accessed January 14, 2006, at www.aaup.org/publications/Academe/2003/03jf/03jfpra.htm

Premfors, R. (1980). *The politics of higher education in a comparative perspective*. Stockholm: Group for the Study of Higher Education and Research Policy of the University of Stockholm.

Prensky, M. (2001). Digital natives, digital immigrants. *On the Horizon, 9*(5). Accessed January 25, 2005, at www.marcprensky.com/writing/

Pynchon, T. (1984, October 28). Is it OK to be a Luddite? *New York Times Book Review, 1*, 40–41.

Rainie, L., & Hitlin, P. (2005, August 2). The Internet at school. *Pew Internet and American Life Project*. Accessed December 16, 2005, at www.pewinternet.org/PPF/r/163/report_display.asp

Rainie, L., Kalehoff, M., & Hess, D. (2002, September 15). College students and the web. *Pew Internet and American Life Project*. Accessed December 16, 2005, at www.pewinternet.org/reports/toc.asp?Report=73

Ramsden, P. (1992). *Learning to teach in higher education*. London: Routledge.

Readings, W. (1996). *The university in ruins*. Cambridge, MA: Harvard University Press.

Reed, M., & Deem, R. (2002). New managerialism: The manager-academic and technologies of management in universities—Looking forward to virtuality? In K. Robins & F. Webster (Eds.), *The virtual university? Knowledge markets and management* (pp.126–147). Oxford: Oxford University Press.

Reeder, K., Macfadyen, L., Roche, J., & Chase, M. (2004). Negotiating cultures in cyberspace: Participation patterns and problematics. *Language Learning and Technology*, 8(2). Accessed November 3, 2005, at llt.msu.edu/vol8num2/pdf/reeder.pdf

Reidenberg, J.R. (2000). Resolving conflicting international data privacy rules in cyberspace. *Stanford Law Review, 52*, 1315–1376.

Reigeluth, C.M. (1992). The imperative for systemic change. *Educational Technology, 32*(1), 9–13.

Reigeluth, C.M., & Garfinkle, R.J. (1992). Envisioning a new system of education. *Educational Technology, 32*(11), 17–23.

Rheingold, H. (2000). *The virtual community: Homesteading on the electronic frontier*. Cambridge, MA: MIT Press.

Rheingold, H. (2002). *Smart mobs: The next social revolution*. Cambridge, MA: Basic Books.

Rhoades, G. (1998). *Managed professionals: Unionized faculty and restructuring academic labor*. Albany, NY: SUNY Press.

Richards, C. (2000). Hypermedia, Internet communication, and the challenge of redefining literacy in the electronic age. *Language Learning and Technology, 4*(2), 59–77. Accessed January 18, 2006, at llt.msu.edu/vol4num2/richards/default.html

Rifkin, J. (2000). *The age of access*. New York: Putman.

Rizvi, F., & Lingard, B. (1997). Foreword. In S. Marginson (Ed.), *Markets in education* (pp.xvii–xix). St. Leonards, NSW: Allen & Unwin.

Robertson, H. (2003). Toward a theory of negativity. *Journal of Teacher Education, 54*, 280–296.

Robins, K., & Webster, F. (1999). *Times of the technoculture: From the information society to the virtual life*. London: Routledge.

Robins, K., & Webster, F. (Eds.) (2002). *The virtual university? Knowledge, markets and management*. Oxford: Oxford University Press.

Roed, J. (2003). Language learner behaviour in a virtual environment. *Computer Assisted Language Learning, 16*(2–3), 155–172.

Rogers, G., Finley, D., & Kline, T. (2001). Understanding individual differences in university undergraduates: A learner needs segmentation approach. *Innovative Higher Education, 25*(3), 183–196.

Romiszowski, A. (1996). Web-based distance learning and teaching: Revolutionary invention or reaction to necessity? In B. Khan (Ed.), *Web-based instruction* (pp.25–40). Englewood Cliffs, NJ: Educational Technology Publications.

Ronan, J. (2003). The reference interview online. *Reference and User Services Quarterly, 43*, 43–47.

Roof, J., & Wiegman, R. (1995). *Who can speak? Authority and critical identity.* Urbana, IL: University of Illinois Press.

Roosevelt, F.D. (1936). *President Franklin Delano Roosevelt before the Democratic Convention accepting nomination for President. Philadelphia—June 27, 1936.* Accessed August 11, 2005, at www.lava.net/cslater/Roosevelt1936.pdf

Roosevelt, F.D. (1944). *1944 State of the Union Address.* Accessed August 11, 2005, at janda.org/politxts/State%20of%20Union%20Addresses/1934-1945%20Roosevelt/FDR44.html

Ropolyi, L. (2000, September 17). Some theses about the reformation of knowledge. Paper delivered at *Internet Research 1.0: The State of the Interdiscipline* (First Conference of the Association of Internet Researchers), University of Kansas, Lawrence, USA.

Rorty, R. (1980). *Philosophy and the mirror of nature.* Oxford: Blackwell.

Rose, M. (1990). *Lives on the boundary.* New York: Penguin.

Rosemont, H. (2001). *Rationality and religious experience: The continuing relevance of the world's spiritual traditions* (with a Commentary by H. Smith). Chicago, IL: Open Court.

Rosenberg, M.J. (2001). *E-learning: Strategies for delivering knowledge in the digital age.* New York: McGraw-Hill.

Rosenzweig, R. (2000). How Americans use and think about the past. Implications from a national survey for the teaching of history. In P. Stearns, P. Seixas, & S. Wineburg (Eds.), *Knowing, teaching and learning history: National and international perspectives.* New York: New York University Press.

Rouse, J. (1994). Power/knowledge. In G. Gutting (Ed.), *The Cambridge companion to Foucault* (pp.92–114). New York: Cambridge University Press.

Rowntree, D. (1999). *A new way with words in distance education.* Accessed November 3, 2005, at www-iet.open.ac.uk/pp/D.G.F.Rowntree/words_in_de.htm

Roy, D.K.S. (2002). Global technology and local culture: Problematics of cultural lag in technological determinism. In H.P. Dikshit, et al. (Eds.), *Access and equity: Challenges for open and distance education* (pp.267–276). New Delhi: Kogan Page.

Rumble, G. (2001). The costs and costing of networked learning. *Journal of Asynchronous Learning Networks, 5*(2), 75–96. Accessed November 1, 2005, at www.aln.org/alnweb/journal/Vol5-issue2/Rumble/Rumb.htm

Russell, T.L. (1999). *The no significant difference phenomenon: As reported in 355 research reports, summaries and papers.* Raleigh, NC: North Carolina State University, 1999.

Ryan, S., Scott, B., Freeman, H., & Patel, D. (2000). *The virtual university: The Internet and resource-based learning.* London: Kogan Page.

Salmon, G. (2000). *E-moderating: The key to teaching and learning online.* London: Kogan Page.

Salpeter, J. (2003). Web literacy and critical thinking: A teacher's tool kit. *Technology and Learning, 23*(8), 22–34.

Sandiford, J. (2001, April). The business of teaching and learning with technology in Florida's Community College. Paper delivered at the *Annual Meeting of the Council for the Study of Community Colleges.*

Sawyer, A. (2004). Challenges facing African universities: Selected issues. *Association of African Universities.* Accessed November 3, 2005, at www.aau.org/english/documents/asa-challengesfigs.pdf

Sayers, R. (2003, November). Managing hybrid collections for the future. *The Australian Library Journal,* 410–411.

Schank, R. (2002). *Designing world-class e-learning.* New York: McGraw-Hill.

Schiller, D. (1999). *Digital capitalism: Networking the global market system.* Cambridge, MA: MIT Press.

Schroeder, C. (2001). *Re-inventing the university.* Logan, UT: University of Utah Press.

Schugurensky, D. (2001–2005). *History of education: Selected moments of the 20th century.* Accessed November 3, 2005, at fcis.oise.utoronto.ca/~daniel_schugurensky/

Scott, P. (1995). *The meanings of mass higher education.* Buckingham, UK: The Society for Research into Higher Education and Open University Press.

Scott, P. (2003, January 14). Moving targets. *Education Guardian.* Accessed November 3, 2005, at education.guardian.co.uk/egweekly/story/0,874163,00.html

Searching without browser, Google-style (2003, November 11). *Australian Business Intelligence.*

Sears, A. (2003). *Retooling the mind factory: Education in a lean state.* Aurora, Ont.: Garamond.

Selfe, C.L. (1999). *Technology and literacy in the twenty-first century: The importance of paying attention.* Carbondale, IL: Southern Illinois University Press.

Semali, L. (2000). Implementing critical media literacy in school curriculum. In A.W. Pailliotet & P.B. Mosenthal (Eds.), *Reconceptualizing literacy in the media age* (pp.277–298). Stanford, CT: JAI Press.

Sfard, A. (1998). On two metaphors for learning and the dangers of choosing just one. *Educational Researcher, 27*(2), 4–13.

Sharma Sen, R. (2002). Access and equity in the context of the differently-abled. In H.P. Dikshit, et al. (Eds.), *Access and equity: Challenges for open and distance education* (pp.72–81). New Delhi: Kogan Page.

Singletary, R. (2003, August). Under the bonnet. *The Australian Library Journal,* 302–303.

Skill, T.D., & Young, B.A. (2002). Embracing the hybrid model: Working at the intersections of virtual and physical learning spaces. *New Directions for Teaching and Learning, 92,* 23–32.

Slaughter, A. (2002). Beware the trumpets of war. *Harvard Journal of Law and Public Policy, 25,* 965–976.

Slaughter, S., & Leslie, L.L. (1997). *Academic capitalism: Politics, policies, and the entrepreneurial university.* Baltimore, MD: Johns Hopkins University Press.

Slosser, S. (2001). ADL and the sharable content object reference model. Accessed January 31, 2005, at www.nectec.or.th/courseware/pdf-documents/adl-scorm.pdf

Smith, C. (2000). Nobody, which means anybody: Audience on the World Wide Web. In S. Gruber (Ed.), *Weaving a virtual web: Practical approaches to new information technologies.* Urbana, IL: NCTE.

Smith, N. (2002, May/June). Teaching as coaching: Helping students to learn in a technological world. *Educause Review,* 38–47.

Smith, S.E. (1958). Educational structure: The English-speaking Canadian universities. In C.T. Bissell (Ed.), *Canada's crisis in higher education* (pp.8–22). Toronto, Ont.: University of Toronto Press.

Smyth, J., & Hattam, R. (2000). Intellectual as hustler: Researching against the grain of the market. *British Educational Research Journal, 26*(2), 157–175.

Solnit, R. (1995). The garden of merging paths. In J. Brook & I. Boal (Eds.), *Resisting the virtual life: The culture and politics of information* (pp.221–234). San Francisco, CA: City Lights.

Sørensen, K.H., & Stewart, J. (Eds.) (2002). *Digital divides and inclusion measures: A review of literature and statistical trends on gender and ICT.* Trondheim, Norway: Senter for Teknologi og samfunn, Institutt for tverrfaglige kulturstudier, Norwegian University of Science and Technology (NTNU).

Sorgo, A. (2003). Searching for information on the Internet: What if your students cannot speak English? *International Journal of Instructional Media, 30*(3), 315–319.

Sosnoski, J.J. (1999). Hyper-readers and their reading engines. In G.E. Hawisher & C.L. Selfe (Eds.), *Passions, pedagogies and 21st century technologies* (pp.161–177). Logan, UT: Utah State University Press.

Spence, J. (1984). *The memory palace of Matteo Ricci.* New York: Viking.

Spicer, D. (2003). Where the rubber meets the road: An on-campus perspective of a CIO. In M.S. Pittinsky (Ed.), *The wired tower: Perspectives on the impact of the Internet on higher education* (pp.145–179). Upper Saddle River, NJ: Prentice Hall.

Steeples, C., & Jones, C. (Eds.) (2002). *Networked learning: Perspectives and issues.* London: Springer.

Steinkuehler, C. A. (2004). Learning in massively multiplayer online games. In Y. B. Kafai, W. A. Sandoval, N. Enyedy, A. S. Nixon, & F. Herrera (Eds.), *Proceedings of the Sixth International Conference of the Learning Sciences* (pp.521–528). Mahwah, NJ: Erlbaum.

Stewart, C.M., Shields, S., & Sen, N. (2001). Diversity in on-line discussions: A study of cultural and gender differences in listservs. In C. Ess & F. Sudweeks (Eds.), *Culture, technology, communication: Towards an intercultural global village* (pp.161–186). Albany, NY: SUNY Press.

Stone, A.R. (1995). *The war of desire and technology at the close of the mechanical age.* Cambridge, MA: MIT Press.

Stone, A.R. (2000). Will the real body please stand up? Boundary stories about virtual cultures. In D. Bell & B.M. Kennedy (Eds.), *The cybercultures reader* (pp.504–528). London: Routledge.

Studt, T. (2003, October 7). Disruption is inevitable. *R&D Magazine.* Accessed January 26, 2006, at www.rdmag.com

Suleri, S. (1992). *The rhetoric of English India.* Chicago, IL: University of Chicago Press.

Sullivan, P. (2002). It's easier to be yourself when you are invisible: Female college students discuss their online classroom experiences. *Innovative Higher Education, 27*(2), 129–144.

Sumner, J. (2000). Serving the system: A critical history of distance education. *Open Learning, 15*(3), 267–285.

Swerdlow, J. (1995, October). Information revolution. *National Geographic, 188,* 5–15.

Sy, P. (2001). Barangays of IT: Filipinizing mediated communication and digital power. *New Media and Society, 3*(3), 297–313.

Szlezák, T.A. (1999). *Reading Plato* (G. Zanker, Trans.). London: Routledge.

Szymanski Sunal, C., Smith, C., Sunal, D.W., & Britt, J. (1998). Using the Internet to create meaningful instruction. *Social Studies, 89*(1), 11–13.

Taylor, J. (1997). Using online seminars to demonstrate the social psychological impacts of computer-mediated communication systems. *Proceedings of the 2nd conference on integrating technology into computer science education* (pp.80–84). Uppsala, Sweden.

Taylor, M.C. (2001). *The moment of complexity.* Chicago, IL: University of Chicago Press.

Taylor, R., Barr, J., & Steele, T. (2002). *For a radical higher education: After postmodernism.* Buckingham, UK: The Society for Research into Higher Education and Open University Press.

Thanasankit, T., & Corbitt, B.J. (2000). Thai culture and communication of decision making processes in requirements engineering. In F. Sudweeks & C. Ess (Eds.), *Proceedings: Cultural attitudes towards technology and communication 2000* (pp.217–242). Perth, Australia: Murdoch University.

Thompson, S.D., Martin, L., Richards L., & Branson, D. (2003). Assessing critical thinking and problem solving using a web-based curriculum for students. *The Internet and Higher Education, 6*(2), 185–191.

Thoreau, H.D. (1993). *Walden and other writings of Henry David Thoreau* (B. Atkinson, Ed.). New York: Modern Library.

Tinto, V., Love, A.G., & Russo, P. (1993). Building community. *Liberal Learning, 79*(4), 32–35.

Tomasevski, K. (2005). Globalizing what: Education as a human right or as a traded service? *Indiana Journal of Global Legal Studies, 12,* 1–78.

Torres, C.A., & Schugurensky, D. (2002). The political economy of higher education in the era of neoliberal globalization: Latin America in comparative perspective. *Higher Education, 43,* 429–455.

Trilling, B., & Hood, P. (1999). Learning, technology, and education reform in the knowledge age or "We're wired, webbed, and windowed, now what?" *Educational Technology, 39*(3), 5–18.

Trufant, L.W. (2003, March). Move over Socrates: Online discussion is here. Paper delivered at *NERCOMP*. Accessed January 20, 2006, at www.educause.edu/ir/library/pdf/NCP0330.pdf

Tufte, E. (2003a). *The cognitive style of PowerPoint*. Cheshire, CT: Graphics Press.

Tufte, E. (2003b, November 9). PowerPoint is evil: Power corrupts. PowerPoint corrupts absolutely. *Wired*. Accessed November 10, 2005, at www.wired.com/wired/archive/11.09/ppt2.html

Turkle, S. (1995). *Life on the screen: Identity in the age of the Internet*. New York: Simon & Schuster.

Twigg, C.A. (2003, September/October). New models for online learning. *Educause, 29*–38.

Twist, J. (2005, November 17). UN debut for $100 laptop for poor. *BBC News*. Accessed December 15, 2005, at news.bbc.co.uk/1/hi/technology/4445060.stm

Twombly, S. (1997). Curricular reform and the changing role of public higher education in Costa Rica. *Higher Education, 33*, 1–28.

UCF (University of Central Florida) (2001). *Research initiative for teaching effectiveness: Distributed learning impact evaluation*. Accessed November 3, 2005, at pegasus.cc.ucf.edu/~rite/impactevaluation.htm

UCLA (University of California, Los Angeles) (2004). *UCLA Online*. Accessed October 11, 2004, at www.registrar.ucla.edu/soc/online.htm

UN (United Nations) (1948, December 10). *Universal Declaration of Human Rights*. Accessed November 3, 2005, at www.un.org/Overview/rights.html

UN (United Nations) (1999, December 8). *Implementation of the International Covenant on Economic, Social, and Political Rights: General Comment No. 13*. Document E/C.12/1999/10. Accessed November 3, 2005, at www.unhchr.ch/tbs/doc.nsf/(symbol)/E.C.12.1999.10.En?OpenDocument

UN (United Nations) (2003a, December 12). *World Summit on the Information Society. Declaration of principles. Building the information society: A global challenge in the new millennium*. Document WSIS-03/GENEVA/DOC/4-E. Accessed October 16, 2005, at www.itu.int/wsis/docs/geneva/official/dop.html

UN (United Nations) (2003b, December 12). *World Summit on the Information Society. Plan of Action*. Document WSIS-03/Geneva/DOC/5-E. Accessed October 16, 2005, at www.itu.int/wsis/docs/geneva/official/poa.html

UNDP (United Nations Development Program) (2001). *Human Development Report 2001*. New York: Oxford University Press.

University of Phoenix (n.d.). *Mission and Purposes*. Accessed November 3, 2005, at ecampus.phoenix.edu/mission.pdf

Usher, R., & Edwards, R. (1994). *Postmodernism and education*. London: Routledge.

UWM (University of Wisconsin-Milwaukee) (n.d.). *Hybrid Course Website*. Accessed October 11, 2004, at www.uwm.edu/Dept/LTC/hybrid/

Vachris, M.A. (1999). Teaching principles of economics without "chalk and talk": The experience of CNU online. *Journal of Economic Education, 30*(3), 292–303.

Vadén, T. (2003). Foreword. In N. Rajani (Ed.), *Free as in education: Significance of the free/libre and open source software for developing countries* (pp.5–9). Helsinki, Finland: Ministry of Foreign Affairs.

Valentine, J. (2004). The mood of networking culture. In G. Cox, J. Krysa, & A. Lewin (Eds.), *Data Browser 01. Economising Culture: On "the (Digital) Culture Industry"* (pp.63–79). New York: Autonomedia.

van Dijk, J. (2000). Widening information gaps and policies of prevention. In K. Hacker & J. van Dijk (Eds.), *Digital democracy: Issues of theory and practice* (pp.166–183). London: Sage.

van Shaik, P., Barker, P., & Beckstrand, S. (2003). A comparison of on-campus and online course delivery methods in Southern Nevada. *Innovations in Education and Teaching International, 40*(1), 5–15.

Vlastos, G. (1991). *Socrates: Ironist and moral philosopher*. Cambridge: Cambridge University Press.

Vlastos, G. (1996a). Socrates. In W.J. Prior (Ed.), *Socrates: Critical assessments. Vol. 1: The Socratic problem and Socratic ignorance* (pp.136–155). London: Routledge.

Vlastos, G. (1996b). Socrates' disavowal of knowledge. In W.J. Prior (Ed.), *Socrates: Critical assessments. Vol. 1: The Socratic problem and Socratic ignorance* (pp.231–260). London: Routledge.

Walker, G. (2005, June). Critical thinking in asynchronous discussions. *International Journal of Instructional Technology and Distance Learning, 2*(6). Accessed December 16, 2005, at www.itdl.org/Journal/Jun_05/article02.htm

Wallhaus, R.A. (2000). E-learning: From institutions to providers, from students to learners. In R.N. Katz & D.G. Oblinger (Eds.), *The "e" is for everything: E-commerce, e-business and e-learning in the future of higher education* (pp.21–52). San Francisco, CA: Jossey-Bass, Educause & PricewaterhouseCoopers.

Walpole, M. (2003). Socioeconomic status and college: How SES affects college experiences and outcomes. *The Review of Higher Education, 27*(1), 45–73.

Warschauer, M. (1999). *Electronic literacies: Language, culture, and power in online education.* Mahwah, NJ: Lawrence Erlbaum.

Warschauer, M. (2000). Language, identity, and the Internet. In B.E. Kolko, L. Nakamura, & G.B. Rodman (Eds.), *Race in cyberspace* (pp.151–170). New York: Routledge.

Wasson, C. (2004). The paradoxical language of enterprise. *Critical Discourse Studies, 1*(2), 175–199.

Watson, D. (2003). *Death sentence: The decay of public language.* Milsons Point, NSW: Random House.

Watson, J. (2001, October). Students and the World Wide Web. *Teacher-Librarian, 29*(1), 15–19.

WBSI (Western Behavioral Sciences Institute) (US) (1986). *Proposal for the creation of a computer-mediated social systems research and development program at the Western Behavioral Sciences Institute jointly with the Digital Equipment Corporation.* LaJolla: WBSI.

WBSI (Western Behavioral Sciences Institute) (US) (1987). *Social factors in computer-mediated communications.* Report prepared for Digital Equipment Corporation.

Weigel, V.B. (2001). *Deep learning for a digital age: Technology's untapped potential to enrich higher education.* San Francisco, CA: Jossey-Bass.

Weissberg, R. (2003). Technology evolution and citizen activism. *The Policy Studies Journal, 31*, 385–395.

Wellman, B., & Gulia, M. (1999). Virtual communities as communities: Net surfers don't ride alone. In M.A. Smith & P. Kollock (Eds.), *Communities in cyberspace* (pp.167–194). London: Routledge.

Wenger, E. (1998). *Communities of practice: Learning, meaning, and identity.* Cambridge: Cambridge University Press.

Werry, C. (2002a). The rhetoric of commercial online education. *Workplace, 5*(1). Accessed December 16, 2005, at www.louisville.edu/journal/workplace/issue5p1/werry.html

Werry, C. (2002b). The work of education in the age of ecollege. *Computers and Composition, 19*(2), 127–149.

White, F. (1999). Digital diploma mills: A dissenting voice. *First Monday, 4*(7). Accessed March 31, 2000, at www.firstmonday.dk/issues/issue4_7/white/

Whittle, J., Morgan, M., & Maltby, J. (2000). Higher learning online: Using constructivist principles to design effective asynchronous discussion. Paper delivered at *NAWeb 2000.* Accessed December 16, 2005, at naweb.unb.ca/2k/papers/whittle.htm

Wiener, N. (1948). *Cybernetics: Or control and communication in the animal and the machine.* New York: John Wiley & Sons.

Wiles, R. (2005, April 17). Arizona's most valuable companies. *The Arizona Republic,* D6.

Wiley, D. (2002). The coming collision between automated instruction and social constructivism. Accessed November 3, 2005, at telr-research.osu.edu/learning_objects/documents/Wiley.pdf

Wiley, D., et al. (2000). *The instructional use of learning objects.* Accessed December 16, 2005, at www.reusability.org/read/

Wilhelm, A. (2000). *Democracy in the digital age: Challenges to political life in cyberspace.* New York: Routledge.

Williams, B. (1998). *Plato: The invention of philosophy.* London: Phoenix.

Williams, J. (2000). Transnational collaboration: Negotiating cultural diversity. In H.P. Baumeister, J. Williams, & K. Wilson (Eds.), *Teaching across frontiers: A handbook for international online seminars* (pp.61–69). Tübingen, Germany: Deutsches Institut für Fernstudienforschung an der Universität Tübingen.

Willinsky, J. (1998). *Learning to divide the world: Education at empire's end.* Minneapolis, MN: University of Minnesota Press.

Willinsky, J. (2005). Public libraries then, open access now. In C. Kapitzke & B.C. Bruce (Eds.), *Libr@ries and the arobase: Changing information space and practice* (pp.237–242). Mahwah, NJ: Lawrence Erlbaum.

Willis, A. (2000). Nerdy no more: A case study of early wired 1993–96. In F. Sudweeks & C. Ess (Eds.), *Proceedings: Cultural attitudes towards technology and communication 2000* (pp.361–372). Perth, Australia: Murdoch University.

Wineburg, S. (2001). *Historical thinking and other unnatural acts.* Philadelphia, PA: Temple University Press.

Winner, L. (1977). *Autonomous technology: Technics-out-of-control as a theme in political thought.* Cambridge, MA: MIT Press.

Winner, L. (1986). *The whale and the reactor: A search for limits in an age of high technology.* Chicago, IL: University of Chicago Press.

Winner, L. (1995). Citizen virtues in a technological order. In A. Feenberg & A. Hannay (Eds.), *Technology and the politics of knowledge* (pp.65–84). Bloomington, IN: Indiana University Press.

Winner, L. (1997). The handwriting on the wall: Resisting technoglobalism's assault on higher education. In M. Moll (Ed.), *Tech high: Globalization and the future of Canadian education.* Ottawa, Ont.: Canadian Centre for Policy Alternatives and Fernwood Publishing.

Winterson, J. (1992). *Written on the body.* New York: Vintage.

Wood, G. (2004). Academic original sin: Plagiarism, the Internet, and librarians. *Journal of Academic Librarianship, 30*(3), 237–242.

Woodruff, P. (1996). Expert knowledge in the *Apology* and *Laches*: What a general needs to know. In W.J. Prior (Ed.), *Socrates: Critical assessments. Vol. 1: The Socratic problem and Socratic ignorance* (pp.275–299). London: Routledge.

Wulf, W.A. (1998). University alert: The information railroad is coming. *Virginia.edu, 2*(2). Accessed March 22, 2004, at www.itc.virginia.edu/virginia.edu/fall98/mills/comments/c1.html

Xin, M.C. (2003). *Validity centered design for the domain of engaged collaborative discourse in computer conferencing.* Unpublished doctoral dissertation, Brigham Young University, Provo, UT. Accessed July 12, 2004, at www.textweaver.org/xin_dissertation.pdf

Yahoo! search adds personal search and collaboration capabilities to web search (2005, April 27) (Press Release). *Yahoo! Media Relations.* Accessed October 4, 2005, at docs.yahoo.com/docs/pr/release1232.html

Yorke, M., & Knight, P. (2002). Employability through the curriculum. *Skills Plus: Employability in higher education* (The Open University). Accessed June 14, 2004, at www.open.ac.uk/vqportal/Skills-Plus/documents/PromotingEmploy.pdf

Young, J. (2002). "Hybrid" teaching seeks to end the divide between traditional and online instruction. *Chronicle of Higher Education, 48*(28), A33–A34.

Young, M. (1958). *The rise of the meritocracy.* Harmondsworth, UK: Penguin.

Zemsky, R., & Massy, W.F. (2004). Why the e-learning boom went bust. *Chronicle of Higher Education, 50*(44), B6.

Contributors

Darin Barney is Canada Research Chair in Technology and Citizenship and Associate Professor of Communication Studies at McGill University. He is the author of *Communication Technology: The Canadian Democratic Audit* (UBC Press, 2005); *The Network Society* (Polity Press, 2004); and *Prometheus Wired: The Hope for Democracy in the Age of Network Technology* (UBC/Chicago/UNSW, 2000). He is also a Co-editor, with Andrew Feenberg, of *Community in the Digital Age: Philosophy and Practice* (Rowman & Littlefield, 2004).

Tara Brabazon is Professor of Media at the University of Brighton and Director of the Popular Culture Collective (popularculturecollective.com). Her popular cultural research includes sport, popular music, creative industries initiatives, city imaging, multiculturalism, and education. She has published six books: *Tracking the Jack: A Retracing of the Antipodes* (UNSW Press, 2000); *Ladies Who Lunge: Celebrating Difficult Women* (UNSW Press, 2002); *Digital Hemlock: Internet Education and the Poisoning of Teaching* (UNSW Press, 2002); *Liverpool of the South Seas: Perth and Its Popular Music* (as editor; UWA Press, 2005); *From Revolution to Revelation: Generation X, Popular Memory and Cultural Studies* (Ashgate, 2005); and *Playing on the Periphery: Sport, Memory and Identity* (Routledge, 2006). She is a previous winner of a National Teaching Award for the Humanities and a finalist for Australian of the Year.

Charles Ess is a Professor of Philosophy and Religion and Distinguished Professor of Interdisciplinary Studies, Drury University (Springfield, MO, USA); and Professor II, Programme for Applied Ethics, Norwegian University of Science and Technology (Trondheim, Norway). He has received awards for teaching excellence and scholarship, and a national award for work in hypermedia. Dr. Ess has published in comparative (East–West) philosophy, applied ethics, discourse ethics, history of philosophy, feminist biblical studies, and computer-mediated communication (CMC). He serves on the editorial board of several journals devoted to CMC and media. With Fay Sudweeks, Dr. Ess co-chairs the biennial international conference series "Cultural Attitudes towards Technology and Communication" (CATaC). He has chaired the Ethics Working Committee of the Association of Internet Researchers (AoIR). He has lectured on and taught information ethics at several universities abroad. He was a Visiting Professor, IT University, Copenhagen, Denmark (2003), and a Fulbright Senior Scholar, University of Trier (2004).

Bettina Fabos is an Assistant Professor of Interactive Media Studies and Journalism at Miami University of Ohio. With a background in journalism, media production, and media literacy pedagogy, she has written extensively about the role of the US media in democracy. Specifically, she has turned to online information access (as it relates to democracy), Internet commercialization, the role of the Internet as a research tool, and the digital archiving/subject gateway movement. She is the author of *Wrong Turn on the Information Superhighway: Education and the Commercialization of the Internet* (Teachers College Press, 2004), and the co-author of a leading college textbook, *Media and Culture* (Bedford/St. Martin's, 5th ed., 2006), which is used in mass communication survey classes across the country. Other research interests include the public relations industry's influence on journalism practices, online newspapers, and the role of objectivity in the news. Fabos is also an award-winning documentary producer and a former print reporter. She received a PhD in Language, Literacy, and Culture from the University of Iowa, and an MA in Telecommunication Arts from the University of Michigan.

Andrew Feenberg is Canada Research Chair in Philosophy of Technology in the School of Communication, Simon Fraser University, Canada. He has also taught in the Philosophy Department at San Diego State University, and at Duke University, the State University of New York at Buffalo, the Universities of California, San Diego and Irvine, the Sorbonne, the University of Paris-Dauphine, the Ecole des Hautes Etudes en Sciences Sociales, and the University of Tokyo. He is the author of *Lukacs, Marx and the Sources of Critical Theory* (OUP, 1986; Rowman & Littlefield, 1981), *Critical Theory of Technology* (OUP, 1991), *Alternative Modernity* (University of California Press, 1995), and *Questioning Technology* (Routledge, 1999). A second edition of *Critical Theory of Technology* has appeared under the title *Transforming Technology* (OUP, 2002). His latest book is *Heidegger, Marcuse and Technology: The Catastrophe and Redemption of Enlightenment* (Routledge, 2004). Dr. Feenberg is Co-editor of *Marcuse: Critical Theory and the Promise of Utopia* (Bergin & Garvey Press, 1988), *Technology and the Politics of Knowledge* (Indiana University Press, 1995), *Modernity and Technology* (MIT Press, 2003), and *Community in the Digital Age* (Rowman & Littlefield, 2004). He has also published on the French May Events of 1968 (*When Poetry Ruled the Streets*, SUNY Press, 2001), and on the work of Japanese philosopher Nishida Kitaro. He is recognized as an early innovator in online education, a field he helped to create. His latest book is *Heidegger and Marcuse: The Catastrophe and Redemption of History* (Routledge, 2005).

Robin Goodfellow is a Senior Lecturer in Teaching with New Technologies at the Open University's Institute of Educational Technology. He is currently a Director of an online Master's course in Understanding Flexible and Distributed Learning. His research interests are in the area of university teaching and learning as social practice, with specific reference to literacy practices in virtual learning environments. He is currently working on a book about e-literacies and the discourses of e-learning.

Edward Hamilton is a Doctoral Candidate and Sessional Instructor in the School of Communication at Simon Fraser University, Canada. His doctoral dissertation, *The Automatic Student and the Robot Professor*, is a critical historical examination of online education as a transformative social movement in the university. He is also a Research Assistant for the Learning Spaces Project, sponsored by the Social Sciences and Humanities Research Council of Canada. The project involves the development and testing of research methodologies derived from phenomenology to study the user experience of technologically mediated and simulated education. He teaches in the areas of technology studies, popular culture, and communication studies.

Tina S. Kazan is an Assistant Professor in the English Department at Elmhurst College. She teaches undergraduate courses in composition and rhetoric, creative non-fiction, film studies and literary theory, as well as graduate seminars in rhetorical theory. She has co-edited *Lore: An E-Journal for Teachers of Writing* (www.bedfordstmartins.com/lore/) since its inception in 2001, and has written on teaching and technology for the National Council of Teachers of English (NCTE) Teach 2000 Cyberbrief Project. Her article "Dancing Bodies in the Classroom: Moving toward an Embodied Pedagogy" in the journal *Pedagogy* (2005, Fall) analyzes discursive and corporeal texts in the classroom and argues for what she calls an "embodied" pedagogy. Her current research interests include constructions of the body in popular culture.

T. Mills Kelly is the Associate Director of the Center for History and New Media (chnm.gmu.edu) and Assistant Professor of History at George Mason

University in Fairfax, Virginia. His research on teaching and learning has focused on the ways that digital media influence student learning in history. This work has resulted in publications in a variety of journals, several book chapters, and awards such as the Commonwealth of Virginia's Outstanding Faculty Award, the highest honor the state bestows for faculty excellence. Since 1999, he has been a Member of the Carnegie Academy for the Scholarship of Teaching and Learning, and is a Founding Member of the International Society for the Scholarship of Teaching and Learning. For the past eleven years, Prof. Kelly has helped to direct the Civic Education Project, an international educational non-governmental organization working to bring about democratic reform and the improvement of higher education in countries emerging from dictatorship.

Marjorie D. Kibby is an Assistant Dean and Lecturer in the School of Humanities and Social Sciences, University of Newcastle, Australia. Her research interests include media representations of class, race, and gender; Internet culture; and online teaching and learning. She has published extensively on issues of sexuality and the Internet. Her recent work is on an Australian Research Council-funded project that explores the impact of the Internet and digital technologies on the young people's music consumption practices. A previous recipient of the Vice-Chancellor's award for teaching excellence, she is currently teaching staff development courses in the use of the Internet to facilitate effective learning.

Kate Kiefer is a Professor of English at Colorado State University, where she teaches graduate composition theory courses (including Computers and Composition; Reading/Writing Connections; and Chaos, Complexity, and Writing) as well as undergraduate composition. She developed her long-standing interest and expertise in computers and writing in the early 1980s when she set up one of the first computer laboratories dedicated to writing, as well as one of the first computer-networked classrooms, in the country. This interest in technology has also resulted in the development and multiple offerings of COCC301C online (Writing in the Social Sciences). She co-founded *Computers and Composition*, of which she is still Emeritus Editor. She has published three textbooks on writing in addition to a book and numerous articles on computers and composition. She continues to research teaching in both physical and virtual contexts, but her most recent work has focused on the ways in which reading, writing, and thinking can be considered complex adaptive systems.

Kerri-Lee Krause is a Higher Education Policy Researcher at the Centre for the Study of Higher Education, University of Melbourne, Australia. Her research expertise and experience is broadly in the area of higher education policy, but her particular research focus is the student experience in higher education and implications for policy and practice. With a team of colleagues at the CSHE, she has recently published a national study of the first year experience in Australian universities. A significant part of her work involves providing policy and practical advice to university academics, administrators, and student support staff, especially regarding managing and responding to the changing student experience in higher education. She has co-edited two books, including *Cyberlines: Languages and Cultures of the Internet* (JNP, 2006, 2nd ed., in press), which reflects her interest in the role of changing technologies in learning, teaching, and higher education policy.

Joe Lockard is an Assistant Professor of English at Arizona State University, where he teaches early American and African American literatures. He obtained a Doctorate in 2000 from the University of California, Berkeley, held a UC Presidential Fellowship at the University of California, Davis, from 2000 to 2002, and has taught at colleges and universities in the United States, Israel, and the Czech Republic. He has published well-known essays on Internet culture and spent 13 years as an editor of the oldest online political journal, *Bad Subjects*. He directs the Antislavery Literature Project (antislavery.eserver.org), an online public education project that digitizes and publishes historical antislavery texts.

Martha Henn McCormick is the Research Coordinator for Indiana State University's Networks Financial Institute, an organization concerned with research pertaining to the financial services sector, education of future financial service professionals, and community outreach regarding financial literacy. Formerly, she served as the English and women's studies librarian for the University Library, and as Director of Information Resources at the Center for Teaching and Learning within the Office of Professional Development at Indiana University–Purdue University, Indianapolis. She received her Master of Library Science degree from Indiana University, and her Master's degree in English and Graduate Certificate in Women's Studies from Emory University.

Mary Low O'Sullivan is an Educational Developer at Monash University, Melbourne, Australia. She has a Ph.D. in Political Science from the University of Hawaii at Manoa, a Master of Arts in International Relations from the Australian National University, and a Master of Education from Monash

University. She has taught in the International Studies program at the University of New England, Australia, and in Comparative Politics and Development at the University of the South Pacific, Fiji. As an educational developer, she facilitates academic development in the Graduate Certificate in Higher Education and in various professional development workshops. Her research interests are in the areas of situating educational development within social structures and power relations; critical pedagogy and its democratic promise; and state intervention in higher education.

Chrysostomos (Tom) Palaskas has worked as an educator in fields ranging from Teaching English as a Foreign Language (TEFL) to instructional design, educational technology, and academic development. His experience in education and training has been gained through employment in the oil and gas, power generation, banking, and higher education sectors. Tom's work has taken him to New Zealand, Papua New Guinea, Thailand, Libya, Indonesia, and the United Arab Emirates in a variety of consultancy and contractual positions. Currently Tom is a Senior Lecturer and E-Learning Coordinator within the Higher Education Development Unit at Monash University in Australia. His research interests include the institutional and pedagogical impact of educational technology in higher education.

Mark Pegrum is a Lecturer in the Graduate School of Education at the University of Western Australia, where he has particular responsibility for the area of Teaching English to Speakers of Other Languages (TESOL). He previously lectured at the University of Dundee, Scotland, where he was the Programme Coordinator of the Master's in Teaching Modern Languages to Adults (TMLA), an online distance learning course for teachers of English as a Foreign Language (EFL) and Modern Foreign Languages (MFL). In addition to working in the area of TESOL, he has taught German and French language, culture and history, and cultural studies. He is the author of *Challenging Modernity: Dada between Modern and Postmodern* (Berghahn, 2000). His current research focuses mainly on e-learning, in particular the management of intercultural issues online, the development of intercultural competence, and the use of World Englishes.

Robert Samuels is a Lecturer in the Writing Programs at the University of California at Los Angeles. He is the author of *Between Philosophy and Psychoanalysis* (Routledge, 1993), *Hitchcock's Bi-Textuality* (SUNY Press, 1998), and *Writing*

Prejudices (SUNY Press, 2000). His most recent book is *Integrating Hypertextual Subjects: Computers, Composition, and Academic Labor* (Hampton Press, 2006).

Index

General Editor: **Steve Jones**

Digital Formations is an essential source for critical, high-quality books on digital technologies and modern life. Volumes in the series break new ground by emphasizing multiple methodological and theoretical approaches to deeply probe the formation and reformation of lived experience as it is refracted through digital interaction. **Digital Formations** pushes forward our understanding of the intersections—and corresponding implications—between the digital technologies and everyday life. The series emphasizes critical studies in the context of emergent and existing digital technologies.

Other recent titles include:

Leslie Shade
  *Gender and Community in the Social
  Construction of the Internet*

John T. Waisanen
  Thinking Geometrically

Mia Consalvo & Susanna Paasonen
  Women and Everyday Uses of the Internet

Dennis Waskul
  Self-Games and Body-Play

David Myers
  The Nature of Computer Games

Robert Hassan
  The Chronoscopic Society

M. Johns, S. Chen, & G. Hall
  Online Social Research

C. Kaha Waite
  *Mediation and the Communication
  Matrix*

Jenny Sunden
  Material Virtualities

Helen Nissenbaum & Monroe Price
  Academy and the Internet

To order other books in this series please contact our Customer Service Department:
  (800) 770-LANG (within the US)
  (212) 647-7706 (outside the US)
  (212) 647-7707 FAX

To find out more about the series or browse a full list of titles, please visit our website:
  WWW.PETERLANG.COM